Programming Google App Engine

Programming Google App Engine

Dan Sanderson

Beijing · Cambridge · Farnham · Köln · Sebastopol · Taipei · Tokyo

Programming Google App Engine

by Dan Sanderson

Copyright © 2010 Dan Sanderson. All rights reserved.
Printed in the United States of America.

Published by O'Reilly Media, Inc., 1005 Gravenstein Highway North, Sebastopol, CA 95472.

O'Reilly books may be purchased for educational, business, or sales promotional use. Online editions are also available for most titles (*http://my.safaribooksonline.com*). For more information, contact our corporate/institutional sales department: (800) 998-9938 or *corporate@oreilly.com*.

Editor: Mike Loukides
Production Editor: Sumita Mukherji
Proofreader: Sada Preisch

Indexer: Ellen Troutman Zaig
Cover Designer: Karen Montgomery
Interior Designer: David Futato
Illustrator: Robert Romano

Printing History:
  November 2009:   First Edition.

 This book uses RepKover™, a durable and flexible lay-flat binding.

ISBN: 978-0-596-52272-8

[M]

1257862215

For Lisa

Table of Contents

Preface

On the Internet, popularity is swift and fleeting. A mention of your website on a popular blog can bring 300,000 potential customers your way at once, all expecting to find out who you are and what you have to offer. But if you're a small company just starting out, your hardware and software aren't likely to be able to handle that kind of traffic. Chances are, you've sensibly built your site to handle the 30,000 visits per hour you're actually expecting in your first 6 months. Under heavy load, such a system would be incapable of showing even your company logo to the 270,000 others that showed up to look around. And those potential customers are not likely to come back after the traffic has subsided.

The answer is *not* to spend time and money building a system to serve millions of visitors on the first day, when those same systems are only expected to serve mere thousands per day for the subsequent months. If you delay your launch to build big, you miss the opportunity to improve your product using feedback from your customers. Building big before allowing customers to use the product risks building something your customers don't want.

Small companies usually don't have access to large systems of servers on day one. The best they can do is to build small and hope meltdowns don't damage their reputation as they try to grow. The lucky ones find their audience, get another round of funding, and halt feature development to rebuild their product for larger capacity. The unlucky ones, well, don't.

But these days, there are other options. Large Internet companies such as Amazon.com, Google, and Microsoft are leasing parts of their high-capacity systems using a pay-per-use model. Your website is served from those large systems, which are plenty capable of handling sudden surges in traffic and ongoing success. And since you pay only for what you use, there is no up-front investment that goes to waste when traffic is low. As your customer base grows, the costs grow proportionally.

Google App Engine, Google's application hosting service, does more than just provide access to hardware. It provides a model for building applications that grow automatically. App Engine runs your application so that each user who accesses it gets the same experience as every other user, whether there are dozens of simultaneous users or thousands. The application uses the same large-scale services that power Google's applications for data storage and retrieval, caching, and network access. App Engine takes care of the tasks of large-scale computing, such as load balancing, data replication, and fault tolerance, automatically.

The App Engine model really kicks in at the point where a traditional system would outgrow its first database server. With such a system, adding load-balanced web servers and caching layers can get you pretty far, but when your application needs to write data to more than one place, you have a hard problem. This problem is made harder when development up to that point has relied on features of database software that were never intended for data distributed across multiple machines. By thinking about your data in terms of App Engine's model up front, you save yourself from having to rebuild the whole thing later, without much additional effort.

Running on Google's infrastructure means you never have to set up a server, replace a failed hard drive, or troubleshoot a network card. And you don't have to be woken up in the middle of the night by a screaming pager because an ISP hiccup confused a service alarm. And with automatic scaling, you don't have to scramble to set up new hardware as traffic increases.

Google App Engine lets you focus on your application's functionality and user experience. You can launch early, enjoy the flood of attention, retain customers, and start improving your product with the help of your users. Your app grows with the size of your audience—up to Google-sized proportions—without having to rebuild for a new architecture. Meanwhile, your competitors are still putting out fires and configuring databases.

With this book, you will learn how to develop applications that run on Google App Engine, and how to get the most out of the scalable model. A significant portion of the book discusses the App Engine scalable datastore, which does not behave like the relational databases that have been a staple of web development for the past decade. The application model and the datastore together represent a new way of thinking about web applications that, while being almost as simple as the model we've known, requires reconsidering a few principles we often take for granted.

This book introduces the major features of App Engine, including the scalable services (such as for sending email and manipulating images), tools for deploying and managing applications, and features for integrating your application with Google Accounts and Google Apps using your own domain name. The book also discusses techniques for optimizing your application, using task queues and offline processes, and otherwise getting the most out of Google App Engine.

Using This Book

As of this writing, App Engine supports two technology stacks for building web applications: Java and Python. The Java technology stack lets you develop web applications using the Java programming language (or most other languages that compile to Java bytecode or have a JVM-based interpreter) and Java web technologies such as servlets and JSPs. The Python technology stack provides a fast interpreter for the Python programming language, and is compatible with several major open source web application frameworks such as Django.

This book covers concepts that apply to both technology stacks, as well as important language-specific subjects. If you've already decided which language you're going to use, you probably won't be interested in information that doesn't apply to that language. This poses a challenge for a printed book: how should the text be organized so information about one technology doesn't interfere with information about the other?

Foremost, we've tried to organize the chapters by the major concepts that apply to all App Engine applications. Where necessary, chapters split into separate sections to talk about specifics for each language. In cases where an example in one language illustrates a concept equally well for other languages, the example is given in Python. If Python is not your language of choice, hopefully you'll be able to glean the equivalent information from other parts of the book or from the official App Engine documentation on Google's website.

The datastore is a large enough subject that it gets multiple chapters to itself. Starting with Chapter 4, datastore concepts are introduced alongside Python and Java APIs related to those concepts. Note that we've taken an unconventional approach to introducing the datastore APIs by starting with the low-level APIs that map directly to datastore concepts. In your applications, you are most likely to prefer the higher level APIs of the data modeling interfaces. Data modeling is discussed separately, in Chapter 7 for Python, and in Chapter 8 for Java.

Google may release additional technology stacks for other languages in the future. If they've done so by the time you read this, the concepts described here should still be relevant. Check this book's website for information about future editions.

This book has the following chapters:

Chapter 1, *Introducing Google App Engine*
    A high-level overview of Google App Engine and its components, tools, and major features. This chapter also includes a brief discussion of features you might expect App Engine to have but that it doesn't have yet.

Chapter 2, *Creating an Application*
    An introductory tutorial for both Python and Java, including instructions on setting up a development environment, setting up accounts and domain names, and deploying the application to App Engine. The tutorial application demonstrates

the use of several App Engine features—Google Accounts, the datastore, and memcache—to implement a pattern common to many web applications: storing and retrieving user preferences.

Chapter 3, *Handling Web Requests*

Contains details about App Engine's architecture, the various features of the frontend, app servers, and static file servers, and details about the app server runtime environments for Python and Java. The frontend routes requests to the app servers and the static file servers, and manages secure connections and Google Accounts authentication and authorization. This chapter also discusses quotas and limits, and how to raise them by setting a budget.

Chapter 4, *Datastore Entities*

The first of several chapters on the App Engine datastore, a strongly consistent scalable object data storage system with support for local transactions. This chapter introduces data entities, keys and properties, and Python and Java APIs for creating, updating, and deleting entities.

Chapter 5, *Datastore Queries*

An introduction to datastore queries and indexes, and the Python and Java APIs for queries. The App Engine datastore's query engine uses prebuilt indexes for all queries. This chapter describes the features of the query engine in detail, and how each feature uses indexes. The chapter also discusses how to define and manage indexes for your application's queries.

Chapter 6, *Datastore Transactions*

How to use transactions to keep your data consistent. The App Engine datastore uses local transactions in a scalable environment. Your app arranges its entities in units of transactionality known as entity groups. This chapter attempts to provide a complete explanation of how the datastore updates data, and how to design your data and your app to best take advantage of these features.

Chapter 7, *Data Modeling with Python*

How to use the Python data modeling API to enforce invariants in your data schema. The datastore itself is schemaless, a fundamental aspect of its scalability. You can automate the enforcement of data schemas using App Engine's data modeling interface. This chapter covers Python exclusively, though Java developers may wish to skim it for advice related to data modeling.

Chapter 8, *The Java Persistence API*

A brief introduction to the Java Persistence API (JPA), how its concepts translate to the datastore, how to use it to model data schemas, and how using it makes your application easier to port to other environments. JPA is a Java EE standard interface. App Engine also supports another standard interface known as Java Data Objects (JDO), though JDO is not covered in this book. This chapter covers Java exclusively.

Chapter 9, *The Memory Cache*

App Engine's memory cache service (aka "memcache"), and its Python and Java APIs. Aggressive caching is essential for high-performance web applications.

Chapter 10, *Fetching URLs and Web Resources*

How to access other resources on the Internet via HTTP using the URL Fetch service. This chapter covers the Python and Java interfaces, including implementations of standard URL fetching libraries. It also describes the asynchronous URL Fetch interface, which as of this writing is exclusive to Python.

Chapter 11, *Sending and Receiving Mail and Instant Messages*

How to use App Engine services to send email and instant messages to XMPP-compatible services (such as Google Talk). This chapter covers receiving email and XMPP chat messages relayed by App Engine using request handlers. It also discusses creating and processing messages using tools in the API.

Chapter 12, *Bulk Data Operations and Remote Access*

How to perform large maintenance operations on your live application using scripts running on your computer. Tools included with the SDK make it easy to back up, restore, load, and retrieve data in your app's datastore. You can also write your own tools using the remote access API for data transformations and other jobs. You can also run an interactive Python command shell that uses the remote API to manipulate a live Python or Java app.

Chapter 13, *Task Queues and Scheduled Tasks*

How to perform work outside of user requests using task queues. Task queues perform tasks in parallel by running your code on multiple application servers. You control the processing rate with configuration. Tasks can also be executed on a regular schedule with no user interaction.

Chapter 14, *The Django Web Application Framework*

How to use the Django web application framework with the Python runtime environment. This chapter discusses setting up a Django project, using the Django App Engine Helper, and taking advantage of features of Django via the Helper such as using the App Engine data modeling interface with forms and test fixtures.

Chapter 15, *Deploying and Managing Applications*

How to upload and run your app on App Engine, how to update and test an application using app versions, and how to manage and inspect the running application. This chapter also introduces other maintenance features of the Administrator Console, including billing. We conclude with a list of places to go for help and further reading.

Conventions Used in This Book

The following typographical conventions are used in this book:

Italic
> Indicates new terms, URLs, email addresses, filenames, and file extensions.

`Constant width`
> Used for program listings, as well as within paragraphs to refer to program elements such as variable or function names, databases, data types, environment variables, statements, and keywords.

`Constant width bold`
> Shows commands or other text that should be typed literally by the user.

`Constant width italic`
> Shows text that should be replaced with user-supplied values or by values determined by context.

 This icon signifies a tip, suggestion, or general note.

Using Code Samples

This book is here to help you get your job done. In general, you may use the code in this book in your programs and documentation. You do not need to contact us for permission unless you're reproducing a significant portion of the code. For example, writing a program that uses several chunks of code from this book does not require permission. Selling or distributing a CD-ROM of examples from O'Reilly books does require permission. Answering a question by citing this book and quoting example code does not require permission. Incorporating a significant amount of example code from this book into your product's documentation does require permission.

We appreciate, but do not require, attribution. An attribution usually includes the title, author, publisher, and ISBN. For example: "*Programming Google App Engine* by Dan Sanderson. Copyright 2010 Dan Sanderson, 978-0-596-52272-8."

If you feel your use of code examples falls outside fair use or the permission given above, feel free to contact us at *permissions@oreilly.com*.

Safari® Books Online

 Safari Books Online is an on-demand digital library that lets you easily search over 7,500 technology and creative reference books and videos to find the answers you need quickly.

With a subscription, you can read any page and watch any video from our library online. Read books on your cell phone and mobile devices. Access new titles before they are available for print, and get exclusive access to manuscripts in development and post feedback for the authors. Copy and paste code samples, organize your favorites, download chapters, bookmark key sections, create notes, print out pages, and benefit from tons of other time-saving features.

O'Reilly Media has uploaded this book to the Safari Books Online service. To have full digital access to this book and others on similar topics from O'Reilly and other publishers, sign up for free at *http://my.safaribooksonline.com*.

How to Contact Us

Please address comments and questions concerning this book to the publisher:

O'Reilly Media, Inc.
1005 Gravenstein Highway North
Sebastopol, CA 95472
800-998-9938 (in the United States or Canada)
707-829-0515 (international or local)
707-829-0104 (fax)

We have a web page for this book, where we list errata, examples, and any additional information. You can access this page at:

http://oreilly.com/catalog/9780596522728

You can also download the examples from the author's website:

http://www.dansanderson.com/appengine

To comment or ask technical questions about this book, send email to:

bookquestions@oreilly.com

For more information about our books, conferences, Resource Centers, and the O'Reilly Network, see our website at:

http://www.oreilly.com

Acknowledgments

I owe a great deal of thanks to the App Engine team, of which I've been a proud member since 2008. This book would not exist without the efforts and leadership of Paul McDonald, Pete Koomen, and App Engine's fearless tech lead, Kevin Gibbs.

I am especially indebted to the App Engine datastore team, who have made significant contributions to the datastore chapters. Ryan Barrett, lead datastore engineer, provided many hours of conversation and detailed technical review. Max Ross, implementor of the Java datastore interfaces and the JDO and JPA adapters, wrote major portions of Chapter 8. Rafe Kaplan, designer of the Python data modeling library, contributed portions of Chapter 7. My thanks to them.

Thanks to Matthew Blain, Michael Davidson, Alex Gaysinsky, Peter McKenzie, Don Schwarz, and Jeffrey Scudder for reviewing portions of the book in detail. Thanks also to Andy Smith for making last-minute improvements to the Django Helper in time to be included here. Many other App Engine contributors had a hand, directly or indirectly, in making this book what it is: Freeland Abbott, Mike Aizatsky, Ken Ashcraft, Anthony Baxter, Chris Beckmann, Andrew Bowers, Matthew Brown, Ryan Brown, Hannah Chen, Lei Chen, Jason Cooper, Mark Dalrymple, Pavni Diwanji, Brad Fitzpatrick, Alfred Fuller, David Glazer, John Grabowski, Joe Gregorio, Raju Gulabani, Justin Haugh, Jeff Huber, Kevin Jin, Erik Johnson, Nick Johnson, Mickey Kataria, Scott Knaster, Marc Kriguer, Alon Levi, Sean Lynch, Gianni Mariani, Mano Marks, Jon McAlister, Sean McBride, Marzia Niccolai, Alan Noble, Brandon Nutter, Karsten Petersen, George Pirocanac, Alexander Power, Mike Repass, Toby Reyelts, Fred Sauer, Jens Scheffler, Robert Schuppenies, Lindsey Simon, John Skidgel, Brett Slatkin, Graham Spencer, Amanda Surya, David Symonds, Joseph Ternasky, Eric Tholomé, Troy Trimble, Guido van Rossum, Nicholas Verne, Michael Winton, and Wenbo Zhu.

Thanks also to Dan Morrill, Mark Pilgrim, Steffi Wu, Karen Wickre, Jane Penner, Jon Murchinson, Tom Stocky, Vic Gundotra, Bill Coughran, and Alan Eustace.

At O'Reilly, I'm eternally grateful to Michael Loukides, who had nothing but good advice and an astonishing amount of patience for a first-time author. Let's do another one!

## CHAPTER 1

Introducing Google App Engine

Google App Engine is a web application hosting service. By "web application," we mean an application or service accessed over the Web, usually with a web browser: storefronts with shopping carts, social networking sites, multiplayer games, mobile applications, survey applications, project management, collaboration, publishing, and all of the other things we're discovering are good uses for the Web. App Engine can serve traditional website content too, such as documents and images, but the environment is especially designed for real-time dynamic applications.

In particular, Google App Engine is designed to host applications with many simultaneous users. When an application can serve many simultaneous users without degrading performance, we say it *scales*. Applications written for App Engine scale automatically. As more people use the application, App Engine allocates more resources for the application and manages the use of those resources. The application itself does not need to know anything about the resources it is using.

Unlike traditional web hosting or self-managed servers, with Google App Engine, you only pay for the resources you use. These resources are measured down to the gigabyte, with no monthly fees or up-front charges. Billed resources include CPU usage, storage per month, incoming and outgoing bandwidth, and several resources specific to App Engine services. To help you get started, every developer gets a certain amount of resources for free, enough for small applications with low traffic. Google estimates that with the free resources, an app can accommodate about 5 million page views a month.

App Engine can be described as three parts: the runtime environment, the datastore, and the scalable services. In this chapter, we'll look at each of these parts at a high level. We'll also discuss features of App Engine for deploying and managing web applications, and for building websites integrated with other Google offerings such as Google Apps and Google Accounts.

The Runtime Environment

An App Engine application responds to web requests. A web request begins when a client, typically a user's web browser, contacts the application with an HTTP request, such as to fetch a web page at a URL. When App Engine receives the request, it identifies the application from the domain name of the address, either an `.appspot.com` subdomain (provided for free with every app) or a subdomain of a custom domain name you have registered and set up with Google Apps. App Engine selects a server from many possible servers to handle the request, making its selection based on which server is most likely to provide a fast response. It then calls the application with the content of the HTTP request, receives the response data from the application, and returns the response to the client.

From the application's perspective, the runtime environment springs into existence when the request handler begins, and disappears when it ends. App Engine provides at least two methods for storing data that persists between requests (discussed later), but these mechanisms live outside of the runtime environment. By not retaining state in the runtime environment between requests—or at least, by not expecting that state will be retained between requests—App Engine can distribute traffic among as many servers as it needs to give every request the same treatment, regardless of how much traffic it is handling at one time.

Application code cannot access the server on which it is running in the traditional sense. An application can read its own files from the filesystem, but it cannot write to files, and it cannot read files that belong to other applications. An application can see environment variables set by App Engine, but manipulations of these variables do not necessarily persist between requests. An application cannot access the networking facilities of the server hardware, though it can perform networking operations using services.

In short, each request lives in its own "sandbox." This allows App Engine to handle a request with the server that would, in its estimation, provide the fastest response. There is no way to guarantee that the same server hardware will handle two requests, even if the requests come from the same client and arrive relatively quickly.

Sandboxing also allows App Engine to run multiple applications on the same server without the behavior of one application affecting another. In addition to limiting access to the operating system, the runtime environment also limits the amount of clock time, CPU use, and memory a single request can take. App Engine keeps these limits flexible, and applies stricter limits to applications that use up more resources to protect shared resources from "runaway" applications.

A request has up to 30 seconds to return a response to the client. While that may seem like a comfortably large amount for a web app, App Engine is optimized for applications that respond in less than a second. Also, if an application uses many CPU cycles, App Engine may slow it down so the app isn't hogging the processor on a machine serving multiple apps. A CPU-intensive request handler may take more clock time to complete than it would if it had exclusive use of the processor, and clock time may vary as App Engine detects patterns in CPU usage and allocates accordingly.

Google App Engine provides two possible runtime environments for applications: a Java environment and a Python environment. The environment you choose depends on the language and related technologies you want to use for developing the application.

The Java environment runs applications built for the Java 6 Virtual Machine (JVM). An app can be developed using the Java programming language, or most other languages that compile to or otherwise run in the JVM, such as PHP (using Quercus), Ruby (using JRuby), JavaScript (using the Rhino interpreter), Scala, and Groovy. The app accesses the environment and services using interfaces based on web industry standards, including Java servlets and the Java Persistence API (JPA). Any Java technology that functions within the sandbox restrictions can run on App Engine, making it suitable for many existing frameworks and libraries. Notably, App Engine fully supports Google Web Toolkit (GWT), a framework for rich web applications that lets you write all of the app's code—including the user interface—in the Java language, and have your rich graphical app work with all major browsers without plug-ins.

The Python environment runs apps written in the Python 2.5 programming language, using a custom version of CPython, the official Python interpreter. App Engine invokes a Python app using CGI, a widely supported application interface standard. An application can use most of Python's large and excellent standard library, as well as rich APIs and libraries for accessing services and modeling data. Many open source Python web application frameworks work with App Engine, such as Django, web2py, and Pylons, and App Engine even includes a simple framework of its own.

The Java and Python environments use the same application server model: a request is routed to an app server, the application is started on the app server (if necessary) and invoked to handle the request to produce a response, and the response is returned to the client. Each environment runs its interpreter (the JVM or the Python interpreter) with sandbox restrictions, such that any attempt to use a feature of the language or a library that would require access outside of the sandbox fails with an exception.

While using a different server for every request has advantages for scaling, it's time-consuming to start up a new instance of the application for every request. App Engine mitigates startup costs by keeping the application in memory on an application server as long as possible and reusing servers intelligently. When a server needs to reclaim resources, it purges the least recently used app. All app servers have the runtime environment (JVM or Python interpreter) preloaded before the request reaches the server, so only the app itself needs to be loaded on a fresh server.

Applications can exploit the app caching behavior to cache data directly on the app server using global (static) variables. Since an app can be evicted between any two requests (and low-traffic apps are evicted frequently), and there is no guarantee that a given user's requests will be handled by a given server, global variables are mostly useful for caching startup resources, like parsed configuration files.

I haven't said anything about which operating system or hardware configuration App Engine uses. There are ways to figure out what operating system or hardware a server is using, but in the end it doesn't matter: the runtime environment is an abstraction *above* the operating system that allows App Engine to manage resource allocation, computation, request handling, scaling, and load distribution without the application's involvement. Features that typically require knowledge of the operating system are either provided by services outside of the runtime environment, provided or emulated using standard library calls, or restricted in logical ways within the definition of the sandbox.

The Static File Servers

Most websites have resources they deliver to browsers that do not change during the regular operation of the site. The images and CSS files that describe the appearance of the site, the JavaScript code that runs in the browser, and HTML files for pages without dynamic components are examples of these resources, collectively known as *static files*. Since the delivery of these files doesn't involve application code, it's unnecessary and inefficient to serve them from the application servers.

Instead, App Engine provides a separate set of servers dedicated to delivering static files. These servers are optimized for both internal architecture and network topology to handle requests for static resources. To the client, static files look like any other resource served by your app.

You upload the static files of your application right alongside the application code. You can configure several aspects of how static files are served, including the URLs for static files, content types, and instructions for browsers to keep copies of the files in a cache for a given amount of time to reduce traffic and speed up rendering of the page.

The Datastore

Most useful web applications need to store information during the handling of a request for retrieval during a later request. A typical arrangement for a small website involves a single database server for the entire site, and one or more web servers that connect to the database to store or retrieve data. Using a single central database server makes it easy to have one canonical representation of the data, so multiple users accessing multiple web servers all see the same and most recent information. But a central server is difficult to scale once it reaches its capacity for simultaneous connections.

By far the most popular kind of data storage system for web applications in the past decade has been the relational database, with tables of rows and columns arranged for space efficiency and concision, and with indexes and raw computing power for performing queries, especially "join" queries that can treat multiple related records as a queryable unit. Other kinds of data storage systems include hierarchical datastores (filesystems, XML databases) and object databases. Each kind of database has pros and cons, and which type is best suited for an application depends on the nature of the application's data and how it is accessed. And each kind of database has its own techniques for growing past the first server.

Google App Engine's database system most closely resembles an object database. It is not a join-query relational database, and if you come from the world of relational-database-backed web applications (as I did), this will probably require changing the way you think about your application's data. As with the runtime environment, the design of the App Engine datastore is an abstraction that allows App Engine to handle the details of distributing and scaling the application, so your code can focus on other things.

Entities and Properties

An App Engine application stores its data as one or more datastore *entities*. An entity has one or more *properties*, each of which has a name, and a value that is of one of several primitive value types. Each entity is of a named *kind*, which categorizes the entity for the purpose of queries.

At first glance, this seems similar to a relational database: entities of a kind are like rows in a table, and properties are like columns (fields). However, there are two major differences between entities and rows. First, an entity of a given kind is not required to have the same properties as other entities of the same kind. Second, an entity can have a property of the same name as another entity has, but with a different type of value. In this way, datastore entities are "schemaless." As you'll soon see, this design provides both powerful flexibility as well as some maintenance challenges.

Another difference between an entity and a table row is that an entity can have multiple values for a single property. This feature is a bit quirky, but can be quite useful once understood.

Every datastore entity has a unique key that is either provided by the application or generated by App Engine (your choice). Unlike a relational database, the key is not a "field" or property, but an independent aspect of the entity. You can fetch an entity quickly if you know its key, and you can perform queries on key values.

A entity's key *cannot* be changed after the entity has been created. Neither can its kind. App Engine uses the entity's kind and key to help determine where the entity is stored in a large collection of servers—though neither the key nor the kind ensure that two entities are stored on the same server.

Queries and Indexes

A datastore query returns zero or more entities of a single kind. It can also return just the keys of entities that would be returned for a query. A query can filter based on conditions that must be met by the values of an entity's properties, and can return entities ordered by property values. A query can also filter and sort using keys.

In a typical relational database, queries are planned and executed in real time against the data tables, which are stored as they were designed by the developer. The developer can also tell the database to produce and maintain indexes on certain columns to speed up certain queries.

App Engine does something dramatically different. With App Engine, *every* query has a corresponding index maintained by the datastore. When the application performs a query, the datastore finds the index for that query, scans down to the first row that matches the query, then returns the entity for each consecutive row in the index until the first row that doesn't match the query.

Of course, this requires that App Engine know ahead of time which queries the application is going to perform. It doesn't need to know the values of the filters in advance, but it does need to know the kind of entity to query, the properties being filtered or sorted, and the operators of the filters and the orders of the sorts.

App Engine provides a set of indexes for simple queries by default, based on which properties exist on entities of a kind. For more complex queries, an app must include index specifications in its configuration. The App Engine SDK helps produce this configuration file by watching which queries are performed as you test your application with the provided development web server on your computer. When you upload your app, the datastore knows to make indexes for every query the app performed during testing. You can also edit the index configuration manually.

When your application creates new entities and updates existing ones, the datastore updates every corresponding index. This makes queries very fast (each query is a simple table scan) at the expense of entity updates (possibly many tables may need updating for a single change). In fact, the performance of an index-backed query is not affected by the number of entities in the datastore, only the size of the result set.

It's worth paying attention to indexes, as they take up space and increase the time it takes to update entities. We discuss indexes in detail in Chapter 5.

Transactions

When an application has many clients attempting to read or write the same data simultaneously, it is imperative that the data always be in a consistent state. One user should never see half-written data or data that doesn't make sense because another user's action hasn't completed.

When an application updates the properties of a single entity, App Engine ensures that either every update to the entity succeeds all at once, or the entire update fails and the entity remains the way it was prior to the beginning of the update. Other users do not see any effects of the change until the change succeeds.

In other words, an update of a single entity occurs in a *transaction*. Each transaction is *atomic*: the transaction either succeeds completely or fails completely, and cannot succeed or fail in smaller pieces.

An application can read or update multiple entities in a single transaction, but it must tell App Engine which entities will be updated together when it creates the entities. The application does this by creating entities in *entity groups*. App Engine uses entity groups to control how entities are distributed across servers, so it can guarantee a transaction on a group succeeds or fails completely. In database terms, the App Engine datastore natively supports *local transactions*.

When an application calls the datastore API to update an entity, control does not return to the application until the transaction succeeds or fails, and the call returns with knowledge of success or failure. For updates, this means the application waits for all entities and indexes to be updated before doing anything else.

If a user tries to update an entity while another user's update of the entity is in progress, the datastore returns immediately with a concurrency failure exception. It is often appropriate for the app to retry a bounced transaction several times before declaring the condition an error, usually retrieving data that may have changed within the transaction before calculating new values and updating it. In database terms, App Engine uses *optimistic concurrency control*.

Reading the entity never fails due to concurrency; the application just sees the entity in its most recent stable state. You can also perform multiple reads in a transaction to ensure that all of the data read in the transaction is current and consistent with itself.

In most cases, retrying a transaction on a contested entity will succeed. But if an application is designed such that many users might update a single entity, the more popular the application gets, the more likely users will get concurrency failures. It is important to design entity groups to avoid concurrency failures even with a large number of users.

An application can bundle multiple datastore operations in a single transaction. For example, the application can start a transaction, read an entity, update a property value based on the last read value, save the entity, then commit the transaction. In this case, the save action does not occur unless the entire transaction succeeds without conflict with another transaction. If there is a conflict and the app wants to try again, the app should retry the entire transaction: read the (possibly updated) entity again, use the new value for the calculation, and attempt the update again.

With indexes and optimistic concurrency control, the App Engine datastore is designed for applications that need to read data quickly, ensure that the data it sees is in a consistent form, and scale the number of users and the size of the data automatically. While these goals are somewhat different from those of a relational database, they are especially well suited to web applications.

The Services

The datastore's relationship with the runtime environment is that of a service: the application uses an API to access a separate system that manages all of its own scaling needs separately from the runtime environment. Google App Engine includes several other self-scaling services useful for web applications.

The memory cache (or *memcache*) service is a short-term key-value storage service. Its main advantage over the datastore is that it is fast, much faster than the datastore for simple storage and retrieval. The memcache stores values in memory instead of on disk for faster access. It is distributed like the datastore, so every request sees the same set of keys and values. However, it is not persistent like the datastore: if a server goes down, such as during a power failure, memory is erased. It also has a more limited sense of atomicity and transactionality than the datastore. As the name implies, the memcache service is best used as a cache for the results of frequently performed queries or calculations. The application checks for a cached value, and if the value isn't there, it performs the query or calculation and stores the value in the cache for future use.

App Engine applications can access other web resources using the URL Fetch service. The service makes HTTP requests to other servers on the Internet, such as to retrieve pages or interact with web services. Since remote servers can be slow to respond, the URL Fetch API supports fetching URLs in the background while a request handler does other things, but in all cases the fetch must start and finish within the request handler's lifetime. The application can also set a deadline, after which the call is canceled if the remote host hasn't responded.

App Engine applications can send messages using the Mail service. Messages can be sent on behalf of the application or on behalf of the user who made the request that is sending the email (if the message is from the user). Many web applications use email to notify users, confirm user actions, and validate contact information.

An application can also receive email messages. If an app is configured to receive email, a message sent to the app's address is routed to the Mail service, which delivers the message to the app in the form of an HTTP request to a request handler.

App Engine applications can send and receive instant messages to and from chat services that support the XMPP protocol, including Google Talk. An app sends an XMPP chat message by calling the XMPP service. As with incoming email, when someone sends a message to the app's address, the XMPP service delivers it to the app by calling a request handler.

The image processing service can do lightweight transformations of image data, such as for making thumbnail images of uploaded photos. The image processing tasks are performed using the same infrastructure Google uses to process images with some of its other products, so the results come back quickly. We won't be covering the image service API in this book because Google's official documentation says everything there is to say about this easy-to-use service.

Google Accounts

App Engine features integration with Google Accounts, the user account system used by Google applications such as Google Mail, Google Docs, and Google Calendar. You can use Google Accounts as your app's account system, so you don't have to build your own. And if your users already have Google accounts, they can sign in to your app using their existing accounts, with no need to create new accounts just for your app. Of course, there is no obligation to use Google Accounts. You can always build your own account system, or use an OpenID provider.

Google Accounts is especially useful for developing applications for your company or organization using Google Apps. With Google Apps, your organization's members can use the same account to access your custom applications as well as their email, calendar, and documents.

Task Queues and Cron Jobs

A web application has to respond to web requests very quickly, usually in less than a second and preferably in just a few dozen milliseconds, to provide a smooth experience to the user sitting in front of the browser. This doesn't give the application much time to do work. Sometimes, there is more work to do than there is time to do it. In such cases it's usually OK if the work gets done within a few seconds, minutes, or hours, instead of right away, as the user is waiting for a response from the server. But the user needs a guarantee that the work will get done.

For this kind of work, App Engine uses task queues. Task queues let request handlers describe work to be done at a later time, outside the scope of the web request. Queues ensure that every task gets done eventually. If a task fails, the queue retries the task until it succeeds. You can configure the rate at which queues are processed to spread the workload throughout the day.

A queue performs a task by calling a request handler. It can include a data payload provided by the code that created the task, delivered to the task's handler as an HTTP request. The task's handler is subject to the same limits as other request handlers, including the 30-second time limit.

An especially powerful feature of task queues is the ability to enqueue a task within a datastore transaction. This ensures that the task will be enqueued only if the rest of the datastore transaction succeeds. You can use transactional tasks to perform additional datastore operations that must be consistent with the transaction eventually, but that do not need the strong consistency guarantees of the datastore's local transactions.

App Engine has another service for executing tasks at specific times of the day. Scheduled tasks are also known as "cron jobs," a name borrowed from a similar feature of the Unix operating system. The scheduled tasks service can invoke a request handler at a specified time of the day, week, or month, based on a schedule you provide when you upload your application. Scheduled tasks are useful for doing regular maintenance or sending periodic notification messages.

We'll look at these features and some powerful uses for them in Chapter 13.

Developer Tools

Google provides free tools for developing App Engine applications in Java or Python. You can download the software development kit (SDK) for your chosen language and your computer's operating system from Google's website. Java users can get the Java SDK in the form of a plug-in for the Eclipse integrated development environment. Python users using Windows or Mac OS X can get the Python SDK in the form of a GUI application. Both SDKs are also available as ZIP archives of command-line tools, for using directly or integrating into your development environment or build system.

Each SDK includes a development web server that runs your application on your local computer and simulates the runtime environment, the datastore, and the services. The development server automatically detects changes in your source files and reloads them as needed, so you can keep the server running while you develop the application.

If you're using Eclipse, you can run the Java development server in the interactive debugger, and can set breakpoints in your application code. You can also use Eclipse for Python app development using PyDev, an Eclipse extension that includes an interactive Python debugger. (Using PyDev is not covered in this book, but there are instructions on Google's site.)

The development version of the datastore can automatically generate configuration for query indexes as the application performs queries, which App Engine will use to pre-build indexes for those queries. You can turn this feature off for testing whether queries have appropriate indexes in the configuration.

The development web server includes a built-in web application for inspecting the contents of the (simulated) datastore. You can also create new datastore entities using this interface for testing purposes.

Each SDK also includes a tool for interacting with the application running on App Engine. Primarily, you use this tool to upload your application code to App Engine. You can also use this tool to download log data from your live application, or manage the live application's indexes.

The Python and Java SDKs include a feature you can install in your app for secure remote programmatic access to your live application. The Python SDK includes tools that use this feature for bulk data operations, such as uploading new data from a text file and downloading large amounts of data for backup or migration purposes. The SDK also includes a Python interactive command-line shell for testing, debugging, and manually manipulating live data. (These tools are in the Python SDK, but also work with Java apps using the Java version of the remote access feature.) You can write your own scripts and programs that use the remote access feature for large-scale data transformations or other maintenance.

The Administration Console

When your application is ready for its public debut, you create an administrator account and set up the application on App Engine. You use your administrator account to create and manage the application, view its access and resource usage statistics and message logs, and more, all with a web-based interface called the Administration Console.

You sign in to the Administration Console using your Google account. You can use your current Google account if you have one, though you may also want to create a Google account just for your application, which you might use as the "from" address on email messages. Once you have created an application using the Administration Console, you can add additional Google accounts as administrators. Any administrator can access the Console, and can upload a new version of the application.

The Console gives you access to real-time performance data about how your application is being used, as well as access to log data emitted by your application. You can also query the datastore for the live application using a web interface, and check on the status of datastore indexes. (Newly created indexes with large data sets take time to build.)

When you upload new code for your application using the SDK, the uploaded version is assigned a version identifier, which you specify in the application's configuration file. The version used for the live application is whichever major version is selected as the "default." You control which version is the "default" using the Administration Console. You can access nondefault versions using a special URL containing the version identifier. This allows you to test a new version of an app running on App Engine before making it official.

You use the Console to set up and manage the billing account for your application. When you're ready for your application to consume more resources beyond the free amounts, you set up a billing account using a credit card and Google Accounts. The owner of the billing account sets a budget, a maximum amount of money that can be charged per calendar day. Within that budget, you can allocate how much additional

CPU time, bandwidth, storage, and email recipients the app can consume. You are only charged for what the application actually uses beyond the free amounts.

Things App Engine Doesn't Do...Yet

When people first start using App Engine, there are several things they ask about that App Engine doesn't do. Some of these are things Google may implement in the near future, and others run against the grain of the App Engine design and aren't likely to be added. Listing such features in a book is difficult, because by the time you read this, Google may have already implemented them. But it's worth noting these features here, especially to note workaround techniques.

App Engine supports secure connections (HTTPS) to .appspot.com subdomains, but does not yet support secure connections to custom domains. Google Accounts sign-ins always use secure connections.

An application can use the URL Fetch service to make an HTTPS request to another site, but App Engine does not verify the certificate used on the remote server.

An app can receive incoming email and XMPP chat messages at several addresses. As of this writing, none of these addresses can use a custom domain name. See Chapter 11 for information on incoming email and XMPP addresses.

An app can accept web requests on a custom domain using Google Apps. Google Apps maps a subdomain of your custom domain to an app, and this subdomain can be www if you choose. This does not yet support requests for "naked" domains, such as http:// example.com/. It also does not support arbitrary tertiary domains on custom domains (http://foo.www.example.com). App Engine *does* support arbitrary subdomains on appspot.com URLs, such as foo.app-id.appspot.com.

App Engine does not host long-running background processes. Task queues and scheduled tasks can invoke request handlers outside of a user request, and can drive some kinds of batch processing. But processing large chores in small batches is different in character and range from full-scale distributed computing tasks. We will discuss batch processing later in Chapter 12.

App Engine does not support streaming or long-term connections. If the client supports it, the app can use XMPP and an XMPP service (such as Google Talk) to deliver state updates to the client. You could also do this using a polling technique, where the client asks the application for updates on a regular basis, but polling is difficult to scale (5,000 simultaneous users polling every 5 seconds = 1,000 queries per second), and is not appropriate for all applications. Also note that request handlers cannot communicate with the client while performing other calculations. The server sends a response to the client's request only after the handler has returned control to the server.

App Engine only supports web requests via HTTP or HTTPS, and email and XMPP messages via the services. It does not support other kinds of network connections. For instance, a client cannot connect to an App Engine application via FTP.

The App Engine datastore does not support full-text search queries, such as for implementing a search engine for a content management system. Long text values are not indexed, and short text values are only indexed for equality and inequality queries. It is possible to implement text search by building search indexes within the application, but this is difficult to do in a scalable way for large amounts of dynamic data.

Getting Started

You can start developing applications for Google App Engine without creating an account. All you need to get started is the App Engine SDK appropriate for your choice of language, which is a free download from the App Engine website:

> *http://code.google.com/appengine/*

While you're there, check out the official "Getting Started Guide" for your language, which demonstrates how to create an application and use several of App Engine's features.

In the next chapter, we'll describe how to create a new project from start to finish, including how to create an account, upload the application, and run it on App Engine.

## CHAPTER 2

Creating an Application

The App Engine development model is as simple as it gets:

1. Create the application.
2. Test the application on your own computer using the web server software included with the App Engine development kit.
3. Upload the finished application to App Engine.

In this chapter, we will walk through the process of creating a new application, testing it with the development server, registering a new application ID and setting up a domain name, and uploading the app to App Engine. We will look at some of the features of the Python and Java software development kits (SDKs) and the App Engine Administration Console. We'll also discuss the workflow for developing and deploying an app.

We will take this opportunity to demonstrate a common pattern in web applications: managing user preferences data. This pattern uses several App Engine services and features.

Setting Up the SDK

All the tools and libraries you need to develop an application are included in the App Engine SDK. There are separate SDKs for Python and Java, each with features useful for developing with each language. The SDKs work on any platform, including Windows, Mac OS X, and Linux.

The Python and Java SDKs each include a web server that runs your app in a simulated runtime environment on your computer. The development server enforces the sandbox restrictions of the full runtime environment and simulates each of the App Engine services. You can start the development server and leave it running while you build your app, reloading pages in your browser to see your changes in effect.

Both SDKs include a multifunction tool for interacting with the app running on App Engine. You use this tool to upload your app's code, static files, and configuration.

The tool can also manage datastore indexes, task queues, and scheduled tasks, and can download messages logged by the live application so you can analyze your app's traffic and behavior.

Because Google launched Python support before Java, the Python SDK has a few tools not available in the Java SDK. Most notably, the Python SDK includes tools for uploading and downloading data to and from the datastore. This is useful for making backups, changing the structure of existing data, and for processing data offline. If you are using Java, you can use the Python-based data tools with a bit of effort.

The Python SDKs for Windows and Mac OS X include a "launcher" application that makes it especially easy to create, edit, test, and upload an app using a simple graphical interface. Paired with a good programming text editor (such as Notepad++ for Windows, or TextMate for Mac OS X), the launcher provides a fast and intuitive Python development experience.

For Java developers, Google provides a plug-in for the Eclipse integrated development environment that implements a complete App Engine development workflow. The plug-in includes a template for creating new App Engine Java apps, as well as a debugging profile for running the app and the development web server in the Eclipse debugger. To deploy a project to App Engine, you just click a button on the Eclipse toolbar.

Both SDKs also include cross-platform command-line tools that provide these features. You can use these tools from a command prompt, or otherwise integrate them into your development environment as you see fit.

We'll discuss the Python SDK first, then the Java SDK in "Installing the Java SDK" on page 20. Feel free to skip the section that does not apply to your chosen language.

Installing the Python SDK

The App Engine SDK for the Python runtime environment runs on any computer that runs Python 2.5.

If you are using Mac OS X or Linux, or if you have used Python previously, you may already have Python on your system. You can test whether Python is installed on your system and check which version is installed by running the following command at a command prompt (in Windows, Command Prompt; in Mac OS X, Terminal):

```
python -V
```

(That's a capital "V.") If Python is installed, it prints its version number, like so:

```
Python 2.5.2
```

You can download and install Python 2.5 for your platform from the Python website:

http://www.python.org/

Be sure to get Python version 2.5 (such as 2.5.4) from the "Download" section of the site. As of this writing, the latest major version of Python is 3.1, and the latest 2.x-compatible release is 2.6. The App Engine Python SDK works with Python 2.6, but it's better to use the same version of Python that's used on App Engine for development so you are not surprised by obscure compatibility issues.

 App Engine Python does not yet support Python 3. Python 3 includes several new language and library features that are not backward compatible with earlier versions. When App Engine adds support for Python 3, it will likely be in the form of a new runtime environment, in addition to the Python 2 environment. You control which runtime environment your application uses with a setting in the app's configuration file, so your application will continue to run as intended when new runtime environments are released.

You can download the App Engine Python SDK bundle for your operating system from the Google App Engine website:

http://code.google.com/appengine/downloads.html

Download and install the file appropriate for your operating system:

- For Windows, the Python SDK is an `.msi` (Microsoft Installer) file. Click on the appropriate link to download it, then double-click on the file to start the installation process. This installs the Google App Engine Launcher application, adds an icon to your Start menu, and adds the command-line tools to the command path.

- For Mac OS X, the Python SDK is a Mac application in a `.dmg` (disk image) file. Click on the link to download it, then double-click on the file to mount the disk image. Drag the GoogleAppEngineLauncher icon to your Applications folder. To install the command-line tools, double-click the icon to start the Launcher, then allow the Launcher to create the "symlinks" when prompted.

- If you are using Linux or another platform, the Python SDK is available as a `.zip` archive. Download and unpack it (typically with the the `unzip` command) to create a directory named *google_appengine*. The command-line tools all reside in this directory. Adjust your command path as needed.

To test that the App Engine Python SDK is installed, run the following command at a command prompt:

```
dev_appserver.py --help
```

The command prints a helpful message and exits. If instead you see a message about the command not being found, check that the installer completed successfully, and that the location of the `dev_appserver.py` command is on your command path.

Windows users, if when you run this command a dialog box opens with the message "Windows cannot open this file... To open this file, Windows needs to know what program created it," you must tell Windows to use Python to open the file. In the dialog box, choose "Select the program from a list," and click OK. Click Browse, then locate your Python installation (such as *C:\Python25*). Select *python* from this folder, then click Open. Select "Always use the selected program to open this kind of file." Click OK. A window will open and attempt to run the command, then immediately close. You can now run the command from the Command Prompt.

A brief tour of the Launcher

The Windows and Mac OS X versions of the Python SDK include an application called the Google App Engine Launcher (hereafter just "Launcher"). With the Launcher, you can create and manage multiple App Engine Python projects using a graphical interface. Figure 2-1 shows an example of the Launcher window in Mac OS X.

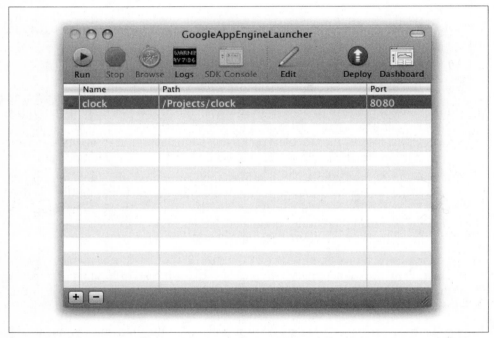

Figure 2-1. The Google App Engine Launcher for Mac OS X main window, with a project selected

To create a new project, select New Project... from the File menu (or click the plus-sign button at the bottom of the window). Browse to where you want to keep your project files, then enter a name for the project. The Launcher creates a new directory at that location, named after the project, to hold the project's files, and creates several starter files. The project appears in the project list in the main launcher window.

To start the development web server, make sure the project is selected, then click the Run button. You can stop the server with the Stop button. To open the home page of the running app in a browser, click the Browse button. The Logs button displays messages logged by the app in the development server.

The SDK Console button opens a web interface for the development server with several features for inspecting the running application, including tools to inspect the contents of the (simulated) datastore and memory cache, and an interactive console that executes Python statements and displays the results.

The Edit button opens the project's files in your default text editor. In the Mac OS X version, this is especially useful with text editors that can open a directory's worth of files, such as TextMate or Emacs. In the Windows version, this just opens *app.yaml* for editing.

The Deploy button uploads the project to App Engine. Before you can deploy a project, you must register an application ID with App Engine and edit the application's configuration file with the registered ID. The Dashboard button opens a browser window with the App Engine Administration Console for the deployed app. We'll look at the configuration file, the registration process, and the Administration Console later in this chapter.

The complete App Engine Python SDK, including the command-line tools, resides in the Launcher's application directory. In the Windows version, the installer adds the appropriate directory to the command path, so you can run these tools from a Command Prompt.

In Mac OS X, when you start the Launcher for the first time it asks for permission to create "symlinks." This creates symbolic links in the directory */usr/local/bin/* that refer to the command-line tools in the application bundle. With the links in this directory, you can type just the name of a command at a Terminal prompt to run it. If you didn't create the symlinks, you can do so later by selecting the Make Symlinks... item from the GoogleAppEngineLauncher menu.

You can set command-line flags for the development server within the Launcher. To do so, select the application, then go to the Edit menu and select Application Settings.... Add the desired command-line options to the "Extra Flags" field, then click Update.

 The Mac OS X version of the Launcher installs Google's software update facility to check for new versions of the App Engine SDK. When a new version is released, this feature notifies you and offers to upgrade.

Immediately after you upgrade, you'll notice the symlinks stop working. To fix the symlinks, reopen the Launcher app and follow the prompts. The upgrade can't do this automatically because it needs your permission to create new symlinks.

Installing the Java SDK

The App Engine SDK for the Java runtime environment runs on any computer that runs the Java SE Development Kit (JDK). The App Engine for Java SDK supports JDK 5 and JDK 6. When running on App Engine, the Java runtime environment uses the Java 6 JVM.

If you don't already have it, you can download and install the Java 6 JDK for most platforms from Sun's website. (Mac users, see the next section.)

   http://java.sun.com/javase/downloads/index.jsp

You can test whether the Java development kit is installed on your system and check which version it is by running the following command at a command prompt (in Windows, Command Prompt; in Mac OS X, Terminal):

    javac -version

If you have the Java 6 JDK installed, the command will print a version number similar to `javac 1.6.0`. If you have the Java 5 JDK installed, the command will print a version number similar to `javac 1.5.0`. The actual output varies depending on which specific version you have.

App Engine Java apps use interfaces and features from Java Enterprise Edition (Java EE). The App Engine SDK includes implementations for the relevant Java EE features. You do not need to install a separate Java EE implementation.

The steps for installing the App Engine SDK for Java depend on whether you wish to use the Google Plugin for the Eclipse IDE. We'll cover these situations separately.

Java on Mac OS X

If you are using Mac OS X, you already have Java and the JDK installed. How you'd use it depends on the version of the operating system, and whether your computer has a 32-bit processor (such as the Intel Core Duo) or a 64-bit processor (Intel Core 2 Duo, Intel Xeon). You can check which processor you have by selecting the Apple menu, About This Mac.

Mac OS X 10.6 Snow Leopard includes Java 6 and its JDK, and it includes separate versions for 32-bit processors and for 64-bit processors. If you have a 64-bit processor, the 64-bit Java 6 is the default. If you have a 32-bit processor, the 32-bit Java 6 is the default.

Mac OS X 10.5 Leopard includes both Java 5 and Java 6. However, in Leopard, Java 5 is the default. This is because Leopard's version of Java 6 only works with 64-bit processors. If you have a 64-bit processor, you can change the default version to the 64-bit Java 6.

To change the version of Java used by the system, open the Java Preferences utility, which you can find under */Applications/Utilities/*. In the "Java Applications" list, drag the desired version (such as "Java SE 6, 64-bit") to the top of the list. OS X uses the topmost version in the list that is compatible with your system.

If you have a 32-bit Mac running Leopard, you're stuck using Java 5. The App Engine SDK works fine under Java 5, and apps built with Java 5 run fine on App Engine. Just be aware that you're using Java 5, and code samples you might find for App Engine may assume Java 6.

If you are using Eclipse, make sure you get the version that corresponds with your processor and selected version of Java. Separate versions of the "Eclipse IDE for Java EE Developers" bundle are available for 32-bit and 64-bit processors.

For more information about Java and Mac OS X, see Apple's developer website:

> *http://developer.apple.com/java/*

Installing the Java SDK with the Google Plugin for Eclipse

One of the easiest ways to develop App Engine applications in Java is to use the Eclipse IDE and the Google Plugin for Eclipse. The plug-in works with Eclipse 3.3 (Europa), Eclipse 3.4 (Ganymede), and Eclipse 3.5 (Galileo). You can get Eclipse for your platform for free at the Eclipse website:

> *http://www.eclipse.org/*

If you're getting Eclipse specifically for App Engine development, get the "Eclipse IDE for Java EE Developers" bundle. This bundle includes several useful components for developing web applications, including the Eclipse Web Tools Platform (WTP) package.

You can tell Eclipse to use the JDK you have installed in the Preferences window. In Eclipse 3.5, select Preferences (Windows and Linux, in the Window menu; Mac OS X, in the Eclipse menu). In the Java category, select "Installed JREs." If necessary, add the location of the SDK to the list, and make sure the checkbox is checked.

To install the App Engine Java SDK and the Google Plugin, use the software installation feature of Eclipse. In Eclipse 3.5, select Install New Software... from the Help menu, then type the following URL in the "Work with" field and click the Add... button:

```
http://dl.google.com/eclipse/plugin/3.5
```

(This URL does not work in a browser; it only works with the Eclipse software installer.)

In the dialog window that opens, enter "Google" for the name, then click OK. Two items are added to the list, one for the plug-in ("Plugin") and a set for the App Engine and Google Web Toolkit SDKs ("SDKs"). Figure 2-2 shows the Install Software window with the appropriate items selected.

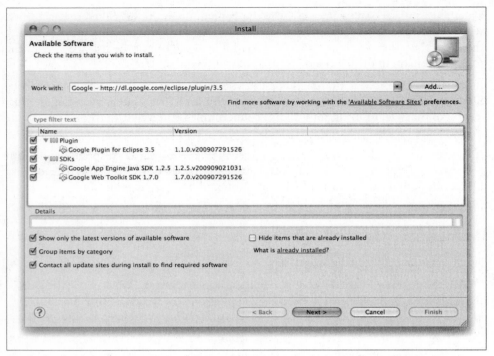

Figure 2-2. The Eclipse 3.5 (Galileo) Install Software window, with the Google Plugin selected

Check the boxes for these two items. Click the Next > button and follow the prompts.

For more information on installing the Google Plugin for Eclipse, including instructions for Eclipse 3.3 or 3.4, see the website for the plug-in:

http://code.google.com/eclipse/

After installation, the Eclipse toolbar has three new buttons, as shown in Figure 2-3.

Figure 2-3. The Eclipse 3.5 toolbar with the Google Plugin installed, with three new buttons: New Web Application Project, GWT Compile Project, and Deploy App Engine Project

The plug-in adds several features to the Eclipse interface:

- The three buttons in the toolbar: New Web Application Project, GWT Compile Project, and Deploy App Engine Project
- A Web Application Project item under New in the File menu

- A Web Application debug profile, for running an app in the development web server under the Eclipse debugger

You can use Eclipse to develop your application, and to deploy it to App Engine. To use other features of the SDK, like downloading log data, you must use the command-line tools from the App Engine SDK. Eclipse installs the SDK in your Eclipse application directory, under *eclipse/plugins/*. The actual directory name depends on the specific version of the SDK installed, but it looks something like this:

```
com.google.appengine.eclipse.sdkbundle_1.2.5.v200909021031/appengine-java-sdk-1.2.5/
```

This directory contains command-line tools in a subdirectory named *bin/*. In Mac OS X or Linux, you may need to change the permissions of these files to be executable in order to use the tools from the command line:

```
chmod 755 bin/*
```

You can add the *bin/* directory to your command path, but keep in mind that the path will change each time you update the SDK.

Installing the Java SDK without Eclipse

If you are not using the Eclipse IDE or otherwise don't wish to use the Google Plugin, you can download the App Engine Java SDK as a `.zip` archive from the App Engine website:

http://code.google.com/appengine/downloads.html

The archive unpacks to a directory with a name such as *appengine-java-sdk-1.2.5*.

The SDK contains command-line launch scripts in the *bin/* subdirectory. You can add this directory to your command path to make the commands easier to run.

Both the AppCfg tool and the development web server execute Java classes to perform their functions. You can integrate these tools into your IDE or build scripts by calling the launch scripts, or by calling the Java classes directly. Look at the contents of the launch scripts to see the syntax.

The App Engine SDK includes a plug-in for Apache Ant that lets you perform functions of the SDK from an Ant build script. See the App Engine documentation for more information about using Ant with App Engine.

Test that the App Engine Java SDK is installed properly by running the following command at a command prompt:

```
dev_appserver --help
```

Mac OS X and Linux users, use `dev_appserver.sh` as the command name.

The command prints a helpful message and exits. If instead you see a message about the command not being found, check that the archive unpacked successfully, and that the SDK's *bin/* directory is on your command path.

Developing the Application

An App Engine application responds to web requests. It does so by calling *request handlers*, routines that accept request parameters and return responses. App Engine determines which request handler to use for a given request from the request's URL, using a configuration file included with the app that maps URLs to handlers.

An app can also include static files, such as images, CSS stylesheets, and browser JavaScript. App Engine serves these files directly to clients in response to requests for corresponding URLs without invoking any code. The app's configuration specifies which of its files are static, and which URLs to use for those files.

The application configuration includes metadata about the app, such as its application ID and version number. When you deploy the app to App Engine, all of the app's files, including the code, configuration files, and static files, are uploaded and associated with the application ID and version number mentioned in the configuration. An app can also have configuration files specific to the services, such as for datastore indexes, task queues, and scheduled tasks. These files are associated with the app in general, not a specific version of the app.

The structure and format of the code and configuration files differ for Python apps and for Java apps, but the concepts are similar. In the next few sections, we will create the files needed for a simple application in both Python and Java, and will look at how to use the tools and libraries included with each SDK.

The User Preferences Pattern

The application we will create in this section is a simple clock. When a user visits the site, the app displays the current time of day according to the server's system clock. By default, the app shows the current time in the Coordinated Universal Time (UTC) time zone. The user can customize the time zone by signing in using Google Accounts and setting a preference.

This app demonstrates three App Engine features:

- The datastore, primary storage for user settings data that is persistent, reliable, and scalable
- The memory cache (or *memcache*), secondary storage that is faster than the datastore, but is not necessarily persistent in the long term
- Google Accounts, the ability to use Google's user account system for authenticating and identifying users

Google Accounts works similarly to most user account systems. If the user is not signed in to the clock application, she sees a generic view with default settings (the UTC time zone) and a link to sign in or create a new account. If the user chooses to sign in or register, the application directs her to a sign-in form managed by Google Accounts. Signing in or creating an account redirects the user back to the application.

Of course, you can implement your own account mechanism instead of using Google Accounts. Using Google Accounts has advantages and disadvantages—the chief advantage being that you don't have to implement your own account mechanism. If a user of your app already has a Google account, the user can sign in with that account without creating a new account for your app.

If the user accesses the application while signed in, the app loads the user's preferences data and uses it to render the page. The app retrieves the preferences data in two steps. First, it attempts to get the data from the fast secondary storage, the memory cache. If the data is not present in the memory cache, the app attempts to retrieve it from the primary storage (the datastore), and if successful, it puts it into the memory cache to be found by future requests.

This means that for most requests, the application can get the user's preferences from the memcache without accessing the datastore. While reading from the datastore is reasonably fast, reading from the memcache is much faster. The difference is substantial when the same data must be accessed every time the user visits a page.

Our clock application has two request handlers. One handler displays the current time of day, along with links for signing in and out. It also displays a web form for adjusting the time zone when the user is signed in. The second request handler processes the time zone form when it is submitted. When the user submits the preferences form, the app saves the changes and redirects the browser back to the main page.

The application gets the current time from the application server's system clock. It's worth noting that App Engine makes no guarantees that the system clocks of all of its web servers are synchronized. Since two requests for this app may be handled by different servers, different requests may see different clocks. The server clock is not consistent enough as a source of time data for a real-world application, but it's good enough for this example.

In the next section, we implement this app using Python. We do the same thing with Java in the section "Developing a Java App" on page 39. As before, feel free to skip the section that doesn't apply to you.

Developing a Python App

The simplest Python application for App Engine is a single directory with two files: a configuration file named *app.yaml*, and a file of Python code for a request handler. The directory containing the *app.yaml* file is the application root directory. You'll refer to this directory often when using the tools.

If you are using the Launcher, you can start a new project by selecting the File menu, New Application.... The Launcher creates a new project with several files, which you may wish to edit to follow along with the example. Alternatively, you can create the project directory and files by hand, then add the project to the Launcher by selecting the File menu, Add Existing Application....

Create a directory named *clock* to contain the project. Using your favorite text editor, create a file inside this directory named *app.yaml* similar to Example 2-1.

Example 2-1. The app.yaml configuration file for a simple application

```
application: clock
version: 1
runtime: python
api_version: 1

handlers:
- url: /.*
  script: main.py
```

This configuration file is in a format called YAML, an open format for configuration files and network messages. You don't need to know much about the format beyond what you see here.

In this example, the configuration file tells App Engine that this is version 1 of an application called clock, which uses version 1 of the Python runtime environment (the "API version"). Every request for this application (every URL that matches the regular expression /.*) is to be handled by a Python script named *main.py*.

Create a file named *main.py* similar to Example 2-2, in the same directory as *app.yaml*.

Example 2-2. A simple Python request handler script

```
import datetime

print 'Content-Type: text/html'
print ''
print '<p>The time is: %s</p>' % str(datetime.datetime.now())
```

This simple Python program imports the datetime module from the Python standard library, prints an HTTP header that indicates the type of the document (HTML), then prints a message containing the current time according to the web server's clock.

Python request handler scripts use the CGI protocol for communicating with App Engine. When App Engine receives a request for your Python application, App Engine establishes a runtime environment with the request data in environment variables, determines which handler script to run using the configuration file, then runs the script with the request body (if any) on the standard input stream. The handler script is expected to perform all necessary actions for the request, then print a response to the standard output stream, including a valid HTTP header. This simple example ignores the request data, prints a header indicating the type of the response data, then prints a message with the current time to be displayed in the browser.

Let's test what we have so far. Start the development server by running the `dev_appserver.py` command, specifying the path to the project directory (*clock*) as an argument:

```
dev_appserver.py clock
```

 If your current working directory is the *clock* directory you just created, you can run the command using a dot (`.`) as the path to the project:

```
dev_appserver.py .
```

The server starts up and prints several messages to the console. If this is the first time you're running the server from the command line, it may ask whether you want it to check for updates; type your answer, then hit Enter. You can safely ignore warnings that say "Could not read datastore data" and "Could not initialize images API." These are expected if you have followed the installation steps so far. The last message should look something like this:

```
INFO ... Running application clock on port 8080: http://localhost:8080
```

This message indicates the server started successfully. If you do not see this message, check the other messages for hints, and double-check that the syntax of your *app.yaml* file is correct.

Test your application by visiting the server's URL in a web browser:

http://localhost:8080/

The browser displays a page similar to Figure 2-4.

Figure 2-4. The first version of the clock application viewed in a browser

You can leave the web server running while you develop your application. The web server notices when you make changes to your files, and reloads them automatically as needed.

 Using the Launcher, you can start the development web server by clicking the Run button. The icon next to the project turns green when the server starts successfully. To open a browser to view the project, click the Browse button.

Introducing the webapp framework

The code in Example 2-2 attempts to implement the CGI protocol directly, but you'd never do this for a real application. The Python standard library includes modules, such as the aptly named `cgi` module, that implement the CGI protocol and perform other common web application tasks. These implementations are complete, fast, and thoroughly tested, and it's nearly always better to use modules like these than to implement your own from scratch.

Web application frameworks go beyond libraries of modules to implement the best practices of web application development as a coherent suite of tools, components, and patterns: data modeling interfaces, template systems, request handling mechanisms, project management tools, and development environments that work together to reduce the amount of code you have to write and maintain. There are dozens of web frameworks written in Python, and several are mature, well documented, and have active developer communities. Django, web2py, and Pylons are examples of well-established Python web frameworks.

Not every Python web application framework works completely with the App Engine Python runtime environment. Constraints imposed by App Engine's sandboxing logic, especially the restriction on modules that use compiled C code, limit which frameworks work out of the box. Django (*http://www.djangoproject.com/*) is known to work well, and others have been adapted with additional software. We'll discuss how to use Django with App Engine in Chapter 14.

To make it easy to get started, App Engine includes a simple web framework called "webapp." The webapp framework is intended to be small and easy to use. It doesn't have the features of more established frameworks, but it's good enough for small projects. If you created the "clock" project using the Launcher, you may have noticed that the starter files use the webapp framework.

For simplicity, most of the Python examples in this book use the webapp framework. We won't cover webapp in detail in this book, but we'll introduce some of its features here. For larger applications, you may want to use a more featureful framework such as Django.

Let's upgrade the clock app to use the webapp framework. Replace the contents of *main.py* with the version shown in Example 2-3. Reload the page in your browser to see the new version in action. (You won't notice a difference other than an updated time. This example is equivalent to the previous version.)

Example 2-3. A simple request handler using the webapp framework

```python
from google.appengine.ext import webapp
from google.appengine.ext.webapp.util import run_wsgi_app
import datetime

class MainPage(webapp.RequestHandler):
    def get(self):
        time = datetime.datetime.now()

        self.response.headers['Content-Type'] = 'text/html'
        self.response.out.write('<p>The time is: %s</p>' % str(time))

application = webapp.WSGIApplication([('/', MainPage)],
                                    debug=True)

def main():
    run_wsgi_app(application)

if __name__ == '__main__':
    main()
```

Example 2-3 imports the module `google.appengine.ext.webapp`, then defines a request handler class called `MainPage`, a subclass of `webapp.RequestHandler`. The class defines methods for each HTTP method supported by the handler, in this case one method for HTTP GET called `get()`. When the application handles a request, it instantiates the handler class, sets `self.request` and `self.response` to values the handler method can access and modify, then calls the appropriate handler method, in this case `get()`. When the handler method exits, the application uses the value of `self.response` as the HTTP response.

The application itself is represented by an instance of the class `webapp.WSGIApplication`. The instance is initialized with a list of mappings of URLs to handler classes. The `debug` parameter tells the application to print error messages to the browser window when a handler returns an exception if the application is running under the development web server. webapp detects whether it is running under the development server or running as a live App Engine application, and will not print errors to the browser when running live even if `debug` is `True`. You can set it to `False` to have the development server emulate the live server when errors occur.

The script defines a `main()` function that runs the application using a utility method. Lastly, the script calls `main()` using the Python idiom of `if __name__ == '__main__': ...`, a condition that is always true when the script is run by the web server. This idiom allows you to import the script as a module for other code, including the classes and functions defined in the script, without running the `main()` routine.

Defining a `main()` function this way allows App Engine to cache the compiled handler script, making subsequent requests faster to execute. For more information on app caching, see Chapter 3.

A single `WSGIApplication` instance can handle multiple URLs, routing the request to different `RequestHandler` classes based on the URL pattern. But we've already seen that the *app.yaml* file maps URL patterns to handler scripts. So which URL patterns should appear in *app.yaml*, and which should appear in the `WSGIApplication`? Many web frameworks include their own URL dispatcher logic, and it's common to route all dynamic URLs to the framework's dispatcher in *app.yaml*. With webapp, the answer mostly depends on how you'd like to organize your code. For the clock application, we will create a second request handler as a separate script to take advantage of a feature of *app.yaml* for user authentication, but we could also put this logic in *main.py* and route the URL with the `WSGIApplication` object.

Users and Google Accounts

So far, our clock shows the same display for every user. To allow each user to customize the display and save her preferences for future sessions, we need a way to identify the user making a request. An easy way to do this is with Google Accounts.

Let's add something to the page that indicates whether the user is signed in, and provides links for signing in and signing out of the application. Edit *main.py* to resemble Example 2-4.

Example 2-4. A version of main.py that displays Google Accounts information and links

```
from google.appengine.api import users
from google.appengine.ext import webapp
from google.appengine.ext.webapp.util import run_wsgi_app
import datetime

class MainPage(webapp.RequestHandler):
    def get(self):
        time = datetime.datetime.now()
        user = users.get_current_user()
        if not user:
            navbar = ('<p>Welcome! <a href="%s">Sign in or register</a> to customize.</p>'
                      % (users.create_login_url(self.request.path)))
        else:
            navbar = ('<p>Welcome, %s! You can <a href="%s">sign out</a>.</p>'
                      % (user.email(), users.create_logout_url(self.request.path)))

        self.response.headers['Content-Type'] = 'text/html'
        self.response.out.write('''
        <html>
            <head>
                <title>The Time Is...</title>
            </head>
```

```
        <body>
        %s
            <p>The time is: %s</p>
        </body>
    </html>
    ''' % (navbar, str(time)))

application = webapp.WSGIApplication([('/', MainPage)],
                                    debug=True)

def main():
    run_wsgi_app(application)

if __name__ == '__main__':
    main()
```

In a real application, you would use a templating system for the output, separating the HTML and display logic from the application code. While many web application frameworks include a templating system, webapp does not. Since the clock app only has one page, we'll put the HTML in the handler code, using Python string formatting to keep things organized.

> The Python runtime environment includes a version of Django, whose templating system can be used with webapp. When Google released version 1 of the Python runtime environment, the latest version of Django was 0.96, so this is what the runtime includes. For more information on using Django templates with webapp, see the App Engine documentation.

Reload the page in your browser. The new page resembles Figure 2-5.

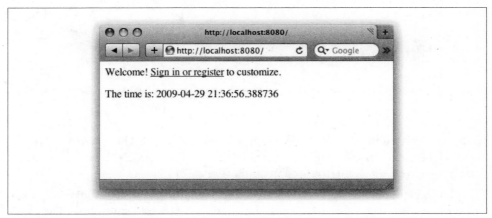

Figure 2-5. The clock app with a link to Google Accounts when the user is not signed in

The Python API for Google Accounts is provided by the module `google.appengine.api.users`. The `get_current_user()` function in this module returns `None` if the user is not signed in, or an object of the class `User` with the user's account information. The `email()` method on the `User` object returns the user's email address.

The `create_login_url()` and `create_logout_url()` methods generate URLs that go to Google Accounts. Each of these methods takes a URL path for the app where the user should be redirected after performing the desired task. The login URL goes to the Google Accounts page where the user can sign in or register for a new account. The logout URL visits Google Accounts to sign out the current user, then immediately redirects back to the given application URL.

If you click on the "Sign in or register" link with the app running in the development server, the link goes to the development server's simulated version of the Google Accounts sign-in screen, as shown in Figure 2-6. At this screen, you can enter any email address, and the development server will proceed as if you are signed in with an account that has that address.

Figure 2-6. The development server's simulated Google Accounts sign-in screen

If this app were running on App Engine, the login and logout URLs would go to the actual Google Accounts locations. Once signed in or out, Google Accounts redirects back to the given URL path for the live application.

Click on "Sign in or register," then click on the Login button on the simulated Google Accounts screen, using the default test email address (`test@example.com`). The clock app now looks like Figure 2-7. To sign out again, click the "sign out" link.

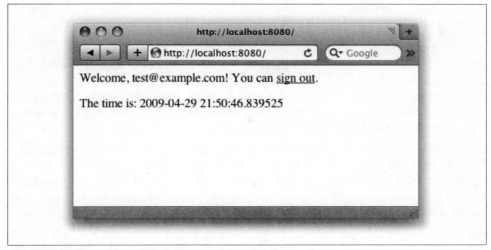

Welcome, test@example.com! You can sign out.

The time is: 2009-04-29 21:50:46.839525

Figure 2-7. The clock app, with the user signed in

Web forms and the datastore

Now that we know who the user is, we can ask her for her preferred time zone, remember her preference, and use it on future visits.

First, we need a way to remember the user's preferences so future requests can access them. The App Engine datastore provides reliable, scalable storage for this purpose. The Python API includes a data modeling interface that maps Python objects to datastore entities. We can use it to write a `UserPrefs` class.

Create a file named *models.py*, as shown in Example 2-5.

Example 2-5. The file models.py, with a class for storing user preferences in the datastore

```python
from google.appengine.api import users
from google.appengine.ext import db

class UserPrefs(db.Model):
    tz_offset = db.IntegerProperty(default=0)
    user = db.UserProperty(auto_current_user_add=True)

def get_userprefs(user_id=None):
    if not user_id:
        user = users.get_current_user()
        if not user:
            return None
        user_id = user.user_id()

    key = db.Key.from_path('UserPrefs', user_id)
    userprefs = db.get(key)
    if not userprefs:
```

```
        userprefs = UserPrefs(key_name=user_id)
    return userprefs
```

The Python data modeling interface is provided by the module google.appengine.ext.db. A data model is a class whose base class is db.Model. The model subclass defines the structure of the data in each object using class properties. This structure is enforced by db.Model when values are assigned to instance properties. For our UserPrefs class, we define two properties: tz_offset, an integer, and user, a User object returned by the Google Accounts API.

Every datastore entity has a primary key. Unlike a primary key in a relational database table, an entity key is permanent and can only be set when the entity is created. A key is unique across all entities in the system, and consists of several parts, including the entity's kind (in this case 'UserPrefs'). An app can set one component of the key to an arbitrary value, known in the API as the *key name*.

The clock application uses the user's unique ID, provided by the user_id() method of the User object, as the key name of a UserPrefs entity. This allows the app to fetch the entity by key, since it knows the user's ID from the Google Accounts API. Fetching the entity by key is faster than performing a datastore query.

In *models.py*, we define a function named get_userprefs() that gets the UserPrefs object for the user. After determining the user ID, the function constructs a datastore key for an entity of the kind 'UserPrefs' with a key name equivalent to the user ID. If the entity exists in the datastore, the function returns the UserPrefs object.

If the entity does not exist in the datastore, the function creates a new UserPrefs object with default settings and a key name that corresponds to the user. The new object is *not* saved to the datastore automatically. The caller must invoke the put() method on the UserPrefs instance to save it.

Now that we have a mechanism for getting a UserPrefs object, we can make two upgrades to the main page. If the user is signed in, we can get the user's preferences (if any) and adjust the clock's time zone. Let's also display a web form so the user can set a time zone preference. Edit *main.py* to resemble Example 2-6 to implement these features.

Example 2-6. A new version of main.py that adjusts the clock to the user's time zone and displays a preferences form

```
from google.appengine.api import users
from google.appengine.ext import webapp
from google.appengine.ext.webapp.util import run_wsgi_app
import datetime
import models

class MainPage(webapp.RequestHandler):
    def get(self):
        time = datetime.datetime.now()
        user = users.get_current_user()
```

```
        if not user:
            navbar = ('<p>Welcome! <a href="%s">Sign in or register</a> to customize.</p>'
                      % (users.create_login_url(self.request.path)))
            tz_form = ''
        else:
            userprefs = models.get_userprefs()
            navbar = ('<p>Welcome, %s! You can <a href="%s">sign out</a>.</p>'
                      % (user.nickname(), users.create_logout_url(self.request.path)))
            tz_form = '''
                <form action="/prefs" method="post">
                    <label for="tz_offset">
                        Timezone offset from UTC (can be negative):
                    </label>
                    <input name="tz_offset" id="tz_offset" type="text"
                        size="4" value="%d" />
                    <input type="submit" value="Set" />
                </form>
            ''' % userprefs.tz_offset
            time += datetime.timedelta(0, 0, 0, 0, 0, userprefs.tz_offset)

        self.response.headers['Content-Type'] = 'text/html'
        self.response.out.write('''
<html>
    <head>
        <title>The Time Is...</title>
    </head>
    <body>
    %s
        <p>The time is: %s</p>
    %s
    </body>
</html>
''' % (navbar, str(time), tz_form))

application = webapp.WSGIApplication([('/', MainPage)],
                                     debug=True)

def main():
    run_wsgi_app(application)

if __name__ == '__main__':
    main()
```

To enable the preferences form, we need a request handler to parse the form data and update the datastore. Let's implement this as a new request handler script. Create a file named *prefs.py* with the contents shown in Example 2-7.

Example 2-7. A new handler script, prefs.py, for the preferences form

```
from google.appengine.ext import webapp
from google.appengine.ext.webapp.util import run_wsgi_app
import models

class PrefsPage(webapp.RequestHandler):
    def post(self):
```

```
        userprefs = models.get_userprefs()
        try:
            tz_offset = int(self.request.get('tz_offset'))
            userprefs.tz_offset = tz_offset
            userprefs.put()
        except ValueError:
            # User entered a value that wasn't an integer.  Ignore for now.
            pass

        self.redirect('/')

application = webapp.WSGIApplication([('/prefs', PrefsPage)],
                                    debug=True)

def main():
    run_wsgi_app(application)

if __name__ == '__main__':
    main()
```

This request handler handles HTTP POST requests to the URL **/prefs**, which is the URL ("action") and HTTP method used by the form. The handler calls the **get_userprefs()** function from *models.py* to get the **UserPrefs** object for the current user, which is either a new unsaved object with default values, or the object for an existing entity. The handler parses the **tz_offset** parameter from the form data as an integer, sets the property of the **UserPrefs** object, then saves the object to the datastore by calling its **put()** method. The **put()** method creates the object if it doesn't exist, or updates the existing object.

If the user enters a noninteger in the form field, we don't do anything. It'd be appropriate to return an error message, but we'll leave this as is to keep the example simple.

Finally, edit *app.yaml* to map the handler script to the URL **/prefs** in the **handlers:** section, as shown in Example 2-8.

Example 2-8. A new version of app.yaml mapping the URL /prefs, with login required

```
application: clock
version: 1
runtime: python
api_version: 1

handlers:
- url: /prefs
  script: prefs.py
  login: required

- url: /.*
  script: main.py
```

The **login: required** line says that the user must be signed in to Google Accounts to access the **/prefs** URL. If the user accesses the URL while not signed in, App Engine automatically directs the user to the Google Accounts sign-in page, then redirects her back to this URL afterward. This makes it easy to require sign-in for sections of your site, and to ensure that the user is signed in before the request handler is called.

Be sure to put the /prefs URL mapping before the /.* mapping. URL patterns are tried in order, and the first pattern to match determines the handler used for the request. Since the pattern /.* matches all URLs, /prefs must come first or it will be ignored.

Reload the page to see the customizable clock in action. Try changing the time zone by submitting the form. Also try signing out, then signing in again using the same email address, and again with a different email address. The app remembers the time zone preference for each user.

Caching with memcache

The code that gets user preferences data in Example 2-5 fetches an entity from the datastore every time a signed-in user visits the site. User preferences are often read and seldom changed, so getting a UserPrefs object from the datastore with every request is more expensive than it needs to be. We can mitigate the costs of reading from primary storage using a caching layer.

We can use the memcache service as secondary storage for user preferences data. We can add caching with just a few changes to *models.py*. Edit this file as shown in Example 2-9.

Example 2-9. A new version of models.py that caches UserPrefs objects in memcache

```python
from google.appengine.api import memcache
from google.appengine.api import users
from google.appengine.ext import db

class UserPrefs(db.Model):
    tz_offset = db.IntegerProperty(default=0)
    user = db.UserProperty(auto_current_user_add=True)

    def cache_set(self):
        memcache.set(self.key().name(), self, namespace=self.key().kind())

    def put(self):
        self.cache_set()
        db.Model.put(self)

def get_userprefs(user_id=None):
    if not user_id:
        user = users.get_current_user()
        if not user:
            return None
        user_id = user.user_id()

    userprefs = memcache.get(user_id, namespace='UserPrefs')
    if not userprefs:
        key = db.Key.from_path('UserPrefs', user_id)
        userprefs = db.get(key)
```

```
        if userprefs:
            userprefs.cache_set()
        else:
            userprefs = UserPrefs(key_name=user_id)

    return userprefs
```

The Python API for the memcache service is provided by the module `google.appengine.api.memcache`. The memcache stores key-value pairs, with an optional namespace for the key. The value can be of any type that can be converted to and from a flat data representation (*serialized*) using the Python `pickle` module, including most data objects.

The new version of the `UserPrefs` class overrides the `put()` method. When the `put()` method is called on an instance, the instance is saved to the memcache, then it is saved to the datastore using the original `put()` method. (`db.Model.put(self)` is one way to call the overridden superclass method in Python.)

A new `UserPrefs` method called `cache_set()` makes the call to `memcache.set()`. `memcache.set()` takes a key, a value, and an optional namespace for the key. Here, we use the entity's key name as the key, the full object (`self`) as the value, and the entity's kind (`'UserPrefs'`) as the namespace. The API takes care of serializing the `UserPrefs` object, so we can put in and take out fully formed objects.

The new version of `get_userprefs()` checks the memcache for the `UserPrefs` object before going to the datastore. If it finds it in the cache, it uses it. If it doesn't, it checks the datastore, and if it finds it there, it stores it in the cache and uses it. If the object is in neither the memcache nor the datastore, `get_userprefs()` returns a fresh `UserPrefs` object with default values.

Reload the page to see the new version work. To make the caching behavior more visible, you can add logging statements in the appropriate places, like so:

```
import logging

class UserPrefs(db.Model):
    # ...
    def cache_set(self):
        logging.info('cache set')
        # ...
```

The development server prints logging output to the console. If you are using the Launcher, you can open a window of development server output by clicking the Logs button.

Next, we'll take a look at the same example using the Java runtime environment. If you're not interested in Java, you can skip ahead to "Registering the Application" on page 55.

Developing a Java App

Java web applications for App Engine use the Java Servlet standard interface for interacting with the application server. An application consists of one or more classes that extend a servlet base class. Servlets are mapped to URLs using a standard configuration file called a "deployment descriptor." When App Engine receives a request for a Java application, it determines which servlet class to use based on the URL and the deployment descriptor, instantiates the class, then calls an appropriate method on the servlet object.

All of the files for a Java application, including the compiled Java classes, configuration files, and static files, are organized in a standard directory structure called a Web Application Archive, or "WAR." Everything in the WAR directory gets deployed to App Engine. It's common to have your development workflow build the contents of the WAR from a set of source files, either using an automated build process or WAR-aware development tools.

If you are using the Eclipse IDE with the Google Plugin, you can create a new project using the Web Application wizard. From the File menu, select New, then Web Application Project. In the window that opens, enter a project name (such as Clock) and package name (such as clock).

Uncheck the "Use Google Web Toolkit" checkbox, and make sure the "Use Google App Engine" checkbox is checked. (If you leave the GWT checkbox checked, the new project will be created with GWT starter files.) Click Finish to create the project.

If you are not using the Google Plugin for Eclipse, you will need to create the directories and files another way. If you are already familiar with Java web development, you can use your existing tools and processes to produce the final WAR. For the rest of this section, we'll assume the directory structure created by the Eclipse plug-in.

Figure 2-8 shows the project file structure, as depicted in the Eclipse Package Explorer.

The project root directory (*Clock*) contains two major subdirectories: *src* and *war*. The *src/* directory contains all of the project's class files in the usual Java package structure. With a package path of clock, Eclipse created source code for a servlet class named ClockServlet in the file *clock/ClockServlet.java*.

The *war/* directory contains the complete final contents of the application. Eclipse compiles source code from *src/* automatically and puts the compiled class files in *war/WEB-INF/classes/*, which is hidden from Eclipse's Package Explorer by default. Eclipse copies the contents of *src/META-INF/* to *war/WEB-INF/classes/META-INF/* automatically, as well. Everything else must be created in the *war/* directory in its intended location.

Let's start our clock application with a simple servlet that displays the current time. Open the file *src/clock/ClockServlet.java* for editing (creating it if necessary), and give it contents similar to Example 2-10.

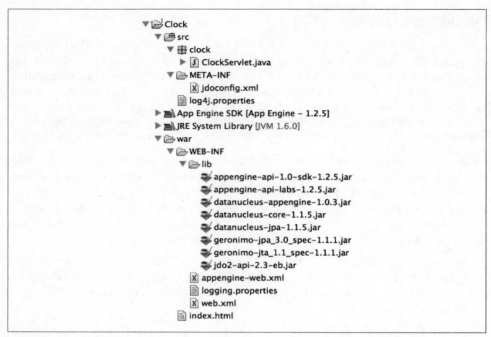

Figure 2-8. A new Java project structure, as shown in the Eclipse Package Explorer

Example 2-10. A simple Java servlet

```java
package clock;

import java.io.IOException;
import java.io.PrintWriter;
import java.text.SimpleDateFormat;
import java.util.Date;
import java.util.SimpleTimeZone;
import javax.servlet.http.*;

@SuppressWarnings("serial")
public class ClockServlet extends HttpServlet {
    public void doGet(HttpServletRequest req,
                      HttpServletResponse resp)
          throws IOException {
        SimpleDateFormat fmt = new SimpleDateFormat("yyyy-MM-dd hh:mm:ss.SSSSSS");
        fmt.setTimeZone(new SimpleTimeZone(0, ""));

        resp.setContentType("text/html");
        PrintWriter out = resp.getWriter();
        out.println("<p>The time is: " + fmt.format(new Date()) + "</p>");
    }
}
```

The servlet class extends `javax.servlet.http.HttpServlet`, and overrides methods for each of the HTTP methods it intends to support. This servlet overrides the **doGet()**

method to handle HTTP GET requests. The server calls the method with an `HttpServletRequest` object and an `HttpServletResponse` object as parameters. The `HttpServletRequest` contains information about the request, such as the URL, form parameters, and cookies. The method prepares the response using methods on the `HttpServletResponse`, such as `setContentType()` and `getWriter()`. App Engine sends the response when the servlet method exits.

To tell App Engine to invoke this servlet for requests, we need a deployment descriptor. Open or create the file *war/WEB-INF/web.xml*, and give it contents similar to Example 2-11.

Example 2-11. The web.xml file, also known as the deployment descriptor, mapping all URLs to ClockServlet

```
<?xml version="1.0" encoding="utf-8"?>
<!DOCTYPE web-app PUBLIC
 "-//Sun Microsystems, Inc.//DTD Web Application 2.3//EN"
 "http://java.sun.com/dtd/web-app_2_3.dtd">

<web-app xmlns="http://java.sun.com/xml/ns/javaee" version="2.5">
  <servlet>
    <servlet-name>clock</servlet-name>
    <servlet-class>clock.ClockServlet</servlet-class>
  </servlet>
  <servlet-mapping>
    <servlet-name>clock</servlet-name>
    <url-pattern>/*</url-pattern>
  </servlet-mapping>
</web-app>
```

Eclipse may open this file in its XML "Design" view, a table-like view of the elements and values. Select the "Source" tab at the bottom of the editor pane to edit the XML source.

web.xml is an XML file with a root element of `<web-app>`. To map URL patterns to servlets, you declare each servlet with a `<servlet>` element, then declare the mapping with a `<servlet-mapping>` element. The `<url-pattern>` of a servlet mapping can be a full URL path, or a URL path with a * at the beginning or end to represent a part of a path. In this case, the URL pattern `/*` matches all URLs.

 Be sure that each of your `<url-pattern>` values starts with a forward slash (/). Omitting the starting slash may have the intended behavior on the development web server but unintended behavior on App Engine.

App Engine needs one additional configuration file that isn't part of the servlet standard. Open or create the file *war/WEB-INF/appengine-web.xml*, and give it contents similar to Example 2-12.

Example 2-12. The appengine-web.xml file, with App Engine-specific configuration for the Java app

```xml
<?xml version="1.0" encoding="utf-8"?>
<appengine-web-app xmlns="http://appengine.google.com/ns/1.0">
  <application>clock</application>
  <version>1</version>
</appengine-web-app>
```

In this example, the configuration file tells App Engine that this is version 1 of an application called clock. You can also use this configuration file to control other behaviors, such as static files and sessions. For more information, see Chapter 3.

The WAR for the application must include several JARs from the App Engine SDK: the Java EE implementation JARs, and the App Engine API JAR. The Eclipse plug-in installs these JARs in the WAR automatically. If you are not using the Eclipse plug-in, you must copy these JARs manually. Look in the SDK directory in the *lib/user/* and *lib/shared/* subdirectories. Copy every *.jar* file from these directories to the *war/WEB-INF/lib/* directory in your project.

Finally, the servlet class must be compiled. Eclipse compiles all of your classes automatically, as needed. If you are not using Eclipse, you probably want to use a build tool such as Apache Ant to compile source code and perform other build tasks. See the official App Engine documentation for information on using Apache Ant to build App Engine projects.

I suppose it's traditional to explain how to compile a Java project from the command line using the javac command. You can do so by putting each of the JARs from *war/WEB-INF/lib/* and the *war/WEB-INF/classes/* directory in the classpath, and making sure the compiled classes end up in the *classes/* directory. But in the real world, you want your IDE or an Ant script to take care of this for you. Also, when we introduce the datastore in the next few sections, we will need to add a step to building the project that makes this even more impractical to do by hand.

It's time to test this application with the development web server. The Eclipse plug-in can run the application and the development server inside the Eclipse debugger. To start it, select the Run menu, Debug As, and Web Application. The server starts, and prints the following message to the Console panel:

```
The server is running at http://localhost:8080/
```

If you are not using Eclipse, you can start the development server using the dev_appserver command (dev_appserver.sh for Mac OS X or Linux). The command takes the path to the WAR directory as an argument, like so:

```
dev_appserver war
```

Test your application by visiting the server's URL in a web browser:

http://localhost:8080

The browser displays a page similar to the Python example, shown earlier in Figure 2-4.

Users and Google Accounts

Right now, our clock displays the time in the UTC time zone. We'd like for our application to let the user customize the time zone, and to remember the user's preference for future visits. To do that, we will use Google Accounts to identify which user is using the application.

Edit *ClockServlet.java* to resemble Example 2-13.

Example 2-13. Code for ClockServlet.java that displays Google Accounts information and links

```java
package clock;

import java.io.IOException;
import java.io.PrintWriter;
import java.text.SimpleDateFormat;
import java.util.Date;
import java.util.SimpleTimeZone;
import javax.servlet.http.*;
import com.google.appengine.api.users.User;
import com.google.appengine.api.users.UserService;
import com.google.appengine.api.users.UserServiceFactory;

@SuppressWarnings("serial")
public class ClockServlet extends HttpServlet {
    public void doGet(HttpServletRequest req,
                      HttpServletResponse resp)
        throws IOException {
        SimpleDateFormat fmt = new SimpleDateFormat("yyyy-MM-dd hh:mm:ss.SSSSSS");
        fmt.setTimeZone(new SimpleTimeZone(0, ""));

        UserService userService = UserServiceFactory.getUserService();
        User user = userService.getCurrentUser();
        String navBar;
        if (user != null) {
            navBar = "<p>Welcome, " + user.getNickname() + "! You can <a href=\"" +
                    userService.createLogoutURL("/") +
                    "\">sign out</a>.</p>";
        } else {
            navBar = "<p>Welcome! <a href=\"" + userService.createLoginURL("/") +
                    "\">Sign in or register</a> to customize.</p>";
        }

        resp.setContentType("text/html");
        PrintWriter out = resp.getWriter();
        out.println(navBar);
        out.println("<p>The time is: " + fmt.format(new Date()) + "</p>");
    }
}
```

In a real application, you wouldn't mix HTML and Java source code like this. You can use JavaServer Pages (JSPs) to represent the page, or you can use a templating engine to render output. To keep things simple, we will continue to write HTML directly from the servlet code for the rest of this example, but keep in mind this is not a best practice.

Using Eclipse, you can leave the development web server running while you edit code. When you save changes to code, Eclipse compiles the class, and if it compiles successfully, Eclipse injects the new class into the already-running server. In most cases, you can simply reload the page in your browser, and it will use the new code.

If you are not using Eclipse, shut down the development server by hitting Ctrl-C. Recompile your project, then start the server again.

Reload the new version of the clock app in your browser. The new page resembles the Python example, shown previously in Figure 2-5.

This version of the clock app uses the interface for Google Accounts provided by the com.google.appengine.api.users package. The app gets a UserService instance by calling the getUserService() method of the UserServiceFactory class. Then it calls the getCurrentUser() method of the UserService, which returns a User object, or null if the current user is not signed in. The getEmail() method of the User object returns the email address for the user.

The createLoginURL() and createLogoutURL() methods of the UserService generate URLs that go to Google Accounts. Each of these methods takes a URL path for the app where the user should be redirected after performing the desired task. The login URL goes to the Google Accounts page where the user can sign in or register for a new account. The logout URL visits Google Accounts to sign out the current user, then immediately redirects back to the given application URL without displaying anything.

If you click on the "Sign in or register" link with the app running in the development server, the link goes to the development server's simulated version of the Google Accounts sign-in screen, similar to the Python version shown earlier in Figure 2-6. At this screen, you can enter any email address, and the development server will proceed as if you are signed in with an account that has that address.

If this app were running on App Engine, the login and logout URLs would go to the actual Google Accounts locations. Once signed in or out, Google Accounts redirects back to the given URL path for the live application.

Click on "Sign in or register," then enter an email address (such as test@example.com) and click on the Login button on the simulated Google Accounts screen. The clock app now looks like Figure 2-7 (shown earlier). To sign out again, click the "sign out" link.

In addition to the UserService API, an app can also get information about the current user with the servlet "user principal" interface. The app can call the getUserPrincipal() method on the HttpServletRequest object to get a java.security.Principal object, or null if the user is not signed in. This object has a getName() method, which in App Engine is equivalent to calling the getEmail() method of a User object.

The main advantage to getting user information from the servlet interface is that the servlet interface is a standard. Coding an app to use standard interfaces makes the app easier to port to alternate implementations, such as other servlet-based web application environments or private servers. As much as possible, App Engine implements standard interfaces for its services and features.

The disadvantage to the standard interfaces is that not all standard interfaces represent all of App Engine's features, and in some cases the App Engine services don't implement every feature of an interface. All of the services include a nonstandard "low-level" API, which you can use directly or use to implement adapters to other interfaces.

Web forms and the datastore

Now that we can identify the user, we can prompt for the user's preferences and remember them for future requests. We can store preferences data in the App Engine datastore.

The App Engine SDK supports two major standard interfaces for accessing the datastore: Java Data Objects (JDO) 2.3 and the Java Persistence API (JPA) 1.0. As with the other services, the datastore also has a low-level API.

Let's use the JPA interface to store the user's time zone setting. JPA requires a configuration file that specifies the JPA implementation to use, and other options. The final location of this file is *war/WEB-INF/classes/META-INF/persistence.xml*. If you are using Eclipse, you can create this file as *src/META-INF/persistence.xml*, and Eclipse will copy it to the final location automatically.

Create the file *src/META-INF/persistence.xml* with the contents shown in Example 2-14.

Example 2-14. The JPA configuration file, persistence.xml, with several useful options

```
<?xml version="1.0" encoding="UTF-8" ?>
<persistence xmlns="http://java.sun.com/xml/ns/persistence"
  xmlns:xsi="http://www.w3.org/2001/XMLSchema-instance"
  xsi:schemaLocation="http://java.sun.com/xml/ns/persistence
    http://java.sun.com/xml/ns/persistence/persistence_1_0.xsd" version="1.0">
  <persistence-unit name="transactions-optional">
    <provider>org.datanucleus.store.appengine.jpa.DatastorePersistenceProvider</provider>
    <properties>
      <property name="datanucleus.NontransactionalRead" value="true"/>
      <property name="datanucleus.NontransactionalWrite" value="true"/>
      <property name="datanucleus.ConnectionURL" value="appengine"/>
    </properties>
  </persistence-unit>
</persistence>
```

The application interacts with the datastore using an `EntityManager` object. It gets this object from an `EntityManagerFactory`. For efficiency, it's best to instantiate the factory only once per servlet. You can store this instance in a static member of a wrapper class.

Create a new class named `EMF` in the `clock` package (*src/clock/EMF.java*) resembling Example 2-15.

Example 2-15. The file EMF.java, a static wrapper class for an EntityManagerFactory instance

```
package clock;

import javax.persistence.EntityManagerFactory;
import javax.persistence.Persistence;

public final class EMF {
    private static final EntityManagerFactory emfInstance =
            Persistence.createEntityManagerFactory("transactions-optional");

    private EMF() {}

    public static EntityManagerFactory get() {
        return emfInstance;
    }
}
```

JPA makes your Java data objects persistent. As far as the rest of your application is concerned, the data objects are just plain old Java objects (POJOs), with members and methods. When you create an instance of a data class, you declare it as persistent by passing it to the EntityManager. From that point on, JPA ensures that changes to the object are saved to the datastore. When you retrieve the object from the datastore later, it still has all of its data, and it retains its persistent behavior.

When you define a JPA data class, you declare it as a persistent-capable class, and optionally tell JPA how to save and restore instances of the class. You do this using Java annotations in the class definition.

Example 2-16 shows the code for a user preferences data class called UserPrefs, using annotations to declare it as persistent-capable by JPA. Create this class (*src/clock/UserPrefs.java*).

Example 2-16. Code for UserPrefs.java, a data class using JPA annotations to make instances persistent

```
package clock;

import javax.persistence.Basic;
import javax.persistence.Entity;
import javax.persistence.EntityManager;
import javax.persistence.Id;
import com.google.appengine.api.users.User;

import clock.EMF;
import clock.UserPrefs;

@Entity(name = "UserPrefs")
public class UserPrefs {
    @Id
    private String userId;

    private int tzOffset;
```

```java
@Basic
private User user;

public UserPrefs(String userId) {
    this.userId = userId;
}

public String getUserId() {
    return userId;
}

public int getTzOffset() {
    return tzOffset;
}

public void setTzOffset(int tzOffset) {
    this.tzOffset = tzOffset;
}

public User getUser() {
    return user;
}

public void setUser(User user) {
    this.user = user;
}

public static UserPrefs getPrefsForUser(User user) {
    UserPrefs userPrefs = null;

    EntityManager em = EMF.get().createEntityManager();
    try {
        userPrefs = em.find(UserPrefs.class, user.getUserId());
        if (userPrefs == null) {
            userPrefs = new UserPrefs(user.getUserId());
            userPrefs.setUser(user);
        }
    } finally {
        em.close();
    }

    return userPrefs;
}

public void save() {
    EntityManager em = EMF.get().createEntityManager();
    try {
        em.persist(this);
    } finally {
        em.close();
    }
}
}
```

The UserPrefs class has three members: the user ID, the user's time zone preference, and the User object representing the current user (which contains the user's email address). The class is declared as persistence-capable using the @Entity annotation. Its name argument specifies the name to be used in JPA queries, typically the same as the class name. By default, the name of the underlying datastore entity kind is derived from the simple name of the class, in this case UserPrefs.

The user field gets an @Basic annotation because JPA does not recognize its field type (User) as persistence-capable by default. String and int are understood by JPA as persistence-capable by default.

The userId field is the primary key for the object, as declared by the @Id annotation. Unlike a relational database, the key is not a field of a record, but a permanent aspect of the underlying datastore entity, set when the object is first saved. When the data class uses a String member as the primary key, JPA expects the member to be set to the *key name*, a value unique across all objects of this class, when the object is saved for the first time. This value cannot be changed once the object is saved.

This application creates a UserPrefs object for each user with preferences set, using the unique user ID provided by Google Accounts as the key name of the object's key. When a user visits the clock, the app attempts to get the UserPrefs object via the key constructed from the user ID, and adjusts the clock display accordingly if such an object is found.

There are other ways to declare the primary key using JPA and App Engine, including a way to let the datastore assign a unique ID automatically. These are discussed in Chapter 8.

JPA attaches its plumbing to the data class after the class is compiled, in a step called "enhancement." The annotations tell the enhancement process how to modify the compiled class bytecode, adding calls to the JPA API in places that ensure the object's persistent members are saved to the datastore. If you are using Eclipse and the plug-in, JPA enhancement happens automatically when data classes are compiled. The App Engine SDK includes an Ant plug-in that performs this step, and you can also run the enhancement process from your own build process by running a tool. See the official App Engine documentation for more information on performing the JPA class enhancement step from a build script.

In anticipation of adding caching logic later on, we've included two methods on this class for getting and saving UserPrefs objects. The static method getPrefsForUser() takes a User object, as returned by the Google Accounts API, and attempts to fetch the UserPrefs object from the datastore for that user. The instance method save() stores the object in the datastore, creating a new datastore entity if one does not already exist for this key, or updating the existing entity if one does. (This save() method goes against JPA's notion of automatic object persistence, but is a convenient way to integrate memcache later with very little code.)

It's time to upgrade the clock application to allow the user to customize the time zone of the clock. Example 2-17 shows a new version of the ClockServlet class that retrieves the UserPrefs object for the currently signed-in user, if any, and uses it to customize the clock display. It also displays a web form that the user can submit to change her time zone preference.

Example 2-17. A new version of ClockServlet.java that adjusts the clock to the user's time zone and displays a preferences form

```
// ...
import clock.UserPrefs;

@SuppressWarnings("serial")
public class ClockServlet extends HttpServlet {
    public void doGet(HttpServletRequest req,
                      HttpServletResponse resp)
        throws IOException {
        SimpleDateFormat fmt = new SimpleDateFormat("yyyy-MM-dd hh:mm:ss.SSSSSS");

        UserService userService = UserServiceFactory.getUserService();
        User user = userService.getCurrentUser();
        String navBar;
        String tzForm;
        if (user == null) {
            navBar = "<p>Welcome! <a href=\"" + userService.createLoginURL("/") +
                "\">Sign in or register</a> to customize.</p>";
            tzForm = "";
            fmt.setTimeZone(new SimpleTimeZone(0, ""));

        } else {
            UserPrefs userPrefs = UserPrefs.getPrefsForUser(user);
            int tzOffset = 0;
            if (userPrefs != null) {
                tzOffset = userPrefs.getTzOffset();
            }

            navBar = "<p>Welcome, " + user.getEmail() + "! You can <a href=\"" +
                userService.createLogoutURL("/") +
                "\">sign out</a>.</p>";
            tzForm = "<form action=\"/prefs\" method=\"post\">" +
                "<label for=\"tz_offset\">" +
                "Timezone offset from UTC (can be negative):" +
                "</label>" +
                "<input name=\"tz_offset\" id=\"tz_offset\" type=\"text\" size=\"4\" " +
                "value=\"" + tzOffset + "\" />" +
                "<input type=\"submit\" value=\"Set\" />" +
                "</form>";
            fmt.setTimeZone(new SimpleTimeZone(tzOffset * 60 * 60 * 1000, ""));
        }

        resp.setContentType("text/html");
        PrintWriter out = resp.getWriter();
        out.println(navBar);
        out.println("<p>The time is: " + fmt.format(new Date()) + "</p>");
```

```
        out.println(tzForm);
    }
}
```

To enable the preferences form, we need a servlet to parse the form data and update the datastore. Let's implement this as a new servlet class. Create a class named PrefsServlet (*src/clock/PrefsServlet.java*) with the contents shown in Example 2-18.

Example 2-18. Code for PrefsServlet.java, a servlet that handles the preferences form

```java
package clock;

import java.io.IOException;
import javax.servlet.http.HttpServlet;
import javax.servlet.http.HttpServletRequest;
import javax.servlet.http.HttpServletResponse;
import com.google.appengine.api.users.User;
import com.google.appengine.api.users.UserService;
import com.google.appengine.api.users.UserServiceFactory;

import clock.UserPrefs;

@SuppressWarnings("serial")
public class PrefsServlet extends HttpServlet {
    public void doPost(HttpServletRequest req,
                       HttpServletResponse resp)
            throws IOException {
        UserService userService = UserServiceFactory.getUserService();
        User user = userService.getCurrentUser();

        UserPrefs userPrefs = UserPrefs.getPrefsForUser(user);

        try {
            int tzOffset = new Integer(req.getParameter("tz_offset")).intValue();
            userPrefs.setTzOffset(tzOffset);
            userPrefs.save();
        } catch (NumberFormatException nfe) {
            // User entered a value that wasn't an integer.  Ignore for now.
        }

        resp.sendRedirect("/");
    }
}
```

Next, we need to change web.xml to map this servlet to the /prefs URL. Edit this file and add the XML shown in Example 2-19.

Example 2-19. Mapping the URL /prefs to the PrefsServlet using a security constraint in web.xml (excerpt)

```xml
  <servlet>
    <servlet-name>prefs</servlet-name>
    <servlet-class>clock.PrefsServlet</servlet-class>
  </servlet>
  <servlet-mapping>
```

```
  <servlet-name>prefs</servlet-name>
  <url-pattern>/prefs</url-pattern>
</servlet-mapping>

<security-constraint>
  <web-resource-collection>
    <web-resource-name>prefs</web-resource-name>
    <url-pattern>/prefs</url-pattern>
  </web-resource-collection>
  <auth-constraint>
    <role-name>*</role-name>
  </auth-constraint>
</security-constraint>
```

The order in which the URL mappings appear in the file does not matter. Longer patterns (not counting wildcards) match before shorter ones.

The `<security-constraint>` block tells App Engine that only users signed in with a Google Account can access the URL /prefs. If a user who is not signed in attempts to access this URL, App Engine redirects the user to Google Accounts to sign in. When the user signs in, she is directed back to the URL she attempted to access. A security constraint is a convenient way to implement Google Accounts authentication for a set of URLs. In this case, it means that `PrefsServlet` does not need to handle the case where someone tries to submit data to the URL without being signed in.

The servlet accesses the form data using the `HttpServletRequest` object passed to the `doPost()` method. For now, if the user enters a noninteger in the form field, we don't do anything. Later, we can implement an error message.

If the form data is valid, the servlet sets the value on the `UserPrefs` object obtained from our `getPrefsForUser()` method, then calls our `save()` method. The `save()` method opens a `PersistenceManager`, attaches the `UserPrefs` object (perhaps making it persistent for the first time), then closes the `PersistenceManager` to save the object in the datastore.

Finally, `PrefsServlet` redirects the user back to the main page. Redirecting after the form submission allows the user to reload the main page without resubmitting the form.

Restart your development server, then reload the page to see the customizable clock in action. Try changing the time zone by submitting the form. Also try signing out, then signing in again using the same email address, and again with a different email address. The app remembers the time zone preference for each user.

Caching with memcache

So far, our application fetches the object from the datastore every time a signed-in user visits the site. Since user preferences data doesn't change very often, we can speed up the per-request data access using the memory cache as secondary storage.

As with the other services, the App Engine SDK includes two interfaces to the memcache service: a featureful proprietary API, and an API that conforms to a proposed Java standard known as JCache (JSR 107). We could use either for this example; for now, we'll use the proprietary API.

Because we limited fetching and saving UserPrefs objects to two methods, we can implement the caching of UserPrefs objects with minimal changes. Example 2-20 shows the needed changes to the UserPrefs class.

Example 2-20. Changes for UserPrefs.java to implement caching of UserPrefs objects

```java
import java.io.Serializable;
import com.google.appengine.api.memcache.MemcacheService;
import com.google.appengine.api.memcache.MemcacheServiceException;
import com.google.appengine.api.memcache.MemcacheServiceFactory;
// ...

@SuppressWarnings("serial")
@Entity(name = "UserPrefs")
public class UserPrefs implements Serializable {
    // ...

    @SuppressWarnings("unchecked")
    public static UserPrefs getPrefsForUser(User myUser) {
        UserPrefs userPrefs = null;

        String cacheKey = "UserPrefs:" + myUser.getUserId();

        try {
            MemcacheService memcache = MemcacheServiceFactory.getMemcacheService();
            if (memcache.contains(cacheKey)) {
                userPrefs = (UserPrefs) memcache.get(cacheKey);
                return userPrefs;
            }
            // If the UserPrefs object isn't in memcache,
            // fall through to the datastore.
        } catch (MemcacheServiceException e) {
            // If there is a problem with the cache,
            // fall through to the datastore.
        }

        EntityManager em = EMF.get().createEntityManager();
        try {
            userPrefs = em.find(UserPrefs.class, myUser.getUserId());
            if (userPrefs == null) {
                userPrefs = new UserPrefs(myUser.getUserId());
                userPrefs.setUser(myUser);
            } else {
                try {
                    MemcacheService memcache = MemcacheServiceFactory.getMemcacheService();
                    memcache.put(cacheKey, userPrefs);
                } catch (MemcacheServiceException e) {
                    // Ignore cache problems, nothing we can do.
                }
```

```
        }
    } finally {
        em.close();
    }

    return userPrefs;
}

public void save() {
    EntityManager em = EMF.get().createEntityManager();
    try {
        em.persist(this);
    } finally {
        em.close();
    }
}
}
```

Any object you store in the memcache must be serializable; that is, it must implement the `Serializable` interface from the `java.io` package. For `UserPrefs`, it suffices to declare that the class implements the interface, since all the relevant members are already serializable.

The new version of the `getPrefsForUser()` static method checks to see whether the `UserPrefs` object for the given user is present in the cache before going to the datastore. Each cache value is stored with a key, which itself can be any serializable object. For `UserPrefs` objects, we use a cache key equivalent to the string `"UserPrefs:"` followed by the email address from the `User` object. If a value with that key is not in the cache, or if there is a problem accessing the cache, the method proceeds to get the object from the datastore, then stores it in the cache by calling a new helper method, `cacheSet()`.

Similarly, the new version of the `save()` method stores the object in the datastore, then also stores it in the cache. There is no way to guarantee that the cache and the datastore contain the same value if one of the services fails and the other succeeds, but it's usually sufficient to save to the datastore first, then save to the cache. For further safety, we could set the cache values to expire after a period of time, so if they do get out of sync, it won't be for long. As written, the cache values persist as long as possible in memory.

Reload the page to see the new version work. To make the caching behavior more visible, you can add logging statements in the appropriate places, like so:

```
import java.util.logging.*;
import javax.persistence.Transient;

// ...
public class UserPrefs implements Serializable {
    @Transient
    private static Logger logger = Logger.getLogger(UserPrefs.class.getName());

    // ...
        if (cache.containsKey(cacheKey)) {
            logger.warning("CACHE HIT");
```

```
            userPrefs = (UserPrefs) cache.get(cacheKey);
            return userPrefs;
        }
        logger.warning("CACHE MISS");
```

The development server prints logging output to the console. If you are using Eclipse, these messages appear in the Console pane.

The Development Console

The Python and Java development web servers include a handy feature for inspecting and debugging your application while testing on your local machine: a web-based development console. With your development server running, visit the following URL in a browser to access the console:

> *http://localhost:8080/_ah/admin*

In the Python Launcher, you can also click the SDK Console button to open the console in a browser window.

The Java development console is currently behind the Python console in features, but it's catching up. Figure 2-9 shows the datastore viewer in the Python console.

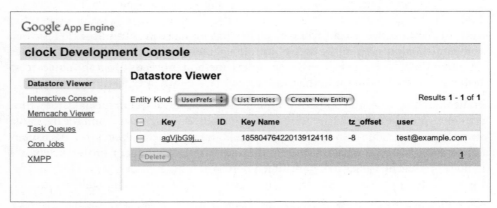

Figure 2-9. The development console's datastore viewer, Python version

The Python development console's datastore viewer lets you list and inspect entities by kind, edit entities, and create new ones. You can edit the values for existing properties, but you cannot delete properties or add new ones, nor can you change the type of the value. For new entities, the console makes a guess as to which properties belong on the entity based on existing entities of that kind, and displays a form to fill in those properties. Similarly, you can only create new entities of existing kinds, and cannot create new kinds from the console.

The Python console also has a viewer for the memcache. You can see cache statistics, and inspect, create, and delete keys. Values are displayed and edited in their serialized ("pickled") form.

An especially powerful feature of the Python console is the "Interactive Console." This feature lets you type arbitrary Python code directly into a web form and see the results displayed in the browser. You can use this to write ad hoc Python code to test and manipulate the datastore, memcache, and global data within the local development server.

Here's an example: run your clock application, sign in with an email address, then set a time zone preference, such as -8. Now open the Python development console, then select "Interactive Console." In the lefthand text box, enter the following, where -8 is the time zone preference you used:

```
from google.appengine.ext import db
import models

q = models.UserPrefs.gql("WHERE tz_offset = -8")

for prefs in q:
    print prefs.user
```

Click the Run Program button. The code runs, and the email address you used appears in the righthand box.

Code run in the development console behaves just like application code. If you perform a datastore query that needs a custom index, the development server adds configuration for that index to the application's *index.yaml* configuration file. Datastore index configuration is discussed in Chapter 5.

You can use the Python console to inspect the application's task queue and cron job configuration in the browser. You can also use the task queue inspector to see tasks currently on the queue (in the local instance of the app), run them, and flush them. (The development server does not run task queues in the background; you must run them from the console. See Chapter 13.)

Lastly, you can test how your app receives email and XMPP messages by sending it mock messages through the console.

The Java development server also has a console. It includes a datastore viewer that lets you list and inspect datastore entities by kind, the ability to run task queues, and the ability to send email and XMPP messages to the app.

Registering the Application

Before you can upload your application to App Engine and share it with the world, you must first create a developer account, then register an application ID. If you intend to use a custom domain name (instead of the free appspot.com domain name included with every app), you must also set up the Google Apps service for the domain. You can do all of this from the App Engine Administration Console.

To access the Administration Console, visit the following URL in your browser:

https://appengine.google.com/

Sign in using the Google account you intend to use as your developer account. If you don't already have a Google account (such as a Gmail account), you can create one using any email address.

Once you have signed in, the Console displays a list of applications you have created, if any, and a button to "Create an Application," similar to Figure 2-10. From this screen, you can create and manage multiple applications, each with its own URL, configuration, and resource limits.

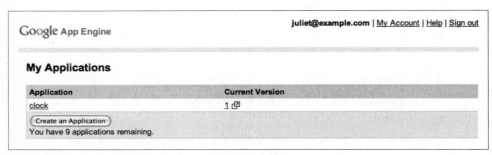

Figure 2-10. The Administration Console application list, with one app

When you register your first application ID, the Administration Console prompts you to verify your developer account using an SMS message sent to your mobile phone. After you enter your mobile phone number, Google sends an SMS to your phone with a confirmation code. Enter this code to continue the registration process. You can verify only one account per phone number, so if you have only one mobile number (like most people), be sure to use it with the account you intend to use with App Engine.

If you don't have a mobile phone number, you can apply to Google for manual verification by filling out a web form. This process takes about a week. For information on applying for manual verification, see the official App Engine website.

You can have up to 10 active application IDs created by a given developer account. If you decide you do not want an app ID, you can disable it using the Administration Console to reclaim one of your 10 available apps. Disabling an app makes the app inaccessible by the public, and disables portions of the Console for the app. Disabling an app does *not* free the application ID for someone else to register. You can request that a disabled app be deleted permanently.

To disable or request deletion of an app, go to "Application Settings" in the Administration Console, and click the Disable Application... button. When you request deletion, all developers of the app are notified by email, and if nobody cancels the request, the app is deleted after 24 hours.

The Application ID and Title

When you click the "Create an Application" button, the Console prompts for an application identifier. The application ID must be unique across all App Engine applications, just like an account username.

The application ID identifies your application when you interact with App Engine using the developer tools. The tools get the application ID from the application configuration file. For Python applications, you specify the app ID in the *app.yaml* file, on the `application:` line. For Java applications, you enter it in the `<application>` element of the *appengine-web.xml* file.

 In the example earlier in this chapter, we chose the application ID "clock" arbitrarily. If you'd like to try uploading this application to App Engine, remember to edit the appropriate configuration file after you register the application to change the application ID to the one you chose.

The application ID is part of the domain name you can use to test the application running on App Engine. Every application gets a free domain name that looks like this:

app-id.appspot.com

The application ID is also part of the email and XMPP addresses the app can use to receive incoming messages. See Chapter 11.

Because the application ID is used in the domain name, an ID can contain only lowercase letters, numbers, or hyphens, and must be shorter than 32 characters. Additionally, Google reserves every Gmail username as an application ID that only the corresponding Gmail user can register. As with usernames on most popular websites, a user-friendly application ID may be hard to come by.

When you register a new application, the Console also prompts for an "application title." This title is used to represent your application throughout the Console and the rest of the system. In particular, it is displayed to a user when the application directs the user to sign in with a Google account. Make sure the title is as you would want your users to see it.

Once you have registered an application, its ID cannot be changed, though you can delete the application and create a new one. You can change the title for an app at any time from the Administration Console.

Setting Up a Domain Name

If you are developing a professional or commercial application, you probably want to use your own domain name instead of the `appspot.com` domain as the official location of your application. You can set up a custom domain name for your App Engine app using Google's "software as a service" service, Google Apps.

Google Apps provides hosted applications for your business or organization, including email (with Gmail and POP/IMAP interfaces), calendaring (Google Calendar), chat (Google Talk), hosted word processing, spreadsheets and presentations (Google Docs), easy-to-edit websites (Google Sites), video hosting, and so forth. You associate these services with your organization's domain name by mapping the domain to Google's servers in its DNS record, either by letting Google manage the DNS for the domain or by pointing subdomains to Google in your own DNS configuration. Your organization's members access the hosted services using your domain name.

With App Engine, you can add your own applications to subdomains of your domain. Even if you do not intend to use the other Google Apps services, you can use Google Apps to associate your own domain with your App Engine application.

 The website for Google Apps indicates that Standard Edition accounts are "ad-supported." This refers to ads that appear on Google products such as Gmail. It does not refer to App Engine: Google does not place ads on the pages of App Engine applications, even those using free accounts. Of course, you can put ads on your own sites, but that's your choice—and your ad revenue.

If you have not set up Google Apps for your domain already, you can do so during the application ID registration process. You can also set up Google Apps from the Administration Console after you have registered the app ID. If you haven't yet purchased a domain name, you can do so while setting up Google Apps, and you can host the domain on Google's name servers for free. To use a domain you purchased previously, follow the instructions on the website to point the domain to Google's servers.

Once you have set up Google Apps for a domain, you can access the Google Apps dashboard at a URL similar to the following:

```
http://www.google.com/a/example.com
```

To add an App Engine application as a service, click the "Add more services" link, then find Google App Engine in the list. Enter the application ID for your app, then click "Add it now." On the following settings screen, you can configure a subdomain of your domain name for the application. All web traffic to this subdomain will go to the application.

Google Apps does not support routing web traffic for the top-level domain (such as `http://example.com/`) directly to an App Engine app. If you bought the domain name through Google, an HTTP request to the top-level domain will redirect to `http://www.example.com`, and you can assign the "www" subdomain to your App Engine app. If Google does not maintain the DNS record for your domain, you will need to set up the redirect yourself using a web server associated with the top-level domain.

By default, the subdomain "www" is assigned to Google Sites, even if you do not have the Sites app activated. To release this subdomain for use with App Engine, first enable the Sites service, then edit the settings for Sites and remove the "www" subdomain.

Google Apps and Authentication

Google Apps allows your organization's members (employees, contractors, volunteers) to create user accounts with email addresses that use your domain name (such as `juliet@example.com`). Members can sign in with these accounts to access services that are private to your organization, such as email or word processing. Using Apps accounts, you can restrict access to certain documents and services to members of the organization, like a hosted intranet that members can access from anywhere.

You can also limit access to your App Engine applications to just those users with accounts on the domain. This lets you use App Engine for internal applications such as project management or sales reporting. When an App Engine application is restricted to an organization's domain, only members of the organization can sign in to the application's Google Accounts prompt. Other Google accounts are denied access.

The authentication restriction must be set when the application is registered, in the "Authentication Options" section of the registration form. The default setting allows any user with a Google account to sign in to the application, leaving it up to the application to decide how to respond to each user. When the app is restricted to a Google Apps domain, only users with Google accounts on the domain can sign in.

After the application ID has been registered, the authentication options cannot be changed. If you want different authentication options for your application, you must register a new application ID.

The restriction applies only to the application's use of Google Accounts. If the application has any URLs that can be accessed without signing in to Google Accounts (such as a welcome page), those URLs will still be accessible by everyone. One of the simplest ways to restrict access to a URL is with application configuration. For example, a Python application can require sign-in for all URLs with the following in the *app.yaml* file:

```
handlers:
- url: /.*
```

```
script: main.py
login: required
```

A Java app can do something similar in the application's deployment descriptor (*web.xml*). See Chapter 3.

The sign-in restriction applies even when the user accesses the app using the `appspot.com` domain. The user does not need to be accessing the app with the Apps domain for the authentication restriction to be enforced.

If you or other members of your organization want to use Google Apps accounts as developer accounts, you must access the Administration Console using a special URL. For example, if your Apps domain is `example.com`, you would use the following URL to access the Administration Console:

```
https://appengine.google.com/a/example.com
```

You sign in to the domain's Console with your Apps account (for instance, `juliet@example.com`).

If you create an app using a non-Apps account, then restrict its authentication to the domain, you will still be able to access the Administration Console using the non-Apps account. However, you will not be able to sign in to the app with that account, including when accessing URLs restricted to administrators.

Uploading the Application

In a traditional web application environment, releasing an application to the world can be a laborious process. Getting the latest software and configuration to multiple web servers and backend services in the right order and at the right time to minimize downtime and prevent breakage is often difficult and delicate. With App Engine, deployment is as simple as uploading the files with a single click or command. You can upload and test multiple versions of your application, and set any uploaded version to be the current public version.

For Python apps, you can upload an app from the Launcher, or from a command prompt. From the Launcher, select the app to deploy, then click the "Deploy" button. From a command prompt, run the `appcfg.py` command as follows, substituting the path to your application directory for *clock*:

```
appcfg.py update clock
```

As with `dev_appserver.py`, `clock` is just the path to the directory. If the current working directory is the *clock/* directory, you can use the relative path, a dot (`.`).

For Java apps, you can upload from Eclipse using the Google plug-in, or from a command prompt. In Eclipse, click the "Deploy to App Engine" button (the little App Engine logo) in the Eclipse toolbar. Or from a command prompt, run the `appcfg` (or `appcfg.sh`) command from the SDK's *bin/* directory as follows, using the path to your application's WAR directory for `war`:

```
appcfg update war
```

When prompted by these tools, enter your developer account's email address and password. The tools remember your credentials for subsequent runs so you don't have to enter them every time.

The upload process determines the application ID and version number from the app configuration file—*app.yaml* for Python apps, *appengine-web.xml* for Java apps—then uploads and installs the files and configuration as the given version of the app. After you upload an application for the first time, you can access the application immediately using either the `.appspot.com` subdomain or the custom Google Apps domain you set up earlier. For example, if the application ID is `clock`, you can access the application with the following URL:

http://clock.appspot.com/

 There is no way to download an application's files from App Engine after they have been uploaded. Make sure you are retaining copies of your application files, such as with a revision control system and regular backups.

Introducing the Administration Console

You manage your live application from your browser using the App Engine Administration Console. You saw the Console when you registered the application, but as a reminder, you can access the Console at the following URL:

https://appengine.google.com/

If your app uses a Google Apps domain name and you are using an Apps account on the domain as your developer account, you must use the Apps address of the Administration Console:

```
https://appengine.google.com/a/example.com
```

Select your application (click its ID) to go to the Console for the app.

The first screen you see is the "dashboard," shown in Figure 2-11. The dashboard summarizes the current and past status of your application, including traffic and load, resource usage, and error rates. You can view charts for the request rate, the amount of time spent on each request, error rates, bandwidth and CPU usage, and whether your application is hitting its resource limits.

If you've already tested your new application, you should see a spike in the requests-per-second chart. The scale of the chart goes up to the highest point in the chart, so the

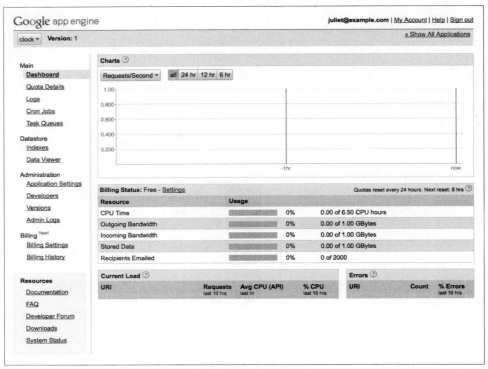

Figure 2-11. The Administration Console dashboard for a new app

spike reaches the top of the graph even though you have only accessed the application a few times.

The Administration Console is your home base for managing your live application. From here, you can examine how the app is using resources, browse the application's request and message logs, and query the datastore and check the status of its indexes. You can also manage multiple versions of your app, so you can test a newly uploaded version before making it the live "default" version. You can invite other people to be developers of the app, allowing them to access the Administration Console and upload new files. And when you're ready to take on large amounts of traffic, you can establish a billing account, set a daily budget, and monitor expenses.

Take a moment to browse the Console, especially the Dashboard, Quota Details, and Logs sections. Throughout this book, we will discuss how an application consumes system resources, and how you can optimize an app for speed and cost effectiveness. The Administration Console is your main resource for tracking resource consumption and diagnosing problems.

## CHAPTER 3

Handling Web Requests

A web application is an application that responds to requests over the Web. Ideally, a web application is an application that responds to web requests quickly, doing the smallest amount of work required to return a response. Most web apps serve users interacting with the application in real time, and a fast response means less time the user is waiting for an action to be completed or information to be displayed. With user-facing web apps, milliseconds matter.

A less obvious advantage to an app that responds quickly is that it's easier to scale. The less work the app does in response to a request, the more efficiently those requests can be distributed across multiple servers. It's like scheduling meetings on a busy day: the shorter the meeting, the more likely you'll be able to fit it in.

Apps with faster responses are also more tolerant of system faults. An app receiving 100 queries per second of traffic will have fewer simultaneous requests in progress at a given moment in time if each request takes 10 milliseconds than if each request takes 100 milliseconds. If a machine goes down and a portion of the requests in progress must be canceled, fewer users will be affected, and more subsequent new requests will be routed to other machines.

App Engine is designed for web applications that respond to requests quickly. An app that can respond within tens of milliseconds is doing pretty well. Occasionally, an app must take hundreds of milliseconds, such as to save data to the datastore or contact a remote server. If an app routinely takes a long time to respond to requests, App Engine triages the slow requests to make room in the schedule for faster ones.

In this chapter, we'll take a look at App Engine's request handling architecture, and follow the path of a web request through the system. We'll discuss how to configure the system to handle different kinds of requests, including requests for static content, requests for the application to perform work, and secure connections (HTTP over SSL, also known as HTTPS). Finally, we'll take a close look at the application runtime environments for Python and Java, how App Engine invokes an application to respond to requests, and how to take advantage of the environment to speed up request handling.

The App Engine Architecture

The architecture of App Engine—and therefore an App Engine application—can be summarized as shown in Figure 3-1.

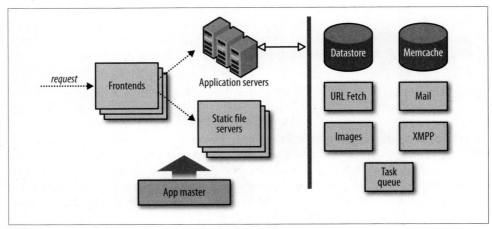

Figure 3-1. The App Engine request handling architecture

The first stop for an incoming request is the App Engine frontend. A load balancer, a dedicated system for distributing requests optimally across multiple machines, routes the request to one of many frontend servers. The frontend determines the app for which the request is intended from the request's domain name, either the Google Apps domain and subdomain or the `appspot.com` subdomain. It then consults the app's configuration to determine the next step.

The app's configuration describes how the frontends should treat requests based on their URL paths. A URL path may map to a static file that should be served to the client directly, such as an image or a file of JavaScript code. Or, a URL path may map to a request handler, application code that is invoked to determine the response for the request. You upload this configuration data along with the rest of your application. We'll look at how to configure URL paths and static files in the next section.

If the URL path for a request does not match anything in the app's configuration, the frontends return an HTTP 404 "Not Found" error response to the client. The frontends return a generic error response. If you want clients to receive a custom response when accessing your app (such as an HTTP 404 error code with a friendly HTML message), you can map a URL pattern that matches all URLs to a request handler that returns the custom response.

If the URL path of the request matches the path of one of the app's static files, the frontend routes the request to the static file servers. These servers are dedicated to the task of serving static files, with network topology and caching behavior optimized for fast delivery of resources that do not change often. You tell App Engine about your app's static files in the app's configuration. When you upload the app, these files are pushed to the static file servers.

If the URL path of the request matches a pattern mapped to one of the application's request handlers, the frontend sends the request to the app servers. The app server pool starts up an instance of the application on a server, or reuses an existing instance if there is one already running from a previous request. The server invokes the app by calling the request handler that corresponds with the URL path of the request, according to the app configuration.

You can configure the frontend to authenticate the user with Google Accounts. The frontend can restrict access to URL paths with several levels of authorization: all users, users who have signed in, and users who are application administrators. With a Google Apps domain, you can also set your application to allow only users on the domain to access URLs. The frontend checks whether the user is signed in, and redirects the user to the Google Accounts sign-in screen if needed. We'll look at authentication and authorization later in this chapter.

The app servers use one of several strategies for distributing requests and starting up instances, depending on the app's traffic and resource usage patterns. As of this writing, the specifics of these strategies are still being developed and tuned, but they are all intended to work best with request handlers that return quickly. The goal is to maximize the throughput of app instances, so as many instances are running as needed to handle the current traffic levels, but not so many that instances are sitting around doing nothing. The app servers are also designed so that one request handler cannot interfere with the behavior or performance of another handler running on the same server.

When an app server receives a request for your application, the server checks the URL configuration to determine which of the application's request handlers should process the request. The server invokes the request handler and awaits its response. The server manages the local resources available to the app, including CPU cycles, memory, and execution time, and ensures that apps do not consume system resources in a way that interferes with other apps.

Your application code executes in a *runtime environment*, an abstraction above the server hardware and operating system that provides access to system resources and other services. The runtime environment is a "sandbox," a walled arena that lets the application use only the features of the server that can scale without interfering with other apps. For instance, the sandbox prevents the application from writing to the server's filesystem, or from making arbitrary network connections to other hosts.

Applications can access various services to perform tasks outside of the runtime environment. For instance, the URL Fetch service allows an app to make HTTP requests to remote machines, using Google's infrastructure for fetching web pages. These services are the same scalable services used by Google's own applications, such as Gmail, Google Reader, and Picasa. They provide a scalable alternative to performing similar tasks directly on the app server. All app servers use the same services, so data saved to the datastore by one request handler can be accessed by another.

The request handler prepares the response, then returns it and terminates. The app server does not send any data to the client until the request handler has terminated, so it cannot stream data or keep a connection open for a long time. When the handler terminates, the app server returns the response, and the request is complete.

The frontend takes the opportunity to tailor the response to the client. Most notably, the frontend will compress the response data using the "gzip" format if the client gives some indication that it supports compressed responses. This applies to both app responses and static file responses, and is done automatically. The frontend uses several techniques to determine when it is appropriate to compress responses, based on web standards and known browser behaviors. (If you are using a custom client that does not support compressed content, simply omit the "Accept-Encoding" request header to disable the automatic gzip behavior.)

The frontends, app servers, and static file servers are governed by an "app master." Among other things, the app master is responsible for deploying new versions of application software and configuration, and updating the "default" version served on an app's user-facing domain. Updates to an app propagate quickly, but are not atomic in the sense that only code from one version of an app is running at any one time. If you switch the default version to new software, all requests that started before the switch are allowed to complete using their version of the software. (An app that makes an HTTP request to itself might find itself in a pickle, but you can manage that situation in your own code, if you really need to.)

Configuring the Frontend

You control how the frontend routes requests for your application using configuration files. These files reside alongside your application's code and static files in your application directory. When you upload your application, all of these files are uploaded together as a single logical unit.

Let's take a look at how to configure the frontend for an application. First, we'll look at the overall layout and syntax for the configuration files for a Python app and for a Java app. Then we'll discuss each frontend feature, with examples for each runtime environment.

Configuring a Python App

A Python application consists of files, including Python code for request handlers and libraries, static files, and configuration files. On your computer, these files reside in the application root directory. Static files and application code may reside in the root directory or in subdirectories. Configuration files always reside in fixed locations in the root directory.

You configure the frontend for a Python application using a file named *app.yaml* in the application root directory. This file is in a format called YAML, a concise human-readable data format with support for nested structures like sequences and mappings.

Example 3-1 shows an example of a simple *app.yaml* file. We'll discuss these features in the following sections. For now, notice a few things about the structure of the file:

- The file is a mapping of values to names. For instance, the value `python` is associated with the name `runtime`.
- Values can be scalars (`python`, `1`), sequences of other values, or mappings of values to names. The value of `handlers` is a sequence of two values, each of which is a mapping containing two name-value pairs.
- Order is significant in sequences, but not mappings.
- YAML uses indentation to indicate scope.
- YAML supports all characters in the Unicode character set. The encoding is assumed to be UTF-8 unless the file uses a byte order mark signifying UTF-16.
- A YAML file can contain comments. All characters on a line after a # character are ignored, unless the # is in a quoted string value.

Example 3-1. An example of an app.yaml configuration file

```
application: ae-book
version: 1
runtime: python
api_version: 1

handlers:
- url: /css
  static_dir: css

- url: /.*
  script: main.py
```

Runtime versions

Among other things, this configuration file declares that this application (or, specifically, this version of this application) uses the Python runtime environment. It also declares which version of the Python runtime environment to use. As of this writing, there is only one version of the Python runtime environment. If Google ever makes changes to the runtime environment that may be incompatible with existing applications, the changes will be released using a new version number. Your app will continue to use the version of the runtime environment specified in your configuration file, giving you a chance to test your app with the new version before uploading the new configuration.

You specify the name and version of the runtime environment in *app.yaml* using the `runtime` and `api_version` elements, like so:

```
runtime: python
api_version: 1
```

Configuring a Java App

A Java application consists of files bundled in a standard format called WAR (short for "Web application archive"). The WAR standard specifies the layout of a directory structure for a Java web application, including the locations of several standard configuration files, compiled Java classes, JAR files, static files, and other auxiliary files. Some tools that manipulate WARs support compressing the directory structure into a single file similar to a JAR. App Engine's tools generally expect the WAR to be a directory on your computer's filesystem.

Java servlet applications use a file called a "deployment descriptor" to specify how the server invokes the application. This file uses an XML format, and is part of the servlet standard specification. In a WAR, the deployment descriptor is a file named *web.xml* that resides in a directory named *WEB-INF/*, which itself is in the WAR's root directory. Example 3-2 shows a very simple deployment descriptor.

Example 3-2. An example of a web.xml deployment descriptor file

```xml
<?xml version="1.0" encoding="utf-8"?>
<!DOCTYPE web-app PUBLIC
 "-//Sun Microsystems, Inc.//DTD Web Application 2.5//EN"
 "http://java.sun.com/dtd/web-app_2_5.dtd">

<web-app xmlns="http://java.sun.com/xml/ns/javaee" version="2.5">
  <servlet>
    <servlet-name>ae-book</servlet-name>
    <servlet-class>aebook.MainServlet</servlet-class>
  </servlet>
  <servlet-mapping>
    <servlet-name>ae-book</servlet-name>
    <url-pattern>/*</url-pattern>
  </servlet-mapping>
</web-app>
```

The deployment descriptor tells the App Engine frontend most of what it needs to know, but not all. For the rest, App Engine uses a file named *appengine-web.xml*, also in the *WEB-INF/* directory and also using XML syntax. If your code editor supports XML validation, you can find the schema definition for this file in the App Engine Java SDK. Example 3-3 shows a brief example.

Example 3-3. An example of an appengine-web.xml configuration file

```xml
<?xml version="1.0" encoding="utf-8"?>
<appengine-web-app xmlns="http://appengine.google.com/ns/1.0">
  <application>ae-book</application>
```

```
    <version>1</version>
</appengine-web-app>
```

When Google releases major new features for the Java API, the release includes a new version of the SDK with an updated *appengine-api-....jar* file. App Engine knows which version of the API the app is expecting by examining the API JAR included in the app's WAR. The server may replace the JAR with a different but compatible implementation when the app is run.

Domain Names

Every app gets a free domain name on `appspot.com`, based on the application ID:

    app-id.appspot.com

Requests for URLs that use your domain name are routed to your app by the frontend.

    http://*app-id*.appspot.com/*url/path...*

You can register your own domain name (such as `example.com`) and set it up with Google Apps to point to your app. You assign a subdomain of your top-level domain to the app. For instance, if your registered domain is `example.com` and you assign the `www` subdomain, the domain name for the app is:

    www.example.com

Google Apps does not support routing requests for the top-level domain without a subdomain. If you want users to see something when they visit `http://example.com/`, you must use your own domain name service (DNS) and web server to handle traffic to that domain name, and point subdomains to Google Apps in the DNS record. If you use the Google Apps DNS service for the domain, Google Apps will automatically redirect web requests for the bare domain to the `www` subdomain.

The `appspot.com` domain has a couple of useful features. One such feature is the ability to accept an additional domain name part:

    anything.app-id.appspot.com

Requests for domain names of this form, where *anything* is any valid single domain name part (that cannot contain a dot, `.`), are routed to the application. This is useful for accepting different kinds of traffic on different domain names, such as for allowing your users to serve content from their own subdomains. Only `appspot.com` domains support the additional part. Google Apps domains do not.

You can determine which domain name was used for the request in your application code by checking the `Host` header on the request. Here's how you check this header using Python and webapp:

```
class MainHandler(webapp.RequestHandler):
    def get(self):
        host = self.request.headers['Host']

        self.response.out.write('Host: %s' % host)
```

App IDs and Versions

Every App Engine application has an application ID that uniquely distinguishes the app from all other applications. As described in Chapter 2, you can register an ID for a new application using the Administration Console. Once you have an ID, you add it to the app's configuration so the developer tools know that the files in the app root directory belong to the app with that ID.

The app's configuration also includes a version identifier. Like the app ID, the version identifier is associated with the app's files when the app is uploaded. App Engine retains one set of files and frontend configuration for each distinct version identifier used during an upload. If you do not change the app version in the configuration when you upload, the existing files for that version of the app are replaced.

Each distinct version of the app is accessible at its own domain name, of the following form:

> *version-id*.latest.*app-id*.appspot.com

When you have multiple versions of an app uploaded to App Engine, you can use the Administration Console to select which version is the one you want the public to access. The Console calls this the "default" version. When a user visits your Google Apps domain (and configured subdomain), or the appspot.com domain without the version ID, he sees the default version.

The appspot.com domain containing the version ID supports an additional domain part, just like the default appspot.com domain:

> *anything*.*version-id*.latest.*app-id*.appspot.com

 Unless you explicitly prevent it, anyone who knows your application ID and version identifiers can access any uploaded version of your application using the appspot.com URLs. You can restrict access to nondefault versions of the application using code that checks the domain of the request and only allows authorized users to access the versioned domains. You can't restrict access to static files this way.

Another way to restrict access to nondefault versions is to use Google Accounts authorization, described later in this chapter. You can restrict access to app administrators while a version is in development, then replace the configuration to remove the restriction just before making that version the default version.

All versions of an app access the same datastore, memcache, and other services, and all versions share the same set of resources. Later on, we'll discuss other configuration files that control these backend services. These files are separate from the configuration files that control the frontend because they are not specific to each app version.

There are several ways to use app versions. For instance, you can have just one version, and always update it in place. Or you can have a "dev" version for testing and a "live" version that is always the public version, and do separate uploads for each. Some developers generate a new app version identifier for each upload based on the version numbers used by a source code revision control system.

You can have up to 10 active versions. You can delete previous versions using the Administration Console.

Application IDs and version identifiers can contain numbers, lowercase letters, and hyphens.

App IDs and versions in Python

For a Python app, the application ID and version identifier appear in the *app.yaml* file. The app ID is specified with the name `application`. The version ID is specified as `version`.

Here is an example of *app.yaml* using `dev` as the version identifier:

```
application: ae-book
version: dev
```

This would be accessible using this domain name:

```
http://dev.latest.ae-book.appspot.com
```

App IDs and versions in Java

The app ID and version identifier of a Java app appear in the *appengine-web.xml* file. The app ID is specified with the XML element `<application>`, and the version identifier is specified with `<version>`. For example:

```
<?xml version="1.0" encoding="utf-8"?>
<appengine-web-app xmlns="http://appengine.google.com/ns/1.0">
  <application>ae-book</application>
  <version>dev</version>
</appengine-web-app>
```

As in the Python example, this version of this app would be accessible using this domain name:

```
http://dev.latest.ae-book.appspot.com
```

Request Handlers

The app configuration tells the frontend what to do with each request, routing it to either the application servers or the static file servers. The destination is determined by the URL path of the request. For instance, an app might send all requests whose URL paths start with /images/ to the static file server, and all requests for the site's home page (the path /) to the app servers. The configuration specifies a list of patterns that match URL paths, with instructions for each pattern.

For requests intended for the app servers, the configuration also specifies the request handler responsible for specific URL paths. A request handler is an entry point into the application code. In Python, a request handler is a script of Python code. In Java, a request handler is a servlet class. Each runtime environment has its own interface for invoking the application.

Request handlers in Python

All URL paths for Python apps are described in the *app.yaml* file using the handlers element. The value of this element is a sequence of mappings, where each item includes a pattern that matches a set of URL paths and instructions on how to handle requests for those paths. Here is an example with four URL patterns:

```
handlers:
- url: /profile/.*
  script: userprofile.py

- url: /css
  static_dir: css

- url: /info/(.*\.xml)
  static_files: /datafiles/\1

- url: /.*
  script: main.py
```

The url element in a handler description is a regular expression that matches URL paths. Every path begins with a forward slash (/), so a pattern can match the beginning of a path by also starting with this character. This URL pattern matches all paths:

```
url: /.*
```

If you are new to regular expressions, here is the briefest of tutorials: the . character matches any single character, and the * character says the previous symbol, in this case any character, can occur zero or more times. There are several other characters with special status in regular expressions. All other characters, like /, match literally. So this pattern matches any URL that begins with a / followed by zero or more of any character.

If a special character is preceded by a backslash (\), it is treated as a literal character in the pattern. Here is a pattern that matches the exact path /home.html:

```
url: /home\.html
```

See the Python documentation for the `re` module for an excellent introduction to regular expressions. The actual regular expression engine used for URL patterns is not Python's, but it's similar.

App Engine attempts to match the URL path of a request to each handler pattern in the order the handlers appear in the configuration file. The first pattern that matches determines the handler to use. If you use the catchall pattern `/.*`, make sure it's the last one in the list, since a later pattern will never match.

To map a URL path pattern to application code, you provide a `script` element. The value is the path to a Python source file, relative to the application root directory. If the frontend gets a request whose path matches a script handler, it routes the request to an application server to invoke the script and produce the response.

In the previous example, the following handler definition routes all URL paths that begin with `/profile/` to a script named *userprofile.py*:

```
- url: /profile/.*
  script: userprofile.py
```

We'll take a closer look at how App Engine invokes a script handler later in this chapter.

Request handlers in Java

A Java web application maps URL patterns to servlets in the deployment descriptor (*web.xml*). You set up a servlet in two steps: the servlet declaration, and the servlet mapping.

The `<servlet>` element declares a servlet. It includes a `<servlet-name>`, a name for the purposes of referring to the servlet elsewhere in the file, and the `<servlet-class>`, the name of the class that implements the servlet. Here's a simple example:

```
<servlet>
  <servlet-name>ae-book</servlet-name>
  <servlet-class>aebook.MainServlet</servlet-class>
</servlet>
```

The servlet declaration can also define initialization parameters for the servlet. This is useful if you want to use the same servlet class in multiple servlet declarations, with different parameters for each one. For example:

```
<servlet>
  <servlet-name>ae-book</servlet-name>
  <servlet-class>aebook.MainServlet</servlet-class>
  <init-param>
    <param-name>colorscheme</param-name>
    <param-value>monochrome</param-value>
  </init-param>
  <init-param>
    <param-name>background</param-name>
    <param-value>dark</param-value>
```

```
        </init-param>
    </servlet>
```

To map a servlet to a URL path pattern, you use the `<servlet-mapping>` element. A mapping includes the `<servlet-name>` that matches a servlet declaration, and a `<url-pattern>`.

```
    <servlet-mapping>
        <servlet-name>ae-book</servlet-name>
        <url-mapping>/home/*</url-mapping>
    </servlet-mapping>
```

The URL pattern matches the URL path. It can use a * character at the beginning or end of the pattern to represent zero or more of any character. Note that this wildcard can only appear at the beginning or end of the pattern, and you can only use one wildcard per pattern.

The order in which URL mappings appear is not significant. The "most specific" matching pattern wins, determined by the number of nonwildcard characters in the pattern. The pattern `/*` matches all URLs, but will only match if none of the other patterns in the deployment descriptor match the URL.

We'll take a closer look at servlets and the Java runtime environment later in this chapter.

JavaServer Pages (JSPs). App Engine includes support for JavaServer Pages (JSPs). JSPs are dynamic web pages defined using a mix of HTML (or other output text) and Java code. JSPs are compiled to Java classes equivalent to servlets that output the static content and evaluate the Java code. You can build large dynamic websites using JSPs for all user-facing servlets.

From the developer's point of view, working with JSPs is a lot like working with files of static HTML content. Like other JSP-capable web servers, App Engine compiles JSP files automatically, so an additional compilation step is usually not necessary. When you upload the app, App Engine compiles the JSPs, and stores the compiled servlet classes. No compilation occurs on the app servers themselves.

JSPs reside in the application directory, outside of the *WEB-INF/* directory. The file-name of a JSP must end with the characters `.jsp`. By default, each JSP is mapped automatically to a URL path equivalent to the path to the JSP file from the application root. So if a JSP file's path is *forum/home.jsp*, it can be accessed with the URL path `/forum/home.jsp`.

As we'll see later in this chapter, this is also how URLs for static files work for Java. This lets you store JSPs and static files together in the application directory, and refer to them using intuitive paths in the HTML.

You can also set an explicit URL mapping for a JSP in the deployment descriptor by declaring it as a servlet. Instead of a `<servlet-class>` element, use a `<jsp-file>` element that contains the path to the file from the application root.

```
<servlet>
  <servlet-name>forum-home</servlet-name>
  <jsp-file>/forum/home.jsp</jsp-file>
</servlet>
<servlet-mapping>
  <servlet-name>forum-home</servlet-name>
  <url-pattern>/forum</url-pattern>
<servlet-mapping>
```

App Engine includes the JavaServer Pages Standard Tag Library (JSTL), a standard library of extensions for use with JSPs. You do not need to add it to your app or install it—and in fact doing so might conflict with the one included with App Engine.

For more information on JSPs and the JSTL, see *Head First Servlets and JSP* by Brian Basham et al. (O'Reilly) and *JavaServer Pages* by Hans Bergsten (O'Reilly).

Static Files and Resource Files

Most web applications have a set of files that are served verbatim to all users, and do not change as the application is used. These can be media assets like images used for site decoration, CSS stylesheets that describe how the site should be drawn to the screen, JavaScript code to be downloaded and executed by a web browser, or HTML for full pages with no dynamic content. To speed up the delivery of these files and improve page rendering time, App Engine uses dedicated servers for static content. Using dedicated servers also means the app servers don't have to spend resources on requests for static files.

Both the deployment process and the frontend must be told which of the application's files are static files. The deployment process delivers static files to the dedicated servers. The frontend remembers which URL paths refer to static files, so it can route requests for those paths to the appropriate servers.

The static file configuration can also include a recommendation for a cache expiration interval. App Engine returns the cache instructions to the client in the HTTP header along with the file. If the client chooses to heed the recommendation, it will retain the file for up to that amount of time, and use its local copy instead of asking for it again. This reduces the amount of bandwidth used, but at the expense of browsers retaining old copies of files that may have changed.

To save space and reduce the amount of data involved when setting up new app instances, static files are not pushed to the application servers. This means application code cannot access the contents of static files using the filesystem.

The files that do get pushed to the application servers are known as "resource files." These can include app-specific configuration files, web page templates, or other static data that is read by the app but not served directly to clients. Application code can access these files by reading them from the filesystem. The code itself is also accessible this way.

There are ways to specify that a file is both a resource file and a static file, depending on which runtime environment you are using.

Static files in Python

We've seen how request handlers defined in the *app.yaml* file can direct requests to scripts that run on the app servers. Handler definitions can also direct requests to the static file servers.

There are two ways to specify static file handlers. The easiest is to declare a directory of files as static, and map the entire directory to a URL path. You do this with the `static_dir` element, as follows:

```
handlers:
- url: /images
  static_dir: myimgs
```

This says that all of the files in the directory *myimgs/* are static files, and the URL path for each of these files is `/images/` followed by the directory path and filename of the file. If the app has a file at the path *myimgs/people/frank.jpg*, App Engine pushes this file to the static file servers, and serves it whenever someone requests the URL path `/images/people/frank.jpg`.

Notice that with `static_dir` handlers, the `url` pattern does not include a regular expression to match the subpath or filename. The subpath is implied: whatever appears in the URL path after the URL pattern becomes the subpath to the file in the directory.

The other way to specify static files is with the `static_files` element. With `static_files`, you use a full regular expression for the `url`. The URL pattern can use regular expression groups to match pieces of the path, then use those matched pieces in the path to the file. The following is equivalent to the `static_dir` handler above:

```
- url: /images/(.*)
  static_files: myimgs/\1
  upload: myimgs/.*
```

The parentheses in the regular expression identify which characters are members of the group. The `\1` in the file path is replaced with the contents of the group when looking for the file. You can have multiple groups in a pattern, and refer to each group by number in the file path. Groups are numbered in the order they appear in the pattern from left to right, where `\1` is the leftmost pattern, `\2` is the next, and so on.

When using `static_files`, you must also specify an `upload` element. This is a regular expression that matches paths to files in the application directory on your computer. App Engine needs this pattern to know which files to upload as static files, since it cannot determine this from the `static_files` pattern alone (as it can with `static_dir`).

While developing a Python app, you keep the app's static files in the application directory along with the code and configuration files. When you upload the app, App Engine determines which files are static files from the handler definitions in *app.yaml*. Files mentioned in static file handler definitions are pushed to the static file servers. All other files in the application directory are considered resource files, and are pushed to the application servers. As such, static files are not accessible to the application code via the filesystem.

The Python SDK treats every file as either a resource file or a static file. If you have a file that you want treated as both a resource file (available to the app via the filesystem) and a static file (served verbatim from the static file servers), you can create a symbolic link in the project directory to make the file appear twice to the deployment tool under two separate names. The file will be uploaded twice, and count as two files toward the file count limit.

MIME types. When the data of an HTTP response is of a particular type, such as a JPEG image, and the web server knows the type of the data, the server can tell the client the type of the data using an HTTP header in the response. The type can be any from a long list of standard type names, known as MIME types. If the server doesn't say what the type of the data is, the client has to guess, and may guess incorrectly.

By default, for static files, App Engine makes its own guess of the file type based on the last few characters of the filename (such as `.jpeg`). If the filename does not end in one of several known extensions, App Engine serves the file as the MIME type `application/ octet-stream`, a generic type most web browsers treat as generic binary data.

If this is not sufficient, you can specify the MIME type of a set of static files using the `mime_type` element in the static file handler configuration. For example:

```
- url: docs/(.*)\.ps
  static_files: psoutput/\1.dat
  upload: psoutput/.*\.dat
  mime_type: application/postscript
```

This says that the application has a set of datafiles in a directory named *psoutput/* whose filenames end in `.dat`, and these should be served using URL paths that consist of `docs/`, followed by the filename with the `.dat` replaced with `.ps`. When App Engine serves one of these files, it declares that the file is a PostScript document.

You can also specify `mime_type` with a `static_dir` handler. All files in the directory are served with the declared type.

Cache expiration. It's common for a static file to be used on multiple web pages of a site. Since static files seldom change, it would be wasteful for a web browser to download the file every time the user visits a page. Instead, browsers can retain static files in a cache on the user's hard drive, and reuse the files when they are needed.

To do this, the browser needs to know how long it can safely retain the file. The server can suggest a maximum cache expiration in the HTTP response. You can configure the cache expiration period App Engine suggests to the client.

To set a default cache expiration period for all static files for an app, you specify a `default_expiration` value. This value applies to all static file handlers, and belongs at the top level of the *app.yaml* file, like so:

```
application: ae-book
version: 1
runtime: python
api_version: 1

default_expiration: "5d 12h"

handlers:
  # ...
```

The value is string that specifies a number of days, hours, minutes, and seconds. As shown here, each number is followed by a unit (d, h, m, or s), and values are separated by spaces.

You can also specify an expiration value for `static_dir` and `static_files` handlers individually, using an `expiration` element in the handler definition. This value overrides the `default_expiration` value, if any. For example:

```
handlers:
- url: /docs/latest
  static_dir: /docs
  expiration: "12h"
```

If the configuration does not suggest a cache expiration period for a set of static files, App Engine does not give an expiration period when serving the files. Browsers will use their own caching behavior in this case, and may not cache the files at all.

Sometimes you want a static file to be cached in the browser as long as possible, but then replaced immediately when the static file changes. A common technique is to add a version number for the file to the URL, then use a new version number from the app's HTML when the file changes. The browser sees a new URL, assumes it is a new resource, and fetches the new version.

You can put the version number of the resource in a fake URL parameter, such as `/js/code.js?v=19`, which gets ignored by the static file server. Alternatively, in Python, you can use regular expression matching to match all versions of the URL and route them to the same file in the static file server, like so:

```
- handlers:
  url: /js/(.*)/code.js
  static_files: js/code.js
  expiration: "90d"
```

This handler serves the static file `js/code.js` for all URLs such as `/js/v19/code.js`, using a cache expiration of 90 days.

If you'd like browsers to reload a static file resource automatically every time you launch a new major version of the app, you can use the multiversion URL handler just discussed, then use the `CURRENT_VERSION_ID` environment variable as the "version" in the static file URLs:

```
self.response.out('<script src="/js/' +
                  os.environ['CURRENT_VERSION_ID'] +
                  '/code.js" />')
```

Static files in Java

As we saw earlier, the WAR directory structure for a Java web application keeps all application code, JARs, and configuration in a subdirectory named *WEB-INF/*. Typically, files outside of *WEB-INF/* represent resources that the user can access directly, including static files and JSPs. The URL paths to these resources are equivalent to the paths to these files within the WAR.

Say an app's WAR has the following files:

```
main.jsp
forum/home.jsp
images/logo.png
images/cancelbutton.png
images/okbutton.png
terms.html
WEB-INF/classes/com/example/Forum.class
WEB-INF/classes/com/example/MainServlet.class
WEB-INF/classes/com/example/Message.class
WEB-INF/classes/com/example/UserPrefs.class
WEB-INF/lib/appengine-api.jar
```

This app has four static files: three PNG images and an HTML file named *terms.html*. When the app is uploaded, these four files are pushed to the static file servers. The frontends know to route requests for URL paths equivalent to these file paths (such as `/images/logo.png`) to the static file servers.

The two `.jsp` files are assumed to be JSPs, and are compiled to servlet classes and mapped to the URL paths equivalent to their file paths. Since these are application code, they are handled by the application servers. The JSP source files themselves are not pushed to the static file servers.

By default, *all* files in the WAR are pushed to the application servers, and are accessible by the application code via the filesystem. This includes the files that are identified as static files and pushed to the static file servers. In other words, all files are considered resource files, and all files except for JSPs and the *WEB-INF/* directory are considered static files.

You can specify which files are considered resource files and which are considered static files using the *appengine-web.xml* file, with the `<resource-files>` and `<static-files>` elements, respectively. These elements can contain an `<include>` element and an `<exclude>` element that modify the default behavior of including all files. For example:

```
<resource-files>
  <exclude path="/images/**" />
</resource-files>
```

This excludes the contents of the *images/* directory and all subdirectories from the set of resource files. This reduces the amount of data that is pushed to the application servers when starting up a new application instance, at the expense of not being able to access those files from within the application (probably fine for site images). The `**` pattern matches any number of characters in file and directory names, including subdirectories.

Another example:

```
<static-files>
  <exclude path="/**.xml" />
  <include path="/sitemap.xml" />
</static-files>
```

This excludes all files with names ending in `.xml` from the set of static files, except for *sitemap.xml*. Perhaps the XML files are intended for the application's eyes only, but we want to make sure search engines can see the site map.

Files in the *WEB-INF/* directory are always considered resource files. They cannot be included as static files or excluded from the set of resource files.

Browsers rely on the web server to tell them the type of the file being served. The static file server determines the MIME content type of a file from the extension on the filename. For instance, a file whose name ends in `.jpeg` is served with a MIME type of `image/jpeg`. The server has a built-in set of mappings from filename extensions to MIME types. You can specify additional mappings using `<mime-mapping>` elements in the deployment descriptor (*web.xml*). See a *web.xml* reference or the App Engine documentation for more information.

Browsers also need to know if a file is safe to cache, and for how long. The static file server can suggest a cache expiration duration when it serves a file (though a browser is not obligated to honor it). You can specify that a set of static files should be cached for a particular duration by including an `expiration` attribute on the `<include>` element in *appengine-web.xml*:

```
<static-files>
  <include path="images/**" expiration="30d" />
</static-files>
```

The value of `expiration` is a duration specified as numbers and units, where `d` is days, `h` is hours, `m` is minutes, and `s` is seconds. You can add values of multiple units by specifying them separated with spaces: `3d 12h`.

Secure Connections

When a client requests and retrieves a web page over an HTTP connection, every aspect of the interaction is transmitted over the network in its final intended form, including the URL path, request parameters, uploaded data, and the complete content of the server's response. For web pages, this usually means human-readable text is flying across the wire, or through the air if the user is using a wireless connection. Anyone else privy to the network traffic can capture and analyze this data, and possibly glean sensitive information about the user and the service.

Websites that deal in sensitive information, such as banks and online retailers, can use a secure alternative for web traffic. With servers that support it, the client can make an HTTPS connection (HTTP over the Secure Socket Layer, or SSL). All data sent in either direction over the connection is encrypted by the sender and decrypted by the recipient, so only the participants can understand what is being transmitted even if the encrypted messages are intercepted. Web browsers usually have an indicator that tells the user when a connection is secure.

App Engine has limited support for secure connections. As of this writing, secure connections are only supported for the `appspot.com` domain, and not custom Google Apps domains. This limitation has to do with how the server proves to the client that he is who he says he is, and not an impostor. Site identification is based on the domain name of the site and the security certificate returned by the App Engine frontend. Because the frontend does not know the domain name this early in the connection process—the browser connects directly to an IP address shared by multiple apps, and only sends the domain name as part of the HTTP header after the connection is made—it cannot verify that the certificate matches the domain.

A newer version of the SSL protocol will allow App Engine to identify the site via other means (using Server Name Indication, or SNI), but not all browsers support the newer protocol yet. When browser support improves (or the use of older browsers diminishes), App Engine will be able to support HTTPS for custom domains.

Since an App Engine app can use both a custom domain and an `appspot.com` domain simultaneously, secure connections are still useful in cases where the domain name of the connection doesn't matter. And you can always redirect users to the `appspot.com` domain to use the secure features of the app. It's not the ideal user experience—most users rightly get suspicious when the domain name for a secure connection is not the one they expect—but it may be appropriate for some apps.

With App Engine, you can enable secure connections for each URL path in the frontend configuration. Secure connections take a bit more time to decrypt requests and encrypt responses. The application code itself doesn't need to know the difference between a secure connection and a standard connection: it just consumes the decrypted request and provides a response that is encrypted by App Engine.

All URL paths can be configured to use secure connections, including those mapped to application code and those mapped to static files. The frontend takes care of the secure connection on behalf of the app servers and static file servers.

App Engine only supports secure connections over TCP port 443, the standard port used by browsers for `https://` URLs. Similarly, App Engine only supports standard connections over port 80. The App Engine frontend returns an error for URLs that specify a port other than the standard port for the given connection method.

The development server does not support secure connections, and ignores the security settings in the configuration. You can test these URLs during development using the nonsecure equivalent URLs.

Because HTTPS uses the domain name to validate the secure connection, requests to versioned `appspot.com` URLs, such as `https://3.latest.ae-book.appspot.com/`, will display a security warning in the browser saying that the domain does not match the security certificate. You can accept the warning to bypass this check against imposters (which guards against "man-in-the-middle" attacks) and continue loading the page.

Secure connections in Python

To configure a URL handler in a Python application to accept secure connections, add a `secure` element to the handler's properties in the *app.yaml* file:

```
handler:
- url: /profile/.*
  script: userprofile.py
  secure: always
```

The value of the `secure` element can be either `always`, `never`, or `optional`. If you don't specify a `secure` element for a URL path, the default is `optional`.

`always` says that requests to this URL path should always use a secure connection. If a user attempts to request the URL path over a nonsecure connection, the App Engine frontend issues an HTTP redirect code telling it to try again using a secure HTTP connection. Browsers follow this redirect automatically.

`never` says that requests to this URL path should never use a secure connection, and requests for an HTTPS URL should be redirected to the HTTP equivalent. Note that browsers often display a warning when a user follows a link from a secure page to a nonsecure page.

`optional` allows either connection method for the URL path, without redirects. The app can use the `HTTPS` environment variable to determine which method was used for the request, and produce a custom response.

Secure connections in Java

For a Java application, anyone can access any URL path with either HTTP or HTTPS. You can use the deployment descriptor to require secure connections for certain URL paths. In the *web.xml* file, you declare a security constraint for a URL path or set of URL paths as follows:

```
<security-constraint>
  <web-resource-collection>
    <web-resource-name>home</web-resource-name>
    <url-pattern>/home/*</url-pattern>
  </web-resource-collection>
  <user-data-constraint>
    <transport-guarantee>CONFIDENTIAL</transport-guarantee>
  </user-data-constraint>
</security-constraint>
```

A security constraint, indicated by the `<security-constraint>` element, describes the minimum security requirements a request must meet to access a resource. You identify the resource using a URL pattern in a `<web-resource-collection>` element containing a `<url-pattern>` element. (According to the spec, `<web-resource-collection>` must have a `<web-resource-name>`, though this name is not used for anything.) As with URL patterns in servlet mappings, the URL pattern can be a single URL path, or a partial URL path with a * wildcard at the beginning or at the end.

You specify a security constraint requiring a secure connection with a `<user-data-constraint>` element containing a `<transport-guarantee>` element, itself containing the value `CONFIDENTIAL`. (The transport guarantee `INTEGRAL` is also supported as a synonym for `CONFIDENTIAL`.) App Engine does not support other transport guarantee constraints.

If you do not want users accessing your app with HTTPS, you can disable secure connections by adding this to your *appengine-web.xml* configuration file:

```
<ssl-enabled>false</ssl-enabled>
```

You can only enable or disable SSL for the entire application. The deployment descriptor standard does not have a concept of accepting secure connections for some URL paths and not others.

Authorization with Google Accounts

Back in Chapter 2, we discussed how an App Engine application can integrate with Google Accounts to identify and authenticate users. We saw how an app can use library calls to check whether the user making a request is signed in, access the user's email address, and calculate the sign-in and sign-out URLs of the Google Accounts system. With this API, application code can perform fine-grained access control and customize displays.

Another way to do access control is to leave it to the frontend. With just a little configuration, you can instruct the frontend to protect access to specific URL handlers such that only signed-in users can request them. If a user who is not signed in requests such a URL, the frontend redirects the user to the Google Accounts sign-in and registration screen. Upon successfully signing in or registering a new account, the user is redirected back to the URL.

You can also tell the frontend that only the registered developers of the application can access certain URL handlers. This makes it easy to build administrator-only sections of your website, with no need for code that confirms the user is an administrator. You can manage which accounts have developer status in the Administration Console, under Developers. If you revoke an account's developer status, that user is no longer able to access administrator-only resources, effective immediately.

Later on, we will discuss App Engine services that call your application in response to events. For example, the scheduled tasks service (the "cron" service) can be configured to trigger a request to a URL at certain times of the day. Typically, you want to restrict access to these URLs so not just anybody can call them. For the purposes of access control enforced by the frontend, these services act as app administrators, so restricting these URLs to administrators effectively locks out meddling outsiders while allowing the services to call the app.

If your app runs on a Google Apps domain for the purposes of serving your organization's members, you can set an access policy for the app such that only Google Apps accounts on the domain can sign in to the app. You set this policy when you register the application ID; it cannot be changed after the app ID has been registered.

This coarse-grained access control is easy to set up in the frontend configuration. And unlike access control in the application code, frontend authentication can restrict access to static files as well as application request handlers.

Authorization in Python

For a Python app, you establish frontend access control for a URL handler with the `login` element in *app.yaml*, like so:

```
handlers:
- url: /myaccount/.*
  script: account.py
  login: required
```

The `login` element has two possible values: `required` and `admin`.

If `login` is `required`, then the user must be signed in to access URLs for this handler. If the user is not signed in, the frontend returns an HTTP redirect code to send the user to the Google Accounts sign-in and registration form.

If `login` is `admin`, then the user must be signed in *and* must be a registered developer for the application.

If no `login` is provided, the default policy is to allow anyone to access the resource, whether or not the client represents a signed-in user, and whether or not the app is set to use a members-only access policy.

You can use the `login` element with both script handlers and static file handlers.

Authorization in Java

For Java, you establish a frontend access control policy using a security constraint in the deployment descriptor. We introduced security constraints earlier when we discussed secure connections. Authentication constraints are similar: they specify the minimum level of a condition required to access a resource.

Here's what an authentication constraint looks like in *web.xml*:

```
<security-constraint>
  <web-resource-collection>
    <url-pattern>/myaccount/*</url-pattern>
  </web-resource-collection>
  <auth-constraint>
    <role-name>*</role-name>
  </auth-constraint>
</security-constraint>
```

As before, the security constraint identifies a resource with a URL pattern, then specifies the constraint to apply. An `<auth-constraint>` element contains a `<role-name>` element that specifies the minimum level of authentication.

`<role-name>` can be one of two values: * (a single asterisk) or `admin`. If the role name is *, then any user that has signed in can access the resource. If the user is not signed in, the frontend sends an HTTP redirect code with the Google Accounts sign-in and registration page as the destination. If the role name is `admin`, then only a user who is both signed in and a registered developer for the application can access the resource.

If a URL does not have an authentication constraint, then anyone can access the URL, whether or not the client represents a signed-in user, and whether or not the app is set to use a members-only access policy.

How the App Is Run

The frontend routes a request whose URL is mapped to an application handler to one of many application servers. When the app server receives the request, it loads the app's code, resource files, and configuration into a runtime environment. The server invokes the request handler for the request, gathers the response data, and sends the response data to the user.

The runtime environment includes the interpreter that executes the code (either the Python interpreter or the Java virtual machine), the application's memory, a read-only filesystem with the application's resource files, and APIs to the App Engine services. The runtime environment also includes the request handler API, which defines how the server and the handler communicate information about the request and the response, and how the handler emits messages to the App Engine logging system. The details differ between the Python and Java environments, but can involve environment variables and the system input and output streams.

The Python Runtime Environment

When an app server receives a request intended for a Python application, it compares the URL path of the request to the URL patterns in in the app's *app.yaml* file. Each URL pattern is associated with a file of Python code (a "script"), and the first pattern to match the path identifies the script that will handle the request.

The server uses the Common Gateway Interface (CGI) standard to communicate with the Python code. CGI is one of the earliest building blocks of the Web, and if you did any web application programming in the 20th century, you may currently be experiencing flashbacks of a slow and cumbersome application model that was common in the days of Apache servers and `mod_cgi`, with a fresh Perl interpreter started from scratch for every request. Thankfully, that execution model has nothing to do with the interface, and CGI is just as useful for modern, high-performance web apps.

The CGI standard specifies how the server communicates the request to the application and how the application returns the response to the server. It uses a combination of environment variables and the application process's input and output streams to handle this communication. While you could write your own code that implements this interface, it's far more productive to let an application framework take care of this for you.

Python developers have many web application frameworks to choose from. Django, Pylons, and web2py are several "full stack" frameworks currently known to work well with App Engine, and App Engine includes Django as part of the runtime environment. You can include other frameworks and libraries with your application simply by adding them to your application directory. As we saw in Chapter 2, App Engine also includes a simple framework of its own, called webapp.

By the time an app server receives the request, it has already fired up the Python interpreter, ready to handle requests. If the server served a request for the application recently, it may have the application in memory as well, but if it hasn't, it loads the handler script for the request. The server evaluates the script with the data for the request, and returns the response the script emits.

If the server already has the application in memory from a previous request, it keeps the application memory, including imported modules and global variables. In this sense, it behaves more like FastCGI than CGI. The Python environment does flush environment variables at the end of each request. We'll discuss app caching later in this chapter.

App Engine's Python interpreter is a modified version of the official Python 2.5 interpreter, sometimes referred to as "CPython" to distinguish it from other Python interpreters. The application code must run entirely within the Python interpreter. That is, the code must be purely Python code, and cannot include or depend upon extensions to the Python interpreter. Python modules that include extensions written in C cannot be uploaded with your app or otherwise added to the runtime environment. The "pure

Python" requirement can be problematic for some third-party libraries, so be sure that libraries you want to use operate without extensions.

The handler script produces a response by writing to the standard output stream (sys.stdout, or however your framework of choice marshals output). The runtime environment buffers the output of the script while it is running. When the handler exits, the server returns the response to the client. (An app cannot stream content to the client as it is doing other work.)

The server runs the handler script as if it were the main program. The __name__ variable is set to '__main__' in the scope of the handler script, so the Python idiom if __name__ == '__main__': ... works as expected.

App Engine sets the following environment variables at the beginning of each request (in addition to the CGI variables), which you can access using os.environ:

APPLICATION_ID
> The ID of the application.

CURRENT_VERSION_ID
> The ID of the version of the app serving this request.

AUTH_DOMAIN
> This is set to gmail.com if the user is signed in using a Google Account, or the domain of the app if signed in with a Google Apps account; not set otherwise.

SERVER_SOFTWARE
> The version of the runtime environment; starts with the word Development when running on the development server.

The Java Runtime Environment

The Java runtime environment behaves like a servlet container. When the app server receives a request, it determines the servlet class to call by comparing the URL path to the servlet mappings in the deployment descriptor. The server uses the standard servlet interface to invoke the servlet, passing it a populated request object and an empty response object. The application's servlet code populates the response object and exits, and the server returns the response to the client.

The Java runtime environment uses the Java 6 virtual machine (JVM). The JVM runs Java bytecode, which is what you get from passing Java code to a Java compiler. It's also what you get from compilers for other languages that produce Java bytecode, such as Scala, and from interpreters for other languages implemented in Java bytecode, such as JRuby (Ruby), Rhino (JavaScript), Groovy, and even Jython (a Python interpreter implemented in Java). You can use any language that compiles to or has an interpreter for the JVM to write applications for App Engine, as long as the result implements a servlet interface.

Having a complete JVM also means you can use many third-party libraries with your application. Some restrictions apply—we'll look at a few in a moment—but in most cases, using a library is a simple matter of including the JAR or class files in the application's WAR.

An app can determine whether it is running on App Engine or in the development server from the servlet info string in the servlet context, returned by `this.getServletContext().getServletInfo()`. This string starts with `Google App Engine Development` when running in the development server. It also contains the release number of the runtime environment.

An app can get its application ID and version ID using the `ApiProxy` class:

```
import com.google.apphosting.api.ApiProxy;

// ...
        String appId =
            ApiProxy.getCurrentEnvironment().getAppId();
        String versionId =
            ApiProxy.getCurrentEnvironment().getVersionId();
```

The Sandbox

The runtime environment does not expose the complete operating system to the application. Some functions, such as the ability to create arbitrary network connections, are restricted. This "sandbox" is necessary to prevent other applications running on the same server from interfering with your application (and vice versa). Instead, an app can perform some of these functions using App Engine's scalable services, such as the URL Fetch service.

The most notable sandbox restrictions include the following:

- An app cannot spawn additional processes or threads. All processing for a request must be performed by the request handler's process.
- An app cannot make arbitrary network connections. Some networking features are provided by the App Engine services, such as URL Fetch and Mail.
- An app can only read from the filesystem, and can only read its own code and resource files. It cannot create or modify files. Instead of files, an app can use the datastore to save data.
- An app cannot see or otherwise know about other applications or processes that may be running on the server. This includes other request handlers from the same application that may be running simultaneously.

These restrictions are implemented on multiple levels, both to ensure that the restrictions are enforced and to make it easier to troubleshoot problems that may be related to the sandbox.

The Python sandbox

In the Python runtime environment, the Python interpreter prevents the app from accessing illegal system resources at a low level. Since a Python app can only consist of Python code, an app must perform all processing within the Python interpreter.

For convenience, portions of the Python standard library whose only use is to access restricted system resources have been disabled. If you attempt to import a disabled module or call a disabled function, the interpreter raises an `ImportError`. The Python development server enforces the standard module import restrictions, so you can test imports on your computer.

Some standard library modules have been replaced with alternate versions for speed or compatibility. Other modules have custom implementations, such as `zipimport`. You can find out more about modules that have been replaced or added from the official documentation.

The Java sandbox

In the Java runtime environment, sandbox restrictions are enforced within the JVM. These restrictions are implemented using a combination of JVM permissions, a Java Runtime Environment (JRE) class whitelist, and alternate implementations for specific functions. This fine-grained approach allows more third-party libraries to work and makes other code easier to port than relying on JVM permissions alone.

The Java runtime environment includes a subset of the JRE classes. You can find a complete list of supported JRE classes in the official documentation. Not every feature of every class in this list works with App Engine. For instance, the `java.lang.Thread` class can be imported successfully, but can only be used to examine the current thread. It cannot be used to create new threads.

Reflection is supported for all of the app's own classes. Custom class loaders are supported, but with all classes granted the same permissions. Native JNI code is not supported.

App Caching

Once an application server loads an app's code and resource files, it keeps them in memory to serve multiple requests. The behavior of this "app cache" differs slightly between the Python and Java runtime environments, but in general, it's as if the application instance is "running" on the server and responding to requests as events. The app can store code and data in memory, and expects it to be available for subsequent requests handled by the app instance. App caching is one of the main mechanisms for speeding up requests, and it's worthwhile to use it as much as possible, when appropriate.

App Engine makes no guarantee that the requests from the same client reach the same server, nor does it guarantee that an app instance will stay in memory for any particular amount of time. If the app is receiving many requests, App Engine may start new instances on additional servers to spread the load. If an app instance does not receive a request in a while, the server may purge it from memory to free resources for other apps. Each server frees the least recently used app when it needs more resources.

The best uses of the app cache are for caching code (Python module imports, Java classes) and processed data that is not specific to a given user or request (such as parsed configuration files). All of the application's memory is retained in the cache, so using the app cache is a simple matter of storing values in global variables.

Because there are no guarantees for how apps are cached or how requests are distributed, the app cache is not a good choice for persisting data that isn't local to the app instance. Instead, use the datastore for permanent reliable storage, and the memcache for app-visible cached data and temporary values.

App caching in Python

The Python runtime environment keeps the global variable space in memory as long as the environment exists. This includes imported modules, as well as the script handler's global variables and function and class definitions.

The first time a Python module is imported, the contents of the module are evaluated. If the module is imported again in the same runtime environment, nothing happens. Typically, evaluating a module's code defines classes, functions, and global variables, and does nothing else, so doing nothing on subsequent tries saves time and otherwise does the right thing. This is how imports normally work during a run of a Python program.

With App Engine, this is also how imports work across multiple requests handled by the same application instance. Once a module has been imported in an instance of an app, subsequent attempts to import it in every request handled by that instance will do nothing.

When to Import Modules

Import caching might suggest that you ought to do something clever with imports. If you import all the modules you would ever need at the top of the request handler, then only the first request for the instance incurs the cost of the imports, and all subsequent requests are faster. Alternatively, if you wait to import a module until just before you use the module, you spread the cost of importing modules across multiple request handlers. (In Python, you can put an `import` statement anywhere, including inside conditionals.)

In practice, neither method of importing offers much advantage. Late importing may actually be slower if the import is inside a loop or frequent code path, since importing an already-imported module takes some time, even if it doesn't load files or evaluate module code. It's best to import modules in the way that makes the most sense for code clarity, typically at the top of each module (source file) that uses the module. Once you've developed your app, if you notice you have a significant slowdown during imports of the first request, you could consider importing selected modules in their code paths if you can demonstrate that doing so would skip a lot of unneeded code in a significant number of cases.

App Engine includes a feature similar to import caching to achieve similar savings for the handler scripts themselves. In general, when the app server invokes a handler script, it evaluates all of the script's code, regardless of whether the script has been invoked by the app instance in the past. But if the script defines a function named `main()` that takes no arguments (or arguments with default values), App Engine treats the handler script like a module. The first invocation evaluates the complete script as usual, but for all subsequent invocations, App Engine just calls the `main()` function.

Consider an early version of the clock application we built in Chapter 2, repeated here as Example 3-4. This handler script imports three modules, defines three global elements (a class, a global variable, and the `main()` function), then calls the `main()` function.

Example 3-4. A simple request handler illustrating the use of app caching

```
from google.appengine.ext import webapp
from google.appengine.ext.webapp.util import run_wsgi_app
import datetime

class MainPage(webapp.RequestHandler):
    def get(self):
        time = datetime.datetime.now()

        self.response.headers['Content-Type'] = 'text/html'
        self.response.out.write('<p>The time is: %s</p>' % str(time))

application = webapp.WSGIApplication([('/', MainPage)],
                                    debug=True)

def main():
    run_wsgi_app(application)

if __name__ == '__main__':
    main()
```

The first time an app instance invokes this script, the full script is evaluated, thereby importing the modules and defining the global elements in the script's namespace within the app instance. Evaluating the script also calls the `main()` function.

The if `__name__` ... condition is a Python idiom that allows you to import the script as if it were a module without side effects, such as to test the code in a separate test script. App Engine ensures this idiomatic condition is true when the script is invoked the first time.

If the app instance receives a request for this handler after the script has already been evaluated, the instance simply calls its `main()` function directly. This avoids the unnecessary overhead of constituting the values of the global elements, since they're already defined and aren't expected to change. This includes the global variable `application`, whose value is an object representing the webapp application run by the `main()` function. This object can be reused by multiple requests, so creating it only on the first invocation and storing it in a global saves time during subsequent requests.

App caching is also useful for reusing calculations that are not specific to the user. When you use regular expressions with the `re` module, each regular expression is compiled the first time it is used. The module remembers compiled versions of up to 100 regular expressions, so subsequent uses of a pattern do not incur processing time to compile the pattern. With app caching, only a fraction of requests spend time compiling regular expressions.

You can store your own data in the app cache using global variables. For instance, if your app loads and parses configuration or datafiles that are uploaded with the app (and therefore do not change), you can store the parsed objects in globals. As long as it's reasonable for two requests coming from different users to use the same data, you can store it in the memory of the app instance for reuse.

 Remember to call your `main()` function in the body of your script handler. If you do not, the first invocation of the handler will appear to do nothing, but subsequent invocations will succeed, because they are calling `main()` directly. This behavior will appear erratic as App Engine creates, reuses, and destroys app instances.

There is no reason not to take advantage of app caching, so make sure all of your Python script handlers define a `main()` function.

App caching in Java

When an app server receives a request for a Java application for the first time, the server creates a new instance of the app environment, then loads the servlet classes. Subsequent requests for the app routed to that server are handled by the same JVM instance, with the app's memory preserved between requests, including imported classes and static variables. You can reduce the amount of time it takes to handle requests by storing values that apply to all requests in statics, such as data structures parsed from configuration files.

When an app accesses data that is global to the JVM, it should do so in a thread-safe manner. App Engine may run multiple request handlers with the same JVM instance simultaneously, each in its own thread. As per the sandbox restriction, request handlers cannot spawn their own threads, but App Engine may use multiple threads to initiate request handlers. Using thread safety with global data in a servlet container is a common practice, and this best practice is no different for App Engine.

If your servlets must be loaded in a particular order for initialization to succeed, you can control this order using the `<load-on-startup>` element in the deployment descriptor. This element appears inside the servlet declaration (`<servlet>`) and contains an integer that describes its load order relative to the other servlets (1 for the first, 2 for the second, and so on).

Note that App Engine loads the servlet classes during the first request, not beforehand. If possible, you may want to delay initialization tasks until the latest moment they are needed to spread out application warm-up across multiple requests.

Logging

Activity and message logs are an essential part of a web application. They are your view into what happens with your application over time as it is being used, who is using it and how, and what problems, if any, your users are having.

App Engine logs all incoming requests for your application, including application requests, static file requests, and requests for invalid URLs (so you can determine whether there is a bad link somewhere). For each request, App Engine logs the date and time, the IP address of the client, the URL requested (including the path and parameters), the domain name requested, the browser's identification string (the "user agent"), the referring URL if the user followed a link, and the HTTP status code in the response returned by the app or by the frontend.

App Engine also logs several important statistics about each request: the amount of time it took to handle each request, the amount of "CPU time" that was spent handling the request, and the size of the response. The CPU time measurement is particularly important to watch because requests that consistently consume a large amount of CPU may be throttled, such that the CPU use is spread over more clock time.

Your application code can log the occurrence of notable events and data using a logging API. Logging a message associates a line of text with the request that emitted it, including all of the data logged for the request. Each message has a *log level* indicating the severity of the message to make it easier to find important messages during analysis. App Engine supports five log levels: debug, info, warning, error, and critical.

You can browse your application's request and message logs using the Administration Console, under Logs. You can also download your log data for offline analysis and recordkeeping. We'll look at these features in detail in Chapter 15.

Logging in Python

Python applications can use the `logging` module from the standard library to log messages. App Engine hooks into this module to relay messages to the logging system, and to get the log level for each message. Example 3-5 shows this module in action.

Example 3-5. The use of the logging Python module to emit messages at different log levels

```python
import logging

# ...
        logging.debug('debug level')
        logging.info('info level')
        logging.warning('warning level')
        logging.error('error level')
        logging.critical('critical level')

        sys.stderr.write('stderr write, logged at the error level\n')
```

In addition to messages logged with the `logging` module, each line of text written to the standard error stream (`sys.stderr`) is logged at the "error" level. (Because Python uses CGI, anything written to the standard output stream becomes part of the response data.)

In a traditional application using the `logging` module, you would configure the module to output only messages above a given level of severity. When running on App Engine, the level of the output is always the "debug" level, and it cannot be changed. You can filter messages by severity after the fact in the Administration Console, or when downloading logs using `appcfg.py`.

When running in the development web server, log messages are written to the Console, and data written to `sys.stderr` is written to the server's error stream. If you are running your server in the Launcher, you can open a window to view log messages by clicking the Logs button.

The development server sets its log level to `INFO` by default. You can change this to `DEBUG` by giving the server the command-line argument `--debug`.

Logging in Java

For Java applications, App Engine supports the `java.util.logging` library from the JRE. App Engine recognizes log levels of messages logged using this library. Example 3-6 illustrates the use of the Logger class and its convenience methods.

Example 3-6. The use of the java.util.logging package to emit messages at different log levels

```java
import java.io.IOException;
import javax.servlet.http.*;

import java.util.logging.Logger;

public class LoggingServlet extends HttpServlet {
```

```
    private static final Logger log = Logger.getLogger(TestServlet.class.getName());

    public void doGet(HttpServletRequest req, HttpServletResponse resp)
            throws IOException {
        log.finest("finest level");
        log.finer("finer level");
        log.fine("fine level");
        log.config("config level");
        log.info("info level");
        log.warning("warning level");
        log.severe("severe level");

        System.out.println("stdout level");
        System.err.println("stderr level");
    }
}
```

The seven log levels of `java.util.logging` correspond to four of App Engine's log levels: "finest," "finer," "fine," and "config" all correspond to the App Engine debug level; "info" is info, "warning" is warning, and "severe" is error. The "critical" log level is reserved for exceptions that are not caught by the servlet; when this happens, the runtime environment logs a message at this level.

If the application writes any data to the standard output or error streams (`System.out` and `System.err`), App Engine adds that data to the log. Each line of text written to standard output becomes a log message at the "info" level, and each line written to standard error is logged at the "warning" level.

You can control which level of message should be written to the log using configuration for `java.util.logging`. This allows you to leave detailed low-level logging statements in your code without having all of that information clutter up the logs unnecessarily in a high-traffic app.

Configuring the log level requires two things: a configuration file and a system property that identifies the configuration file. For the configuration, create a resource file, such as *war/WEB-INF/logging.properties*, containing a line like this:

```
.level=INFO
```

You can configure the log level on a per-class basis by adding lines like this with the package path before the `.level`. Be sure to use the `logging` level name (such as `FINEST`) and not the App Engine level name.

Next, set a system property telling the logging library where to find its configuration file. You do this by including a `<system-properties>` element in your *appengine-web.xml* file, like so:

```
        <system-properties>
          <property name="java.util.logging.config.file"
                    value="WEB-INF/logging.properties" />
        </system-properties>
```

If you created your Java project using the Google Plugin for Eclipse, your app already has this configuration file and this system property. This configuration comes pre-loaded with log levels for the DataNucleus interface (an interface for the datastore), so you can leave those set to the "warning" level while the rest of your app uses another level.

The `java.util.logging` and the standard output and error streams are the only ways to log messages at specific log levels. If you or a component of your app prefers a different logging library, such as log4j, messages emitted by that library will work as long as the library can write to the standard streams. If you want to be able to use the Administration Console to filter logs by levels other than "info" and "warning," you will need an adapter of some kind that calls `java.util.logging` behind the scenes. You get complete log messages when you download log data, so you can always analyze alternate log formats in downloaded data.

When running in the development web server, log messages are written to the console, and text written to the standard streams is written to the corresponding streams for the server. In Eclipse, these messages appear in the Console pane.

Quotas and Limits

The runtime environment monitors the system resources used by the application and limits how much the app can consume. For the resources you pay for, such as CPU time and storage, you set these limits yourself by allocating a budget in the Administration Console. App Engine also enforces several system-wide limits that protect the integrity of the servers and their ability to serve multiple apps.

In App Engine parlance, "quotas" are resource limits that refresh at the beginning of each calendar day (at midnight, Pacific Time). You can monitor your application's daily consumption of quotas using the Administration Console, in the Quota Details section.

Since Google may change how the limits are set as the system is tuned for performance, we won't state some of the specific values of these limits in this book. You can find the actual values of these limits in the official App Engine documentation. Google has said it will give 90 days' notice before changing limits in a way that would affect existing apps.

Request Limits

Several system-wide limits specify how requests can behave. These include the size and number of requests over a period of time, and the bandwidth consumed by inbound and outbound network traffic.

One important request limit is the request timer. An application has 30 seconds to respond to a request.

Near the end of the 30 seconds, the server raises an exception that the application can catch for the purposes of exiting cleanly or returning a user-friendly error message. For Python, the request timer raises a `google.appengine.runtime.DeadlineExceededError`. For Java, the request timer throws a `com.google.apphosting.api.DeadlineExceededException`.

If the request handler has not returned a response or otherwise exited after 30 seconds, the server terminates the process and returns a generic system error (HTTP code 500) to the client.

The 30-second limit applies to every request, including user web requests, enqueued tasks, scheduled tasks, and other web hooks such as incoming XMPP and email requests.

The size of a request is limited to 10 megabytes, as is the size of the request handler's response.

CPU Limits

Naturally, when application code is executing, it uses the CPU of the server. The CPU is shared by multiple request handlers running on a given server at the same time. App Engine prevents one request handler's use of the CPU from affecting the performance of other apps by allocating more resources as needed, such as serving apps from alternate servers. Use of the CPU is an important commodity in App Engine, so it is a billable quota. It is also limited to prevent bursts of usage from causing problems.

Use of a CPU could be measured by the number of processor cycles it takes to do the work, in units such as megacycles (millions of CPU operations per second). However, the speed of a CPU may vary from one app server to the next. While the same amount of work gets done on any CPU for a given number of megaflops, the total impact to performance may vary (though not in a way you'd notice).

So instead of megaflops, App Engine measures CPU usage in "CPU minutes." A CPU minute is the number of megaflops that can be performed by a standard processor in one minute. The standard processor in this case is a 1.2 GHz Intel x86 processor.

In other words, if your app were running by itself on a single 1.2 GHz processor, it would do a CPU minute's worth of work in one clock minute. The actual amount of clock time to perform that work can vary, depending on how App Engine allocates resources.

App Engine tries to balance the load so each app gets a consistent rate of CPU attention. But if a request handler uses too much CPU time, the app server may throttle the allocation of CPU. In that case, the request handler consumes the same number of CPU minutes, but it takes more clock time to do it.

The CPU time quota includes two sets of resources: CPU time used on the app server, and CPU rime used in the datastore. Other services do not contribute to the CPU time quota; they manage CPU resources in other ways. An app server does not consume CPU time while it is waiting for a service call to return.

The Python runtime environment provides a function you can call to analyze the CPU usage in a request handler. The `get_request_cpu_usage()` function in the `google.appengine.api.quota` package returns the number of megacycles (not CPU minutes) used by the request handler so far. You can call this function before and after a calculation to determine how much CPU time the calculation used.

Service Limits

Each service has its own set of quotas and limits. As with system-wide limits, some can be raised using a billing account and a budget, such as the number of recipients the application has sent emails to. Other limits are there to protect the integrity of the service, such as the number of image transformations performed by the image service.

We won't list all of the service limits here. See the official documentation for a complete list, including values.

In Python, when an app exceeds a service-specific limit or quota, the runtime environment raises a `...runtime.apiproxy_errors.OverQuotaError`. In Java, the service call throws a `com.google.apphosting.api.ApiProxy.OverQuotaException` (note the `apphosting` package name, not `appengine`).

Two particular limits apply to all services: the size of a service call and the size of the service response are each limited to 1 megabyte. This imposes an inherent limit on the size of datastore entities and memcache values. Even though an incoming request can contain up to 10 megabytes, only 1 megabyte of that data can be stored using a single call to the datastore or memcache.

The service call size limits also apply to the datastore's batch API. Batch calls fetch or store multiple entities in one service call. The total size of a batch call must fit within the 1-megabyte service call limit.

Deployment Limits

Two limits affect the size and structure of your application's files. An application file cannot be larger than 10 megabytes. This applies to resource files (code, configuration) as well as static files. Also, the total number of files for an application cannot be larger than 3,000, including resource files and static files.

These limits aren't likely to cause problems in most cases, but some common tasks can push on these numbers. Some third-party libraries or frameworks can be many hundreds of files. Sites consisting of many pages of text or images can reach 3,000 pretty quickly. A site offering video or software for download might have difficulty with the 10-megabyte limit.

The Python runtime offers two ways to mitigate the file count limit. If you have many files of Python code, you can store the code files in a ZIP archive file, then add the path to the ZIP archive to `sys.path` at the top of your request handler scripts. The request handler scripts themselves must not be in a ZIP archive. Thanks to `zipimport`, a feature built into Python, the Python interpreter will recognize the ZIP file automatically and unpack it as needed when importing modules. Unpacking takes additional CPU time, but since imports are cached, the app only incurs this cost the first time the module is imported in a given app instance.

```
import sys
sys.path.insert(0, 'locales.zip')

import locales.es
```

The Python App Engine runtime includes a similar mechanism for serving static files from a ZIP archive file, called `zipserve`. Unlike `zipimport`, this feature is specific to App Engine. To serve static files from a ZIP archive, add the `zipserve` request handler to your *app.yaml*, associated with a URL path that represents the path to the ZIP file:

```
- url: /static/images/.*
  script: $PYTHON_LIB/google/appengine/ext/zipserve
```

This declares that all requests for a URL starting with `/static/images/` should resolve to a path in the ZIP file `/static/images.zip`.

The string `$PYTHON_LIB` in the script path refers to the location of the App Engine libraries, and is the only such substitution available (so far). It's useful precisely for this purpose, to set up a request handler whose code is in the App Engine Python modules included with the runtime environment.

When using `zipserve`, keep in mind that the ZIP archive is uploaded as a resource file, not a static file. Files are served by application code, not the static file infrastructure. By default, the handler advises browsers to cache the files for 20 minutes. You can customize the handler's cache duration using the wrapper `WSGIApplication`. See the source code for `google/appengine/ext/zipserve/__init__.py` in the SDK for details.

Java applications have a common solution for reducing the file count for application code: JARs. If your app has too many `.class` files, simply put them in a JAR file using the `jar` utility included with the Java development kit. As with Python, app caching reduces the overhead of unpacking JARs. There is no equivalent to `zipserve` for static files in Java included with the SDK, but it's easy to write something that behaves similarly using JAR files.

Also, with Java, make sure to use `<static-files>` and `<resource-files>` directives in your *appengine-web.xml* file to exclude the appropriate files. By default, all files outside of *WEB-INF/* belong to both groups, and so are counted *twice*, once for each group. The file count limit is the total count for both groups.

An application can only be uploaded a limited number of times per day, currently 250. You may not notice this limit during normal application development. If you are using app deployments to upload data to the application on a regular schedule, you may want to keep this limit in mind. See Chapter 12 for a better way to upload data.

Billable Quotas

Every application gets a limited amount of computing resources for free, so you can start developing and testing your application right away. You can purchase additional computing resources at competitive rates. You only pay for what you actually use: you specify the maximum amount of money you want to spend, and allocate those funds to the various resources to increase those limits. The amount App Engine bills is for the resources your application actually consumes, and it never exceeds your declared budget.

The first step is to establish a billing account for the app. To enable billing, sign in to the Administration Console with the developer account that is to become the billing account, then select Billing Settings from the sidebar. Click the Enable Billing button, and follow the prompts.

Billing is managed through Google Checkout, Google's payment service. When you set a budget, you are prompted to go through Google Checkout to approve the maximum charge. Setting a budget does not apply a charge to your account, it only sets the maximum. Billing occurs once a day.

When you set up billing, you are prompted to specify a budget and the resource allocations for that budget. You can accept the default settings, pick another preset, or set custom allocations for each of the resources. The billable resources include:

- CPU time, in CPU hours
- Outgoing bandwidth, in gigabytes sent
- Incoming bandwidth, in gigabytes received
- Data stored, in gigabytes per day
- Recipients emailed (the number of total recipients in all email messages sent)

The bandwidth limits apply to incoming requests, outgoing responses, bandwidth used in a URL Fetch, and other network activity in and out of Google's data centers. The data storage limit comprises the datastore, including automatic and custom indexes, as well as the memcache. As mentioned earlier, CPU time includes CPU usage on the app servers and on the datastore servers.

Each billable resource has a maximum amount you can set in the Console. If your application needs more resources than the allowed maximum settings, you can request an increase of these maximums. See the official documentation for the link to the request form.

The owner of the billing account can change the budget and the resource allocations for the app at any time using the Administration Console. A change to your budget takes about 10 minutes to complete, and you will not be able to change the setting again during those 10 minutes.

The resources you purchase with your budget are in addition to the free resources included with every app. In fact, when you enable billing, App Engine increases the free resource levels for the app. You can enable billing, then set the budget to $0 to claim the free quota increase without additional charges, though you still need to associate a method of payment with the billing account.

The official documentation includes a complete list of the free quota limits, the increased free quota limits with billing enabled, the maximum allocation amounts, and the latest billing rates.

Resource Usage Headers

If you are signed in to your app via Google Accounts using your developer account when you request an app URL, App Engine includes HTTP headers in the response that give you information about resources consumed by that request. You can view these headers using a browser plug-in, such as the Web Developer extension for Firefox (Information menu, View Response Headers). Figure 3-2 shows an example of viewing these response headers using the Web Developer extension.

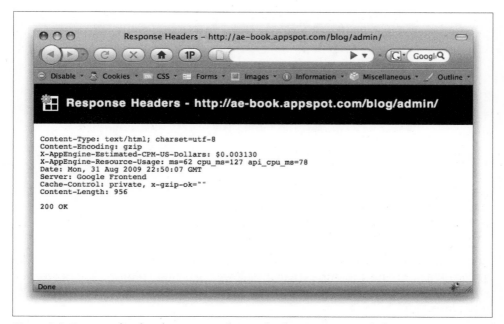

Figure 3-2. Response headers for a request from a developer account, including resource usage, as viewed with the Firefox Web Developer extension

The X-AppEngine-Estimated-CPM-US-Dollars header represents the monetary cost of the request times 1,000, at the current price in U.S. dollars. That is, it's an estimate of what 1,000 requests similar to this one would cost.

The X-AppEngine-Resource-Usage header summarizes various resource usage metrics for the request, including clock time and CPU time spent on the app server and APIs. Each number is in milliseconds.

If your app does not use Google Accounts for authentication, you can create a request handler restricted to administrators for the sole purpose of signing in. After you visit that handler and sign in, subsequent requests to the app will return the resource usage headers.

## CHAPTER 4

Datastore Entities

Most scalable web applications use separate systems for handling web requests and for storing data. The request handling system routes each request to one of many machines, each of which handles the request without knowledge of other requests going to other machines. Each request handler behaves as if it is *stateless*, acting solely on the content of the request to produce the response. But most web applications need to maintain state, whether it's remembering that a customer ordered a product, or just remembering that the user who made the current request is the same user who made an earlier request handled by another machine. For this, request handlers must interact with a central database to fetch and update the latest information about the state of the application.

Just as the request handling system distributes web requests across many machines for scaling and robustness, so does the database. But unlike the request handlers, databases are by definition *stateful*, and this poses a variety of questions. Which machine remembers which piece of data? How does the system route a data query to the machine—or machines—that can answer the query? When a client updates data, how long does it take for all machines that know that data to get the latest version, and what does the system return for queries about that data in the meantime? What happens when two clients try to update the same data at the same time? What happens when a machine goes down?

As with request handling, Google App Engine manages the scaling and maintenance of data storage automatically. Your application interacts with an abstract model that hides the details of managing and growing a pool of data servers. This model and the service behind it provide answers to the questions of scalable data storage specifically designed for web applications.

App Engine's abstraction for data is easy to understand, but it is not obvious how to best take advantage of its features. In particular, it is surprisingly different from the kind of database with which most of us are most familiar, the relational database. It's different enough, in fact, that Google doesn't call it a "database," but a "datastore."

We will dedicate the next several chapters to this important subject.

Entities, Keys, and Properties

The App Engine datastore is best understood as an object database. An object in the datastore is known as an *entity*.

An entity has a *key* that uniquely identifies the object across the entire system. If you have a key, you can fetch the entity for the key quickly. Keys can be stored as data in entities, such as to create a reference from one entity to another. A key has several parts, some of which we'll discuss here and some of which we'll cover later.

One part of the key is the application's ID, which ensures that nothing else about the key can collide with the entities of any other application. It also ensures that no other app can access your app's data, and that your app cannot access data for other apps. You won't see the app ID mentioned in the datastore API; this is automatic.

An important part of the key is the *kind*. An entity's kind categorizes the entity for the purposes of queries, and for ensuring the uniqueness of the rest of the key. For example, a shopping cart application might represent each customer order with an entity of the kind "Order." The application specifies the kind when it creates the entity.

The key also contains an *entity ID*. This can be an arbitrary string specified by the app, or it can be generated automatically by the datastore. The API calls an entity ID given by the app a *key name*, and an entity ID generated by the datastore an *ID*. An entity has either a key name or an ID, but not both.

Once an entity has been created, its key cannot be changed. This applies to all parts of its key, including the kind and the key name or ID.

The data for the entity is stored in one or more *properties*. Each property has a name and at least one value. Each value is of one of several supported data types, such as a string, an integer, a date-time, or a null value. We'll look at property value types in detail later in this chapter.

A property can have multiple values, and each value can be of a different type. As you will see in "Multivalued Properties" on page 113, multivalued properties have unusual behavior, but are quite useful for modeling some kinds of data, and surprisingly efficient.

It's tempting to compare these concepts with similar concepts in relational databases: kinds are tables; entities are rows; properties are fields or columns. That's a useful comparison, but watch out for differences.

Unlike a table in a relational database, there is no relationship between an entity's kind and its properties. Two entities of the same kind can have different properties set or not set, and can each have a property of the same name but with values of different types. You can (and often will) enforce a data schema in your own code, and App Engine includes libraries to make this easy, but this is not required by the datastore.

Also unlike relational databases, keys are not properties. You can perform queries on key names just like properties, but you cannot change a key name after the entity has been created.

And of course, a relational database cannot store multiple values in a single cell, while an App Engine property can have multiple values.

Introducing the Python Datastore API

In the Python API for the App Engine datastore, Python objects represent datastore entities. The class of the object corresponds to the entity's kind, where the name of the class is the name of the kind. You define kinds by creating classes that extend one of the provided base classes.

Each attribute of the object corresponds with a property of the entity. To create a new entity in the datastore, you call the class constructor, set attributes on the object, then call a method to save it. To update an existing entity, you call a method that returns the object for the entity (such as via a query), modify its attributes, then save it.

Example 4-1 defines a class named Book to represent entities of the kind Book. It creates an object of this class by calling the class constructor, then sets several property values. Finally, it calls the put() method to save the new entity to the datastore. The entity does not exist in the datastore until it is put() for the first time.

Example 4-1. Python code to create an entity of the kind Book

```
from google.appengine.ext import db
import datetime

class Book(db.Expando):
    pass

obj = Book()
obj.title = 'The Grapes of Wrath'
obj.author = 'John Steinbeck'
obj.copyright_year = 1939
obj.author_birthdate = datetime.date(1902, 2, 27)

obj.put()
```

The `Book` class inherits from the class `Expando` in App Engine's `db` package. The `Expando` base class says `Book` objects can have any of their properties assigned any value. The entity "expands" to accommodate new properties as they are assigned to attributes of the object. Python does not require that an object's member variables be declared in a class definition, and this example takes advantage of this using an empty class definition—the `pass` keyword indicates the empty definition—and assigns values to attributes of the object after it is created. The `Expando` base class knows to use the object's attributes as the values of the corresponding entity's properties.

The `Expando` class has a funny name because this isn't the way the API's designers expect us to create new classes in most cases. Instead, you're more likely to use the `Model` base class with a class definition that ensures each instance conforms to a structure, so a mistake in the code doesn't accidentally create entities with malformed properties. Here is how we might implement the `Book` class using `Model`:

```
class Book(db.Model):
    title = db.StringProperty()
    author = db.StringProperty()
    copyright_year = db.IntegerProperty()
    author_birthdate = db.DateProperty()
```

The `Model` version of `Book` specifies a structure for `Book` objects that is enforced while the object is being manipulated. It ensures that values assigned to an object's properties are of appropriate types, such as string values for `title` and `author` properties, and raises a runtime error if the app attempts to assign a value of the wrong type to a property. With `Model` as the base class, the object does not "expand" to accommodate other entities: an attempt to assign a value to a property not mentioned in the class definition raises a runtime error. `Model` and the various `Property` definitions also provide other features for managing the structure of your data, such as automatic values, required values, and the ability to add your own validation and serialization logic.

It's important to notice that these validation features are provided by the `Model` class and your application code, *not* the datastore. Even if part of your app uses a `Model` class to ensure a property's value meets certain conditions, another part of your app can still retrieve the entity without using the class and do whatever it likes to that value. The bad value won't raise an error until the app tries to load the changed entity into a new instance of the `Model` class. This is both a feature and a burden: your app can manage entities flexibly and enforce structure where needed, but it must also be careful when those structures need to change. Data modeling and the `Model` class are discussed in detail in Chapter 7.

The `Book` constructor accepts initial values for the object's properties as keyword arguments. The constructor code earlier could also be written like this:

```
obj = Book(title='The Grapes of Wrath',
           author='John Steinbeck',
           copyright_year=1939,
           author_birthdate=datetime.date(1902, 2, 27))
```

As written, this code does not set a key name for the new entity. Without a key name, the datastore generates a unique ID when the object is saved for the first time. If you prefer to use a key name generated by the app, you call the constructor with the key_name parameter:

```
obj = Book(key_name='0143039431',
           title='The Grapes of Wrath',
           author='John Steinbeck',
           copyright_year=1939,
           author_birthdate=datetime.date(1902, 2, 27))
```

 Because the Python API uses keyword arguments, object attributes, and object methods for purposes besides entity properties, there are several property names that are off-limits. For instance, you cannot use the Python API to set a property named key_name, because this could get confused with the key_name parameter for the object constructor. Names reserved by the Python API are enforced in the API, but *not* in the datastore itself. Google's official documentation lists the reserved property names.

The datastore reserves all property names beginning and ending with two underscores (such as __internal__). This is true for the Python API and the Java API, and will be true for future APIs as well.

The Python API ignores all object attributes whose names begin with a single underscore (such as _counter). You can use such attributes to attach data and functionality to an object that should not be saved as properties for the entity.

The complete key of an entity, including the key name and kind, must be unique. (We'll discuss another part to keys that contributes to a key's uniqueness, called ancestors, in Chapter 6.) If you build a new object with a key that is already in use, then try to save it, the save will replace the existing object. For when you don't want to overwrite existing data, the datastore API provides an alternate way to create an object. The get_or_insert() class method takes a key name and either returns an existing entity with that key name, or creates a new entity with that key name and no properties and returns it. Either way, the method is guaranteed to return an object that represents an entity in the datastore:

```
obj = Book.get_or_insert('0143039431')

if obj.title:
    # Book already exists.
    # ...
else:
```

```
obj.title = 'The Grapes of Wrath'
obj.author = 'John Steinbeck'
obj.copyright_year = 1939
obj.author_birthdate = datetime.date(1902, 2, 27)

obj.put()
```

Introducing the Java Datastore API

App Engine for Java includes support for two major standard interfaces for databases: Java Data Objects (JDO) and the Java Persistence API (JPA). Like the other standards-based interfaces in the App Engine Java API, using one of these interfaces makes it easier to move your application from and to another platform. JDO and JPA support different kinds of databases, including object databases and relational databases. They provide an object-oriented interface to your data, even if the underlying database is not an object store.

Many of the concepts of these interfaces translate directly to App Engine datastore concepts: classes are kinds, objects are entities, fields are properties. App Engine's implementation also supports several advanced features of these interfaces, such as object relationships. Inevitably, some concepts do not translate directly and have behaviors that are specific to App Engine.

We'll discuss one of these interfaces, JPA, in Chapter 8. For now, here is a simple example of a data class using JPA:

```
import java.util.Date;
import javax.persistence.Entity;
import javax.persistence.GeneratedValue;
import javax.persistence.GenerationType;
import javax.persistence.Id;

@Entity
public class Book {
    @Id
    @GeneratedValue(strategy = GenerationType.IDENTITY)
    private Long id;

    private String title;
    private String author;
    private int copyrightYear;
    private Date authorBirthdate;

    public Long getId() {
        return id;
    }

    public String getTitle() {
        return title;
    }
    public void setTitle(String title) {
        this.title = title;
```

```
    }

    public String getAuthor() {
        return author;
    }
    public void setAuthor(String author) {
        this.author = author;
    }

    public int getCopyrightYear() {
        return copyrightYear;
    }
    public void setCopyrightYear(int copyrightYear) {
        this.copyrightYear = copyrightYear;
    }

    public Date getAuthorBirthdate() {
        return authorBirthdate;
    }
    public void setAuthorBirthdate(Date authorBirthdate) {
        this.authorBirthdate = authorBirthdate;
    }
}
```

The JDO and JPA implementations are built on top of a low-level API for the App Engine datastore. The low-level API exposes all of the datastore's features, and corresponds directly to datastore concepts. For instance, you must use the low-level API to manipulate entities with properties of unknown names or value types. You can also use the low-level API directly in your applications out of preference, or to implement your own data management layer.

The following code creates a **Book** entity using the low-level API:

```
import java.io.IOException;
import java.util.Calendar;
import java.util.Date;
import java.util.GregorianCalendar;

import javax.servlet.http.HttpServlet;
import javax.servlet.http.HttpServletRequest;
import javax.servlet.http.HttpServletResponse;

import com.google.appengine.api.datastore.DatastoreService;
import com.google.appengine.api.datastore.DatastoreServiceFactory;
import com.google.appengine.api.datastore.Entity;

// ...
        DatastoreService ds = DatastoreServiceFactory.getDatastoreService();

        Entity book = new Entity("Book");

        book.setProperty("title", "The Grapes of Wrath");
        book.setProperty("author", "John Steinbeck");
        book.setProperty("copyrightYear", 1939);
        Date authorBirthdate =
```

```
        new GregorianCalendar(1902, Calendar.FEBRUARY, 27).getTime();
    book.setProperty("authorBirthdate", authorBirthdate);

    ds.put(book);

    // ...
```

Notice that the application code, not the datastore, is responsible for managing the structure of the data. JDO and JPA impose this structure using classes whose fields are persisted to the datastore behind the scenes. This can be both a benefit and a burden when you need to change the structure of existing data.

To illustrate the datastore concepts, we will use the low-level API for Java examples in the next few chapters. In Chapter 8, we will reintroduce JPA, and discuss how JPA concepts correspond with App Engine concepts. For more information on the Java Data Objects interface, see the official App Engine documentation.

Property Values

Each value data type supported by the datastore is represented by a primitive type in the language for the runtime or a class provided by the API. The data types and their language-specific equivalents are listed in Table 4-1. In this table, `db` is the Python package `google.appengine.ext.db`, and `datastore` is the Java package `com.google.appengine.api.datastore`.

Table 4-1. Datastore property value types and equivalent language types

Data type	Python type	Java type
Unicode text string (up to 500 bytes, indexed)	unicode or str (converted to uni code as ASCII)	java.lang.String
Long Unicode text string (not indexed)	db.Text	datastore.Text
Short byte string (up to 500 bytes, indexed)	db.ByteString	datastore.ShortBlob
Long byte string (not indexed)	db.Blob	datastore.Blob
Boolean	bool	boolean
Integer (64-bit)	int or long (converted to 64-bit long)	byte, short, int, or long (converted to long)
Float (double precision)	float	float or double (converted to double)
Date-time	datetime.datetime	java.util.Date
Null value	None	null
Entity key	db.Key	datastore.Key
A Google account	users.User	...api.users.User
A category (GD)	db.Category	datastore.Category

Data type	Python type	Java type
A URL (GD)	db.Link	datastore.Link
An email address (GD)	db.Email	datastore.Email
A geographical point (GD)	db.GeoPt	datastore.GeoPt
An instant messaging handle (GD)	db.IM	datastore.IMHandle
A phone number (GD)	db.PhoneNumber	datastore.PhoneNumber
A postal address (GD)	db.PostalAddress	datastore.PostalAddress
A user rating (GD)	db.Rating	datastore.Rating

The datastore types in this table labeled "(GD)" are types borrowed from the Google Data protocol. These are supported as distinct native data types in the datastore, though most of them are implemented as text strings. Notable exceptions are GeoPt, which is a pair of floating-point values for latitude (−90 to +90) and longitude (−180 to +180), and Rating, which is an integer between 1 and 100.

Example 4-2 demonstrates the use of several of these data types in Python.

Example 4-2. Python code to set property values of various types

```
from google.appengine.ext import webapp
from google.appengine.ext import db
from google.appengine.api import users
import datetime

class Comment(db.Expando):
    pass

class CommentHandler(webapp.RequestHandler):
    def post(self):
        c = Comment()
        c.commenter = users.get_current_user()  # returns a users.User object
        c.message = db.Text(self.request.get('message'))
        c.date = datetime.datetime.now()
        c.put()

        # Display the result page...
```

When you use Python's db.Expando or Java's low-level datastore API, types that are widened to other types when stored come back as the wider datastore types when you retrieve the entity. For instance, a Java Integer comes back as a Long. If you use these APIs in your app, it's best to use the native datastore types, so the value types stay consistent.

The data modeling interfaces offer a way to store values in these alternate types and convert them back automatically when retrieving the entity. See Chapters 7 and 8.

Strings, Text, and Blobs

The datastore has two distinct data types for storing strings of text: short strings and long strings. Short strings are indexed; that is, they can be the subject of queries, such as a search for every `Person` entity with a given value for a `last_name` property. Short string values must be less than 500 bytes in length. Long strings can be longer than 500 bytes, but are not indexed.

Text strings, short and long, are strings of characters from the Unicode character set. Internally, the datastore stores Unicode strings using the UTF-8 encoding, which represents some characters using multiple bytes. This means that the 500-byte limit for short strings is not necessarily the same as 500 Unicode characters. The actual limit on the number of characters depends on which characters are in the string.

The Python API distinguishes between short strings and long strings using Python data types. The Python built-in types `unicode` and `str` represent short string values. `str` values are assumed to be text encoded as ASCII, and are treated as UTF-8 (which is equivalent to ASCII for the first 128 characters in the character set). For long strings, the Python API includes a `db.Text` class, which takes a `unicode` or `str` value as an argument for its constructor.

```
# Short strings.
e.prop = "a short string, as an ASCII str"
e.prop = unicode("a short string, as a unicode value")

# A long string.
e.prop = db.Text("a long string, can be longer than 500 bytes")
```

The Java API makes a similar distinction, treating `String` values as short strings, and using the `datastore.Text` class to represent long text strings.

The datastore also supports two additional classes for strings of bytes, or "blobs." Blobs are not assumed to be of any particular format, and their bytes are preserved. This makes them good for nontext data, such as images, movies, or other media. As with text strings, the blob types come in indexed and nonindexed varieties. The Python API provides the `db.Blob` class to represent blob values, which takes a `str` value as an argument for its constructor.

```
# A blob.  self.request.body is the body of the request in a
# webapp request handler, such as an uploaded file.
e.prop = db.Blob(self.request.body)
```

In Java, the blob types are `datastore.ShortBlob` and `datastore.Blob`.

Unset Versus the Null Value

One possible value of a property is the null value. In Python, the null value is represented by the Python built-in value `None`. In Java, this value is `null`.

A property with the null value is not the same as an unset property. Consider the following Python code:

```python
class Entity(db.Expando):
    pass

a = Entity()
a.prop1 = 'abc'
a.prop2 = None
a.put()

b = Entity()
b.prop1 = 'def'
b.put()
```

This creates two entities of the kind `Entity`. Both entities have a property named `prop1`. The first entity has a property named `prop2`; the second does not.

Of course, an unset property can be set later:

```python
b.prop2 = 123
b.put()

# b now has a property named "prop2."
```

Similarly, a set property can be made unset. In the Python API, you delete the property by deleting the attribute from the object, using the `del` keyword:

```python
del b.prop2
b.put()

# b no longer has a property named "prop2."
```

In Java, the low-level datastore API's `Entity` class has methods to set properties (`setProperty()`) and unset properties (`removeProperty()`).

Multivalued Properties

As we mentioned earlier, a property can have multiple values. We'll discuss the more substantial aspects of multivalued properties when we talk about queries and data modeling. But for now, it's worth a brief mention.

A property can have one or more values. A property cannot have zero values; a property without a value is simply unset. Each value for a property can be of a different type, and can be the null value.

The datastore preserves the order of values as they are assigned. The Python API returns the values in the same order as they were set.

In Python, a property with multiple values is represented as a single Python `list` value:

```python
e.prop = [1, 2, 'a', None, 'b']
```

Because a property must have at least one value, it is an error to assign an empty list ([] in Python) to a property on an entity whose Python class is based on the Expando class.

```
class Entity(db.Expando):
    pass

e = Entity()
e.prop = []  # ERROR
```

In contrast, the Model base class includes a feature that automatically translates between the empty list value and "no property set." You'll see this feature in Chapter 7.

In the Java low-level datastore API, you can store multiple values for a property using a Collection type. The low-level API returns the values as a java.util.List. The items are stored in the order provided by the Collection type's iterator. For many types, such as SortedSet or TreeSet, this order is deterministic. For others, such as HashSet, it is not. If the app needs the original data structure, it must convert the List returned by the datastore to the appropriate type.

Keys and Key Objects

The key for an entity is a value that can be retrieved, passed around, and stored like any other value. If you have the key for an entity, you can retrieve the entity from the datastore quickly, much more quickly than with a datastore query. Keys can be stored as property values, as an easy way for one entity to refer to another.

The Python API represents an entity key value as an instance of the Key class, in the db package. To get the key for an entity, you call the entity object's key() method. The Key instance provides access to its several parts using accessor methods, including the kind, key name (if any), and system-assigned ID (if the entity does not have a key name).

The Java low-level API is similar: the getKey() method of the Entity class returns an instance of the Key class.

When you construct a new entity object and do not provide a key name, the entity object has a key, but the key does not yet have an ID. The ID is populated when the entity object is saved to the datastore for the first time. You can get the key object prior to saving the object, but it will be incomplete.

```
e = Entity()
e.prop = 123

k = e.key()  # key is incomplete, has neither key name nor ID
kind = k.kind()  # 'Entity'

e.put()  # ID is assigned
```

```
k = e.key()  # key is complete, has ID
id = k.id()  # the system-assigned ID
```

If the entity object was constructed with a key name, the key is complete before the object is saved—though if the entity has not been saved, the key name is not guaranteed to be unique. (In Python, the entity class method get_or_insert(), mentioned earlier, always returns a saved entity, either one that was saved previously or a new one created by the call.)

You can test whether a key is complete using a method on the Key object. In Python, this is the has_id_or_name() method. The id_or_name() method returns either the object's key name or its ID, whichever one it has.

In Java, you can call isComplete() to test the Key for completeness, and getId() or getName() to get the numeric ID or the string name.

Once you have a complete key, you can assign it as a property value on another entity to create a reference.

```
e2 = Entity()
e2.ref = k
e2.put()
```

If you know the kind and either the key name or ID of an entity in the datastore, you can construct the key for that entity without its object. In Python, you use the from_path() class method of the Key class. A complete explanation of this feature involves another feature we haven't mentioned yet (paths), but the following suffices for the examples you've seen so far:

```
e = Entity(key_name='alphabeta')
e.prop = 123
e.put()

# ...

k = db.Key.from_path('Entity', 'alphabeta')
```

In Java, you can build a Key object from parts using KeyFactory. The static method KeyFactory.createKey() takes the kind and the ID or name as arguments:

```
Key k = KeyFactory.createKey("Entity", "alphabeta");
```

Paths are related to how the datastore does transactions. We'll get to them in Chapter 6. For the entities we have created so far, the path is just the kind followed by the ID or name.

Keys can be converted to string representations for the purposes of passing around as textual data, such as in a web form or cookie. The string representation avoids characters considered special in HTML or URLs, so it is safe to use without escaping characters. The encoding of the value to a string is simple and easily reversed, so make sure you do not use any information that ought to be secret as part of a key whose string form will be sent to users, such as a key name or kind. In Python:

```
k_str = str(k)

# ...

k = db.Key(k_str)
```

And in Java:

```
String k_str = KeyFactory.keyToString(k);

// ...

Key k = KeyFactory.stringToKey(k_str);
```

The Java Key class's toString() method does not return the key's string encoding. You must use KeyFactory.keyToString() to get the string encoding of a key.

Using Entities

Let's look briefly at how to retrieve entities from the datastore using keys, how to inspect the contents of entities, and how to update and delete entities. The API methods for these features are straightforward.

Getting Entities Using Keys

Given a complete key for an entity, you can retrieve the entity from the datastore.

In the Python API, you can call the get() function in the db package with the Key object as an argument:

```
from google.appengine.ext import db

k = db.Key('Entity', 'alphabeta')

e = db.get(k)
```

If you know the kind of the entity you are fetching, you can also use the get() class method on the appropriate entity class. This does a bit of type checking, ensuring that the key you provide is of the appropriate kind:

```
class Entity(db.Expando):
    pass

e = Entity.get(k)
```

To fetch multiple entities in a batch, you can pass the keys to get() as a list. Given a list, the method returns a list containing entity objects, with None values for keys that do not have a corresponding entity in the datastore.

```
entities = db.get([k1, k2, k3])
```

Getting a batch of entities in this way performs a single service call to the datastore for the entire batch. This is faster than getting each entity in a separate call. It is also subject to the service call size limit (one megabyte), so make sure the total size of all of the entities will not exceed this limit when doing a batch get. Batch gets are also subject to an entity count limit.

For convenience, entity classes include methods that take just the IDs or key names and retrieve the corresponding entities, inferring the kind from the class name. See get_by_id() and get_by_key_name() in the official reference documentation.

In the Java low-level API, you get an entity by its key using a DatastoreService instance (returned by DatastoreServiceFactory.getDatastoreService()). The instance provides a get() method that takes a Key for a single entity get, or an Iterable<Key> for a batch get. If given an iterable of keys, get() returns a Map of Key to Entity:

```
DatastoreService ds = DatastoreServiceFactory.getDatastoreService();

Map<Key, Entity> entities = ds.get(new ArrayList(Arrays.asList(k1, k2, k3)));

Entity e1 = entities.get(k1);
```

Of course, you won't always have the keys for the entities you want to fetch from the datastore. To retrieve entities that meet other criteria, you use datastore queries. Queries are discussed in Chapter 5.

Inspecting Entity Objects

Entity objects have methods for inspecting various aspects of the entity.

In the Java API, the methods of the Entity class provide straightforward access to the key (getKey()) and kind (getKind()) of the entity. The getProperty() method returns the value of a property given its name. The hasProperty() method tests whether a property is set. setProperty() takes a name and a value and sets the property, replacing any existing value.

The Python API has several features for inspecting entities worth mentioning here. You've already seen the key() method of an entity object, which returns the db.Key.

The is_saved() method returns False if the object has not been saved to the datastore since the object was constructed. If the object has been saved since it was constructed, or if the object was retrieved from the datastore, the method returns True. The method continues to return True even if the object's properties have been modified, so do not rely on this method to track changes to properties of previously saved entities.

```
e = Entity()
# e.is_saved() == False

e.put()
# e.is_saved() == True
```

The Java API does not have an equivalent to is_saved().

In Python, entity properties can be accessed and modified just like object attributes:

```
e.prop1 = 1
e.prop2 = 'two'

print "prop2 has the value " + e.prop2
```

You can use Python built-in functions for accessing object attributes to access entity properties. For instance, to test that an entity has a property with a given name, use the hasattr() built-in:

```
if hasattr(e, 'prop1'):
    # ...
```

To get or set a property whose name is a string, use getattr() and setattr(), respectively:

```
# Set prop1, prop2, ..., prop9.
for n in range(1, 10):
    value = n * n
    setattr(e, 'prop' + str(n), value)

value = getattr(e, 'prop' + str(7))
```

While entity objects support accessing properties using these methods, the objects do not actually store property values as object attributes. For instance, you cannot use Python's dir() built-in to get a list of an entity's properties. Instead, entity objects provide their own method, instance_properties(), for this purpose:

```
for name in e.instance_properties():
    value = getattr(e, name)
```

Saving Entities

In Python, calling the put() method on an entity object saves the entity to the datastore. If the entity does not yet exist in the datastore, put() creates the entity. If the entity exists, put() updates the entity so that it matches the object.

```
e = Entity()
e.prop = 123

e.put()
```

When you update an entity, the app sends the complete contents of the entity to the datastore. The update is all or nothing: there is no way to send just the properties that have changed to the datastore. There is also no way to update a property on an entity without retrieving the complete entity, making the change, then sending the new entity back.

You use the same API to create an entity as you do to update an entity. The datastore does not make a distinction between creates and updates. If you save an entity with a complete key (such as a key with a kind and a key name) and an entity already exists with that key, the datastore replaces the existing entity with the new one.

 If you want to test that an entity with a given key does not exist before you create it, you can do so using the transaction API. You must use a transaction to ensure that another process doesn't create an entity with that key after you test for it and before you create it. For more information on transactions, see Chapter 6.

If you have several entity objects to save, you can save them all in one call using the put() function in the db package. The put() function can also take a single entity object.

```
db.put(e)
db.put([e1, e2, e3])
```

As with a batch get, a batch put performs a single call to the service. The total size of the call is subject to the API call limits for the datastore. The entity count is also subject to a limit.

In Java, you can save entities using the put() method of a DatastoreService instance. As with get(), the method takes a single Entity for a single put, or an Iterable<Entity> for a batch put.

When the call to put() returns, the datastore is up to date, and all future queries in the current request handler and other handlers will see the new data. The specifics of how the datastore gets updated are discussed in detail in Chapter 6.

Deleting Entities

Deleting entities works similarly to putting entities. In Python, you can call the delete() method on the entity object, or you can pass entity objects or Key objects to the delete() function.

```
e = db.get('Entity', 'alphabeta')
e.delete()

db.delete(e)
db.delete([e1, e2, e3])

# Deleting without first fetching the entity:
k = db.Key('Entity', 'alphabeta')
db.delete(k)
```

In Java, you call the delete() method of the DatastoreService with either a single Key or an Iterable<Key>.

As with gets and puts, a delete of multiple entities occurs in a single batch call to the service, and is faster than making multiple service calls.

## CHAPTER 5

Datastore Queries

Inevitably, an application that manages data must do more than store and retrieve that data one record at a time. It must also answer questions about that data: which records meet certain criteria, how records compare to one another, what a set of records represents in aggregate. Web applications in particular are expected not only to know the answers to questions about large amounts of data, but to provide them quickly in response to web requests.

Most database systems provide a mechanism for executing queries, and the App Engine datastore is no exception. But App Engine's technique differs significantly from that of traditional database systems. When the application asks a question, instead of rifling through the original records and performing calculations to determine the answer, App Engine simply finds the answer in a list of possible answers prepared in advance. App Engine can do this because it knows which questions are going to be asked.

This kind of list, or *index*, is common to many database technologies, and some relational databases can be told to maintain a limited set of indexes to speed up some kinds of queries. But App Engine is different: it maintains an index for *every* query the application is going to perform. Since the datastore need only do a simple scan of an index for every query, the application gets results back quickly. And for large amounts of data, App Engine can spread the data and the indexes across many machines, and get results back from all of them without an expensive aggregate operation.

This indexing strategy has significant drawbacks. The datastore's built-in query engine is downright weak compared to some relational databases, and is not suited to sophisticated data processing applications that would prefer slow but powerful runtime queries to fast simple ones. But most web applications need fast results, and the dirty secret about those powerful query engines is that they can't perform at web speeds with large amounts of data distributed across many machines. App Engine uses a model suited to scalable web applications: calculate the answers to known questions when the data is written, so reading is fast.

In this chapter, we will explain how queries and indexes work, how the developer tools help you configure indexes automatically, and how to manage indexes as your application evolves. By understanding indexes, you will have an intuition for how to design your application and your data to make the most of the scalable datastore.

Queries and Kinds

You've seen how to retrieve an entity from the datastore given its key. But in most cases, the application does not know the keys of the entities it needs; it has only a general idea that it needs entities that meet certain criteria. For example, a leader board for the game app would need to retrieve the 10 Player entities with the highest score property values.

To retrieve entities this way, the app performs a *query*. A query includes:

- The kind of the entities to query
- Zero or more *filters*, criteria that property values must meet for an entity to be returned by the query
- Zero or more *sort orders* that determine the order in which results are returned based on property values

A query based on property values can only return entities of a single kind. This is the primary purpose of kinds: to determine which entities are considered together as possible results for a query. In practice, kinds correspond to the intuitive notion that each entity of the same nominal kind represents the same kind of data. But unlike other database systems, it's up to the app to enforce this consistency if it is desired, and the app can diverge from it if it's useful.

It is also possible to perform a limited set of queries on entities regardless of kind. Kindless queries can use a filter on the ID or key name, or on ancestors. We'll discuss ancestors and kindless queries in Chapter 6.

Query Results and Keys

When retrieving results for a query, the datastore returns the full entity for each result to the application. There is no way to query for a subset of the properties, as you might with fields in a relational database.

For large entities, this may mean more data is transmitted between the datastore and the app than is needed. If you have objects with large property values or very many properties and you only need to access a subset of this data most of the time, you can speed up access by storing the data across multiple entities. One entity stores the oft-accessed properties and properties used in queries, as well as a reference to another entity carrying the larger data (the key of the other entity). When the app needs the larger data, it queries for the small entity, then follows the reference to the large entity.

The datastore can return just the keys for the entities that match your query instead of fetching the full entities. A keys-only query is useful for determining the entities that match query criteria separately from when the entities are used. Keys can be remembered in the memcache or in a datastore property, and vivified as full entities when needed. We'll look at keys-only queries when we discuss each query API.

GQL

The Python and Java runtime environments provide several ways to formulate queries. They all do the same thing: they ask the datastore to return the entities (or keys for entities) whose keys and properties meet the given filter criteria, returned in an order determined by sorting the given properties.

One way to formulate a query is with *GQL*. GQL is a text-based query language that is intended to resemble SQL, the query language of relational databases. It supports only the features of the datastore's query engine, and therefore lacks many features common to SQL. But it is expressive and concise enough to be useful for datastore queries.

Say we have entities of the kind **Player** representing players in an online role-playing game. The following GQL query retrieves all **Player** entities whose "level" property is an integer between 5 and 20, sorted by level in ascending order, then by score in descending order:

```
SELECT * FROM Player
        WHERE level > 5
          AND level < 20
      ORDER BY level ASC, score DESC
```

You can use GQL to browse the contents of the datastore of your live application using the Administration Console. To do this, select Data Viewer from the sidebar. You can browse entities by kind, or enter a GQL query. You can also create new entities through the Console, though new entities are limited to the kinds, properties, and value types of existing entities. You can also edit the properties of an entity by clicking on its ID. Figure 5-1 shows the results of running a GQL query in the Console.

 You can only perform a query in the Administration Console if the query does not require a custom index, or if the app already has the requisite index for the query. We discuss indexes in depth later in this chapter.

Python apps can also perform queries using GQL from code. We'll look at this API in a moment. The Java datastore API does not yet support GQL. As you'll see later, Java apps using JDO or JPA have other textual query languages at their disposal.

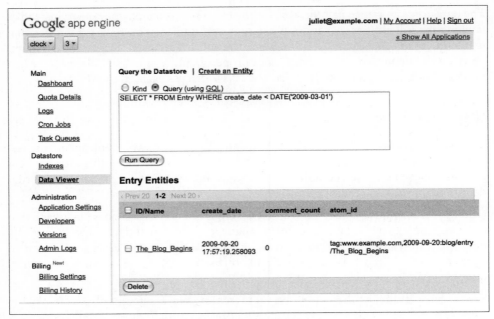

Figure 5-1. The Data Viewer panel of the Administration Console

The first part of the SQL-like syntax in the GQL query above, `SELECT * FROM Player`, says that the datastore should return complete entities as results, and that it should only consider entities of the kind `Player`. This is the most common kind of query.

Despite its similarity with SQL, GQL can only represent queries, and cannot perform updates, inserts, or deletes. In other words, every GQL query begins with `SELECT`.

The rest of the query syntax also resembles SQL, and translates directly to filters and sort orders. The `WHERE` clause, if present, represents one or more filter conditions, separated by `AND`. The `ORDER BY` clause, if present, represents one or more sort orders, separated by commas, applied from left to right.

Each condition in a `WHERE` clause consists of the name of a property, a comparison operator, and a value. You can also specify a condition that matches an entity's ID or key name by using the reserved name `__key__` (that's two underscores, the word "key," and two underscores) like a property name. GQL does not support expressions fancier than this: the lefthand side can only be a property name or `__key__`, and the righthand side can only be a simple value.

The datastore query engine supports five comparison operators for filters: `=`, `<`, `<=`, `>`, and `>=`. GQL also supports two additional operators: `!=`, meaning "not equal to," and `IN`, which tests that the value equals any in a set of values.

For IN, the values are represented by a comma-delimited list of values surrounded by parentheses:

```
SELECT * FROM Player WHERE level IN (5, 6, 7)
```

Internally, GQL translates the != and IN operators into multiple datastore queries that have the same effect. If a query contains an IN clause, the query is evaluated once for each value in the clause, using an = filter. The results of all of the queries are aggregated. The != operator performs the query once using a < filter and once using a >, then aggregates the results. Using these operators more than once in a GQL statement requires a query for each combination of the required queries, so be judicious in their use.

The WHERE clause is equivalent to one or more filters. It is not like SQL's WHERE clause, and does not support arbitrary logical expressions. In particular, it does not support testing the logical-OR of two conditions.

The value on the righthand side of a condition can be a literal value that appears inside the query string. Seven of the datastore value types have string literal representations, as shown in Table 5-1.

Table 5-1. GQL value literals for datastore types

Type	Literal syntax	Examples
String	Single-quoted string; escape the quote by doubling it	`'Haven''t You Heard'`
Integer or float	Sign, digits; float uses decimal point	`-7 3.14`
Boolean	True or false keywords	`TRUE FALSE`

Date-time, date or time	Type, and value as numbers or a string
	`DATETIME(year, month, day, hour, minute, second)`
	`DATETIME('YYYY-MM-DD HH:MM:SS')`
	`DATE(year, month, day)`
	`DATE('YYYY-MM-DD')`
	`TIME(hour, minute, second)`
	`TIME('HH:MM:SS')`
		`DATETIME(1999, 12, 31, 23, 59, 59)`
		`DATETIME('1999-12-31 23:59:59')`
		`DATE(1999, 12, 31)`
		`DATE('1999-12-31')`
		`TIME(23, 59, 59)`
		`TIME('23:59:59')`

Entity key	Entity kind, and name or ID; can be a path
	`KEY('kind', 'name'/id)`
	`KEY('kind', 'name'/id, 'kind', 'name'/id, ...)`
		`KEY('Player', 1287)`

User object	`User('email-address')`	`User('edward@example.com')`
GeoPt object	`GEOPT(lat, long)`	`GEOPT(37.4219, -122.0846)`

As we'll see later, the type of a filter's value is significant in a datastore query. If you use the wrong type for a value, such as by specifying a `'string_key'` when you meant to specify a `KEY('kind', 'key_name')`, your query may not return the results you intend, or may unexpectedly return no results.

A GQL query can specify a LIMIT, a maximum number of results to return. A query can also specify an OFFSET, a number of results to skip before returning the remaining results. The following example returns the third, fourth, and fifth results, and may return fewer if the query has fewer than five results:

```
SELECT * FROM Player LIMIT 3 OFFSET 2
```

GQL keywords, shown here in uppercase as is traditional with SQL, are case-insensitive. Kind and property names, however, are case-sensitive.

The datastore can return results as complete entities, or just the keys for those entities. Unlike SQL's ability to select specific columns from tables, the datastore cannot return a subset of an entity's properties, nor can it "join" properties from entities of multiple kinds into a single set of results. In GQL, SELECT * says to return full entities. SELECT __key__ says to return just the keys.

The Python Query API

Recall that the Python datastore API represents entities using objects of classes named after kinds. Example 5-1 shows Python code that creates three Player entities for an online role-playing game.

Example 5-1. Python code to create several entities of the kind Player

```python
from google.appengine.ext import db
import datetime

class Player(db.Expando):
    pass

player1 = Player(name='wizard612',
                 level=1,
                 score=32,
                 charclass='mage',
                 create_date=datetime.datetime.now())
player1.put()

player2 = Player(name='druidjane',
                 level=10,
                 score=896,
                 charclass='druid',
                 create_date=datetime.datetime.now())
player2.put()

player3 = Player(name='TheHulk',
                 level=7,
                 score=500,
                 charclass='warrior',
                 create_date=datetime.datetime.now())
player3.put()
```

Once again, we'll use `Expando` to keep the examples simple. As we start talking about queries, the importance of using a consistent layout, or *schema*, for entities of a kind will become apparent.

The Python API provides two ways to formulate queries, one using an object-oriented interface and one based on GQL.

The Query Class

The first way to formulate a query is with an instance of the `Query` class. A `Query` object can be constructed in one of two ways, with equivalent results:

```
q = db.Query(Player)
```

```
q = Player.all()
```

In both cases, `q` is assigned a new `Query` instance that represents all entities of the kind `Player`. The query is not executed right away; right now it's just a question waiting to be asked. Without filters or sort orders, the object represents a query for all objects of the given kind.

To apply a filter to the query, you call the `filter()` method on the `Query` object. It takes two arguments. The first argument is a string containing the name of a property, a space character, and a comparison operator. The second argument is the value for the comparison, of a type appropriate for the situation.

```
q.filter("level >", 5)
```

You specify multiple filters by calling the `filter()` method multiple times. An entity must meet all filter criteria in order to be a result for the query. That is, filters have a logical-AND relationship with one another.

```
q.filter("level >", 5)
q.filter("level <", 20)
```

For convenience, the `filter()` method returns the `Query` object, so you can chain multiple calls to `filter()` in a single line:

```
q.filter("level >", 5).filter("level <", 20)
```

The `filter()` method supports the equality (=) operator, and the four inequality operators (<, <=, >, and >=). The `Query` class also supports the != (not-equal) and `IN` operators from GQL, and does so in the same way, using multiple datastore queries and aggregating the results.

To apply a sort order, you call the `order()` method. This method takes one argument, a string containing the name of a property to sort by. If the string begins with a hyphen character (-), the sort will be in descending order; otherwise, the sort will be in ascending order. Like `filter()`, `order()` returns the `Query` object, for chaining.

```
q.order("-score")
```

The datastore can sort query results by multiple properties. First, it sorts by the property and order from the first call to order(), then from the next call, and so on. For example, the following sorts first by level ascending, then by score descending:

```
q.order("level").order("-score")
```

The query engine supports limiting the number of results returned, and skipping ahead a number of results. You specify the limit and offset when you retrieve the results, described later.

GQL in Python

The Python environment includes a rich API for preparing queries using GQL. In addition to the pure textual syntax, the Python API supports additional syntax for parameterized substitution of filter values.

To use GQL from Python, you instantiate an instance of the GqlQuery class with the text of the query:

```
q = db.GqlQuery("SELECT * FROM Player
                WHERE level > 5
                  AND level < 20
              ORDER BY level ASC, score DESC")
```

You can also instantiate a GqlQuery from the kind class directly, using its gql() class method. When using this method, omit the SELECT * FROM Kind from the string, since this is implied by the use of the method:

```
q = Player.gql("WHERE level > 5
                AND level < 20
            ORDER BY level ASC, score DESC")
```

You can specify values for conditions using parameter substitution. With parameter substitution, the query string contains a placeholder with either a number or a name, and the actual value is passed to GqlQuery() or gql() as either a positional argument or a keyword argument.

```
q = db.GqlQuery("SELECT * FROM Player
                WHERE level > :1
                  AND level < :2",
              5, 20)
```

```
q = db.GqlQuery("SELECT * FROM Player
                WHERE level > :min_level
                  AND level < :max_level",
            min_level=5, max_level=20)
```

One advantage to parameter substitution is that each argument value is of the appropriate datastore type, so you don't need to bother with the string syntax. For the datastore types that do not have string literal syntax (mostly the Google Data value types mentioned in Table 4-1), parameter substitution is the only way to use values of those types in a GQL query.

You can rebind new values to a GQL query using parameter substitution after the `GqlQuery` object has been instantiated using the `bind()` method. This means you can reuse the `GqlQuery` object for multiple queries that have the same structure but different values. This saves time because the query string only needs to be parsed once. The `bind()` method takes the new values as either positional arguments or keyword arguments.

You can save more time by caching parameterized `GqlQuery` objects in global variables. This way, the query string is parsed only when a server loads the application for the first time, and the application reuses the object for all subsequent calls handled by that server.

```
_LEADERBOARD_QUERY = db.GqlQuery(
  "SELECT * FROM Player
          WHERE level > :min_level
            AND level < :max_level
        ORDER BY level ASC, score DESC")

class LeaderboardHandler(webapp.RequestHandler):
    def get(self):
        _LEADERBOARD_QUERY.bind(min_level=5, max_level=20)
        # ...
```

Retrieving Results

Once you have a `Query` or `GqlQuery` object configured with filters, sort orders, and value bindings (in the case of `GqlQuery`), you can execute the query using one of several methods. The query is not executed until you call one of these methods, and you can call these methods repeatedly on the same query object to reexecute the query and get new results.

The `fetch()` method returns a number of results, up to a specified limit. `fetch()` returns a list of entity objects, which are instances of the kind class.

```
q = db.Query(Player).order('-score')

results = q.fetch(10)
```

When serving web requests, it's always good to limit the amount of data the datastore might return, so an unexpectedly large result set doesn't cause the request handler to exceed its deadline. This is so often the case that App Engine imposes a maximum limit of 1,000 results for all queries, which is the default if no smaller limit is given.

The `fetch()` method also accepts an optional `offset` parameter. If provided, the method skips that many results, then returns subsequent results, up to the specified limit.

```
q = db.Query(Player).order('-score')

results = q.fetch(10, offset=20)
```

For a `GqlQuery`, the fetch result limit and offset are equivalent to the `LIMIT` and `OFFSET` that can be specified in the query itself. The arguments to `fetch()` override those specified in the GQL statement. The limit argument to `fetch()` is required, so it always overrides a GQL `LIMIT` clause.

In order to perform a fetch with an offset, the datastore must collect the complete result set from all of its servers, then scan down the compiled list to the offset. The amount of time this takes depends on the size of the offset. To prevent the transient result set from getting too large and the query from taking too long, App Engine imposes the same maximum on the offset as it does on the limit: 1,000 results.

This makes fetch offsets unsuitable for retrieving records in batches, such as for a paginated display. Later pages will take much longer to retrieve results than earlier pages, and when the offset gets too large, pages won't display at all. If you're used to using a single-server database's result offset feature to power paginated displays, you'll want to consider another strategy.

One viable strategy is to maintain a property that can be used with an inequality filter to find the entity at the top of each page. As you'll see later in this chapter, index scans are much more efficient than result offsets, and can operate on very large data sets. You can also perform inequality queries on entity keys.

It's common for an app to perform a query expecting to get just one result, or nothing. You can do this with `fetch(1)`, then test whether the list it returns is empty. For convenience, the query object also provides a `get()` method, which returns either the first result, or the Python value `None` if the query did not return any results.

```
q = db.Query(Player).filter('name =', 'django97')

player = q.get()
if player:
    # ...
```

The `count()` method executes the query, then returns the number of results that would be returned instead of the results themselves. `count()` must perform the query to count the results, and so it is subject to the same 1,000 result maximum as `fetch()`. `count()` accepts a limit as a parameter, and providing one causes the method to return immediately once that many results have been counted.

```
q = db.Query(Player).filter('level >', 10)
if q.count(100) == 100:
    # 100 or more players are above level 10.
```

Query objects provide one other mechanism for retrieving results, and it's quite powerful. In the Python API, query objects are *iterable*. If you use the object in a context that accepts iterables, such as in a `for` loop, the object executes the query, then provides a Python standard iterator that returns each result one at a time, starting with the first result.

```
q = db.Query(Player).order('-score')

for player in q:
    # ...
```

Unlike `fetch()`, the iterator interface does *not* impose a maximum limit. As the app uses the iterator, the iterator fetches the results in small batches. The iterator could return results beyond 1,000, though in practice, the app request handler will probably reach its deadline before that happens. It's up to the app to stop requesting results from the iterator (to `break` from the `for` loop) when it has had enough.

If you want to use the iterator interface for fetching results but also want to use a limit or an offset, you can specify the limit or offset in a GQL query:

```
q = db.GqlQuery("SELECT * FROM Player LIMIT 10 OFFSET 5")

# Iterate over Players 5 through 10.
for player in q:
    # ...
```

You can pass the iterator to something that expects one, such as a templating engine, and the iterator will honor the limit and offset specified in the GQL query.

Keys-Only Queries

As we mentioned earlier, instead of returning complete entities, the datastore can return just the keys of the entities that match the query.

In the Python query API, you can query for keys using either the `Query` interface or the `GqlQuery` interface. To request just the keys with `Query`, provide the `keys_only` argument set to `True` to the `Query` constructor:

```
q = db.Query(Player, keys_only=True)
```

To specify a keys-only query using GQL, begin the GQL query with `SELECT __key__` instead of `SELECT *`:

```
q = db.GqlQuery('SELECT __key__ FROM Player')
```

When performing a keys-only query, each result returned by the query object is a `Key` object instead of an instance of the model class.

```
q = db.Query(Player, keys_only=True)
for result_key in q:
    # result_key is a Key...
```

There is no way to perform keys-only queries using the `Model` class methods `all()` and `gql()`. This makes sense: the return values of the `Model` methods represent collections of instances of the model class, not keys.

The Java Query API

If you are using the JPA interface or the JDO interface, you will use the query facilities of those interfaces to perform datastore queries: JPQL or JDOQL, respectively. The concepts of those interfaces map nicely to the concepts of datastore queries: a query has a kind (a class), filters, and sort orders. We'll look at the calling conventions for JPQL when we look at JPA in Chapter 8.

Naturally, the low-level Java datastore API includes a query interface as well. Here is a brief example:

```java
import com.google.appengine.api.datastore.DatastoreService;
import com.google.appengine.api.datastore.DatastoreServiceFactory;
import com.google.appengine.api.datastore.Entity;
import com.google.appengine.api.datastore.PreparedQuery;
import com.google.appengine.api.datastore.Query;

// ...
        DatastoreService ds = DatastoreServiceFactory.getDatastoreService();

        Query q = new Query("Book");
        q.addFilter("copyrightYear",
                    Query.FilterOperator.LESS_THAN_OR_EQUAL,
                    1950);
        q.addSort("title");

        PreparedQuery pq = ds.prepare(q);
        for (Entity result : pq.asIterable()) {
            String title = result.getProperty("title");

            // ...
        }
```

To perform a query, you instantiate the `Query` class (from the `com.google.appengine.api.datastore` package), providing the name of the kind of the entities to query as an argument to the constructor. You call methods on the query object to add filters and sort orders. To perform the query, you pass the query object to a method of the `DatastoreService` instance. This method returns a `PreparedQuery` object, which you can manipulate to retrieve the results.

The query is not actually performed until you attempt to access results using the `PreparedQuery` object. If you access the results using an iterator via the `asIterable()` or `asIterator()` methods, the act of iterating causes the API to fetch the results in batches. When these methods are called without arguments, the resulting iterator will keep going until all results for the query have been returned. If a query has a large number of results, this may take longer than the time allowed for the request.

The `asIterable()` and `asIterator()` methods accept an optional argument, a `FetchOptions` object, that controls which results are returned. Options can include an *offset*, a number of results to skip prior to returning any, and a *limit*, a maximum number of results to return. `FetchOptions` uses a builder-style interface, as follows:

```
import com.google.appengine.api.datastore.Entity;
import com.google.appengine.api.datastore.FetchOptions;
import com.google.appengine.api.datastore.PreparedQuery;
import com.google.appengine.api.datastore.Query;

// ...
        // Query q = ...
        PreparedQuery pq = ds.prepare(q);

        Iterable<Entity> results =
            pq.asIterable(FetchOptions.Builder.limit(10).offset(20));

        for (Entity result : results) {
            String title = result.getProperty("title");

            // ...
        }
```

This tells the datastore to skip the first 20 results, and return up to the next 10 results (if any).

 As with the Python interface, offsets require calculation within the service after the results have been gathered from across the datastore. This means the performance of an offset is proportional to the size of the offset, which makes offsets unsuitable for rendering paginated lists. See the similar note in the description of the Python query API, within the section "Retrieving Results" on page 129.

Instead of fetching results in batches, you can get all results in a list by calling the `asList()` method of the `PreparedQuery` class. Unlike the iterator interface, which gets results in batches, this method retrieves all results with a single service call. The method requires that a limit be specified using `FetchOptions`, up to the maximum of 1,000 entities.

If a query is likely to have only one result, or if only the first result is desired, calling the `asSingleEntity()` method retrieves the result and returns an `Entity` object, or `null`.

If you just want a count of the results and not the entities themselves, you can call the `countEntities()` method of the `PreparedQuery`. Because the datastore has to perform the query to get the count, the speed of this call is proportional to the count, though faster than actually fetching the results by a constant factor. Like an `asList()` fetch, the count is also limited to a maximum of 1,000 entities.

Keys-Only Queries in Java

You can fetch just the keys for the entities that match a query instead of the full entities using the low-level Java datastore API. To declare that a query should return just the keys, call the `setKeysOnly()` method on the `Query` object:

```
Query q = new Query("Book");

q.setKeysOnly();
```

When a query is set to return only keys, the results of the query are `Entity` objects without any properties set. You can get the key from these objects using the `getKey()` method:

```
PreparedQuery pq = ds.prepare(q);
for (Entity result : pq.asIterable()) {
    Key k = result.getKey();

    // ...
}
```

You can also perform keys-only queries using the JDO and JPA interfaces. See Chapter 8.

Introducing Indexes

For every query an application performs, App Engine maintains an index, a single table of possible answers for the query. Specifically, it maintains an index for a set of queries that use the same filters and sort orders, possibly with different values for the filters. Consider the following simple query:

```
SELECT * FROM Player WHERE name = 'druidjane'
```

To perform this query, App Engine uses an index containing the keys of every `Player` entity and the value of each entity's `name` property, sorted by the `name` property values in ascending order. Such an index is illustrated in Figure 5-2.

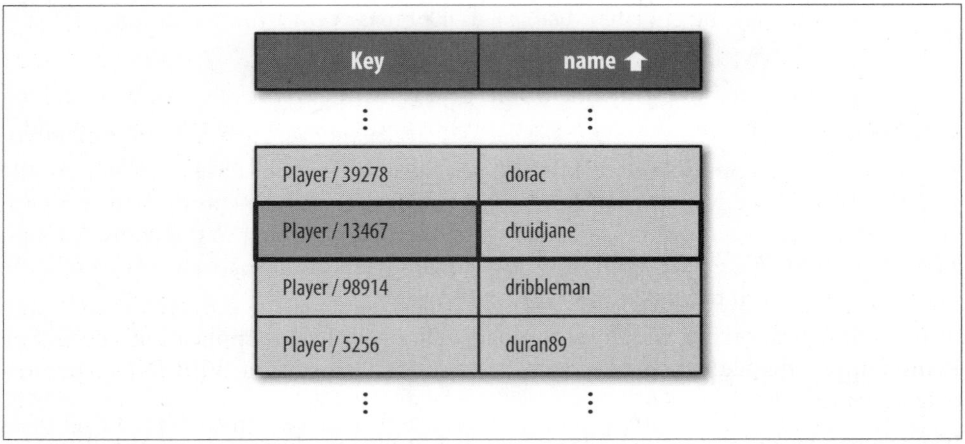

Figure 5-2. An index of Player entity keys and "name" property values, sorted by name in ascending order, with the result for WHERE name = 'druidjane'

To find all entities that meet the conditions of the query, App Engine finds the first row in the index that matches, then it scans down to the first row that doesn't match. It returns the entities mentioned on all rows in this range (not counting the nonmatching row), in the order they appear in the index. Because the index is sorted, all results for the query are guaranteed to be on consecutive rows in the table.

App Engine would use this same index to perform other queries with a similar structure but different values, such as the following query:

```
SELECT * FROM Player WHERE name = 'duran89'
```

This query mechanism is fast, even with a very large number of entities. Entities and indexes are distributed across multiple machines, and each machine scans its own index in parallel with the others. Each machine returns results to App Engine as it scans its own index, and App Engine delivers the final result set to the app, in order, as if all of the results were in one large index.

Another reason queries are fast has to do with how the datastore finds the first matching row. Because indexes are sorted, the datastore can use an efficient algorithm to find the first matching row. In the common case, finding the first row takes approximately the same amount of time regardless of the size of the index. In other words, the speed of a query is not affected by the size of the data set.

App Engine updates all relevant indexes when property values change. In this example, if an application retrieves a `Player` entity, changes the `name`, then saves the entity with a call to the `put()` method, App Engine updates the appropriate row in the previous index. It also moves the row if necessary so the ordering of the index is preserved. The call to `put()` does not return until all appropriate indexes are updated.

Similarly, if the application creates a new `Player` entity with a `name` property, or deletes a `Player` entity with a `name` property, App Engine updates the index. In contrast, if the application updates a `Player` but does not change the `name` property, or creates or deletes a `Player` that does not have a `name` property, App Engine does not update the `name` index because no update is needed.

App Engine maintains two indexes like the previous example above for every property name and entity kind, one with the property values sorted in ascending order and one with values in descending order. App Engine also maintains an index of entities of each kind. These indexes satisfy some simple queries, and App Engine also uses them internally for bookkeeping purposes.

For other queries, you must tell App Engine which indexes to prepare. You do this using a configuration file, which gets uploaded along with your application's code. For Python apps, this file is named *index.yaml*. For Java, this file is *WEB-INF/datastore-indexes.xml*.

It'd be a pain to write this file by hand, but thankfully you don't have to. While you're testing your application using the development web server from the SDK, when the app performs a datastore query, the server checks that the configuration file has an appropriate entry for the needed index. If it doesn't find one, it adds one. As long as the app performs each of its queries at least once during testing, the resulting configuration file will be complete.

The index configuration file must be complete, because when the app is running on App Engine, if the application performs a query for which there is no index, the query returns an error. You can tell the development web server to behave similarly if you want to test for these error conditions. (How to do this depends on which SDK you are using; see "Configuring Indexes" on page 159.)

Indexes require a bit of discipline to maintain. While the development tools can help add index configuration, they cannot know when an index is unused and can be deleted from the file. Extra indexes consume storage space and slow down updates of properties mentioned in the index. And while the version of the app you're developing may not need a given index, the version of the app still running on App Engine may still need it. The App Engine SDK and the Administration Console include tools for inspecting and maintaining indexes. We'll look at these tools in Chapter 15.

Before we discuss index configuration, let's look more closely at how indexes support queries. We just saw an example where the results for a simple query appear on consecutive rows in a simple index. In fact, this is how most queries work: the results for every query that would use an index appear on consecutive rows in the index. This is both surprisingly powerful in some ways and surprisingly limited in others, and it's worth understanding why.

Automatic Indexes and Simple Queries

As we mentioned, App Engine maintains two indexes for every single property of every entity kind, one with values in ascending order and one with values in descending order. App Engine builds these indexes automatically, whether or not they are mentioned in the index configuration file. These automatic indexes satisfy the following kinds of queries using consecutive rows:

- A simple query for all entities of a given kind, no filters or sort orders
- One filter on a property using the equality (=) operator
- Filters using greater-than or less-than operators (>, >=, <, <=) on a single property
- One sort order, ascending or descending, and no filters, or with filters only on the same property used with the sort order
- Filters or a sort order on the entity key
- Kindless queries with or without key filters

Let's look at each of these in action.

All Entities of a Kind

The simplest datastore query asks for every entity of a given kind, in any order. Stated in GQL, a query for all entities of the kind `Player` looks like this:

```
SELECT * FROM Player
```

App Engine maintains an index mapping kinds to entity keys. This index is sorted using a deterministic ordering for entity keys, so this query returns results in "key order." The kind of an entity cannot be changed after it is created, so this index is updated only when entities are created and deleted.

Since a query can only refer to one kind at a time, you can imagine this index as simply a list of entity keys for each kind. Figure 5-3 illustrates an example of this index.

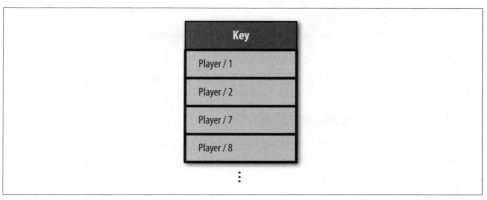

*Figure 5-3. An index of all Player entity keys, with results for SELECT * FROM Player*

When the query results are fetched, App Engine uses the entity keys in the index to find the corresponding entities, and returns the full entities to the application.

One Equality Filter

Consider the following query, which asks for every `Player` entity with a `level` property with a value of the integer 10:

```
SELECT * FROM Player WHERE level = 10
```

This query uses an index of `Player` entities with the `level` property, ascending—one of the automatic indexes. It uses an efficient algorithm to find the first row with a `level` equal to 10. Then it scans down the index until it finds the first row with a `level` not equal to 10. The consecutive rows from the first matching to the last matching represent all of the `Player` entities with a `level` property equal to the integer 10. This is illustrated in Figure 5-4.

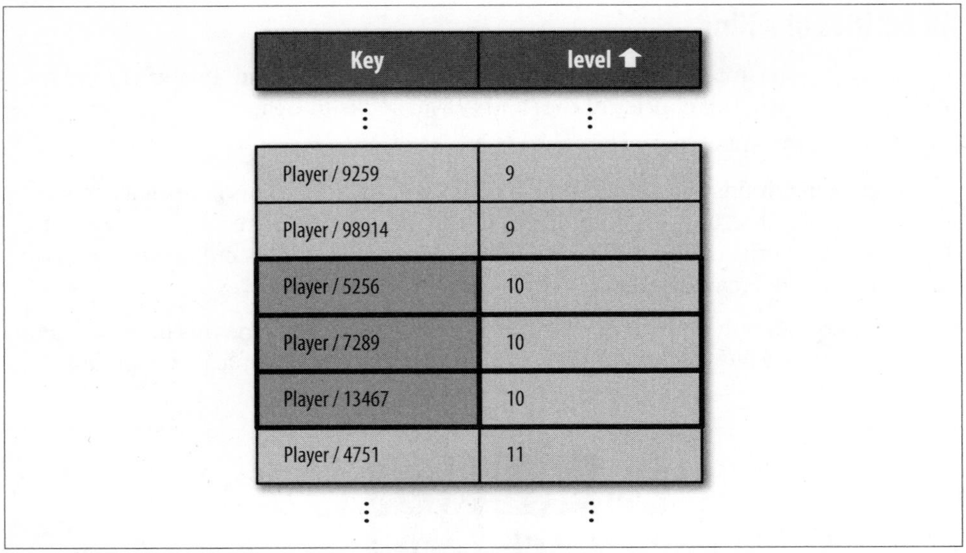

Key	level ⬆
⋮	⋮
Player / 9259	9
Player / 98914	9
Player / 5256	10
Player / 7289	10
Player / 13467	10
Player / 4751	11
⋮	⋮

Figure 5-4. An index of the Player entity "level" properties, sorted by level then by key, with results for WHERE level = 10

Greater-Than and Less-Than Filters

The following query asks for every `Player` entity with a `score` property whose value is greater than the integer 500:

```
SELECT * FROM Player WHERE score > 500
```

This uses an index of `Player` entities with the `score` property, ascending, also an automatic index. As with the equality filter, it finds the first row in the index whose `score` is greater than 500. In the case of greater-than, since the table is sorted by `score` in ascending order, every row from this point to the bottom of the table is a result for the query. See Figure 5-5.

Similarly, consider a query that asks for every `Player` with a `score` less than 1,000:

```
SELECT * FROM Player WHERE score < 1000
```

App Engine uses the same index (`score`, ascending), and the same strategy: it finds the first row that matches the query, in this case the first row. Then it scans to the next row that doesn't match the query, the first row whose `score` is greater than or equal to 1000. The results are represented by everything above that row.

Finally, consider a query for `score` values between 500 and 1,000:

```
SELECT * FROM Player WHERE score > 500 AND score < 1000
```

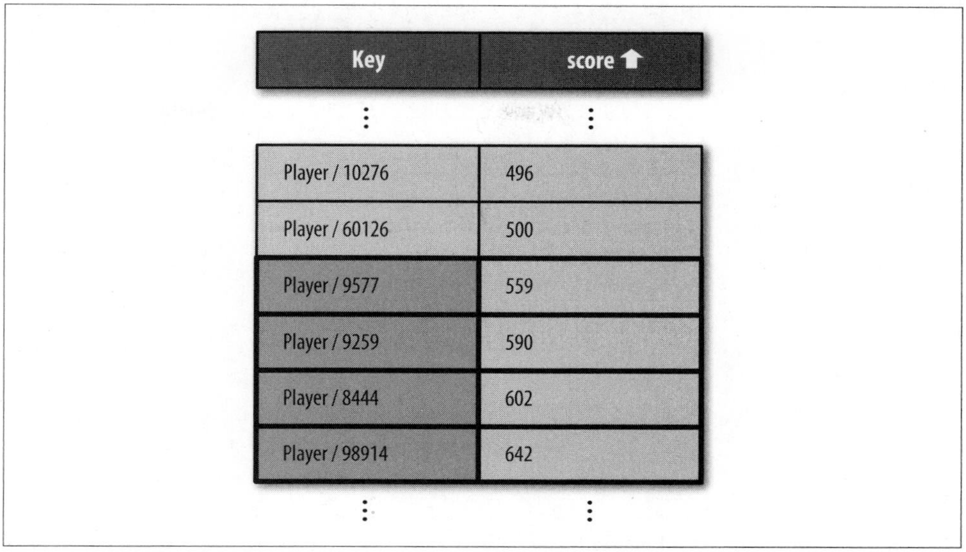

Figure 5-5. An index of the Player entity "score" properties, sorted by "score" then by key, with results for WHERE score > 500

Once again, the same index and strategy prevail: App Engine scans from the top down, finding the first matching and next nonmatching rows, returning the entities represented by everything in between. This is shown in Figure 5-6.

If the values used with the filters do not represent a valid range, such as `score < 500 AND score > 1000`, the query planner notices this and doesn't bother performing a query, since it knows the query has no results.

One Sort Order

The following query asks for every `Player` entity, arranged in order by `level`, from lowest to highest:

```
SELECT * FROM Player ORDER BY level
```

As before, this uses an index of `Player` entities with `level` properties in ascending order. If both this query and the previous equality query were performed by the application, both queries would use the same index. This query uses the index to determine the order in which to return `Player` entities, starting at the top of the table and moving down until the application stops fetching results, or until the bottom of the table. Recall that every `Player` entity with a `level` property is mentioned in this table. See Figure 5-7.

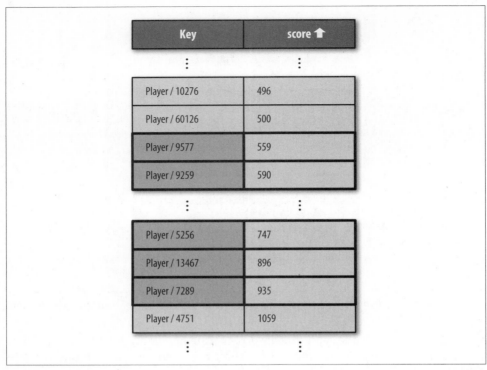

Figure 5-6. An index of the Player entity "score" properties, sorted by score, with results for WHERE score > 500 AND score < 1000

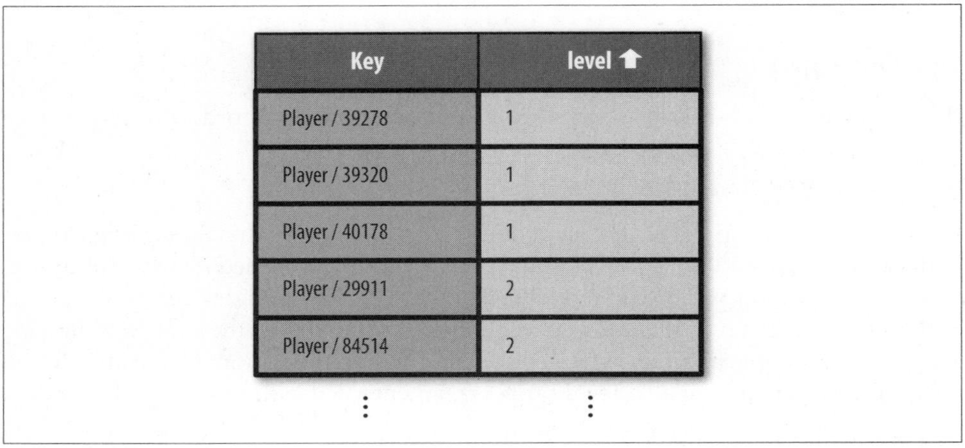

Key	level ⬆
Player / 39278	1
Player / 39320	1
Player / 40178	1
Player / 29911	2
Player / 84514	2

Figure 5-7. An index of the Player entity "level" properties sorted by level in ascending order, with results for ORDER BY level

The following query is similar to the previous one, but asks for the entities arranged by level from highest to lowest:

```
SELECT * FROM Player ORDER BY level DESC
```

This query cannot use the same index as before, because the results are in the wrong order. For this query, the results should start at the entity with the highest level, so the query needs an index where this result is in the first row. App Engine provides an automatic index for single properties in descending order for this purpose. See Figure 5-8.

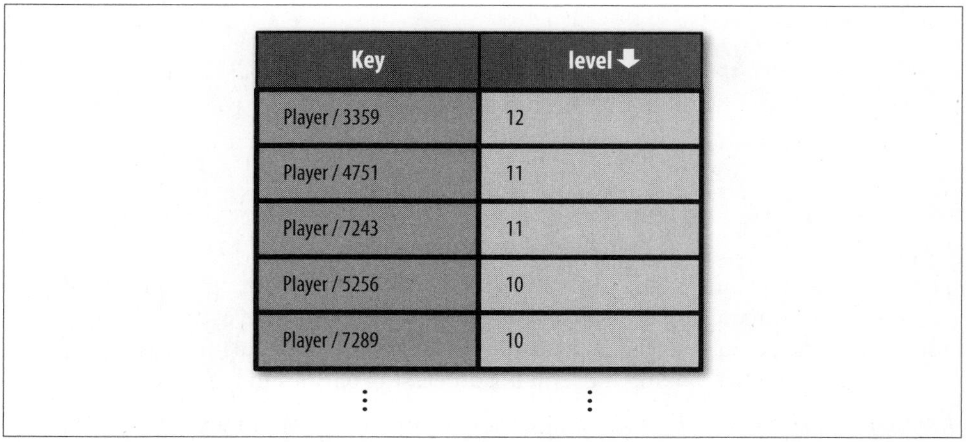

Key	level ⬇
Player / 3359	12
Player / 4751	11
Player / 7243	11
Player / 5256	10
Player / 7289	10
⋮	⋮

Figure 5-8. An index of the Player entity "level" properties sorted by level in descending order, with results for ORDER BY level DESC

If a query with a sort order on a single property also includes filters on that property, and no other filters, App Engine still needs only the one automatic index to fulfill the query. In fact, you may have noticed that for these simple queries, the results are returned sorted by the property in ascending order, whether or not the query specifies the sort order explicitly. In these cases, the ascending sort order is redundant.

Queries on Keys

In addition to filters and sort orders on properties, you can also perform queries with filters and sort orders on entity keys. You can refer to an entity's key in a filter or sort order using the special name __key__.

An equality filter on the key isn't much use. Only one entity can have a given key, and if the key is known, it's faster to perform a get() than a query. But an inequality filter on the key is especially useful, and in fact it's a good way to perform a common task: to fetch all of the entities of a given kind in batches.

Notice that given an entity key and an index of keys sorted by key, an app can fetch a batch of entities using an inequality filter. Python code to fetch a batch in this way might look like this:

```
# ...
# next_key is the db.Key object of the first entity in the batch.

if next_key:
    q = Player.gql("WHERE __key__ >= :1", next_key)
else:
    q = Player.all()

players = q.fetch(11)
if len(players) == 11:
    # Remove the last entity, then use its key
    # as the start of the next batch.
    next_key = players.pop().key
else:
    next_key = None

# Process the players, and give next_key to the
# client for the next call.
# ...
```

The query in this example uses the built-in index of keys in ascending order. App Engine provides an automatic indexes of kinds and keys, sorted by key in ascending order. The query returns the results sorted in key order. This order isn't useful for display purposes, but it's deterministic, making it useful for processing entities in batches.

A query that sorts keys in descending order requires a custom index.

App Engine uses indexes for filters on keys in the same way as filters on properties, with a minor twist: a query using a key filter in addition to other filters can use an automatic index if a similar query without the key filter could use an automatic index. Automatic indexes for properties already include the keys, so such queries can just use the same indexes. And of course, if the query has no other filters beyond the key filter, it can use the automatic key index.

Kindless Queries

In addition to performing queries on entities of a given kind, the datastore lets you perform a limited set of queries on entities of all kinds. Kindless queries cannot use filters or sort orders on properties. They can, however, use equality and inequality filters on keys (IDs or names).

Kindless queries are mostly useful in combination with ancestors, which we'll discuss in Chapter 6. They can also be used to get every entity in the datastore, using an inequality filter on keys and a limit to get them a batch at a time.

Using the Python `Query` class, you perform a kindless query by omitting the model class argument from the constructor:

```
q = db.Query()

q.filter('__key__ >', last_key)
```

Similarly in the Java low-level API, you perform a kindless query by instantiating the `Query` class using the no-argument constructor.

In GQL, you specify a kindless query by omitting the `FROM Kind` part of the statement:

```
q = db.GqlQuery('SELECT * WHERE __key__ > :1', last_key)
```

The results of a kindless query are returned in key order, ascending. Kindless queries use an automatic index.

Custom Indexes and Complex Queries

All queries not covered by the automatic indexes must have a corresponding index defined in the app's index configuration file. We'll refer to these as "custom indexes," in contrast with "automatic indexes." App Engine needs these hints because building every possible index for every combination of property and sort order would take a gargantuan amount of space and time, and an app isn't likely to need more than a fraction of those possibilities.

In particular, the following queries require custom indexes:

- A query with multiple sort orders
- A query with an inequality filter on a property and filters on other properties

A query that uses just equality filters on properties does not need a custom index in most cases thanks to a specialized query algorithm for this case, which we'll look at in a moment. Also, filters on keys do not require custom indexes; they can operate on whatever indexes are used to fulfill the rest of the query.

Let's examine these queries and the indexes they require.

Multiple Sort Orders

The automatic single-property indexes provide enough information for one sort order. When two entities have the same value for the sorted property, the entities appear in the index in adjacent rows, ordered by their entity keys. If you want to order these entities using other criteria, you need an index with more information.

The following query asks for all `Player` entities, sorted first by the `level` property in descending order, then, in the case of ties, sorted by the `score` property in descending order:

```
SELECT * FROM Player ORDER BY level DESC, score DESC
```

The index this query needs is straightforward: a table of `Player` entity keys, `level` values, and `score` values, sorted according to the query. This is not one of the indexes provided by the datastore automatically, so it is a custom index, and must be mentioned in the index configuration file. If you performed this query in the Python development web server, the server would add the following lines to the *index.yaml* file:

```
- kind: Player
  properties:
  - name: level
    direction: desc
  - name: score
    direction: desc
```

The order the properties appear in the configuration file matters. This is the order in which the rows are sorted: first by `level` descending, then by `score` descending.

This configuration creates the index shown in Figure 5-9. The results appear in the table, and are returned for the query in the desired order.

Key	level ⬇	score ⬇
Player / 3359	12	1366
Player / 7243	11	1280
Player / 4751	11	1059
Player / 7289	10	935
Player / 13467	10	896
⋮	⋮	⋮

Figure 5-9. An index of the Player entity "level" and "score" properties, sorted by level descending, then score descending, then by key ascending

Filters on Multiple Properties

Consider the following query, which asks for every `Player` with a `level` less than the integer `10` and a `charclass` of the string `'mage'`:

```
SELECT * FROM Player WHERE charclass='mage' AND level < 10
```

To be able to scan to a contiguous set of results meeting both filter criteria, the index must contain columns of values for these properties. The entities must be sorted first by `charclass`, then by `level`.

For Python, the index configuration for this query would appear as follows in the *index.yaml* file:

```
- kind: Player
  properties:
  - name: charclass
    direction: asc
  - name: level
    direction: asc
```

This index is illustrated in Figure 5-10.

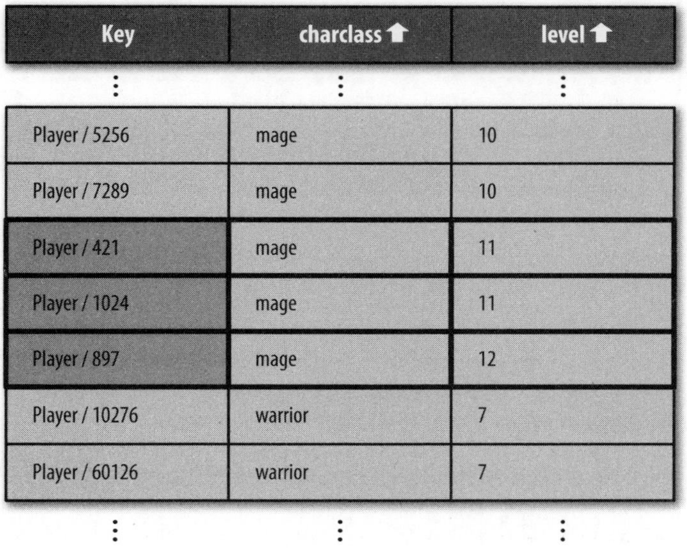

Key	charclass ⬆	level ⬆
⋮	⋮	⋮
Player / 5256	mage	10
Player / 7289	mage	10
Player / 421	mage	11
Player / 1024	mage	11
Player / 897	mage	12
Player / 10276	warrior	7
Player / 60126	warrior	7
⋮	⋮	⋮

Figure 5-10. An index of the Player entity "charclass" and "level" properties, sorted by charclass, then level, then key, with results for WHERE charclass = "mage" AND level < 10

The ordering sequence of these properties is important! Remember: the results for the query must all appear on adjacent rows in the index. If the index for this query were sorted first by `level` then by `charclass`, it would be possible for valid results to appear on nonadjacent rows. Figure 5-11 demonstrates this problem.

The index ordering requirement for combining inequality and equality filters has several implications that may seem unusual when compared to the query engines of other databases. Heck, they're downright weird. The first implication, illustrated previously, can be stated generally:

The First Rule of Inequality Filters: If a query uses inequality filters on one property and equality filters on one or more other properties, the index must be ordered first by the properties used in equality filters, then by the property used in the inequality filters.

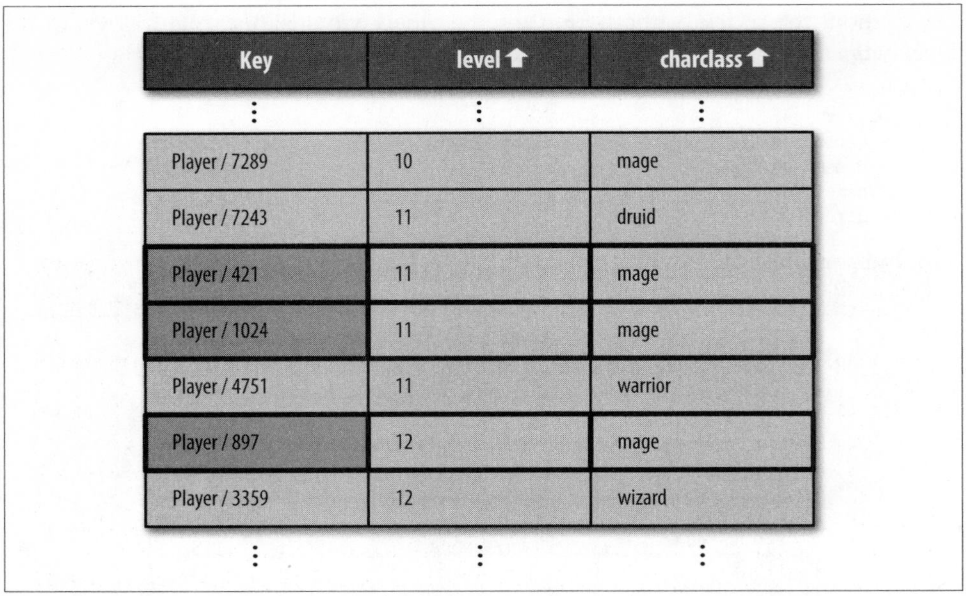

Key	level ⬆	charclass ⬆
⋮	⋮	⋮
Player / 7289	10	mage
Player / 7243	11	druid
Player / 421	11	mage
Player / 1024	11	mage
Player / 4751	11	warrior
Player / 897	12	mage
Player / 3359	12	wizard
⋮	⋮	⋮

Figure 5-11. An index of the Player entity "charclass" and "level" properties, sorted first by level then by charclass, which cannot satisfy WHERE charclass = "mage" AND level < 10 with consecutive rows

This rule has a corollary regarding queries with both an inequality filter and sort orders. Consider the following possible query:

```
SELECT * FROM Player WHERE level < 10 ORDER BY score DESC
```

What would the index for this query look like? For starters, it would have a column for the `level`, so it can select the rows that match the filter. It would also have a column for the `score`, to determine the order of the results. But which column is ordered first?

The First Rule implies that `level` must be ordered first. But the query requested that the results be returned sorted by `score`, descending. If the index were sorted by `score`, then by `level`, the rows may not be adjacent.

To avoid confusion, App Engine requires that the correct sort order be stated explicitly in the query:

```
SELECT * FROM Player WHERE level < 10 ORDER BY level, score DESC
```

In general:

> **The Second Rule of Inequality Filters:** If a query uses inequality filters on one property and sort orders of one or more other properties, the index must be ordered first by the property used in the inequality filters (in either direction), then by the other desired sort orders. To avoid confusion, the query must state all sort orders explicitly.

There's one last implication to consider with regard to inequality filters. The following possible query attempts to get all `Player` entities with a `level` less than 10 and a `score` less than 500:

```
SELECT * FROM Player WHERE level < 10 AND score < 500
```

Consider an index ordered first by `level`, then by `score`, as shown in Figure 5-12.

Key	level ↑	score ↑
⋮	⋮	⋮
Player / 5052	8	498
Player / 5176	8	500
Player / 5844	9	499
Player / 8311	10	498
⋮	⋮	⋮

Key	score ↑	level ↑
⋮	⋮	⋮
Player / 5052	498	8
Player / 8311	498	10
Player / 5844	499	9
Player / 5178	500	8
⋮	⋮	⋮

Figure 5-12. Neither possible index of the Player entity "level" and "score" properties can satisfy WHERE level < 10 AND score < 500 with consecutive rows

In fact, there is no possible index that could satisfy this query completely using consecutive rows. This is not a valid App Engine datastore query.

The Third Rule of Inequality Filters: A query cannot use inequality filters on more than one property.

A query *can* use multiple inequality filters on the same property, such as to test for a range of values.

Multiple Equality Filters

For queries using just equality filters, it's easy to imagine custom indexes that satisfy them. For instance:

```
SELECT * FROM Player WHERE charclass='mage' AND level=10
```

A custom index containing these properties, ordered in any sequence and direction, would meet the query's requirements. But App Engine has another trick up its sleeve for this kind of query. For queries using just equality filters and no sort orders, instead of scanning a single table of all values, App Engine can scan the automatic single-property indexes for each property, and return the results as it finds them. App Engine can perform a "merge join" of the single-property indexes to satisfy this kind of query.

In other words, the datastore doesn't need a custom index to perform queries using just equality filters and no sort orders. If you add a suitable custom index to your configuration file, the datastore will use it. But a custom index is not required, and the development server's automatic index configuration feature will not add one if it doesn't exist.

More specifically, the datastore *usually* doesn't need a custom index for such queries. The algorithm that assembles the results performs well enough in typical cases, but in extreme cases it cannot fulfill the query in a reasonable amount of time. If an amount of time has passed and the algorithm has not assembled the requested number of results, the query will return an error. In Python, this raises a `db.NeedIndexError` exception.

To understand the problematic extreme case, let's consider how the algorithm would perform the following query using single-property indexes:

```
SELECT * FROM Kind WHERE a=1 AND b=2 AND c=3
```

Recall that each of these tables contains a row for each entity with the property set, with fields for the entity's key and the property's value. The table is sorted first by the value, then by the key. The algorithm takes advantage of the fact that rows with the same value are consecutive, and within that consecutive block, rows are sorted by key.

To perform the query, the datastore uses the following steps:

1. The datastore checks the **a** index for the first row with a value of **1**. The entity whose key is on this row is a candidate, but not yet a confirmed result.

2. It then checks the **b** index for the first row whose value is **2** *and* whose key is greater than or equal to the candidate's key. Other rows with a value of **2** may appear above this row in the **b** index, but the datastore knows those are not candidates because the first **a** scan determined the candidate with the smallest key.

3. If the datastore finds the candidate's key in the matching region of **b**, that key is still a candidate, and the datastore proceeds with a similar check in the index for **c**. If the datastore does not find the candidate in the **b** index but does find another larger key with a matching value, that key becomes the new candidate, and it proceeds to check for the new candidate in the **c** index. (It'll eventually go back to check **a** with the new candidate before deciding it is a result.) If it finds neither the candidate nor a matching row with a larger key, the query is complete.

4. If a candidate is found to match all criteria in all indexes, the candidate is returned as a result. The datastore starts the search for a new candidate, using the previous candidate's key as the minimum key.

Figure 5-13 illustrates this zigzag search across the single-property indexes, first with a failed candidate, then two successful candidates.

A key feature of this algorithm is that it finds results in the order in which they are to be returned: key order. The datastore does not need to compile a complete list of possible results for the query—possibly millions of entities—then sort them to determine

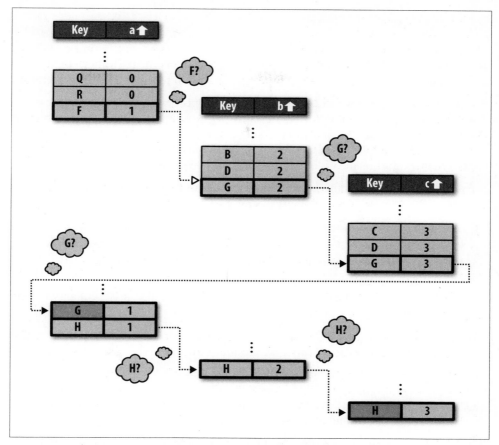

Figure 5-13. The merge join algorithm finding two entities WHERE a=1 AND b=2 AND c=3

which results ought to be first. Also, the datastore can stop scanning as soon as it has enough results to fulfill the query, which is always a limited number of entities.

The problem case, the one that cannot be handled by this algorithm before the datastore times out the operation, arises when the algorithm has to reject too many candidates. Each scan takes time, and a rejected candidate represents several scans that do not produce a result. If too much time elapses before the algorithm has found enough results to satisfy the query, the datastore terminates the query.

Using a custom index for a query with only equality filters and no sort orders speeds up the query, but it slows down updates to the properties mentioned in the query. If a query raises `NeedIndexError`, you must use a custom index.

A zigzag-capable query using equality filters on properties can also use inequality filters on keys without needing a custom index. This is useful for fetching a large number of results in batches, using inequality filters on keys to define the range of the batch.

Not-Equal and IN Filters

The Python API supports two operators we haven't discussed yet: != (not-equal) and IN. These operators are not actually supported by the datastore itself. Instead, they are implemented by the datastore API as multiple queries in terms of the other operators.

The filter `prop != value` matches every entity whose property does not equal the value. The datastore API determines the result set by performing two queries: one using `prop < value` in place of the not-equal filter, and one using `prop > value` in place of the filter. It returns both sets of results as one result set, which it can do reasonably quickly because the results are already in order.

Because not-equal is actually implemented in terms of the inequality operators, it is subject to the three rules of inequality operators:

1. The query's index must be ordered by the property used with the not-equal filter before other sort orders.
2. If the query uses other explicit sort orders, the not-equal filter's property must be explicitly ordered first.
3. And finally, any query using a not-equal filter cannot also use inequality or not-equal filters on other properties.

A not-equal filter will never return an entity that doesn't have the filtered property. This is true for all filters, but can be especially counterintuitive in the case of not-equal.

The filter `prop IN (value1, value2, value3)` matches every entity whose property equals any of the values. The datastore API implements this as a series of equality queries, one for each value to test. The more values that appear in the list, the longer the full set of queries will take to execute.

If a single query includes multiple IN filters on multiple properties, the datastore API must perform equality queries for every combination of values in all of the filters. `prop1 IN (value1, value2, value3, value4) AND prop2 IN (value5, value6, value7)` is equivalent to 12 queries using equality filters.

The != and IN operators are useful shortcuts. But because they actually perform multiple queries, they take longer to execute than the other operators. It's worth understanding their performance implications before using them.

Unset and Nonindexed Properties

As you've seen, an index contains columns of property values. Typically, an app creates entities of the same kind with the same set of properties: every Player in our game has a name, a character class, a level, and a score. If every entity of a kind has a given property, then an index for that kind and property has a row corresponding to each entity of the kind.

But the datastore neither requires nor enforces a common layout of properties across entities of a kind. It's quite possible for an entity to not have a property that other entities of the same kind have. For instance, a `Player` entity might be created without a character class, and go without until the user chooses one.

App Engine does not have a notion of an "empty field." It is possible to set a property with a null value (Python's `None`, Java's `null`), but a property set to the null value is distinct from the property not being set at all. This is different from a tabular database, which requires a value (possibly null) for every cell in a row.

If an entity does not have a property used in an index, the entity does not appear in the index. Stated conversely, an entity must have *every* property mentioned in an index to appear in the index. If a `Player` does not have a `charclass` property, it does not appear in any index with a `charclass` column.

If an entity is not mentioned in an index, it cannot be returned as a result for a query that uses the index. Remember that queries use indexes for both filters and sort orders. A query that uses a property for any kind of filter or any sort order can never return an entity that doesn't have that property. The `charclass`-less Player can never be a result for a `Player` query that sorts results by `charclass`.

In "Strings, Text, and Blobs" on page 112, we mentioned that text and blob values are not indexed. Another way of saying this is that, for the purposes of indexes, a property with a text or blob value is treated as if it is unset. If an app performs a query using a filter or sort order on a property that is always set to a text or blob value, that query will always return no results.

It is sometimes useful to store property values of other types, and exempt them from indexes. This saves space in index tables, and reduces the amount of time it takes to save the entity.

In the Python API, the only way to declare a property as unindexed is with the `Model` API. There is currently no other way to set a specific property as unindexed in this API. We'll look at this feature when we discuss the modeling API in Chapter 7.

In the Java API, you can set a property as unindexed using the `setUnindexedProperty()` method of the `Entity` object, instead of the `setProperty()` method. An entity can only have one property of a given name, so an unindexed property overwrites an indexed one, and vice versa. You can also declare properties as unindexed in the JDO and JPA interfaces; see Chapter 8.

If you need an entity to qualify as a result for a query, but it doesn't make sense in your data model to give the entity every property used in the query, use the null value to represent the "no value" case, and always set it. The Python modeling API and the Java JDO and JPA interfaces make it easy to ensure that properties always have values.

Sort Orders and Value Types

App Engine keeps the rows of an index sorted in an order that supports the corresponding query. Each type of property value has its own rules for comparing two values of the same type, and these rules are mostly intuitive: integers are sorted in numeric order, strings in Unicode order, and so forth.

Two entities can have values of different types for the same property, so App Engine also has rules for comparing such values, though these rules are not so intuitive. Values are ordered first by type, then within their type. For instance, all integers are sorted above all strings.

One effect of this that might be surprising is that all floats are sorted below all integers. The datastore treats floats and integers as separate value types, and so sorts them separately. If your app relies on the correct ordering of numbers, make sure all numbers are stored using the same type of value.

The datastore stores eight distinct types of values, not counting the nonindexed types (text and blob). The datastore supports several additional types by storing them as one of the eight types, then marshaling them between the internal representation and the value your app sees automatically. These additional types are sorted by their internal representation. For instance, a date-time value is actually stored as an integer, and will be sorted amongst other integer values in an index.

Table 5-2 describes the eight indexable types supported by the datastore. The types are listed in their relative order, from first to last.

Table 5-2. How the datastore value types are sorted

Data type	Python type	Java type	Ordering
The null value	None	null	-
Integer and date-time	long, datetime.datetime, db.Rating	long (other integer types are widened), java.util.Date, datastore.Rating	Numeric (datetime is chronological)
Boolean	bool (True or False)	boolean (true or false)	False, then true
Byte string	db.ByteString	datastore.ShortBlob	Byte order
Unicode string	unicode, db.Category, db.Email, db.IM, db.Link, db.PhoneNumber, db.PostalAddress	java.lang.String, datastore.Category, datastore.Email, datastore.IMHandle, datastore.Link, datastore.PhoneNumber, datastore.PostalAddress	Unicode character order
Floating-point number	float	double	Numeric

Data type	Python type	Java type	Ordering
Geographical point	db.GeoPt	datastore.GeoPt	By latitude, then longitude (floating-point numbers)
A Google account	users.User	users.User	By email address, Unicode order
Entity key	db.Key	datastore.Key	Kind (byte string), then ID (numeric) or name (byte string)

Queries and Multivalued Properties

In a typical database, a field in a record stores a single value. A record represents a data object, and each field represents a single, simple aspect of the object. If a data object can have more than one of a particular thing, each of those things is typically represented by a separate record of an appropriate kind, associated with the data object using the object's key as a field value. App Engine supports both of these uses of fields: a property can contain a simple value, or the key of another entity.

But the App Engine datastore can do something most other databases can't: it can store more than one value for a single property. With multivalued properties (MVPs), you can represent a data object with more than one of something without resorting to creating a separate entity for each of those things, if each thing could be represented by a simple value.

One of the most useful features of multivalued properties is how they match an equality filter in a query. The datastore query engine considers a multivalued property equal to a filter value if any of the property's values is equal to the filter value. This ability to test for membership means MVPs are useful for representing sets.

Multivalued properties maintain the order of values, and can have repeated items. The values can be of any datastore type, and a single property can have values of different types.

A Simple Example

Consider the following example. The players of our online game can earn trophies for particular accomplishments. The app needs to display a list of all of the trophies a player has won, and the app needs to display a list of all of the players who have won a particular trophy. The app doesn't need to maintain any data about the trophies themselves; it's sufficient to just store the name of the trophy.

One option is to store the list of trophy names as a single delimited string value for each Player entity. This makes it easy to get the list of trophies for a particular player, but impossible to get the list of players for a particular trophy. (A query filter can't match patterns within string values.)

Another option is to record each trophy win in a separate property named after the trophy. To get the list of players with a trophy, you just query for the existence of the corresponding property. However, getting the list of trophies for a given player would require either coding the names of all of the trophies in the display logic, or iterating over all of the Player entity's properties looking for trophy names.

With multivalued properties, we can store each trophy name as a separate value for the trophies property. To access a list of all trophies for a player, we simply access the property of the entity. To get a list of all players with a trophy, we use a query with an equality filter on the property.

Here's what this example looks like in Python:

```
p = Player.get_by_key_name(user_id)
p.trophies = ['Lava Polo Champion',
              'World Building 2008, Bronze',
              'Glarcon Fighter, 2nd class']
p.put()

# List all trophies for a player.
for trophy in p.trophies:
    # ...

# Query all players that have a trophy.
q = Player.gql("WHERE trophies = 'Lava Polo Champion'")
for p in q:
    # ...
```

MVPs in Python

The Python API represents the values of a multivalued property as a Python list. Each member of the list must be of one of the supported datastore types.

```
class Entity(db.Expando):
  pass

e = Entity()

e.prop = [ 'value1', 123, users.get_current_user() ]
```

Remember that list is not a datastore type; it is only the mechanism for manipulating multivalued properties. A list cannot contain another list.

A property must have at least one value, otherwise the property does not exist. To enforce this, the Python API does not allow you to assign an empty list to a property. Notice that the API can't do otherwise: if a property doesn't exist, then the API cannot know to represent the missing property as an empty list when the entity is retrieved from the datastore. (This being Python, the API could return the empty list whenever a nonexistent property is accessed, but that might be more trouble than it's worth.)

Because it is often useful for lists to behave like lists, including the ability to contain zero items, the Python data modeling API provides a mechanism that supports assigning the empty list to a property. We'll look at this mechanism in Chapter 7.

MVPs and Equality Filters

As you've seen, when a multivalued property is the subject of an equality filter in a query, the entity matches if any of the property's values are equal to the filter value.

```
e1 = Entity()
e1.prop = [ 3.14, 'a', 'b' ]
e1.put()

e2 = Entity()
e2.prop = [ 'a', 1, 6 ]
e2.put()

# Returns e1 but not e2:
q = Entity.gql('WHERE prop = 3.14')

# Returns e2 but not e1:
q = Entity.gql('WHERE prop = 6')

# Returns both e1 and e2:
q = Entity.gql("WHERE prop = 'a'")
```

Recall that a query with a single equality filter uses an index that contains the keys of every entity of the given kind with the given property and the property values. If an entity has a single value for the property, the index contains one row that represents the entity and the value. If an entity has multiple values for the property, the index contains one row for each value. The index for this example is shown in Figure 5-14.

This brings us to the first of several odd-looking queries that nonetheless make sense for multivalued properties. Since an equality filter is a membership test, it is possible for multiple equality filters to use the same property with different values and still return a result. An example in GQL:

```
SELECT * FROM Entity WHERE prop = 'a' AND prop = 'b'
```

App Engine uses the "merge join" algorithm described earlier for multiple equality filters to satisfy this query using the prop single-property index. This query returns the e1 entity because the entity key appears in two places in the index, once for each value requested by the filters.

The way multivalued properties appear in an index gives us another way of thinking about multivalued properties: an entity has one or more properties, each with a name and a single value, and an entity can have multiple properties with the same name. The API represents the values of multiple properties with the same name as a list of values associated with that name.

Key	prop ⬆
e2	1
e2	6
e1	a
e2	a
e1	b
e2	3.14

Figure 5-14. An index of two entities with multiple values for the "prop" property, with results for WHERE prop='a'

The datastore does not have a way to query for the exact set of values in a multivalued property. You can use multiple equality filters to test that each of several values belongs to the list, but there is no filter that ensures that those are the only values that belong to the list, or that each value appears only once.

MVPs and Inequality Filters

Just as an equality filter tests that any value of the property is equal to the filter value, an inequality filter tests that any value of the property meets the filter criterion.

```
e1 = Entity()
e1.prop = [ 1, 3, 5 ]
e1.put()

e2 = Entity()
e2.prop = [ 4, 6, 8 ]
e2.put()

# Returns e1 but not e2:
q = Entity.gql("WHERE prop < 2")

# Returns e2 but not e1:
q = Entity.gql("WHERE prop > 7")

# Returns both e1 and e2:
q = Entity.gql("WHERE prop > 3")
```

Figure 5-15 shows the index for this example, with the results of **prop > 3** highlighted.

In the case of an inequality filter, it's possible for the index scan to match rows for a single entity multiple times. When this happens, the first occurrence of each key in the

Figure 5-15. An index of two entities with multiple values for the "prop" property, with results for WHERE prop > 3

index determines the order of the results. If the index used for the query sorts the property in ascending order, the first occurrence is the smallest matching value. For descending, it's the largest. In the example above, prop > 3 returns e2 before e1 because 4 appears before 5 in the index.

MVPs and Sort Orders

To summarize things we know about how multivalued properties are indexed:

- A multivalued property appears in an index with one row per value.
- All rows in an index are sorted by the values, possibly distributing property values for a single entity across the index.
- The first occurrence of an entity in an index scan determines its place in the result set for a query.

Together, these facts explain what happens when a query orders its results by a multivalued property. When results are sorted by a multivalued property in ascending order, the smallest value for the property determines its location in the results. When results are sorted in descending order, the largest value for the property determines its location.

This has a counterintuitive—but consistent—consequence:

```
e1 = Entity()
e1.prop = [ 1, 3, 5 ]
e1.put()

e2 = Entity()
```

```
e2.prop = [ 2, 3, 4 ]
e2.put()

# Returns e1, e2:
q = Entity.gql("ORDER BY prop ASC")

# Also returns e1, e2:
q = Entity.gql("ORDER BY prop DESC")
```

Because **e1** has both the smallest value and the largest value, it appears first in the result set in ascending order *and* in descending order. See Figure 5-16.

Key	prop ⬆
e1	1
e2	2
e1	3
e2	3
e2	4
e1	5

Key	prop ⬇
e1	5
e2	4
e1	3
e2	3
e2	2
e1	1

Figure 5-16. Indexes of two entities with multiple values for the "prop" property, one ascending and one descending

MVPs and the Query Planner

The query planner tries to be smart by ignoring aspects of the query that are redundant or contradictory. For instance, a = 3 AND a = 4 would normally return no results, so the query planner catches those cases and doesn't bother doing work it doesn't need to do. However, most of these normalization techniques don't apply to multivalued properties. In this case, the query could be asking, "Does this MVP have a value that is equal to 3 and another value equal to 4?" The datastore remembers which properties are MVPs (even those that end up with one or zero values), and never takes a shortcut that would produce incorrect results.

But there is one exception. A query that has both an equality filter and a sort order will drop the sort order. If a query asks for a = 3 ORDER BY a DESC and a is a single-value property, the sort order has no effect because all of the values in the result are identical. For an MVP, however, a = 3 tests for membership, and two MVPs that meet that condition are not necessarily identical.

The datastore drops the sort order in this case anyway. To do otherwise would require too much index data and result in exploding indexes in cases that could otherwise survive. As always, the actual sort order is deterministic, but it won't be the requested order.

Exploding Indexes

There's one more thing to know about indexes when considering multivalued properties for your data model.

When an entity has multiple values for a property, each index that includes a column for the property must use multiple rows to represent the entity, one for each possible combination of values. In a single property index on the multivalued property, this is simply one row for each value, two columns each (the entity key and the property value).

In an index of multiple properties where the entity has multiple values for one of the indexed properties and a single value for each of the others, the index includes one row for each value of the multivalued property. Each row has a column for each indexed property, plus the key. The values for the single-value properties are repeated in each row.

Here's the kicker: if an entity has more than one property with multiple values, and more than one multivalued property appears in an index, the index must contain one row for each combination of values to represent the entity completely.

If you're not careful, the number of index rows that need to be updated when the entity changes could grow very large. It may be so large that the datastore cannot complete an update of the entity before it reaches its safety limits, and returns an error.

To help prevent "exploding indexes" from causing problems, App Engine limits the number of property values—that is, the number of rows times the number of columns—a single entity can occupy in an index. The limit is 5,000 property values, high enough for normal use, but low enough to prevent unusual index sizes from inhibiting updates.

If you do include a multivalued property in a custom index, be careful about the possibility of exploding indexes.

Configuring Indexes

An application specifies the custom indexes it needs in a configuration file. Each index definition includes the kind, and the names and sort orders of the properties to include. A configuration file can contain zero or more index definitions.

Most of the time, you can leave the maintenance of this file to the development web server. The development server watches the queries the application makes, and if a query needs a custom index and that index is not defined in the configuration file, the server adds appropriate configuration automatically.

The development server will not remove index configuration. If you are sure your app no longer needs an index, you can edit the file manually and remove it.

You can disable the automatic index configuration feature. Doing so causes the development server to behave like App Engine: if a query doesn't have an index and needs one, the query fails. How to do this is particular to the runtime environment, so we'll get to that in a moment.

Index configuration is global to all versions of your application. All versions of an app share the same datastore, including indexes. If you deploy a version of the app and the index configuration has changed, App Engine will use the new index configuration for all versions.

Index Configuration for Python

For Python apps, the index configuration file is named *index.yaml*, and is in the YAML format (similar to *app.yaml*). It appears in the application root directory.

The structure is a single YAML list named `indexes`, with one element per index. Each index definition has a `kind` element (the kind name, a string) and a `properties` element. If the index supports queries with ancestor filters, it has an `ancestor` element with a value of `yes`.

`properties` is a list, one element per column in the index, where each column has a `name` and an optional `direction` that is either `asc` (ascending order, the default) or `desc` (descending order). The order of the properties list is significant: the index is sorted by the first column first, then by the second column, and so on.

Here's an example *index.yaml* file using indexes from earlier in this chapter:

```
indexes:
- kind: Player
  properties:
  - name: charclass
  - name: level
    direction: desc

- kind: Player
  properties:
  - name: level
    direction: desc
  - name: score
    direction: desc
```

By default, the development server adds index configuration to this file as needed. When it does, it does so beneath this line, adding it (and a descriptive comment) if it doesn't find it:

```
# AUTOGENERATED
```

You can move index configuration above this line to take manual control over it. This isn't strictly necessary, since the development server will never delete index configuration, not even that which was added automatically.

To disable automatic index configuration in the development server, start the server with the `--require_indexes` command-line option. If you are using the Launcher, select the application, then go to the Edit menu and select Application Settings. Add the command-line option to the "Extra Flags" field, then click Update.

Index Configuration for Java

For Java apps, you add index configuration to a file named *datastore-indexes.xml*, in the directory *WEB-INF/* in the WAR. This is an XML file with a root element named `<datastore-indexes>`. This contains zero or more `<datastore-index>` elements, one for each index.

Each `<datastore-index>` specifies the kind using the `kind` attribute. It also has an `ancestor` attribute, which is `true` if the index supports queries with ancestor filters, and `false` otherwise.

A `<datastore-index>` contains one or more `<property>` elements, one for each column in the index. Each `<property>` has a `name` attribute (the name of the property) and a `direction` attribute (`asc` for ascending, `desc` for descending). The order of the `<property>` elements is significant: the index is sorted by the first column first, then by the second column, and so on.

An example:

```xml
<datastore-indexes autoGenerate="true">
  <datastore-index kind="Player" ancestor="false">
    <property name="charclass" direction="asc" />
    <property name="level" direction="desc" />
  </datastore-index>

  <datastore-index kind="Player" ancestor="false">
    <property name="level" direction="desc" />
    <property name="score" direction="desc" />
  </datastore-index>
</datastore-indexes>
```

The `<datastore-indexes>` root element has an attribute named `autoGenerate`. If `true`, or if the app does not have a *datastore-indexes.xml* file, the Java development server will generate new index configuration when needed for a query. If `false`, the development server behaves like App Engine: if a query needs an index that is not defined, the query fails.

The development server does not modify *datastore-indexes.xml*. Instead, it generates a separate file named *datastore-indexes-auto.xml*, in the directory *WEB-INF/appengine-generated/*. The complete index configuration is the total of the two configuration files.

The Java server will never remove index configuration from the automatic file, so if you need to delete an index, you may need to remove it from the automatic file. You can move configuration from the automatic file to the manual file if that's easier to manage, such as to check it into a revision control repository.

## CHAPTER 6

Datastore Transactions

With web applications, many users access and update data concurrently. Often, multiple users need to read or write to the same unit of data at the same time. This requires a data system that can give some assurances that simultaneous operations will not corrupt any user's view of the data. Most data systems guarantee that a single operation on a single unit of data maintains the integrity of the data, typically by scheduling operations that act on the same unit of data to be performed one at a time.

Many applications need similar data integrity guarantees when performing a set of multiple operations, possibly over multiple units of data. Such a set of operations is called a *transaction*. A data system that supports transactions guarantees that if a transaction succeeds, all of the operations in the transaction are executed completely. If any step of the transaction fails, then none of its effects are applied to the data. The data remains in a consistent and predictable state before and after the transaction, even if other processes are attempting to modify the data concurrently.

For example, say you want to post a message to the bulletin board in the town square inviting other players to join your guild. The bulletin board maintains a count of how many messages have been posted to the board, so readers can see how many messages there are without reading every message object in the system. Posting a message requires three datastore operations: the app must read the old message count, update the message count with an incremented value, and create the new message object.

Without transactions, these operations may succeed or fail independently. The count may be updated but the message object may not be created. Or, if you create the message object first, the object may be created, but the count not updated. In either case, the resulting count is inaccurate. By performing these operations in a single transaction, if any step fails, none of the effects are applied, and the application can try the entire transaction again.

Also consider what happens when two players attempt to post to the message board at the same time. To increment the message count, each player process must read the old value, then update it with a new value calculated from the old one. Without transactions, these operations may be interleaved: the first process reads the original count (say, 10), the second process reads the count (also 10), the first process adds 1 and updates the count with the new value (11), then finally the second process adds 1 to its value and updates the count (11). Because the second process doesn't know that the first process updated the value, the final count is 1 less than it ought to be (12). With transactions, the second process knows right away that the first process is updating the count and can do the right thing.

A scalable web application has several requirements that are at odds with transactions. For one, the application needs access to data to be fast, and not be affected by how much data is in the system or how it is distributed across multiple servers. The longer it takes for a transaction to complete, the longer other processes have to wait to access the data reserved by the transaction. The combined effect on how many transactions can be completed in a period of time is called *throughput*. For web apps, high throughput is important.

A web app also needs transactions to finish completely and consistently, so it knows that the effects of the transaction can be relied upon by other processes for further calculations. The promise that all processes can see the changes once a transaction is complete is known as *strong consistency*. (Alternatives such as *eventual consistency* trade this promise for greater flexibility in how changes are applied, but this makes life difficult for an app that needs to present the user with a consistent view of the world with each request.)

The App Engine datastore provides transactions with strong consistency and low overhead. It does this by limiting the scope of transactions: a single transaction can only read or write to entities that belong to a single *entity group*. Every entity belongs to an entity group, by default a group of its own. The app assigns an entity to a group when the entity is created, and the assignment is permanent.

By having the app arrange entities into groups, the datastore can treat each group independently when applying concurrent transactions. Two transactions that use different groups can occur simultaneously without harm. With a bit of thought, an app can ensure that entities are arranged to minimize the likelihood that two processes will need to access the same group, and thereby maximize throughput.

In this chapter, we will discuss what happens when you update an entity group, how to create entities in entity groups, and how to perform multiple operations on an entity group using a transaction. We'll also discuss batch operations, how query indexes are built, and the consistency guarantees of the datastore.

Entities and Entity Groups

When you create, update, or delete a single entity, the change occurs in a transaction: either all of your changes to the entity succeed, or none of them do. If you change two properties of an entity and save it, every request handler process that fetches the entity will see both changes. At no point during the save will a process see the new value for one property and the old value for the other. And if the update fails, the entity stays as it was before the save. In database terms, the act of updating an entity is *atomic*.

It is often useful to update multiple entities atomically, such that any process's view of the data is consistent across the entities. In the bulletin board example, the message count and each of the messages may be stored as separate entities, but the combined act of creating a new message entity and updating the count ought to be atomic. We need a way to combine multiple actions into a single transaction, so they all succeed or all fail.

To do this in a scalable way, App Engine must know in advance which entities may be involved in a single transaction. These entities are stored and updated together, so the datastore can keep them consistent and still access them quickly. You tell App Engine which entities may be involved in the same transaction using entity groups.

Every entity belongs to an entity group, possibly a group containing just itself. An entity can only belong to one group. You assign an entity to a group when the entity is created. Group membership is permanent; an entity cannot be moved to another group once it has been created.

The datastore uses entity groups to determine what happens when two processes attempt to update data in the entity group at the same time. When this happens, the first update that completes "wins," and the other update is canceled. App Engine notifies the process whose update is canceled by raising an exception. In most cases, the process can just try the update again and succeed. But the app must decide for itself how to go about retrying, since important data may have changed between attempts.

This style of managing concurrent access is known as *optimistic concurrency control*. It's "optimistic" in the sense that the database tries to perform the operations without checking whether another process is working with the same data (such as with a "locking" mechanism), and only checks for collisions at the end, optimistic that the operations will succeed. The update is not guaranteed to succeed, and the app must reattempt the operations or take some other course of action if the data changes during the update.

Optimistic concurrency control is a good choice for web applications because reading data is fast—a reader never waits for updates—and almost always succeeds. If an update fails due to concurrency, it's usually easy to try again, or return an error message to the user. Most web applications have only a small number of users updating the same piece of data, so concurrency failures are rare.

Updating an entity in a group can potentially cancel updates to *any* other entity in the group by another process. You should design your data model so that entity groups do not need to be updated by many users simultaneously.

Be especially careful if the number of simultaneous updates to a single group grows as your application gets more users. In this case, you usually want to spread the load across multiple entity groups, and increase the number of entity groups automatically as the user base grows. Scalable division of a data resource like this is known as *sharding*.

Also be aware that some data modeling tasks may not be practical on a large scale. Incrementing a value in a single datastore entity every time any user visits the site's home page is not likely to work well with a distributed strong consistency data system.

Keys, Paths, and Ancestors

To create an entity in a group with other entities, you associate it with the key of another entity from that group. The existing entity becomes the new entity's *parent*, forming a path of ancestor relationships down to a *root* entity that does not have a parent. This path becomes part of the new entity's key. Every entity whose key begins with the same root is in the same group, including the root entity itself.

When you create an entity and do not specify a parent, the entity is created in a new group by itself. The new entity is the root of the new group.

We alluded to paths earlier when we discussed keys, so let's complete the picture. An entity's key consists of the path of ancestors in the entity's group, starting from the group's root. Each entity in the path is represented by the entity's kind followed by either the system-assigned numeric ID or the app-assigned string name. The full path is a sequence of kind and ID/name pairs.

The following Python code creates four entities in the same group. The model class constructor accepts either an entity object or a `Key` object as the parent.

```python
# Creating a new entity group with a root entity:
board = MessageBoard(key_name='The_Archonville_Times')
board.title = 'The Archonville Times'
board.put()

# Using the object for the "parent" argument:
msg1 = Message(parent=board, key_name='first!')
msg1.put()

# Using a Key for the "parent" argument:
p_key = board.key()
msg2 = Message(parent=p_key, key_name='pk_fest_aug_21')
msg2.put()

# Using an entity that isn't the root as the parent:
```

```
msg3 = Message(parent=msg1, key_name='keep_clean')
msg3.put()
```

When you're deriving the key of an entity with a parent, you must use the complete ancestor path. For example, in Python:

```
k = db.Key.from_path('MessageBoard', 'The_Archonville_Times',
                     'Message', 'first!',
                     'Message', 'keep_clean')
```

Similarly, GQL supports key literals with ancestors, as follows:

```
SELECT * FROM MessageAttachment
        WHERE message = KEY(MessageBoard, 'The_Archonville_Times',
                            Message, 'first!',
                            Message, 'keep_clean')
```

Notice that entities of different kinds can be in the same entity group. In the datastore, there is no relationship between kinds and entity groups. (You can enforce such a relationship in your app's code, if you like.)

Ancestors do not have to exist for a key to be valid. If you create an entity with a parent, then delete the parent, the key for the child is still valid and can still be assembled from its parts (such as with Python's `from_path()` method). This is true even for a group's root entity: the root can be deleted and other entities in the group remain in the group.

You can even use a key for an entity that doesn't exist as the parent for a new entity. Neither the kind nor the name/ID of an ancestor need to represent an actual entity. Group membership is defined by the first key part in the ancestor path, regardless of whether that part corresponds to an entity. Here is Python code that creates two entities in the same group without a root entity:

```
root = db.Key.from_path('MessageBoard', 'The_Baskinville_Post')

msg1 = Message(parent=root)
msg1.put()

msg2 = Message(parent=root)
msg2.put()
```

Ancestor Queries

Though the full path on an entity key is not considered to determine group membership, ancestor paths are useful thanks to another datastore feature: ancestor queries.

A datastore query can include a filter that limits the results to just those entities with a given ancestor. This can match any ancestor, not just the immediate parent. In other words, a query can match a sequence of key parts starting from the root.

Continuing the town square bulletin board example, where each `MessageBoard` is the root of an entity group containing things attached to the board, the following GQL query returns the 10 most recent `Message` entities attached to a specific board:

```
SELECT * FROM Message
        WHERE ANCESTOR IS KEY(MessageBoard, 'The_Archonville_Times')
        ORDER BY post_date DESC
        LIMIT 10
```

Most queries that use an ancestor filter need custom indexes. There is one unusual exception: a query does not need a custom index if the query also contains equality filters on properties (and no inequality filters or sort orders). In this exceptional case, the "merge join" algorithm can use a built-in index of keys along with the built-in property indexes. In cases where the query would need a custom index anyway, the query can match the ancestor to the keys in the custom index.

As we mentioned in Chapter 5, the datastore supports queries over entities of all kinds. Kindless queries are limited to key filters and ancestor filters. Since ancestors can have children of disparate kinds, kindless queries are useful for getting every child of a given ancestor, regardless of kind:

```
SELECT * WHERE ANCESTOR IS KEY('MessageBoard', 'The_Archonville_Times')
```

While ancestor queries can be useful, don't get carried away building large ancestor trees. Remember that every entity with the same root belongs to the same entity group, and more simultaneous users that need to write to a group mean a greater likelihood of concurrency failures.

If you want to model hierarchical relationships between entities without the consequences of entity groups, consider using multivalued properties to store paths. For example, if there's an entity whose path in your hierarchy can be represented as /A/B/C/D, you can store this path as: `e.parents = ['/A', '/A/B', '/A/B/C']` Then you can perform a query similar to an ancestor query on this property: `... WHERE parents = '/A/B'`.

What Can Happen in a Transaction

Entity groups ensure that the operations performed within a transaction see a consistent view of the entities in a group. For this to work, a single transaction must limit its operations to entities in a single group. The entity group determines the scope of the transaction.

Within a transaction, you can fetch, update, or delete an entity using the entity's key. You can also create a new entity that either is a root entity of a new group that becomes the subject of the transaction, or that has a member of the transaction's entity group as its parent.

You can perform queries over the entities of a single entity group in a transaction. A query in a transaction must have an ancestor filter that matches the transaction's entity group. The results of the query, including both the indexes that provide the results as well as the entities themselves, are guaranteed to be consistent with the rest of the transaction.

In the Python and Java APIs, you do not need to declare the entity group for a transaction explicitly. You simply perform datastore actions on entities of the same group. If you attempt to perform actions that involve different entity groups within a transaction, the API raises an exception. The API also raises an exception if you attempt to perform a query in a transaction that does not have an ancestor filter. (We'll discuss the specific exception that is raised in the next few sections.)

Transactional Reads

Sometimes it is useful to fetch entities in a transaction even if the transaction does not update any data. Reading multiple entities in a transaction ensures that the entities are consistent with one another. As with updates, entities fetched in a transaction must be members of the same entity group.

A transaction that only reads entities never fails due to concurrency. As with reading a single entity, a read-only transaction sees the data as it appears at the beginning of the transaction, even if other processes make changes after the transaction starts and before it completes.

The same is true for ancestor-only queries within a transaction. If the transaction does not create, update, or delete data from the entity group, it will not fail due to concurrency.

The datastore can do this because it remembers previous versions of entities, using timestamps associated with the entity groups. The datastore notes the current time at the beginning of every operation and transaction, and this determines which version of the data the operation or transaction sees. This is known as *multiversion concurrency control*, a form of optimistic concurrency control. This mechanism is internal to the datastore; the application cannot access previous versions of data, nor can it see the timestamps.

This timestamp mechanism has a minor implication for reading data within transactions. When you read an entity in a transaction, the datastore returns the version of the entity most recent to the beginning of the transaction. If you update an entity, then refetch the same entity within the same transaction, the datastore returns the entity as it appeared *before* the update. In most cases, you can just reuse the in-memory object you modified (which has your changes) instead of refetching the entity.

Transactions in Python

As we've seen, to create an entity in an entity group in Python, you provide either the Key object or the model object of the parent to the model class constructor, as the parent argument:

```
p = Entity()

e = Entity(parent=p)
```

The parent key does not have to represent an entity that exists. You can construct a fake key using db.Key.from_path() and use it as the parent:

```
p_key = db.Key.from_path('Entity', 'fake_parent')

e = Entity(parent=p_key)
```

You can use methods on the model object to get the key for the entity's parent, or fetch the entity's parent from the datastore. These methods return None if the entity is a root entity for its entity group.

```
p = e.parent()

p_key = e.parent_key()
```

Similarly, the Key object can return the Key of its parent, or None:

```
e_key = e.key()

p_key = e_key.parent()
```

The Python API uses function objects to handle transactions. To perform multiple operations in a transaction, you define a function that executes the operations, then you pass it to the run_in_transaction() function (in the ...ext.db module).

```
import datetime
from google.appengine.ext import db

class MessageBoard(db.Expando):
    pass

class Message(db.Expando):
    pass

def create_message_txn(board_name, message_name, message_title, message_text):
    board = db.get(db.Key.from_path('MessageBoard', board_name))
    if not board:
        board = MessageBoard(key_name=board_name)
        board.count = 0

    message = Message(key_name=message_name, parent=board)
    message.title = message_title
    message.text = message_text
    message.post_date = datetime.datetime.now()

    board.count += 1

    db.put([board, message])

# ...
    try:
        db.run_in_transaction(create_message_txn,
```

```
                    board_name=board_name,
                    message_name=message_title,
                    message_title=message_title,
                    message_text=message_text)

      except db.TransactionFailedError, e:
          # Report an error to the user.
          # ...
```

run_in_transaction() takes the transaction function as its first argument, and any positional or keyword arguments intended for the transaction function as its remaining arguments. To perform the transaction, it starts a new transaction in the datastore, calls the function, then commits the transaction. If the transaction function returns a value, run_in_transaction() returns that value.

All calls to the datastore to create, update, or delete entities within the transaction function take effect when the transaction is committed. Typically, you would update an entity by fetching or creating the model object, modifying it, then saving it, and continue to use the local object to represent the entity. In the rare case where the transaction function fetches an entity after saving it, the fetch will see the entity as it was *before* the update, because the update has not yet been committed.

If the transaction function raises an exception, the transaction is aborted, and run_in_transaction() reraises the exception. If you need to abort the transaction but do not want run_in_transaction() to raise an exception, raise the db.Rollback exception. run_in_transaction() catches and does not reraise this exception.

If the transaction cannot be completed due to a concurrency failure, run_in_transaction() retries the transaction again automatically up to three times. For each attempt, it calls the transaction function again with the same arguments. Make sure the transaction function can be called multiple times safely without undesirable side effects.

If you don't want the transaction to be retried in the event of the concurrency failure, or if you'd like it retried more than three times, you can use the alternate function run_in_transaction_custom_retries(). This function behaves identically to run_in_transaction() except for the custom number of retries. You pass it the number of retries as the first argument and the function as the second argument, followed by arguments for the function.

If the transaction cannot be completed due to concurrency failures after all of the retries have been exhausted, run_in_transaction() (or ...custom_retries()) raises a db.TransactionFailedError. Since this condition can happen with any datastore update, you should catch it and provide an appropriate response to the user.

Transactions in Java

The JDO and JPA interfaces provide their own mechanisms for formulating transactions. Google's online documentation describes JDO, and we'll cover the JPA interface in Chapter 8.

Using the low-level datastore interface, you create an entity in an entity group by providing a `Key` object that represents an entity in that group to the `Entity` constructor. You can create this key using the `KeyFactory` class, or by calling the `getKey()` method on an `Entity` instance:

```
Key parentKey = KeyFactory.createKey("MessageBoard", "The_Archonville_Times");
Entity message = new Entity("Message", parentKey);
```

To create a key for a root entity (an entity without a parent), you call the `KeyFactory.createKey()` method with a kind (as a string) and the numeric ID or the string key name. To create a key with ancestors using `createKey()`, you also provide the `Key` of the parent.

For convenience, the `KeyFactory` class provides an alternate mechanism for constructing keys with ancestors. The `KeyFactory.Builder` class represents a key path, which you can extend by calling its `addChild()` method. The method returns the object, so you can chain multiple calls on a single line. Once the path is complete, you call `getKey()` to get the `Key` object:

```
Key k = new Builder("MessageBoard", "The_Archonville_times")
        .addChild("Message", 1427)
        .getKey();
```

To perform multiple operations within a single transaction, you call the `beginTransaction()` method of the `DatastoreService` instance. This method returns a `Transaction` object that represents the transaction. You perform the datastore operations as usual, calling the `put()`, `get()`, and `delete()` methods of the `DatastoreService`. Finally, you call the `commit()` method of the `Transaction` object to complete the transaction.

Updates (`put()` and `delete()`) do not take effect until you commit the transaction. Fetching an entity using `get()` after it has been updated in the same transaction will return an `Entity` object that represents the state of the entity *before* the update.

If the transaction cannot be committed due to a concurrency failure (or other datastore error), the commit throws a `DatastoreFailureException`:

```
DatastoreService ds = DatastoreServiceFactory.getDatastoreService();

Key boardKey;
Entity messageBoard;

try {
    Transaction txn = ds.beginTransaction();
```

```
    try {
        boardKey = KeyFactory.createKey("MessageBoard", boardName);
        messageBoard = ds.get(boardKey);

    } catch (EntityNotFoundException e) {
        messageBoard = new Entity("MessageBoard", boardName);
        messageBoard.setProperty("count", 0);
        boardKey = ds.put(messageBoard);
    }

    txn.commit();

} catch (DatastoreFailureException e) {
    // Report an error...
}
```

If you do not commit the transaction, the transaction is rolled back automatically after the servlet exits, and changes are not applied. You can roll back the transaction explicitly by calling the rollback() method of the Transaction object.

By default, each datastore operation is associated with the transaction started by the most recent call to beginTransaction(), known in the API as the "current" transaction. If you call beginTransaction() more than once, each Transaction is remembered in a stack. Calling commit() or rollback() removes the Transaction from the stack. If you commit or roll back the current transaction and there is another transaction on the stack, the next most recent transaction becomes the current transaction.

You can associate a datastore operation with a specific transaction explicitly by passing the Transaction object to the operation method:

```
Transaction txn = ds.beginTransaction();

ds.put(txn, messageBoard);

txn.commit();
```

If there is no current transaction on the stack, calling an operation method performs the operation without a transaction. Updates occur immediately. If there is a current transaction but you would like the operation performed immediately and outside of the transaction, provide null as the first argument to the operation:

```
Transaction txn = ds.beginTransaction();

// Add an update of entityOne to the transaction.
ds.put(txn, entityOne);

// Update entityTwo immediately, outside of the transaction.
ds.put(null, entityTwo);

// Commit the transaction, updating entityOne.
txn.commit();
```

With optimistic concurrency control, it is usually appropriate for the application to try the transaction again in the event of a concurrency failure. The following example retries the transaction up to three times before reporting an error to the user:

```java
import com.google.appengine.api.datastore.DatastoreFailureException;
import com.google.appengine.api.datastore.DatastoreService;
import com.google.appengine.api.datastore.DatastoreServiceFactory;
import com.google.appengine.api.datastore.Entity;
import com.google.appengine.api.datastore.EntityNotFoundException;
import com.google.appengine.api.datastore.Key;
import com.google.appengine.api.datastore.KeyFactory;
import com.google.appengine.api.datastore.PreparedQuery;
import com.google.appengine.api.datastore.Query;
import com.google.appengine.api.datastore.Transaction;

// ...
        DatastoreService ds = DatastoreServiceFactory.getDatastoreService();

        int retries = 3;
        boolean success = false;
        while (!success && retries > 0) {
            --retries;
            try {
                Transaction txn = ds.beginTransaction();

                Key boardKey;
                Entity messageBoard;
                try {
                    boardKey = KeyFactory.createKey("MessageBoard", boardName);
                    messageBoard = ds.get(boardKey);

                } catch (EntityNotFoundException e) {
                    messageBoard = new Entity("MessageBoard", boardName);
                    messageBoard.setProperty("count", 0);
                    boardKey = ds.put(messageBoard);
                }

                Entity message = new Entity("Message", boardKey);
                message.setProperty("message_title", messageTitle);
                message.setProperty("message_text", messageText);
                message.setProperty("post_date", postDate);
                ds.put(message);

                long count = (Long) messageBoard.getProperty("count");
                ++count;
                messageBoard.setProperty("count", count);
                ds.put(messageBoard);

                log.info("Posting msg, updating count to " + count);

                txn.commit();

                // Break out of retry loop.
                success = true;
```

```
        } catch (DatastoreFailureException e) {
            // Allow retry to occur.
        }
    }
    if (!success) {
        // Tell the user it didn't work out...
        resp.getWriter().println
            ("<p>A new message could not be posted.  Try again later.</p>");
    }

    // ...

    Key boardKey = KeyFactory.createKey("MessageBoard", boardName);
    try {
        Entity messageBoard = ds.get(boardKey);
        long count = (Long) messageBoard.getProperty("count");
        resp.getWriter().println("<p>Latest messages posted to
                " + boardName + " (" + count + " total):</p>");

        Query q = new Query("Message", boardKey);
        PreparedQuery pq = ds.prepare(q);
        for (Entity result : pq.asIterable()) {
            resp.getWriter().println("<h3>"
                    + result.getProperty("message_title")
                    + "</h3><p>"
                    + result.getProperty("message_text")
                    + "</p>");
        }
    } catch (EntityNotFoundException e) {
        resp.getWriter().println("<p>No message board found.</p>");
    }
```

How Entities Are Updated

To fully understand how the datastore guarantees that your data stays consistent, it's worth discussing how transactions are performed behind the scenes. To do so, we must mention BigTable, Google's distributed data system that is the basis of the App Engine datastore. We won't go into the details of how entities, entity groups, and indexes are stored in BigTable, but we will refer to BigTable's own notion of atomic transactions in our explanation.

Figure 6-1 shows the phases of a successful transaction.

The datastore uses a "journal" to keep track of changes that need to be applied to entities in an entity group. Each journal entry has a unique timestamp that indicates the order in which the changes were made. The datastore remembers the timestamp of the most recent change that has been committed, and guarantees that attempts to read the data will see all changes up to that point.

When an app begins a transaction for an entity group, the datastore makes a note of the current last-committed timestamp for the group (point A in Figure 6-1). As the app

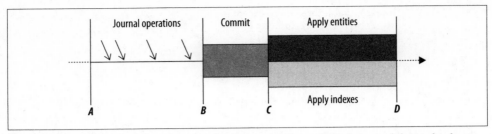

Figure 6-1. The timeline of a transaction: the operations, the commit phase, and the apply phase

calls the datastore to update entities, the datastore writes the requested changes to the journal. Each change is marked as "uncommitted."

When the app finishes the transaction (point B), the datastore checks the group's last-committed timestamp again. If the timestamp hasn't changed since the transaction began, it marks all of the transaction's changes as "committed," then advances the group's timestamp. Otherwise, the timestamp was advanced by another request handler since the beginning of the transaction, so the datastore aborts the current transaction and reports a concurrency failure to the app.

Verifying the timestamp, committing the journal entries, and updating the timestamp all occur in an atomic BigTable operation. If another process attempts to commit a transaction to the same entity group while the first transaction's commit is in progress, the other process waits for the first commit to complete. This guarantees that if the first commit succeeds, the second process sees the updated timestamp and reports a concurrency failure. This is illustrated in Figure 6-2.

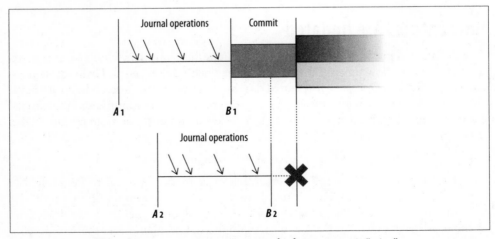

Figure 6-2. A timeline of two concurrent transactions; the first to commit "wins"

Once the journal entries have been committed (point C in Figure 6-1), the datastore applies each committed change to the appropriate entity and appropriate indexes, then marks the change as "applied." If there are multiple unapplied changes for an entity in the journal, they are applied in the order they were performed.

Here's the sneaky bit. If the apply phase fails for whatever reason (hard drive failure, power outage, meteorite), the committed transaction is still considered successful. If there are committed but unapplied changes the next time someone performs an operation on an entity in the entity group (within or without an explicit transaction), the datastore reruns the apply phase before performing the operation. This ensures that operations and transactions always see all changes that have been committed prior to the start of the operation or transaction. The datastore also uses background processes to roll forward unapplied operations, as well as purge old journal entries.

The roll-forward mechanism also ensures that subsequent operations can see all committed changes even if the apply phase is still in progress. At the beginning of an operation or transaction, the datastore notes the current time, then waits for all changes committed prior to that time to be applied before continuing.

Notice that the apply phase does not need to occur inside a BigTable transaction. Because of this, the datastore can spread multiple entities in the same group across multiple machines, and can allow an entity group to get arbitrarily large. Only the group's last-committed timestamp and journal need to be stored close enough together for a BigTable transaction. The datastore makes an effort to store entities of the same group "near" each other for performance reasons, but this does not limit the size or speed of entity groups.

When an app updates an entity outside of a transaction, the datastore performs the update using the same transactional mechanism, as if it were a transaction of just one operation. The datastore assumes that an update performed outside of a transaction is safe to perform at any time, and will retry the update automatically in the event of a concurrency failure. If several attempts fail, the datastore throws the concurrency exception. In contrast, an explicit transaction throws a concurrency exception on the first failure, because the datastore does not know if it is safe to commit the same changes. The app must retry the explicit transaction on its own. (The Python API's `run_in_transaction()` function knows how to rerun the function that performs the transaction, but this occurs as part of the application code.)

The App Engine datastore replicates all data to at least three places in each of at least two different data centers. An application uses one location as the "master" location, and replicates data to the others for use during failover or system maintenance. An update completes when the master location meets the consistency guarantees, and does not wait for replication to complete before returning.

When an app calls the datastore to update data, the call does not return until the apply phase is complete. If an error occurs at any point in the process, the datastore call raises an exception in the application.

This is true even if the error occurs during the apply phase, after the commit phase is complete and the update is guaranteed to be applied before the next transaction. Because the application can't tell the difference between an error during the commit phase and an error during the apply phase, the application should react as if the update has not taken place.

In most cases, the app can simply retry the update. More care is needed if retrying the update relies on the previous attempt to have been unsuccessful, but these cases usually require testing the state of the data in a transaction, and the solution is to just retry the entire transaction. If the transaction creates a new entity, one way to avoid creating a duplicate entity is to use a key name instead of a system-supplied numeric ID, precalculating and testing for the nonexistence of a global unique ID (GUID) if necessary.

Failures during the apply phase are very rare, and most errors represent a failure to commit. One of the most important principles in scalable app design is to be tolerant of the most rare kinds of faults.

How Entities Are Read

The timestamp mechanism explains what happens when two processes attempt to write to the same entity group at the same time. When one process commits, it updates the timestamp for the group. When the other process tries to commit, it notices the timestamp has changed, and aborts. The app can retry the transaction with fresh data, or give up.

The transaction is aborted only if the app attempted to update an entity during the transaction and another process has since committed changes. If the app only reads data in the transaction and does not make changes, the app simply sees the entities as they were at the beginning of the transaction. To support this, the datastore retains several old versions of each entity, marked with the timestamp of the most recently applied journal entry. Reading an entity in a transaction returns the version of the entity most recent to the timestamp at the beginning of the transaction.

Reading an entity outside of a transaction does *not* roll forward unapplied but committed changes. Instead, the read returns the entity as it appears on disk, as of the most recently applied changes. This is faster than waiting for pending changes to be applied, and usually not a concern for reads outside of transactions. But this means the entity may appear older or newer than other entities. If you need any consistency guarantees when reading multiple entities, use transactions.

Batch Updates

When you read, create, update, or delete an entity, the runtime environment makes a service call to the datastore. Each service call has some overhead, including serializing and deserializing parameters and transmitting them between machines in the data center. If you need to update multiple entities, you can save time by performing the updates together as a batch in one service call.

We introduced batch calls in Chapter 4. Here's a quick example of the Python batch API:

```
# Creating multiple entities:
e1 = Message(key_name='m1', text='...')
e2 = Message(key_name='m2', text='...')
e3 = Message(key_name='m3', text='...')
message_keys = db.put([e1, e2, e3])

# Getting multiple entities using keys:
message_keys = [db.Key('Message', 'm1'),
                db.Key('Message', 'm2'),
                db.Key('Message', 'm2')]
messages = db.get(message_keys)
for message in messages:
    # ...

# Deleting multiple entities:
db.delete(message_keys)
```

When the datastore receives a batch call, it bundles the keys or entities by their entity groups, which it can determine from the keys. Then it dispatches calls to the datastore machines responsible for each entity group. The datastore returns results to the app when it has received all results from all machines.

If the call includes changes for multiple entities in a single entity group, those changes are performed in a single transaction. There is no way to control this behavior, but there's no reason to do it any other way. It's faster to commit multiple changes to a group at once than to commit them individually, and no less likely to result in concurrency failures.

Each entity group involved in a batch update may fail to commit due to a concurrency failure. If a concurrency failure occurs for any update, the API raises the concurrency failure exception—even if updates to other groups were committed successfully.

Batch updates in disparate entity groups are performed in separate threads, possibly by separate datastore machines, executed in parallel to one another. This can make batch updates especially fast compared to performing each update one at a time.

Remember that if you use the batch API during a transaction, every entity or key in the batch must use the same entity group as the rest of the transaction. Also, be aware that App Engine puts a maximum size on service calls and responses, and the total size of the call or its responses must not exceed these limits. The number of items in a batch also has a fixed limit, so a single batch operation cannot consume more than a fixed amount of memory. See Google's official documentation for more information on these limits.

How Indexes Are Updated

As we saw in Chapter 5, datastore queries are powered by indexes. The datastore updates these indexes as entities change, so results for queries can be determined without examining the entity properties directly. This includes an index of keys, an index for each kind and property, and custom indexes described by your app's configuration files that fulfill complex queries. When an entity is created, updated, or deleted, each relevant index is updated and sorted so subsequent queries match the new state of the data.

The datastore updates indexes after changes have been committed, during the apply phase. Changes are applied to indexes and entities in parallel. Updates of indexes are themselves performed in parallel, so the number of indexes to update doesn't necessarily affect how fast the update occurs.

As with entities, the datastore retains multiple versions of index data, labeled with timestamps. When you perform a query, the datastore notes the current time, then uses the index data that is most current up to that time. However, unless the query has an ancestor filter, the datastore has no way to know which entity groups are involved in the result set and so cannot wait for changes in progress to be applied.

This means that, for a brief period during an update, a query may return results that do not match the query criteria. While another process is updating an entity, the query may see the old version of its index but return the new version of the entity. And since changes to entities and changes to indexes are applied in parallel, it is possible for a query to see the new version of its index but return the old version of the entity.

Figure 6-3 illustrates one possibility of what nontransactional reads and queries may see while changes are being applied.

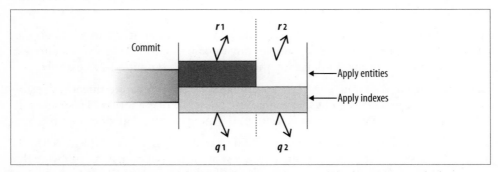

Figure 6-3. What nontransactional fetches and queries may see while changes are applied

Even though both fetches *r-1* and *r-2* occur after the commit, because they do not occur within transactions, they see different data: *r-1* fetches the entity as it is before the update, and *r-2* fetches the entity as it is after the update has been applied. Queries *q-1* and *q-2* may use the same (preupdate) index data to produce a list of results, but they return different entity data depending on whether changes have been applied to the entities.

In rare cases, it's also possible for changes to indexes to be applied prior to changes to entities, and for the apply phase to fail and leave committed changes unapplied until the next transaction on the entity group. If you need stronger guarantees, fetch or query entities within transactions to ensure all committed changes are applied before the data is used.

A query with an ancestor filter knows its entity group, and can therefore offer the same strong consistency guarantees within transactions as fetches. But many useful queries span entity groups, and therefore cannot be performed in transactions. If it is important to your application that a result for a nontransactional query match the criteria exactly, verify the result in the application code before using it.

## CHAPTER 7

Data Modeling with Python

Data modeling is the process of translating the data requirements of your application to the features of your data storage technology. While the application deals in players, towns, weapons, potions, and gold, the datastore knows only entities, entity groups, keys, properties, and indexes. The data model describes how the data is stored and how it is manipulated. Entities represent players and game objects; properties describe the status of objects and the relationships between them. When an object changes location, the data is updated in a transaction, so the object cannot be in two places at once. When a player wants to know about the weapons in her inventory, the application performs a query for all weapon objects whose location is the player, possibly requiring an index.

In the last few chapters, we've been using the Python class `db.Expando` to create and manipulate entities and their properties. As we've been doing it, this class illustrates the flexible nature of the datastore. The datastore itself does not impose or enforce a structure on entities or their properties, giving the application control over how individual entities represent data objects. This flexibility is also an essential feature for scalability: changing the structure of millions of records is a large task, and the proper strategy for doing this is specific to the task and the application.

But structure is needed. Every player has a number of health points, and a `Player` entity without a `health` property, or with a `health` property whose value is not an integer, is likely to confuse the battle system. The data ought to conform to a structure, or *schema*, to meet the expectations of the code. Because the datastore does not enforce this schema itself—the datastore is *schemaless*—it is up to the application to ensure that entities are created and updated properly.

App Engine includes a data modeling library for defining and enforcing data schemas in Python. This library resides in the `google.appengine.ext.db` package. It includes several related classes for representing data objects, including `db.Model`, `db.Expando` and `db.PolyModel`. To give structure to entities of a given kind, you create a subclass of one of these classes. The definition of the class specifies the properties for those objects, their allowed value types, and other requirements.

In this chapter, we'll introduce the Python data modeling library and discuss how to use it to enforce a schema for the otherwise schemaless datastore. We'll also discuss how the library works and how to extend it.

Models and Properties

The `db.Model` superclass lets you specify a structure for every entity of a kind. This structure can include the names of the properties, the types of the values allowed for those properties, whether the property is required or optional, and a default value. Here is a definition of a `Book` class similar to the one we created in Chapter 4:

```
from google.appengine.ext import db
import datetime

class Book(db.Model):
    title = db.StringProperty(required=True)
    author = db.StringProperty(required=True)
    copyright_year = db.IntegerProperty()
    author_birthdate = db.DateProperty()

obj = Book(title='The Grapes of Wrath',
           author='John Steinbeck')
obj.copyright_year = 1939
obj.author_birthdate = datetime.date(1902, 2, 27)

obj.put()
```

This `Book` class inherits from `db.Model`. In the class definition, we declare that all `Book` entities have four properties, and we declare their value types: `title` and `author` are strings, `copyright_year` is an integer, and `author_birthdate` is a date-time. If someone tries to assign a value of the wrong type to one of these properties, the assignment raises a `db.BadValueError`.

We also declare that `title` and `author` are required properties. If someone tries to create a `Book` without these properties set as arguments to the `Book` constructor, the attempt raises a `db.BadValueError`. `copyright_year` and `author_birthdate` are optional, so we can leave them unset on construction, and assign values to the properties later. If these properties are not set by the time the object is saved, the resulting entity will not have these properties—and that's allowed by this model.

A property declaration ensures that the entity created from the object has a value for the property, possibly `None`. As we'll see in the next section, you can further specify what values are considered valid using arguments to the property declaration.

A model class that inherits from `db.Model` ignores all attributes that are not declared as properties when it comes time to save the object to the datastore. In the resulting entity, all declared properties are set, and no others.

This is the sole difference between `db.Model` and `db.Expando`. A `db.Model` class ignores undeclared properties. A `db.Expando` class saves all attributes of the object as properties of the corresponding entity. That is, a model using a `db.Expando` class "expands" to accommodate assignments to undeclared properties.

You can use property declarations with `db.Expando` just as with `db.Model`. The result is a data object that validates the values of the declared properties, and accepts any values for additional undeclared properties.

> The official documentation refers to properties with declarations as *static properties* and properties on a `db.Expando` without declarations as *dynamic properties*. These terms have a nice correspondence with the notions of static and dynamic typing in programming languages. Property declarations implement a sort of runtime validated static typing for model classes, on top of Python's own dynamic typing.
>
> As we'll see, property declarations are even more powerful than static typing, because they can validate more than just the type of the value.

For both `db.Model` and `db.Expando`, object attributes whose names begin with an underscore (_) are always ignored. You can use these private attributes to attach transient data or functions to model objects. (It's possible to create an entity with a property whose name starts with an underscore; this convention only applies to object attributes in the modeling API.)

Because model objects also have attributes that are methods and other features, you cannot use certain names for properties in the Python model API. Some of the more pernicious reserved names are `key`, `kind`, and `parent`. The official documentation has a complete list of reserved names. In the next section, we'll see a way to use these reserved names for datastore properties even though they aren't allowed as attribute names in the API.

Beyond the model definition, `db.Model` and `db.Expando` have the same interface for saving, fetching, and deleting entities, and for performing queries and transactions. `db.Expando` is a subclass of `db.Model`.

Property Declarations

You declare a property for a model by assigning a property declaration object to an attribute of the model class. The name of the attribute is the name of the datastore property. The value is an object that describes the terms of the declaration. As discussed earlier, the `db.StringProperty` object assigned to the `title` class attribute says that the entity that an instance of the class represents can only have a string value for its `title` property. The `required=True` argument to the `db.StringProperty` constructor says that the object is not valid unless it has a value for the `title` property.

This can look a little confusing if you're expecting the class attribute to shine through as an attribute of an instance of the class, as it normally does in Python. Instead, the `db.Model` class hooks into the attribute assignment mechanism so it can use the property declaration to validate a value assigned to an attribute of the object. In Python terms, the model uses *property descriptors* to enhance the behavior of attribute assignment.

Property declarations act as intermediaries between the application and the datastore. They can ensure that only values that meet certain criteria are assigned to properties. They can assign default values when constructing an object. They can even convert values between a data type used by the application and one of the datastore's native value types, or otherwise customize how values are stored.

Property Value Types

`db.StringProperty` is an example of a property declaration class. There are several property declaration classes included with the Python SDK, one for each native datastore type. Each one ensures that the property can only be assigned a value of the corresponding type:

```
class Book(db.Model):
    title = db.StringProperty()

b = Book()

b.title = 99  # db.BadValueError, title must be a string

b.title = 'The Grapes of Wrath'  # OK
```

Table 7-1 lists the datastore native value types and their corresponding property declaration classes.

Table 7-1. Datastore property value types and the corresponding property declaration classes

Data type	Python type	Property class
Unicode text string (up to 500 bytes, indexed)	unicode or str (converted to unicode as ASCII)	db.StringProperty
Long Unicode text string (not indexed)	db.Text	db.TextProperty
Short byte string (up to 500 bytes, indexed)	db.ByteString	db.ByteStringProperty
Long byte string (not indexed)	db.Blob	db.BlobProperty
Boolean	bool	db.BooleanProperty
Integer (64-bit)	int or long (converted to 64-bit long)	db.IntegerProperty
Float (double precision)	float	db.FloatProperty
Date-time	datetime.date	db.DateProperty
	datetime.datetime	db.DateTimeProperty
	datetime.time	db.TimeProperty

Data type	Python type	Property class
Entity key	db.Key or a model instance	db.ReferenceProperty, db.SelfReferenceProperty
A Google account	users.User	db.UserProperty

Property Validation

You can customize the behavior of a property declaration by passing arguments to the declaration's constructor. We've already seen one example: the **required** argument.

All property declaration classes support the **required** argument. If **True**, the property is required and must not be **None**. You must provide an initial value for each required property to the constructor when creating a new object. (You can provide an initial value for any property this way.)

```
class Book(db.Model):
    title = db.StringProperty(required=True)

b = Book()  # db.BadValueError, title is required

b = Book(title='The Grapes of Wrath')  # OK
```

The datastore makes a distinction between a property that is not set and a property that is set to the null value (**None**). Property declarations do not make this distinction, because all declared properties must be set (possibly to **None**). Unless you say otherwise, the default value for declared properties is **None**, so the **required** validator treats the **None** value as an unspecified property.

You can change the default value with the **default** argument. When you create an object without a value for a property that has a default value, the constructor assigns the default value to the property.

A property that is required and has a default value uses the default if constructed without an explicit value. The value can never be **None**.

```
class Book(db.Model):
    rating = db.IntegerProperty(default=1)

b = Book()  # b.rating == 1

b = Book(rating=5)  # b.rating == 5
```

By default, the name of the class attribute is used as the name of the datastore property. If you wish to use a different name for the datastore property than is used for the attribute, specify a **name** argument. This allows you to use names already taken by the API for class or instance attributes as datastore properties.

```
class Song(db.Model):
    song_key = db.StringProperty(name='key')

s = Song()
```

```
    s.song_key = 'C# min'

    # The song_key attribute is stored as the
    # datastore property named 'key'.
    s.put()
```

You can declare that a property should contain only one of a fixed set of values by providing a list of possible values as the **choices** argument. If None is not one of the choices, this acts as a more restrictive form of **required**: the property must be set to one of the valid choices using a keyword argument to the constructor.

```
_KEYS = ['C', 'C min', 'C 7',
         'C#', 'C# min', 'C# 7',
         # ...
         ]

class Song(db.Model):
    song_key = db.StringProperty(choices=_KEYS)

s = Song(song_key='H min')  # db.BadValueError

s = Song()  # db.BadValueError, None is not an option

s = Song(song_key='C# min')  # OK
```

All of these features validate the value assigned to a property, and raise a **db.BadValueError** if the value does not meet the appropriate conditions. For even greater control over value validation, you can define your own validation function and assign it to a property declaration as the **validator** argument. The function should take the value as an argument, and raise a **db.BadValueError** (or an exception of your choosing) if the value should not be allowed.

```
def is_recent_year(val):
    if val < 1923:
        raise db.BadValueError

class Book(db.Model):
    copyright_year = db.IntegerProperty(validator=is_recent_year)

b = Book(copyright_year=1922)  # db.BadValueError

b = Book(copyright_year=1924)  # OK
```

Nonindexed Properties

In Chapter 5, we mentioned that you can set properties of an entity in such a way that they are available on the entity, but are considered unset for the purposes of indexes. In the Python API, you establish a property as nonindexed using a property declaration. If the property declaration is given an **indexed** argument of **False**, entities created with that model class will set that property as nonindexed.

```
class Book(db.Model):
    first_sentence = db.StringProperty(indexed=False)

b = Book()
b.first_sentence = "On the Internet, popularity is swift and fleeting."
b.put()

# Count the number of Book entities with
# an indexed first_sentence property...
c = Book.all().order('first_sentence').count(1000)

# c = 0
```

Automatic Values

Several property declaration classes include features for setting values automatically.

The db.DateProperty, db.DateTimeProperty, and db.TimeProperty classes can populate the value automatically with the current date and time. To enable this behavior, you provide the auto_now or auto_now_add arguments to the property declaration.

If you set auto_now=True, the declaration class overwrites the property value with the current date and time when you save the object. This is useful when you want to keep track of the last time an object was saved.

```
class Book(db.Model):
    last_updated = db.DateTimeProperty(auto_now=True)

b = Book()
b.put()  # last_updated is set to the current time

# ...

b.put()  # last_updated is set to the current time again
```

If you set auto_now_add=True, the property is set to the current time only when the object is saved for the first time. Subsequent saves do not overwrite the value.

```
class Book(db.Model):
    create_time = db.DateTimeProperty(auto_now_add=True)

b = Book()
b.put()  # create_time is set to the current time

# ...

b.put()  # create_time stays the same
```

The db.UserProperty declaration class also includes an automatic value feature. If you provide the argument auto_current_user=True, the value is set to the user accessing the current request handler if the user is signed in. If you provide auto_current_user_add=True, the value is only set to the current user when the entity is saved for the first time, and left untouched thereafter. If the current user is not signed in, the value is set to None.

```
class BookReview(db.Model):
    created_by_user = db.UserProperty(auto_current_user_add=True)
    last_edited_by_user = db.UserProperty(auto_current_user=True)

br = BookReview()
br.put()  # created_by_user and last_edited_by_user set

# ...

br.put()  # last_edited_by_user set again
```

 At first glance, it might seem reasonable to set a default for a db.UserProperty this way:

```
from google.appengine.api import users

class BookReview(db.Model):
    created_by_user = db.UserProperty(
        default=users.get_current_user())
    # WRONG
```

This would set the default value to be the user who is signed in *when the class is imported*. Requests that use a cached instance of the application may end up using a previous user instead of the current user as the default.

To guard against this mistake, db.UserProperty does not accept the default argument. You can use only auto_current_user or auto_current_user_add to set an automatic value.

List Properties

The data modeling API provides a property declaration class for multivalued properties, called db.ListProperty. This class ensures that every value for the property is of the same type. You pass this type to the property declaration, like so:

```
class Book(db.Model):
    tags = db.ListProperty(basestring)

b = Book()
b.tags = ['python', 'app engine', 'data']
```

The type argument to the db.ListProperty constructor must be the Python representation of one of the native datastore types. Refer back to Table 4-1 for a complete list.

The datastore does not distinguish between a multivalued property with no elements and no property at all. As such, an undeclared property on a db.Expando object can't store the empty list. If it did, when the entity is loaded back into an object, the property simply wouldn't be there, potentially confusing code that's expecting to find an empty list. To avoid confusion, `db.Expando` disallows assigning an empty list to an undeclared property.

The `db.ListProperty` declaration makes it possible to keep an empty list value on a multivalued property. The declaration interprets the state of an entity that doesn't have the declared property as the property being set to the empty list, and maintains that distinction on the object. This also means that you cannot assign None to a declared list property—but this isn't of the expected type for the property anyway.

The datastore *does* distinguish between a property with a single value and a multivalued property with a single value. An undeclared property on a `db.Expando` object can store a list with one element, and represent it as a list value the next time the entity is loaded.

The example above declares a list of string values. (`basestring` is the Python base type for `str` and `unicode`.) This case is so common that the API also provides `db.StringListProperty`.

You can provide a default value to `db.ListProperty` using the `default` argument. If you specify a nonempty list as the default, a shallow copy of the list value is made for each new object that doesn't have an initial value for the property.

`db.ListProperty` does not support the `required` validator, since every list property technically has a list value (possibly empty). If you wish to disallow the empty list, you can provide your own `validator` function that does so:

```
def is_not_empty(lst):
    if len(lst) == 0:
        raise db.BadValueError

class Book(db.Model):
    tags = db.ListProperty(basestring, validator=is_not_empty)

b = Book(tags=[])  # db.BadValueError

b = Book()  # db.BadValueError, default "tags" is empty

b = Book(tags=['awesome'])  # OK
```

`db.ListProperty` does not allow None as an element in the list because it doesn't match the required value type. It is possible to store None as an element in a list for an undeclared property.

Models and Schema Migration

Property declarations prevent the application from creating an invalid data object, or assigning an invalid value to a property. If the application always uses the same model classes to create and manipulate entities, then all entities in the datastore will be consistent with the rules you establish using property declarations.

In real life, it is possible for an entity that does not fit a model to exist in the datastore. When you change a model class—and you will change model classes in the lifetime of your application—you are making a change to your application code, not the datastore. Entities created from a previous version of a model stay the way they are.

If an existing entity does not comply with the validity requirements of a model class, you'll get a `db.BadValueError` when you try to fetch the entity from the datastore. Fetching an entity gets the entity's data, then calls the model class constructor with its values. This executes each property's validation routines on the data.

Some model changes are "backward compatible" such that old entities can be loaded into the new model class and be considered valid. Whether it is sufficient to make a backward-compatible change without updating existing entities depends on your application. Changing the type of a property declaration or adding a required property are almost always incompatible changes. Adding an optional property will not cause a `db.BadValueError` when an old entity is loaded, but if you have indexes on the new property, old entities will not appear in those indexes (and therefore won't be results for those queries) until the entities are loaded and then saved with the new property's default value.

The most straightforward way to migrate old entities to new schemas is to write a script that queries all of the entities and applies the changes. We'll discuss how to implement this kind of batch operation in Chapter 12.

Modeling Relationships

You can model relationships between entities by storing entity keys as property values. The Python data modeling interface includes several powerful features for managing relationships.

The `db.ReferenceProperty` declaration describes a relationship between one model class and another. It stores the key of an entity as the property value. The first argument to the `db.ReferenceProperty` constructor is the model class of the kind of entity referenced by the property. If someone creates a relationship to an entity that is not of the appropriate kind, the assignment raises a `db.BadValueError`.

You can assign a data object directly to the property. The property declaration stores the key of the object as the property's value to create the relationship. You can also assign a `db.Key` directly.

```
class Book(db.Model):
    title = db.StringProperty()
    author = db.StringProperty()

class BookReview(db.Model):
    book = db.ReferenceProperty(Book, collection_name='reviews')

b = Book()
```

```
b.put()

br = BookReview()

br.book = b        # sets br's 'book' property to b's key

br.book = b.key() # same thing
```

We'll explain what collection_name does in a moment.

The referenced object must have a "complete" key before it can be assigned to a reference property. A key is complete when it has all of its parts, including the string name or the system-assigned numeric ID. If you create a new object without a key name, the key is not complete until you save the object. When you save the object, the system completes the key with a numeric ID. If you create the object (or a db.Key) with a key name, the key is already complete, and you can use it for a reference without saving it first.

```
b = Book()
br = BookReview()
br.book = b  # db.BadValueError, b's key is not complete

b.put()
br.book = b  # OK, b's key has system ID

b = Book(key_name='The_Grapes_of_Wrath')
br = BookReview()
br.book = b  # OK, b's key has a name

db.put([b, br])
```

A model class must be defined before it can be the subject of a db.ReferenceProperty. To declare a reference property that can refer to another instance of the same class, you use a different declaration, db.SelfReferenceProperty.

```
class Book(db.Model):
    previous_edition = db.SelfReferenceProperty()

b1 = Book()
b2 = Book()
b2.previous_edition = b1
```

Reference properties have a powerful and intuitive syntax for accessing referenced objects. When you access the value of a reference property, the property fetches the entity from the datastore using the stored key, then returns it as an instance of its model class. A referenced entity is loaded "lazily": it is not fetched from the datastore until the property is dereferenced.

```
br = db.get(book_review_key)
# br is a BookReview instance

title = br.book.title  # fetches book, gets its title property
```

This automatic dereferencing of reference properties occurs the first time you access the reference property. Subsequent uses of the property use the in-memory instance of the data object. This caching of the referenced entity is specific to the object with the property. If another object has a reference to the same entity, accessing its reference fetches the entity anew.

db.ReferenceProperty does another clever thing: it creates automatic back-references from a referenced object to the objects that refer to it. If a BookReview class has a reference property that refers to the Book class, the Book class gets a special property whose name is specified by the collection_name argument to the declaration (e.g., reviews). This property is special because it isn't actually a property stored on the entity. Instead, when you access the back-reference property, the API performs a datastore query for all BookReview entities whose reference property equals the key of the Book. Since this is a single-property query, it uses the built-in indexes, and never requires a custom index.

```
b = db.get(book_key)
# b is a Book instance

for review in b.reviews:
    # review is a BookReview instance
    # ...
```

If you don't specify a collection_name, the name of the back-reference property is the name of the referring class followed by _set. If a class has multiple reference properties that refer to the same class, you *must* provide a collection_name to disambiguate the back-reference properties.

```
class BookReview(db.Model):
    # Book gets a BookReview_set special property.
    book = db.ReferenceProperty(Book)

    # Book gets a recommended_book_set special property.
    recommended_book = db.ReferenceProperty(Book,
                                collection_name='recommended_book_set')
```

Because the back-reference property is implemented as a query, it incurs no overhead if you don't use it.

As with storing db.Key values as properties, neither the datastore nor the property declaration requires that a reference property refer to an entity that exists. Dereferencing a reference property that points to an entity that does not exist raises an error. (As of this writing, there is no specific exception for this case, just an Error with a descriptive message.) Keys cannot change, so a relationship is only severed when the referenced entity is deleted from the datastore.

One-to-Many Relationships

A reference property and its corresponding back-reference represent a *one-to-many relationship* between classes in your data model. The reference property establishes a one-way relationship from one entity to another, and the declaration sets up the back-reference mechanism on the referenced class. The back-reference uses the built-in query index, so determining which objects refer to the referenced object is reasonably fast. It's not quite as fast as storing a list of keys on a property, but it's easier to maintain.

A common use of one-to-many relationships is to model ownership. In the previous example, each BookReview was related to a single Book, and a Book could have many BookReviews. The BookReviews belong to the Book.

One-to-One Relationships

You can also use a reference property to model a *one-to-one relationship.* The property declaration doesn't enforce that only one entity can refer to a given entity, but this is easy to maintain in the application code. Because the performance of queries scales with the size of the result set and not the size of the data set, it's usually sufficient to use the back-reference query to follow a one-to-one relationship back to the object with the reference.

If you'd prefer not to use a query to traverse the back-reference, you could also store a reference on the second object back to the first, at the expense of having to maintain the relationship in two places. This is tricky, because the class has to be defined before it can be the subject of a ReferenceProperty. One option is to use db.Expando and an undeclared property for one of the classes.

A one-to-one relationship can be used to model partnership. A good use of one-to-one relationships in App Engine is to split a large object into multiple entities to provide selective access to its properties. A player might have an avatar image up to 64 kilobytes in size, but the application probably doesn't need the 64 KB of image data every time it fetches the Player entity. You can create a separate PlayerAvatarImage entity to contain the image, and establish a one-to-one relationship by creating a reference property from the Player to the PlayerAvatarImage. The application must know to delete the related objects when deleting a Player:

```
class PlayerAvatarImage(db.Model):
    image_data = db.BlobProperty()
    mime_type = db.StringProperty()

class Player(db.Model):
    name = db.StringProperty()
    avatar = db.ReferenceProperty(PlayerAvatarImage)

# Fetch the name of the player (a string) a
# reference to the avatar image (a key).
p = db.get(player_key)
```

```
# Fetch the avatar image entity and access its
# image_data property.
image_data = p.avatar.image_data
```

Many-to-Many Relationships

A *many-to-many relationship* is a type of relationship between entities of two kinds where entities of either kind can have that relationship with many entities of the other kind, and vice versa. For instance, a player may be a member of one or more guilds, and a guild can have many members.

There are at least two ways to implement many-to-many relationships using the datastore. Let's consider two of these. The first method we'll call "the key list method," and the second we'll call "the link model method."

The key list method

With the key list method, you store a list of entity keys on one side of the relationship using a `db.ListProperty`. Such a declaration does not have any of the features of a `db.ReferenceProperty` such as back-references or automatic dereferencing, because it does not involve that class. To model the relationship in the other direction, you can implement the back-reference feature using a method and the Python annotation `@property`:

```
class Player(db.Model):
    name = db.StringProperty()
    guilds = db.ListProperty(db.Key)

class Guild(db.Model):
    name = db.StringProperty()

    @property
    def members(self):
        return Player.all().filter('guilds', self.key())

# Guilds to which a player belongs:
p = db.get(player_key)
guilds = db.get(p.guilds)  # batch get using list of keys
for guild in guilds:
    # ...

# Players that belong to a guild:
g = db.get(guild_key)
for player in g.members:
    # ...
```

Instead of manipulating the list of keys, you could implement automatic dereferencing using advanced Python techniques to extend how the values in the list property are accessed. A good way to do this is with a custom property declaration. We'll consider this in a later section.

The key list method is best suited for situations where there are fewer objects on one side of the relationship than on the other, and the short list is small enough to store directly on an entity. In this example, many players each belong to a few guilds; each player has a short list of guilds, while each guild may have a long list of players. We put the list property on the Player side of the relationship to keep the entity small, and use queries to produce the long list when it is needed.

The link model method

The link model method represents each relationship as an entity. The relationship entity has reference properties pointing to the related classes. You traverse the relationship by going through the relationship entity via the back-references.

```
class Player(db.Model):
    name = db.StringProperty()

class Guild(db.Model):
    name = db.StringProperty()

class GuildMembership(db.Model):
    player = db.ReferenceProperty(Player, collection_name='guild_memberships')
    guild = db.ReferenceProperty(Guild, collection_name='player_memberships')

p = Player()
g = Guild()
db.put([p, g])

gm = GuildMembership(player=p, guild=g)
db.put(gm)

# Guilds to which a player belongs:
for gm in p.guild_memberships:
    guild_name = gm.guild.name
    # ...

# Players that belong to a guild:
for gm in g.player_memberships:
    player_name = gm.player.name
    # ...
```

This technique is similar to how you'd use "join tables" in a SQL database. It's a good choice if either side of the relationship may get too large to store on the entity itself. You can also use the relationship entity to store metadata about the relationship (such as when the player joined the guild), or model more complex relationships between multiple classes.

The link model method is more expensive than the key list method. It requires fetching the relationship entity to access the related object.

Remember that App Engine doesn't support SQL-style join queries on these objects. You can achieve a limited sort of join by repeating information from the data objects on the link model objects, using code on the model classes to keep the values in sync. To do this with strong consistency, the link model object and the two related objects would need to be in the same entity group, which is not always possible or practical.

If eventual consistency would suffice, you could use task queues to propagate the information. See Chapter 13.

Model Inheritance

In data modeling, it's often useful to derive new kinds of objects from other kinds. The game world may contain many different kinds of carryable objects, with shared properties and features common to all objects you can carry. Since you implement classes from the data model as Python classes, you'd expect to be able to use inheritance in the implementation to represent inheritance in the model. And you can, sort of.

If you define a class based on either db.Model or db.Expando, you can create other classes that inherit from that data class, like so:

```
class CarryableObject(db.Model):
    weight = db.IntegerProperty()
    location = db.ReferenceProperty(Location)

class Bottle(CarryableObject):
    contents = db.StringProperty()
    amount = db.IntegerProperty()
    is_closed = db.BooleanProperty()
```

The subclass inherits the property declarations of the parent class. A Bottle has five property declarations: weight, location, contents, amount, and is_closed.

Objects based on the child class will be stored as entities whose kind is the name of the child class. The datastore has no notion of inheritance, and so by default will not treat Bottle entities as if they are CarryableObject entities. This is mostly significant for queries, and we have a solution for that in the next section.

If a child class declares a property already declared by a parent class, the class definition raises a db.DuplicatePropertyError. The data modeling API does not support overriding property declarations in subclasses.

A model class can inherit from multiple classes, using Python's own support for multiple inheritance:

```
class PourableObject(GameObject):
    contents = db.StringProperty()
    amount = db.IntegerProperty()
```

```
class Bottle(CarryableObject, PourableObject):
    is_closed = db.BooleanProperty()
```

Each parent class must not declare a property with the same name as declarations in the other parent classes, or the class definition raises a `db.DuplicatePropertyError`. However, the modeling API does the work to support "diamond inheritance," where two parent classes themselves share a parent class:

```
class GameObject(db.Model):
    name = db.StringProperty()
    location = db.ReferenceProperty(Location)

class CarryableObject(GameObject):
    weight = db.IntegerProperty()

class PourableObject(GameObject):
    contents = db.StringProperty()
    amount = db.IntegerProperty()

class Bottle(CarryableObject, PourableObject):
    is_closed = db.BooleanProperty()
```

In this example, both `CarryableObject` and `PourableObject` inherit two property declarations from `GameObject`, and are both used as parent classes to `Bottle`. The model API allows this because the two properties are defined in the same class, so there is no conflict. `Bottle` gets its `name` and `location` declarations from `GameObject`.

Queries and PolyModels

The datastore knows nothing of our modeling classes and inheritance. Instances of the `Bottle` class are stored as entities of the kind `'Bottle'`, with no inherent knowledge of the parent classes. It'd be nice to be able to perform a query for `CarryableObject` entities and get back `Bottle` entities and others. That is, it'd be nice if a query could treat `Bottle` entities as if they were instances of the parent classes, as Python does in our application code. We want *polymorphism* in our queries.

For this, the data modeling API provides a special base class: `db.PolyModel`. Model classes using this base class support polymorphic queries. Consider the `Bottle` class defined previously. Let's change the base class of `GameObject` to `db.PolyModel`, like so:

```
from google.appengine.ext.db import PolyModel

class GameObject(db.PolyModel):
    # ...
```

We can now perform queries for any kind in the hierarchy, and get the expected results:

```
here = db.get(location_key)

q = CarryableObject.all()
q.filter('location', here)
q.filter('weight >', 100)
```

```
for obj in q:
    # obj is a carryable object that is here
    # and weighs more than 100 kilos.
    # ...
```

This query can return any `CarryableObject`, including `Bottle` entities. The query can use filters on any property of the specified class (such as `weight` from `CarryableObject`) or parent classes (such as `location` from `GameObject`).

Behind the scenes, `db.PolyModel` does three clever things differently from its cousins:

- Objects of the class `GameObject` or any of its child classes are all stored as entities of the kind `'GameObject'`.

- All such objects are given a property named `class` that represents the inheritance hierarchy starting from the root class. This is a multivalued property, where each value is the name of an ancestor class, in order.

- Queries for objects of any kind in the hierarchy are translated by the `db.PolyModel` class into queries for the base class, with additional equality filters that compare the class being queried to the `class` property's values.

In short, `db.PolyModel` stores information about the inheritance hierarchy on the entities, then uses it for queries to support polymorphism.

Each model class that inherits directly from `db.PolyModel` is the root of a class hierarchy. All objects from the hierarchy are stored as entities whose kind is the name of the root class. As such, your data will be easier to maintain if you use many root classes to form many class hierarchies, as opposed to putting all classes in a single hierarchy. That way, the datastore viewer and bulk loading tools can still use the datastore's built-in notion of entity kinds to distinguish between kinds of objects.

Creating Your Own Property Classes

The property declaration classes serve several functions in your data model:

Value validation
> The model calls the class when a value is assigned to the property, and the class can raise an exception if the value does not meet its conditions.

Type conversion
> The model calls the class to convert from the value type used by the app to one of the core datastore types for storage, and back again.

Default behavior
> The model calls the class if no value was assigned to determine an appropriate default value.

Every property declaration class inherits from the `db.Property` base class. This class implements features common to all property declarations, including support for the

---

common constructor arguments (such as `required`, `name`, and `indexed`). Declaration classes override methods and members to specialize the validation and type conversion routines.

Validating Property Values

Here is a very simple property declaration class. It accepts any string value, and stores it as a datastore short string (the default behavior for Python string values).

```
from google.appengine.ext import db

class PlayerNameProperty(db.Property):
    data_type = basestring

    def validate(self, value):
        value = super(PlayerNameProperty, self).validate(value)
        if value is not None and not isinstance(value, self.data_type):
            raise db.BadValueError('Property %s must be a %s.' %
                                    (self.name, self.data_type.__name__))
        return value
```

And here is how you would use the new property declaration:

```
class Player(db.Model):
    player_name = PlayerNameProperty()

p = Player()
p.player_name = 'Ned Nederlander'

p.player_name = 12345  # db.BadValueError
```

The `validate()` method takes the value as an argument, and either returns the value, returns a different value, or raises an exception. The value returned by the method becomes the application-facing value for the attribute, so you can use the `validate()` method for things like type coercion. In this example, the method raises a `db.BadValueError` if the value is not a string or `None`. The exception message can refer to the name of the property using `self.name`.

The `data_type` member is used by the base class. It represents the core datastore type the property uses to store the value. For string values, this is `basestring`.

The `validate()` method should call the superclass's implementation before checking its own conditions. The base class's validator supports the `required`, `choices`, and `validator` arguments of the declaration constructor.

If the app does not provide a value for a property when it constructs the data object, the property starts out with a default value. This default value is passed to the `validate()` method during the object constructor. If it is appropriate for your property declaration to allow a default value of `None`, make sure your `validate()` method allows it.

So far, this example doesn't do much beyond `db.StringProperty`. This by itself can be useful to give the property type a class for future expansion. Let's add a requirement that player names be between 6 and 30 characters in length by extending the `validate()` method:

```python
class PlayerNameProperty(db.Property):
    data_type = basestring

    def validate(self, value):
        value = super(PlayerNameProperty, self).validate(value)
        if value is not None:
            if not isinstance(value, self.data_type):
                raise db.BadValueError('Property %s must be a %s.' %
                                       (self.name, self.data_type.__name__))
            if (len(value) < 6 or len(value) > 30):
                raise db.BadValueError(('Property %s must be between 6 and ' +
                                        '30 characters.') % self.name)

        return value
```

The new validation logic disallows strings with an inappropriate length:

```python
p = Player()
p.player_name = 'Ned'     # db.BadValueError
p.player_name = 'Ned Nederlander'     # OK

p = Player(player_name = 'Ned')  # db.BadValueError
```

Marshaling Value Types

The datastore supports a fixed set of core value types for properties, listed in Table 4-1. A property declaration can support the use of other types of values in the attributes of model instances by marshaling between the desired type and one of the core datastore types. For example, the `db.ListProperty` class converts between the empty list of the app side and the condition of being unset on the datastore side.

The `get_value_for_datastore()` method converts the application value to the datastore value. Its argument is the complete model object, so you can access other aspects of the model when doing the conversion.

The `make_value_from_datastore()` method takes the datastore value and converts it to the type to be used in the application. It takes the datastore value and returns the desired object attribute value.

Say we wanted to represent player name values within the application using a `PlayerName` class instead of a simple string. Each player name has a surname and an optional first name. We can store this value as a single property, using the property declaration to convert between the application type (`PlayerName`) and a core datastore type (such as `unicode`).

```python
class PlayerName(object):
    def __init__(self, first_name, surname):
```

```
        self.first_name = first_name
        self.surname = surname

    def is_valid(self):
        return (isinstance(self.first_name, unicode)
                and isinstance(self.surname, unicode)
                and len(self.surname) >= 6)

class PlayerNameProperty(db.Property):
    data_type = basestring

    def validate(self, value):
        value = super(PlayerNameProperty, self).validate(value)
        if value is not None:
            if not isinstance(value, PlayerName):
                raise db.BadValueError('Property %s must be a PlayerName.' %
                                       (self.name))

            # Let the data class have a say in validity.
            if not value.is_valid():
                raise db.BadValueError('Property %s must be a valid PlayerName.' %
                                       self.name)

            # Disallow the serialization delimiter in the first field.
            if value.surname.find('|') != -1:
                raise db.BadValueError(('PlayerName surname in property %s cannot ' +
                                        'contain a "|".') % self.name)
        return value

    def get_value_for_datastore(self, model_instance):
        # Convert the data object's PlayerName to a unicode.
        return (getattr(model_instance, self.name).surname + u'|'
                + getattr(model_instance, self.name).first_name)

    def make_value_for_datastore(self, value):
        # Convert a unicode to a PlayerName.
        i = value.find(u'|')
        return PlayerName(first_name=value[i+1:],
                          surname=value[:i])
```

And here's how you'd use it:

```
p = Player()
p.player_name = PlayerName('Ned', 'Nederlander')

p.player_name = PlayerName('Ned', 'Neder|lander')
    # db.BadValueError, surname contains serialization delimiter

p.player_name = PlayerName('Ned', 'Neder')
    # db.BadValueError, PlayerName.is_valid() == False
```

Here, the application value type is a **PlayerName** instance, and the datastore value type is that value encoded as a Unicode string. The encoding format is the **surname** field, followed by a delimiter, followed by the **first_name** field. We disallow the delimiter character in the surname using the **validate()** method. (Instead of disallowing it, we could also escape it in `get_value_for_datastore()` and unescape it in `make_value_for_datastore()`.)

In this example, `PlayerName('Ned', 'Nederlander')` is stored as this Unicode string:

```
Nederlander|Ned
```

The datastore value puts the surname first so that the datastore will sort `PlayerName` values first by surname, then by first name. In general, you choose a serialization format that has the desired ordering characteristics for your custom property type. (The core type you choose also impacts how your values are ordered when mixed with other types, though if you're modeling consistently this isn't usually an issue.)

 If the conversion from the application type to the datastore type may fail, put a check for the conversion failure in the `validate()` method. This way, the error is caught when the bad value is assigned, instead of when the object is saved.

Customizing Default Values

When the app constructs a data object and does not provide a value for a declared property, the model calls the property declaration class to determine a default value. The base class implementation sets the default value to `None`, and allows the app to customize the default value in the model using the `default` argument to the declaration.

A few of the built-in declaration classes provide more sophisticated default values. For instance, if a `db.DateTimeProperty` was set with `auto_now_add=True`, the default value is the current system date and time. (`db.DateTimeProperty` uses `get_value_for_datastore()` to implement `auto_now=True`, so the value is updated whether or not it has a value.)

The default value passes through the validation logic after it is set. This allows the app to customize the validation logic and disallow the default value. This is what happens when `required=True`: the base class's validation logic disallows the `None` value, which is the base class's default value.

To specify custom default behavior, override the `default_value()` method. This method takes no arguments and returns the desired default value.

Here's a simple implementation of `default_value()` for `PlayerNameProperty`:

```python
class PlayerNameProperty(db.Property):
    # ...

    def default_value(self):
        default = super(PlayerNameProperty, self).default()
        if default is not None:
            return default

        return PlayerName('', 'Anonymous')
```

In this example, we call the superclass `default()` method to support the `default` argument to the constructor, which allows the app to override the default value in the model. If that returns `None`, we create a new `PlayerName` instance to be the default value.

Without further changes, this implementation breaks the `required` feature of the base class, because the value of the property is never `None` (unless the app explicitly assigns a `None` value). We can fix this by amending our validation logic to check `self.required` and disallow the anonymous `PlayerName` value if it's `True`.

Accepting Arguments

If you want the application to be able to control the behavior of your custom property declaration class using arguments, you override the `__init__()` method. The method should call the superclass `__init__()` method to enable the features of the superclass that use arguments (like `required`). The `Property` API requires that the `verbose_name` property come first, but after that all `__init__()` arguments are keyword values.

```
class PlayerNameProperty(db.Property):
    # ...

    def __init__(self, verbose_name=None,
                 require_first_name=False, **kwds):
        super(PlayerNameProperty, self).__init__(verbose_name, **kwds)
        self.require_first_name = require_first_name

    def validate(self, value):
        value = super(PlayerNameProperty, self).validate(value)
        if value is not None:
            # ...

            if self.require_first_name and not value.first_name:
                raise db.BadValueError('Property %s PlayerName needs a first_name.' %
                                       self.name)

        # ...
```

You'd use this feature like this:

```
class Player(db.Model):
    player_name = PlayerNameProperty(require_first_name=True)

p = Player(player_name=PlayerName('Ned', 'Nederlander'))

p.player_name = PlayerName(u'', u'Charo')
# db.BadValueError, first name required

p = Player()
# db.BadValueError, default value PlayerName('', 'Anonymous') has empty first_name
```

## CHAPTER 8

The Java Persistence API

The App Engine Java SDK includes implementations of two data access interface standards: the Java Persistence API (JPA) and Java Data Objects (JDO). These interfaces provide two essential features.

For one, these interfaces define a mechanism for describing the structure of data objects in terms of Java classes. You can use them to define and enforce consistent data schemas on top of App Engine's schemaless datastore, and take advantage of type safety in the Java language. These interfaces serve as a data modeling layer.

Because each interface is a standard supported by other popular data storage solutions, using a standard interface makes it easier to port an application to and from these other solutions. Different databases have varying degrees of support for these standards. Since the standards were developed with SQL-based relational databases in mind, the App Engine datastore can only be said to support a portion of the standard, and it is often easier to port away from App Engine than to it. But this alone adds value, as you can reserve the right to move your app to your company's own servers at any time. These interfaces are a portability layer.

The App Engine SDK uses an open source product called DataNucleus Access Platform as the basis for its implementations of JDO and JPA. Access Platform uses an adapter layer that translates both standards to an underlying implementation. The App Engine SDK includes an Access Platform adapter based on its low-level datastore API. Access Platform version 1.1 supports version 1.0 of the JPA specification and version 2.3 of JDO.

The JDO and JPA standards are similar, and share similar roots. The concepts that apply to the App Engine datastore have similar interfaces in both standards but with different terminology and minor behavioral differences. Which one you choose may depend on how familiar you are with it, or how well it is implemented for your most likely porting target, if you have one in mind.

In this chapter, we'll look at how to use JPA with App Engine. If you'd prefer to use JDO, check out the official documentation for App Engine, which includes a JDO tutorial.

A quick note on terminology: JPA refers to data objects as "entities." This similarity to datastore entities is convenient in some ways, and not so convenient in others. For this chapter, we'll refer to JPA entities as "data objects" (or just "objects") to avoid confusion with datastore entities.

Setting Up JPA

Using JPA requires a few steps common to all App Engine applications. We performed these steps back in Chapter 2.

JPA needs a configuration file that specifies that you want to use the App Engine implementation of the interface. This file is named *persistence.xml*, and should appear in your WAR's *WEB-INF/classes/META-INF/* directory. If you're using Eclipse, you can create this file in the *src/META-INF/* directory, and Eclipse will copy it to the final location automatically. We saw the contents of this file in Example 2-14, but here it is again for reference:

```
<?xml version="1.0" encoding="UTF-8" ?>
<persistence xmlns="http://java.sun.com/xml/ns/persistence"
  xmlns:xsi="http://www.w3.org/2001/XMLSchema-instance"
  xsi:schemaLocation="http://java.sun.com/xml/ns/persistence
      http://java.sun.com/xml/ns/persistence/persistence_1_0.xsd" version="1.0">
  <persistence-unit name="transactions-optional">
      <provider>
        org.datanucleus.store.appengine.jpa.DatastorePersistenceProvider
      </provider>
      <properties>
          <property name="datanucleus.NontransactionalRead" value="true"/>
          <property name="datanucleus.NontransactionalWrite" value="true"/>
          <property name="datanucleus.ConnectionURL" value="appengine"/>
      </properties>
  </persistence-unit>
</persistence>
```

This configuration tells Access Platform to use the **"appengine"** adapter. It also says to allow reads and writes outside of transactions (`NontransactionalRead` and `NontransactionalWrite` are `true`), which fits the semantics of the datastore that we described earlier. We named this configuration set **"transactions-optional"** to match.

Your application uses an `EntityManager` object to perform a set of datastore operations. The application creates an `EntityManager` using an `EntityManagerFactory`. The factory loads the configuration file and uses it for subsequent datastore interactions. You get an instance of the factory by calling a static method and passing it the name of the configuration set ("transactions-optional"):

```java
import javax.persistence.EntityManagerFactory;
import javax.persistence.Persistence;

// ...
    EntityManagerFactory emfInstance =
        Persistence.createEntityManagerFactory("transactions-optional");
```

The `createEntityManagerFactory()` static method performs a nontrivial amount of work. You can think of the factory as a connection pool, and each `EntityManager` as an individual connection. Since you only need one factory for the entire existence of the application, a best practice is to call the method only once, store the factory in a static member, and reuse it for multiple web requests. We did this in Chapter 2 with the EMF class, repeated here for reference:

```java
package clock;

import javax.persistence.EntityManagerFactory;
import javax.persistence.Persistence;

public final class EMF {
    private static final EntityManagerFactory emfInstance =
        Persistence.createEntityManagerFactory("transactions-optional");

    private EMF() {}

    public static EntityManagerFactory get() {
        return emfInstance;
    }
}
```

Access Platform hooks up the persistence plumbing to your JPA data classes in a post-compilation process that it calls "enhancement." If you are using Eclipse with the Google Plugin, the plug-in performs this step automatically. If you are not using Eclipse, you must add the enhancement step to your build process. See the official documentation for information about performing this build step using Apache Ant.

Entities and Keys

In JPA, you define data classes as plain old Java objects (POJOs). You use annotations to tell JPA which classes to persist to the datastore, and how to store its members. Defining your data exclusively in terms of the Java classes your application uses makes it easy to manipulate your persistent data. It also makes it easy to test your application, since you can create mock data objects directly from the classes.

JPA also lets you use an XML file instead of annotations to describe how to persist data classes. We'll only cover the annotation style here, but if you are familiar with the XML file mechanism, you can use it with Access Platform.

Here's a simple example of a data class:

```
import java.util.Date;
import javax.persistence.Entity;
import javax.persistence.Id;

@Entity(name = "Book")
public class Book {
    @Id
    private String isbn;

    private String title;
    private String author;
    private int copyrightYear;
    private Date authorBirthdate;

    // ... constructors, accessors ...
}
```

JPA knows instances of the `Book` class can be made persistent (saved to the datastore) because of the `@Entity` annotation. This annotation takes a `name` argument that specifies the name to be used in JPA queries for objects of this class. The `name` must be unique across all data classes in the application.

By default, the name of the datastore kind is derived from the name of the class. Specifically, this is the simple name of the class, without the package path (everything after the last `.`, e.g., `"Book"`). If you have two data classes with the same simple name in different packages, you can specify an alternate kind name using the `@Table` annotation. (JPA was designed with tabular databases in mind, but the concept is equivalent.)

```
import javax.persistence.Entity;
import javax.persistence.Table;

@Entity(name = "Book")
@Table(name = "BookItem")
public class Book {
    // ...
}
```

The `Book` class has five members. Four of these members are stored as properties on the datastore entity: `title`, `author`, `copyrightYear`, and `authorBirthdate`. The fifth member, `isbn`, represents the key name for the entity. JPA knows this because the member has the `@Id` annotation, and because the type of the member is `String`.

Every data class needs a member that represents the object's primary key, annotated with `@Id`. If the type of this member is `String` and it has no other annotations, then the key has no ancestors, and the value of the member is the string key name. The application must set this field before saving the object for the first time.

To tell JPA to let the datastore assign a unique numeric ID instead of using an app-provided key name string, you declare the member with a type of `Long` and give it the annotation `@GeneratedValue(strategy = GenerationType.IDENTITY)`, like so:

```
import javax.persistence.Entity;
import javax.persistence.GeneratedValue;
import javax.persistence.GenerationType;
import javax.persistence.Id;

@Entity(name = "Book")
public class Book {
    @Id
    @GeneratedValue(strategy = GenerationType.IDENTITY)
    private Long id;

    // ...
}
```

The member is set with the system-assigned ID when the object is saved to the datastore for the first time.

These simple key member types are sufficient for entities without ancestors. Together with the entity kind ("Book"), the member represents the complete key of a root entity. If an instance of the class may represent an entity with ancestors, the key member must be able to represent the full key path. There are two ways to do this.

One way is to declare the type of the key member to be the com.google.appengine.api.datastore.Key class:

```
import javax.persistence.Entity;
import javax.persistence.Id;
import com.google.appengine.api.datastore.Key;

@Entity(name = "Book")
public class Book {
    @Id
    private Key id;

    // ...
}
```

You can use this key member type to create a complete Key with a string name. You can also use system-assigned numeric IDs with ancestors by using the @GeneratedValue annotation, then assigning a Key value with neither the name nor the ID set.

If you'd prefer not to create a dependency on an App Engine–specific class, there is another way to implement a key with ancestors: declare the ID field's type as String and use a DataNucleus JPA extension that encodes the complete key as a string value, like so:

```
import javax.persistence.Entity;
import javax.persistence.Id;
import org.datanucleus.jpa.annotations.Extension;
import com.google.appengine.api.datastore.Key;

@Entity(name = "Book")
public class Book {
    @Id
```

```
        @Extension(vendorName = "datanucleus",
                   key = "gae.encoded-pk",
                   value = "true")
        private Key id;

        // ...
    }
```

You can convert between a Key and a string-encoded key using the KeyFactory class's keyToString() and stringToKey() methods. (Note that the Key class's toString() method returns something else.)

You can use a Key ID field or a string-encoded ID field in combination with the @GeneratedValue annotation to produce keys with ancestors and system-assigned numeric IDs.

Entity Properties

The fields of the object become the properties of the corresponding entity. The name of a field is used as the name of the property. The @Id field is not stored as a property value, only as the key.

JPA and App Engine support many types of fields. Any of the types mentioned in Table 4-1 can be used as a field type. A field can contain a serializable object, stored as a single property. A field can also be a collection of one of the core datastore types or a serializable class, to be stored as a multivalued property. Additionally, App Engine supports JPA embedded data objects and relationships between entities using fields.

In some cases, JPA must be told which fields to save to the datastore. For the Java standard types (such as Long or String or Date), JPA assumes that fields of those types should be saved. For other types, especially the datastore-specific classes such as datastore.ShortBlob, you must tell JPA to save the field by giving it the @Basic annotation. If you have a field that should not be saved to the datastore, give it the @Transient annotation.

```
import java.util.List;
import javax.persistence.Basic;
import javax.persistence.Id;
import javax.persistence.Transient;
import com.google.appengine.api.datastore.ShortBlob;

@Entity(name = "Book")
public class Book {
    // ...

    private String title;     // saved

    @Basic                    // saved
    private ShortBlob coverIcon;

    @Basic                    // saved
```

```
        private List<String> tags;

        @Transient                      // not saved
        private int debugAccessCount;
}
```

As with the low-level API, some types are widened before being stored. `int` and `Integer` are converted to `Long`, and `float` and `Float` become `Double`. With the JPA interface, these values are converted back to the declared field types when loaded into an object.

A `Serializable` class can be used as a field type, using the `@Lob` annotation. These values are stored in serialized form as `datastore.Blob` values. As such, these values are not indexed, and cannot be used in queries.

Collection types are stored as multivalued properties in iteration order. When loaded into the data class, multivalued properties are converted back into the specified collection type.

By default, the name of a field is used as the name of the corresponding property. You can override this using the `@Column` annotation:

```
import javax.persistence.Column;
import javax.persistence.Entity;

@Entity(name = "Book")
public class Book {
    // ...

    @Column(name = "long_description")
    private String longDescription;
}
```

You can declare that the datastore property of a field should not be mentioned in indexes—the property of each entity should be created as a nonindexed property—using an `@Extension` annotation:

```
import org.datanucleus.jpa.annotations.Extension;

@Entity(name = "Book")
public class Book {
    // ...

    @Extension(vendorName = "datanucleus",
               key = "gae.unindexed",
               value = "true")
    private String firstSentence;
}
```

Embedded Objects

App Engine supports JPA embedded classes by storing the fields of the embedded class as properties on the same datastore entity as the fields of the primary class. You must declare the class to embed using the @Embeddable annotation. To embed the class, simply use it as a field type:

```
import javax.persistence.Embeddable;
import javax.persistence.Entity;

@Embeddable
public class Publisher {
    private String name;
    private String address;
    private String city;
    private String stateOrProvince;
    private String postalCode;

    // ...
}

@Entity(name = "Book")
public class Book {
    // ...

    private Publisher publisher;
}
```

Because fields of embedded classes are stored as separate properties, they are queryable just like other properties. You can refer to an embedded field in a property with the name of the outer field with a dot-notation, such as publisher.name. The actual property name is just the name of the inner field, and you can change this if needed using an @Column annotation.

Saving, Fetching, and Deleting Objects

To start a session with the datastore, you use the EntityManagerFactory to create an EntityManager. You must create a new EntityManager for each request handler, and close it when you're done.

```
import javax.persistence.EntityManager;
// ...
        // emf is the EntityManagerFactory
        EntityManager em;
        try {
            em = emf.createEntityManager();
            // ... do datastore stuff ...
        } finally {
            em.close();
        }
```

To create a new data object, you construct the data class, then call the EntityManager's persist() method with the object:

```
        EntityManager em;
        try {
            em = emf.createEntityManager();
```

```
        book = new Book();
        book.title = "The Grapes of Wrath";
        // ...
        em.persist(book);
    } finally {
        em.close();
    }
```

If you create an object with a complete key, and an entity with that key already exists in the datastore, saving the new object will overwrite the old one. In App Engine's implementation, JPA's merge() method is equivalent to persist() in this way. (Other implementations may do something different in this case.)

To fetch an entity with a known key, you use the find() method. This method takes the class of the object in which to load the entity, and the key of the object. The key can be any appropriate type: a string key name, a numeric ID, a datastore.Key object, or a string-encoded complete key. The method returns an object of the given class, or null if no object with that key is found:

```
Book book = em.find(Book.class, "9780596156732");
if (book == null) {
    // not found
}
```

 The ability of find() to accept all four key types is nonstandard. To make your code more portable, only call find() using the type of key you used in the data class.

When you create or fetch an entity (or get an entity back from a query), the data object becomes "attached" to (or managed by) the entity manager. If you make changes to an attached object and do not save them by calling the persist() method explicitly, the object is saved automatically when you close the entity manager. As we'll see in the next section, if you need the entity to be updated in a transaction, you pass the updated object to the persist() method at the moment it needs to be saved.

To delete an entity, you call the remove() method. This method takes the data object as its sole argument. The object still exists in memory after it is removed from the datastore.

```
em.remove(book);
```

The remove() method requires a loaded data object. There is no way to delete an entity with this method without fetching its object first. (You can delete entities without fetching them using a JPQL delete query. See the section "Queries and JPQL" on page 217.)

Remember to close the `EntityManager` by calling its `close()` method. If you don't, changes to objects will not be saved to the datastore. The best way to do this is in a `finally` block, as shown above, so the manager still gets closed in the event of an uncaught exception.

Transactions in JPA

The API for performing transactions in JPA is similar to the low-level datastore API. You call a method on the entity manager to create a `Transaction` object, then call methods on the object to begin and commit or roll back the transaction.

```java
import javax.persistence.EntityTransaction;

// ...
        EntityTransaction txn = em.getTransaction();
        txn.begin();
        try {
            Book book = em.find(Book.class, "9780596156732");
            BookReview bookReview = new BookReview();
            bookReview.setRating(5);
            book.getBookReviews().add(bookReview);

            // Persist all updates and commit.
            txn.commit();
        } finally {
            if (txn.isActive()) {
                txn.rollback();
            }
        }
```

The JPA transaction interface was designed for databases that support global transactions, so it knows nothing of App Engine's local transactions and entity groups. It's up to the application to know which operations are appropriate to perform in a single transaction. You can manage entity groups and ancestors using App Engine's extensions to JPA.

One way to set up a data class that can represent entities with parents is to use either a `datastore.Key` or a string-encoded key for the `@Id` field. When you create a new object, you can construct the complete key, including ancestors, and assign it to this field.

Alternatively, you can establish a second field to contain the parent key as either a `Key` or string-encoded key, using an extension:

```java
import javax.persistence.Basic;
import javax.persistence.Entity;
import javax.persistence.GeneratedValue;
import javax.persistence.GenerationType;
import javax.persistence.Id;

import org.datanucleus.jpa.annotations.Extension;
```

```
@Entity
public class BookReview {
    @Id
    @GeneratedValue(strategy = GenerationType.IDENTITY)
    @Extension(vendorName = "datanucleus",
               key = "gae.encoded-pk",
               value = "true")
    private String keyString;

    @Basic
    @Extension(vendorName = "datanucleus",
               key = "gae.parent-pk",
               value = "true")
    private String bookKeyString;
}
```

The parent key field makes it easier to port your application to another database at a later time. It declares a slot in the data class for the ancestor relationship that is separate from the entity's key name.

The parent key field is required if you want to perform queries using ancestor filters. As we'll see in the next section, JPA queries must refer to fields on the data class.

The App Engine implementation of JPA includes features for managing entity groups automatically using object relationships. We'll discuss relationships later in this chapter.

Queries and JPQL

JPA includes a SQL-like query language called JPQL. JPQL provides access to the underlying database's query functionality at the level of abstraction of JPA data objects. You form queries for data objects in terms of the data classes, and get objects as results.

To perform a query, you call the entity manager's **createQuery()** method with the text of the JPQL query. This returns a **Query** object. To get the results, you call getResultList() on the **Query** object.

```
import java.util.List;
import javax.persistence.Query;

// ...

    Query query = em.createQuery("SELECT b FROM Book b");

    @SuppressWarnings("unchecked")
    List<Book> results = (List<Book>) query.getResultList();
```

In this example, the cast to List<Book> generates a compiler warning, so we suppress this warning using an @SuppressWarnings annotation.

JPA knows which class to use for each result from the @Entity(name = "...") annotation on the class. You can also use the full package path of the class in the query.

You can use parameters in your JPQL query, and replace the parameters with values by calling setParameter():

```
Query query = em.createQuery(
    "SELECT b FROM Book b WHERE copyrightYear >= :earliestYear");
query.setParameter("earliestYear", 1923);
```

getResultList() returns a special App Engine–specific implementation of List that knows how to fetch results in batches. If you iterate over the entire list, the List implementation may make multiple calls to the datastore to fetch results.

If you are only expecting one result, you can call getSingleResult() instead. This gets the first result if any, or null if there are no results.

```
Book book = (Book) query.getSingleResult();
```

You can fetch a range of results by setting an offset and a maximum number of results, using the setFirstResult() and setMaxResults() methods before calling getResultList().

```
// Get results 5-15.
query.setFirstResult(4);
query.setMaxResults(10);

@SuppressWarnings("unchecked")
List<Book> results = (List<Book>) query.getResultList();
```

The syntax of JPQL is straightforward, and similar to SQL or the Python API's GQL. JPQL keywords can be all uppercase or all lowercase, and are shown as uppercase here, as is tradition. Class and field names are case-sensitive. The query begins by identifying the simple name of the class of objects to query, corresponding to the kind of the entities:

```
SELECT b FROM Book b
```

This query returns all Book data objects, where Book is the value of the name argument to the @Entity annotation on the data class (which happens to also be named Book). The class name is followed by an identifier (b); stating that identifier after the word SELECT tells JPA to return objects of that class as results.

To perform a keys-only query, give the name of the key field instead of the class identifier. The methods that return results return values of the type used for the @Id field in the data class.

```
Query query = em.createQuery("SELECT isbn FROM Book");

@SuppressWarnings("unchecked")
List<String> results = (List<String>) query.getResultList();
```

The App Engine implementation of JPQL supports queries for specific fields, though perhaps not in the way you'd expect. For a query for specific fields, the datastore returns the complete data for each entity to the application, and the interface implementation selects the requested fields and assembles the results. This is only true if one of the requested fields is a datastore property, and is not true if the only field is a key field (@Id).

If the query is for one field, each result is a value of the type of that field. If the query is for multiple fields, each result is an Object[] whose elements are the field values in the order specified in the query.

```
Query query = em.createQuery("SELECT isbn, title, author FROM Book");

// Fetch complete Book objects, then
// produce result objects from 3 fields
// of each result
@SuppressWarnings("unchecked")
List<Object[]> results = (List<Object[]>) query.getResultList();
for (Object[] result : results) {
    String isbn = result[0];
    String title = result[1];
    String author = result[2];

    // ...
}
```

You specify filters on fields using a WHERE clause and one or more conditions:

```
SELECT b FROM Book b WHERE author = "John Steinbeck"
                     AND copyrightYear >= 1940
```

To filter on the entity key, refer to the field that represents the key in the data class (the @Id field):

```
SELECT b FROM Book b WHERE author = "John Steinbeck"
                     AND isbn > :firstKeyToFetch
```

You can perform an ancestor filter by establishing a parent key field (as we did in the previous section) and referring to that field in the query:

```
SELECT br FROM BookReview br WHERE bookKey = :pk
```

As with find(), you can use any of the four key types with parameterized queries, but the most portable way is to use the type used in the class.

You specify sort orders using an ORDER BY clause. Multiple sort orders are comma-delimited. Each sort order can have a direction of ASC (the default) or DESC.

```
SELECT b FROM Book b ORDER BY rating DESC title
```

The App Engine implementation of JPQL includes a couple of additional tricks that the datastore can support natively. One such trick is the string prefix trick:

```
SELECT b FROM Book b WHERE title LIKE 'The Grape%'
```

The implementation translates this to WHERE title >= 'The Grape', which does the same thing: it returns all books with a title that begins with the string The Grape, including "The Grape", "The Grapefruit", and "The Grapes of Wrath".

This trick only supports a single wildcard at the end of a string. It does not support a wildcard at the beginning of the string.

Another trick App Engine's JPQL implementation knows how to do is to translate queries on key fields into batch gets. For example:

```
SELECT b FROM Book b WHERE isbn IN (:i1, :i2, :i3)
```

This becomes a batch get using three keys, and does not perform a query at all.

In addition to these SELECT queries, App Engine's JPA implementation supports deleting entities that meet criteria with JPQL. A delete query can include filters on keys and properties to specify the entities to delete.

```
DELETE FROM Book b WHERE isbn >= "TEST_000" AND isbn <= "TEST_999"
```

As with other mechanisms for modifying data, if you perform a delete query outside of a transaction, it is possible for a delete of one entity to fail while the others succeed. If you perform it inside a transaction, it'll be all or nothing, but all entities must be in the same entity group, and the delete query must use an ancestor filter.

The JPA specification supports many features of queries that are common to SQL databases, but are not supported natively in the App Engine datastore. With a SQL database, using one of these features calls the database directly, with all of the performance implications (good and bad) of the datastore's implementation.

When an app uses a feature of JPQL that the underlying database does not support, DataNucleus Access Platform tries to make up the difference using its own in-memory query evaluator. It attempts to load all of the information it needs to perform the query into memory, execute the nonnative operations itself, then return the result.

Because such features are potential scalability hazards—an AVG() query would require fetching every entity of the kind, for example—the App Engine implementation disables the Access Platform in-memory query evaluator.

Relationships

Most useful data models involve relationships between classes of data objects. Players are members of guilds, book reviews are about books, messages are posted to message boards, customers place orders, and orders have multiple line items. For logical reasons or architectural reasons, two concepts may be modeled as separate but related classes. Those relationships are as much a part of the data model as the data fields of the objects.

In the App Engine datastore (and most databases), one easy way to model a relationship between two objects is to store the entity key of one object as a property of the other, and (if needed) vice versa. The datastore supports Key values as a native property value type, and also provides a way to encode key values as strings. You don't need any help from JPA to model relationships this way.

But relationships are so important to data modeling that JPA has a family of features to support them. In JPA, you can define *owned relationships* in the data model that enforce constraints by managing changes. With owned relationships, you can say that a book has zero or more book reviews, and JPA ensures that you can't have a book review without a book. If you delete a `Book` object, JPA knows to also delete all of its `BookReview` objects. In the Java code, the relationship is represented by a field whose type is of the related data class, ensuring that only the appropriate classes are used on either side of the relationship.

The App Engine implementation of JPA supports one-to-one and one-to-many relationships. It does not yet support JPA's notion of many-to-many relationships.

An *unowned relationship* is a relationship without these constraints. App Engine supports unowned relationships through the storing of literal key values, but does not yet support them through JPA. You can use multivalued properties of `Key` values to model unowned one-to-one, one-to-many and many-to-many relationships.

To completely support the semantics of JPA owned relationships, App Engine stores objects with owned relationships in the same entity group. It's easy to see why this has to be the case. If one object is deleted within a transaction, the relationship says the related object must also be deleted. But to do that in the same transaction requires that both objects be in the same entity group. If one object is deleted outside of a transaction, then the other object must be deleted in a separate operation, and if one delete or the other fails, an object remains that doesn't meet the relationship requirement.

While the use of entity groups may sound constraining, it's also a powerful feature. You can use JPA owned relationships to perform transactions on related entities, and the JPA implementation will manage entity groups for you automatically.

You specify an owned one-to-one relationship by creating a field whose type is of the related class, and giving the field an `@OneToOne` annotation. For example, you could associate each book with a cover image, like so:

```
import javax.persistence.Entity;
import javax.persistence.OneToOne;
import bookstore.BookCoverImage;

@Entity(name = "Book")
public class Book {
    // ...

    @OneToOne(cascade=CascadeType.ALL)
    private BookCoverImage bookCoverImage;
}
```

This annotation declares a one-to-one relationship between the `Book` and `BookCoverImage` classes.

In every relationship, one class "owns" the relationship. The owner of a relationship is responsible for propagating changes to related objects. In this example, the Book class is the "owner" of the relationship.

The cascade=CascadeType.ALL argument annotation says that all kinds of changes should propagate to related objects (including PERSIST, REFRESH, REMOVE, and MERGE). For example:

```
// EntityManager em;
// ...

Book book = new Book();
book.setBookCoverImage(new BookCoverImage());

book.setTitle("The Grapes of Wrath");
book.bookCoverImage.setType("image/jpg");

EntityTransaction txn = em.getTransaction();
txn.begin();
try {
    em.persist(book);
    txn.commit();
} finally {
    if (txn.isActive()) {
        txn.rollback();
    }
}
em.close();
```

This code creates a Book and a related BookCoverImage. When it makes the Book persistent, the BookCoverImage is made persistent automatically (the PERSIST action cascades). Similarly, if we were to delete the Book, the BookCoverImage would also be deleted (the DELETE action cascades). Cascading actions follow all ownership paths from "owner" to "owned," and do the right thing if the objects they find have changed since they were loaded from the datastore.

You can have JPA populate a field on the "owned" class that points back to the owner automatically, like so:

```
import javax.persistence.Entity;
import javax.persistence.OneToOne;
import bookstore.Book;

@Entity(name = "BookCoverImage")
public class BookCoverImage {
    // ...

    @OneToOne(mappedBy="bookCoverImage")
    private Book book;
}
```

The `mappedBy` argument tells JPA that the `book` field refers to the `Book` object that is related to this object. This is managed from the "owner" side of the relationship: when the `BookCoverImage` is assigned to the `Book`'s field, JPA knows that the back-reference refers to the `Book` object.

To specify a one-to-many relationship, you use a field type that is a `List` or `Set` of the related class, and use the `@OneToMany` annotation on the "one" class:

```
import java.util.List;
import javax.persistence.CascadeType;
import javax.persistence.Entity;
import javax.persistence.OneToMany;
import bookstore.BookReview;

@Entity(name = "Book")
public class Book {
    // ...

    @OneToMany(cascade=CascadeType.ALL)
    private List<BookReview> bookReviews;
}
```

To create a back-reference from the "many" class to the "one" class, you use a `@ManyToOne` annotation, then specify a `mappedBy` on the "one" class's `@OneToMany`:

```
// BookReview.java
@Entity(name = "BookReview")
public class BookReview {
    // ...

    @ManyToOne(mappedBy="bookReviews")
    private Book book;
}
// Book.java
@Entity(name = "Book")
public class Book {
    // ...

    @OneToMany(cascade=CascadeType.ALL,
               mappedBy="book")
    private List<BookReview> bookReviews;
}
```

In a one-to-many relationship, the "one" is always the owner class, and the "many" is the owned class. In a one-to-one relationship, JPA knows which is the "owned" class by the absence of a back-reference field, or a back-reference field mentioned by a `mappedBy` annotation argument.

When you fetch a data object that has a relationship field, JPA does not fetch the related objects right away. Instead, it waits until you access the field to fetch the object (or objects). This is called "lazy" fetching, and it saves your app from unnecessary datastore operations. The App Engine implementation of JPA only supports lazy fetching

(FetchType.LAZY), and does not yet support its opposite, "eager" fetching (FetchType.EAGER). Note that you must access related objects prior to closing the EntityManager, so they are fetched into memory.

```
// Fetch a Book, but not its BookCoverImage.
Book book = em.find(Book.class, "9780596156732");
// ...

// The BookCoverImage is fetched when it is first accessed.
resp.setContentType(book.bookCoverImage.type);
```

In the datastore, the relationship is represented using ancestors. The owner object is the parent, and all owned objects are children. When you access the relationship field on the owner object, the interface uses an ancestor query to get the owned objects. When you access a back-reference to the owner from the owned object, the interface parses the owned object's key to get the parent.

Related objects are created in the same entity group, so they can all be updated within the same transaction if necessary. The owner's entity is created first (if necessary) and becomes the parent of the owned objects' entities. If you declare a back-reference using mappedBy, no property is stored on the owned object's entity. Instead, when the field is dereferenced, the implementation uses the owned object's key path to determine the owner's key and fetches it.

The App Engine implementation does not support many-to-one relationships where the "many" is the owner. That is, it does not support a one-to-many relationship where actions cascade from the many to the one.

Creating new relationships between existing data classes can be tricky, because the entity group requirements must be met in the migrated data. Adding a relationship to the owner class is like adding a field: the entities that represent instances of the owner class must be updated to have appropriate key properties. The "owned" side is trickier: since an owned object's entity must have the owner as its parent, if the owned object already exists in the datastore, it must be deleted and re-created with the new parent. You can't change an entity's parent after the entity has been created.

This use of datastore ancestors means you cannot reassign an owned object to another owner after it has been saved to the datastore. This also means that one object cannot be on the "owned" side of more than one relationship, since the entity can have only one parent.

Relationships and cascading actions imply that an operation on a data object can translate to multiple datastore operations on multiple entities, all in the same entity group. If you want these operations to occur in a single transaction, you must perform the initial operation (such as em.merge(...)) within an explicit transaction.

If you perform a cascading action outside of an explicit transaction, each of the datastore operations performed by JPA occurs in a separate operation. Some of these operations may fail while others succeed. As such, it's a best practice to perform all JPA updates within explicit transactions, so there is no confusion as to what succeeded and what failed.

You can perform queries on relationship fields in JPQL using key values. For a query on the owner class, the query is a simple key property query:

```
SELECT FROM Book b WHERE bookCoverImage = :bci AND publishDate > :pdate
```

For a query on an owned class, a query on the back-reference field becomes an ancestor filter:

```
SELECT FROM BookCoverImage bci WHERE book = :b
```

You cannot refer to properties of the related entity in the query filter. App Engine does not support join queries.

For More Information

The JDO and JPA interfaces have many useful features that work with the App Engine implementation. One excellent source of documentation on these interfaces is the DataNucleus Access Platform website:

http://www.datanucleus.org/products/accessplatform/

The App Engine implementation is an open source project hosted on Google Code. The source includes many unit tests that exercise and demonstrate many features of JDO and JPA. You can browse the source code at the project page:

http://code.google.com/p/datanucleus-appengine/

To read the unit tests, click the Source tab, then click Browse in the navigation bar. The path is svn/trunk/tests/org/datanucleus/store/appengine/.

## CHAPTER 9

The Memory Cache

Durable data storage requires a storage medium that retains data through power loss and system restarts. Today's medium of choice is the hard drive, a storage device composed of circular platters coated with magnetic material on which data is encoded. The platters spin at a constant rate while a sensor moves along the radius, reading and writing bits on the platters as they travel past. Reading or writing a specific piece of data requires a *disk seek* to position the sensor at the proper radius and wait for the platter to rotate until the desired data is underneath. Hard drives are astonishingly fast, all things considered, but for web applications, disk seeks can be costly. Fetching an entity from the datastore by key can take time on the order of tens of milliseconds.

Most high-performance web applications use a *memory cache*. A memory cache uses a volatile storage medium, usually the RAM of the cache machines, for very fast read and write access to values. A *distributed memory cache* provides scalable, consistent temporary storage for distributed systems, so many processes can access the same data. Because memory is volatile—it gets erased during an outage—the cache is not useful for long-term storage, or even short-term primary storage for important data. But it's excellent as a secondary system for fast access to data also kept elsewhere, such as the datastore. It's also sufficient as global high-speed memory for some uses.

The App Engine distributed memory cache service, known as *memcache* in honor of the original memcached system that it resembles, stores key-value pairs. You can set a value with a key, and get the value given the key. A value can be up to a megabyte in size. A key is up to 250 bytes, and the API accepts larger keys and uses a hash algorithm to convert them to 250 bytes.

Setting a single value in the cache is atomic: the key either gets the new value or retains the old one (or remains unset). The memcache does not support transactions like the datastore does. If you get a value, then try to set a value based on what you got, the first value may have changed since it was fetched. The App Engine memcache includes the ability to increment and decrement numeric values as an atomic operation.

A common way to use the memcache with the datastore is to cache datastore entities by their keys. When you want to fetch an entity by key, you first check the memcache for a value with that key, and use it if found (known as a *cache hit*). If it's not in the memcache (a *cache miss*), you fetch it from the datastore, then put it in the memcache so future attempts to access it will find it there. At the expense of a small amount of overhead during the first fetch, subsequent fetches become much faster.

If the entity changes in the datastore, you can attempt to update the memcache when the entity is updated in the datastore, so subsequent requests can continue to go to the cache but see fresh data. This mostly works, but it has two minor problems. For one, it is possible that the memcache update will fail even if the datastore update succeeds, leaving old data in the cache. Also, if two processes update the same datastore entity, then update the memcache, the datastore will have correct data (thanks to datastore transactions), but the memcache update will have the value of whichever update occurs last. Because of this possibility, it's somewhat better to just delete the memcache key when the datastore changes, and let the next read attempt populate the cache with a current value. Naturally, the delete could also fail.

Because there is no way to update both the datastore and the memcache in a single transaction, there is no way to avoid the possibility that the cache may contain old data. To minimize the duration that the memcache will have a stale value, you can give the value an expiration time when you set it. When the expiration time elapses, the cache unsets the key, and a subsequent read results in a cache miss and triggers a fresh fetch from the datastore.

Of course, this caching pattern works for more than just datastore entities. You can use it for datastore queries, web service calls made with URL Fetch, expensive calculations, or any other data that can be replaced with a slow operation, where the benefits of fast access outweigh the possibility of staleness.

This is so often the case with web applications that a best practice is to cache aggressively. Look through your application for opportunities to make this trade-off, and implement caching whenever the same value is needed an arbitrary number of times, especially if that number increases with traffic. Site content such as an article on a news website often falls into this category. Caching speeds up requests and saves CPU time, and reduces the likelihood of datastore read failures impacting your application.

The APIs for the memcache service are straightforward. We'll look at the Python interface first, then the Java interface, with an emphasis on caching datastore entities.

The Python Memcache API

The Python API to the memcache service is designed to be compatible with the Python interface to memcached. It includes a Client class with static methods you can call to interact with the service. The App Engine API also provides these methods as straight functions in the google.appengine.api.memcache package.

Keys are strings. The API also accepts a memcached-style tuple of a hash code and a string as a key for compatibility, but it ignores the hash code. The string can be any size; strings larger than 250 bytes are hashed to 250 bytes.

Values can be any Python value that can be serialized using the pickle module. This includes most simple values, and data structures and objects whose members are pickleable values. Pretty much any db.Model instance falls into this category. You can check the documentation for the pickle module for a more complete description.

Setting and Getting Values in Python

To store a value in memcache, you call the set() function (or method, if you're using the Client class) with the key and the value:

```
from google.appengine.api import memcache

# headlines is a pickle-able object
headlines = ['...', '...', '...']

success = memcache.set("headlines", headlines)
if not success:
    # Problem accessing memcache...
```

set() returns True on success, or False if the value could not be stored.

If there already exists a value with the given key, set() overwrites it. If there is no value for the key, set() sets it.

To set a value only if there is no value for the key, you call the add() function with similar arguments:

```
success = memcache.add("headlines", headlines)
if not success:
    # Key already set, or another problem setting...
```

add() works like set(), but does not update the value and returns False if a value is currently set for the given key.

To update a value only if it's already set, you call the replace() function, also with similar arguments:

```
success = memcache.replace("headlines", headlines)
if not success:
    # Key not set, or another problem setting...
```

To get a value, you call the get() method with the key:

```
headlines = memcache.get("headlines")
if headlines is None:
    # Key not set, or another problem getting...
```

get() returns the value, or None if there is no value set for the given key.

Setting and Getting Multiple Values

You can set and get multiple values at a time using the batch interface. A batch call to memcache is performed as a single call to the service, which is faster than multiple individual calls for many items. Like the datastore batch operations, the total amount of data sent to or received from memcache in a single call must not exceed one megabyte.

`set_multi()`, `add_multi()`, and `replace_multi()` are similar to their singular counterparts, except instead of taking a key and a value as arguments, they take a Python mapping (such as a `dict`) of keys to values.

```
article_summaries = {'article00174': '...',
                     'article05234': '...',
                     'article15820': '...',
                    }

failed_keys = memcache.set_multi(article_summaries)
if failed_keys:
    # One or more keys failed to update...
```

These methods return a list of keys that failed to be set. A completely successful batch update returns the empty list.

To get multiple values in a single batch, you call the `get_multi()` method with a list of keys:

```
article_summary_keys = ['article00174',
                        'article05234',
                        'article15820',
                       ]

article_summaries = memcache.get_multi(article_summary_keys)
```

`get_multi()` returns a `dict` of keys and values that were present and retrieved successfully.

All of the batch operations accept a `key_prefix` keyword argument that prepends every key with the given prefix string. When used with `get_multi()`, the keys on the returned values do not include the prefix.

```
article_summaries = {'00174': '...',
                     '05234': '...',
                     '15820': '...',
                    }

failed_keys = memcache.set_multi(article_summaries,
                                 key_prefix='article')
if failed_keys:
    # ...

# ...

article_summary_keys = ['00174',
```

```
                           '05234',
                           '15820',
                           ]

article_summaries = memcache.get_multi(article_summary_keys,
                                       key_prefix='article')
```

 Batch calls to the memcache service are not atomic actions. set_multi() may be successful for some items and not others. get_multi() will return the data seen at the time of each individual get, and does not guarantee that all retrieved data is read at the same time.

Memcache Namespaces

You can specify an optional namespace for a memcache key with any setter or getter call. Namespaces let you segment the key space by the kind of thing you are storing, so you don't have to worry about key collisions between disparate uses of the cache.

All of the setter and getter functions accept a namespace argument, a string that declares the namespace for all keys involved in the call. The batch functions use one namespace for all keys in the batch.

```
article_summaries = {'article00174': '...',
                     'article05234': '...',
                     'article15820': '...',
                     }

failed_keys = memcache.set_multi(article_summaries,
                                 namespace='News')
if failed_keys:
    # ...

# ...

summary = memcache.get('article05234',
                       namespace='News')
```

Namespaces are different from key prefixes in batch calls. Key prefixes merely prepend keys in a batch with a common string, as a convenience for batch processing. The namespace is a separate part of the key, and must be specified with an explicit namespace argument in all calls.

Cache Expiration

You can tell the memcache to delete (or *evict*) a value automatically after a period of time when you set or update the value.

All of the setter methods accept a time argument. Its value is either a number of seconds from the current time up to one month (up to 2,678,400 seconds), or it is a Unix epoch time (seconds since January 1, 1970, such as returned by time.time()) in the future.

(The API knows the difference by the size of the value, since it's been longer than one month since the epoch.)

```
# Refresh the headlines cache once every 5 minutes.
success = memcache.set('headlines', headlines,
                        time=300)
```

A key's expiration timer is reset every time it is updated using set() or replace() (or the _multi() equivalents).

If no time argument is provided to a setter, the default behavior is to keep the values in the memcache as long as possible.

Deleting Keys

You can delete keys immediately by calling the delete() or delete_multi() functions. delete() takes a key as its argument, and delete_multi() takes a list of keys.

```
# Force the headlines cache to refresh.
result = memcache.delete('headlines')
if not result:
    # Delete failed...
```

For compatibility with the Python memcached interface, the delete() function returns one of three success values, represented by constants in the API: DELETE_NETWORK_FAILURE means there was a problem caused by a network failure; DELETE_ITEM_MISSING means there was no value with the given key to delete; and DELETE_SUCCESSFUL means the key was deleted. If you don't care about the distinction between a successfully deleted value and a value that was never there, you can treat the return value as a true-or-false value, since the network failure case is equivalent to zero and the others are nonzero.

The delete_multi() method returns True if all keys were successfully deleted or did not exist, and False if at least one key was not deleted successfully.

delete() and delete_multi() accept the namespace parameter. delete_multi() also accepts the key_prefix parameter, similar to the other _multi() functions.

You can specify an amount of time during which processes are not allowed to readd the key. This is useful for ensuring that multiple simultaneous worker processes working with the same data do not accidentally undo cache deletes with an update. To specify a readd lock duration, you provide the seconds argument to either delete() or delete_multi(). This argument is either a relative number of seconds up to one month, or a date in the future as a Unix epoch time.

```
result = memcache.delete('tempnode91512',
                          seconds=5)
```

You can delete every memcache value for your application by calling the flush_all() function. It takes no arguments, and returns True on success or False on failure.

```
memcache.flush_all()
```

Memcache Counters

The App Engine memcache includes a feature that lets you increment and decrement numeric values in the cache using atomic operations. The memcache is not transactional otherwise, so this is the only way to modify an existing value atomically.

In Python, you call the `incr()` method to increment a value, and the `decr()` method to decrement a value. These methods accept a key, and an optional amount to increment or decrement as the `delta` argument (the default is 1). As with the other methods, these methods accept the `namespace` argument.

```
work_done = memcache.incr('work_done')
if not work_done:
    # ...

work_done = memcache.incr('work_done', delta=5)
if not work_done:
    # ...
```

As shown, the methods return the new value, or `None` if the key was not set, if it was not set to an integer, or if there was another problem.

You can specify a starting value to use if the key is unset by providing the `initial_value` argument. If the key is found, its value is used as the starting value. Otherwise, the provided initial value is used as the starting value for the operation. If you don't provide an initial value and the key is not set, the call does nothing and returns `None`. (This is the default.)

```
work_done = memcache.incr('work_done', initial_value=0)
```

Cache Statistics

The memcache maintains a set of statistics about cache hits and misses, items in the cache, and data transferred out of the cache. You can inspect this data programmatically by calling the `get_stats()` method. This method returns a dictionary containing the statistics. Note that these statistics are just a best effort, and may be reset by the system at any time.

```
import logging

stats = memcache.get_stats()

logging.info('Memcache statistics:')
for stat in stats.iteritems():
    logging.info('%s = %d' % stat)
```

Available statistics include:

hits
> The number of cache hits counted.

misses
> The number of cache misses counted.

items
> The number of items currently in the cache.

bytes
> The total size of items currently in the cache.

byte_hits
> The total of bytes returned in response to cache hits, including keys and values.

oldest_item_age
> The age of the least recently accessed item in the cache, in milliseconds.

The Python development server includes a memcache viewer in its Console. The viewer lets you query, set, and delete values, and also displays statistics. Refer back to "The Development Console" on page 54 for more information.

The Java Memcache API

As with other services, App Engine includes two Java interfaces to the memcache service. One is a proprietary interface that provides direct access to the features of the service. The other is an implementation of JCache, an interface standard proposed by JSR 107.

As of this writing, JSR 107 is not a ratified standard, and the recommended way to use it on App Engine is in flux. So for now, we'll just consider the proprietary interface. For more information on using the JCache interface with App Engine, consult the App Engine documentation.

The memcache service Java API allows for the use of any serializable object as the key or the value of a key-value pair stored in the cache. Keys whose serialized form is larger than 250 bytes are hashed to 250 bytes. Values can be up to one megabyte in size.

In many cases, you can make a JPA data class serializable simply by declaring that the class implements `Serializable`, with no other changes. If you're using the low-level datastore API, the `Entity` class and all of the property value classes implement the `Serializable` interface.

With App Engine's memcache service Java API, you interact with the service using a `MemcacheService` object, which you get from `MemcacheServiceFactory.getMemcacheService()`. The basic operations are available as methods of `MemcacheService`: `put()`, `get()`, and `delete()`.

```
import com.google.appengine.api.memcache.MemcacheService;
import com.google.appengine.api.memcache.MemcacheServiceFactory;

// ...
        List<String> headlines;
```

```
MemcacheService memcache = MemcacheServiceFactory.getMemcacheService();

memcache.put("headlines", headlines);

headlines = (List<String>) memcache.get("headlines");

memcache.delete("headlines");
```

The put() method takes a key and a value, either of which can be serializable objects. Called with just these two arguments, the new value is stored with no expiration time, and will either create a new value with the given key or replace an existing one, if any.

To set a value with an expiration time, you pass put() an Expiration object as its third argument. You produce this value with a static method in the Expiration class:

```
import com.google.appengine.api.memcache.Expiration;

// ...
        memcache.put("headlines", headlines,
                Expiration.byDeltaSeconds(300));
```

You can use the alternate methods byDeltaMillis(int) for an expiration time in milliseconds, or onDate(java.util.Date) for an expiration time at an absolute time in the future.

To change how put() deals with an existing value with the given key, provide a MemcacheService.SetPolicy enumeration value as the fourth argument. You can use null for the third argument if you don't want to set an expiration.

```
import com.google.appengine.api.memcache.MemcacheService.SetPolicy;

// ...
        memcache.put("headlines", headlines, null,
                SetPolicy.ADD_ONLY_IF_NOT_PRESENT);
```

The three set-policy options are SET_ALWAYS (the default), ADD_ONLY_IF_NOT_PRESENT (only create, do not overwrite), and REPLACE_ONLY_IF_PRESENT (only overwrite, do not create).

You can test whether the cache contains a value with a given key without fetching the value using the contains() method. This method takes a key as its argument, and returns true or false.

```
        boolean headlinesAreCached = memcache.contains("headlines");
```

To delete a value for a given key, you call the delete() method with the key as its argument. You can specify an amount of time during which processes are not allowed to readd the key, as a long integer number of milliseconds in the second argument. This is useful for ensuring that multiple simultaneous worker processes working with the same data do not accidentally undo cache deletes with an update.

```
        memcache.delete("tempnode91512", 5);
```

The low-level API includes methods for setting, fetching, or deleting multiple items in a single batch call. This is faster than making one service call per item. However, the total size of the call and its response is limited to one megabyte.

The `putAll()` method stores multiple values in a batch. It accepts a `Map<Object, Object>` of keys and values as its first argument. It optionally accepts `Expiration` and `SetPolicy` values, like its single-item counterpart.

```java
import java.util.HashMap;
import java.util.Map;

// ...
        Map<Object, Object> articleSummaries = new HashMap<Object, Object>();
        articleSummaries.put("article00174", "...");
        articleSummaries.put("article05234", "...");
        articleSummaries.put("article15820", "...");

        memcache.putAll(articleSummaries);
```

The `getAll()` method fetches multiple items in a batch. It accepts a `Collection<Object>` of keys as its argument, and returns a `Map<Object, Object>` of keys and values for all of the provided keys that were found in the cache.

```java
import java.util.List;

// ...
        List<Object> articleSummaryKeys = Arrays.<Object>asList(
            "article00174",
            "article05234",
            "article15820");

        Map<Object, Object> articleSummaries = memcache.getAll(articleSummaryKeys);
```

The `deleteAll()` method deletes multiple items in a batch. It accepts a `Collection` of keys as its argument. It also optionally accepts a readd lock time in milliseconds as its second argument.

```java
        memcache.deleteAll(articleSummaryKeys);
```

Any memcached value can be stored in a namespace. Namespaces let you segment the key space by the kind of thing you are storing, so you don't have to worry about key collisions between disparate uses of the cache. To use namespaces in the low-level Java API, you set the namespace on the `MemcacheService` by calling its `setNamespace()` method. All subsequent operations use the given namespace when manipulating values.

```java
        memcache.setNamespace("News");
        memcache.put("headlines", headlines);

        memcache.setNamespace("User");
        memcache.put("headlines", userHeadlines);

        // Get User:"headlines".
        userHeadlines = (List<String>) memcache.get("headlines");
```

```
        // Get News:"headlines".
        memcache.setNamespace("News");
        headlines = (List<String>) memcache.get("headlines");
```

If a memcache value is an integer (`int` or `long`), you can increase or decrease the amount atomically—that is, without colliding with other processes doing the same thing—using the `increment()` method. The method takes the key and the amount to increment (which can be negative). It returns the new value (a `Long`), or `null` if there is no value already stored with that key.

```
        memcache.put("work_done", 0);

        // ...

        Long workDone = memcache.increment("work_done", 1);
```

 As of this writing, the Java interface does not support supplying an initial value for an unset cache counter in the same atomic action.

The low-level Java API provides access to more statistics than the JCache API. The `getStatistics()` method returns a `Stats` object, with a method for each of the available stats.

```
    import com.google.appengine.api.memcache.Stats;

    // ...

        Stats stats = memcache.getStatistics();

        int ageOfOldestItemMillis = stats.getMaxTimeWithoutAccess();
```

Available statistics include:

`getHitCount()`
    The number of cache hits counted.

`getMissCount()`
    The number of cache misses counted.

`getItemCount()`
    The number of items currently in the cache.

`getTotalItemBytes()`
    The total size of items currently in the cache.

`getBytesReturnedForHits()`
    The total of bytes returned in response to cache hits, including keys and values.

`getMaxTimeWithoutAccess()`
    The age of the least recently accessed item in the cache, in seconds.

There is no way to explicitly reset the memcache statistics. They are accumulated over the uptime of the service, and so are mostly useful for relative comparisons over brief periods of time.

By default, if the memcache service is unavailable or there is an error accessing the service, the low-level API and the JCache API behave as if keys do not exist. Attempts to put new values fail silently; the four-argument `put()` method will return `false` in this case as if the put failed due to the set policy. Attempts to get values will behave as cache misses.

In the low-level Java API, you can change this behavior by installing an alternate error handler. The `setErrorHandler()` method of `MemcacheService` takes an object that implements the `ErrorHandler` interface. Two such implementations are provided: `LogAndContinueErrorHandler` and `StrictErrorHandler`. The default is `LogAndContinueErrorHandler` with its log level set to `FINE` (the "debug" level in the Administration Console). `StrictErrorHandler` throws `MemcacheServiceException` for all transient service errors.

```
import com.google.appengine.api.memcache.StrictErrorHandler;

// ...
        memcache.setErrorHandler(new StrictErrorHandler());
```

Error handlers can have custom responses for invalid values and service errors. Other kinds of exceptions thrown by the API behave as usual.

## CHAPTER 10

Fetching URLs and Web Resources

An App Engine application can connect to other sites on the Internet to retrieve data and communicate with web services. It does this not by opening a connection to the remote host from the application server, but through a scalable service called the URL Fetch service. This takes the burden of maintaining connections away from the app servers, and ensures that resource fetching performs well regardless of how many request handlers are fetching resources simultaneously. As with other parts of the App Engine infrastructure, the URL Fetch service is used by other Google applications to fetch web pages.

The service supports fetching URLs using the HTTP protocol, and using HTTP with SSL (HTTPS). Other methods sometimes associated with URLs (such as FTP) are not supported. Note that with HTTPS connections, the service can't authenticate the destination of the connection, because there is no certificate trust chain. The service accepts all certificates. This means the connection protocol itself can't protect against "man-in-the-middle" attacks, though the traffic is still encrypted.

Because the URL Fetch service is based on Google infrastructure, the service inherits a few restrictions that were put in place in the original design of the underlying HTTP proxy. The service supports the five most common HTTP actions (GET, POST, PUT, HEAD, and DELETE) but does not allow for others or for using a nonstandard action. Also, it can only connect to the standard TCP ports for each method (80 for HTTP, and 443 for HTTPS). The proxy uses HTTP 1.1 to connect to the remote host.

As a safety measure against accidental request loops in an application, the URL Fetch service cannot fetch the URL that maps to the request handler doing the fetching. An app can make connections to other URLs of its own, so request loops are still possible, but this restriction provides a simple sanity check.

The outgoing request can contain URL parameters, a request body, and HTTP headers. A few headers cannot be modified for security reasons, which mostly means that an app cannot issue a malformed request, such as a request whose Content-Length header does not accurately reflect the actual content length of the request body. In these cases, the service uses the correct values, or does not include the header.

Both the Python and Java runtime environments include interfaces to the URL Fetch service that emulate standard library routines. The Python environment replaces the `urllib` and `urllib2` modules with workalike equivalents that use the URL Fetch service instead of making direct connections. Similarly, the Java environment replaces `java.net.URLConnection` with a service-based implementation. These standard interfaces allow for existing code and third-party components to function in an App Engine app and still meet App Engine's scaling requirements.

These interfaces (and their low-level counterparts) implement *synchronous* URL fetching, where the application waits for the remote host to respond before continuing. The URL Fetch service also supports an *asynchronous* interface that allows the app to trigger fetch requests, do other work, then retrieve results when the requests are ready. This can significantly reduce the amount of clock time spent in a request that relies on a remote host, and allows an app to make multiple URL Fetch connections simultaneously.

 As of this writing, only the Python environment has an asynchronous URL Fetch interface. A similar interface is being developed for Java apps. Check the official App Engine website for updates.

In this chapter, we will introduce the standard and low-level interfaces for fetching URLs synchronously in Python and Java, as well as the asynchronous interface for Python apps.

Fetching URLs in Python

The Python runtime environment overrides portions of the `urllib`, `urllib2`, and `httplib` modules in the Python standard library so that HTTP and HTTPS connections made with these modules use the URL Fetch service. This allows existing software that depends on these libraries to function on App Engine, as long as the requests function within the limitations of the service.

In most cases, if you are writing Python code that fetches URLs, you will want to use the `urllib2` module. This module provides rich extensible support for features of remote web servers such as HTTP authentication and cookies. We won't go into the details of this module here, but Example 10-1 shows a brief example using the module's `urlopen()` convenience function.

Example 10-1. A simple example of using the urllib2 module to access the URL Fetch service

```
import urllib2
from google.appengine.api import urlfetch

# ...
    try:
```

```
        newsfeed = urllib2.urlopen('http://ae-book.appspot.com/blog/atom.xml/')
        newsfeed_xml = newsfeed.read()
    except urllib2.URLError, e:
        # Handle urllib2 error...

    except urlfetch.Error, e:
        # Handle urlfetch error...
```

In this example, we catch both exceptions raised by `urllib2` and exceptions raised from the URL Fetch Python API, `google.appengine.api.urlfetch`. The service may throw one of its own exceptions for conditions that `urllib2` doesn't catch, such as a request exceeding its deadline.

Naturally, not all of the URL Fetch service's features are available in these libraries, and vice versa. When using the standard libraries, the service has the following default behaviors:

- If the remote host doesn't respond within five seconds, the request is canceled and a service exception is raised.
- The service follows HTTP redirects up to five times before returning the response to the application. (A `urllib2` redirect handler will not see most redirects.)
- Responses from remote hosts that exceed one megabyte in size are truncated to one megabyte. The application is not told whether the response is truncated.

If you use the service API directly, you can customize these behaviors. Example 10-2 shows a similar example using the `urlfetch` module, with several options changed.

Example 10-2. Customizing URL Fetch behaviors using the urlfetch module

```
from google.appengine.api import urlfetch

# ...
    try:
        newsfeed = urlfetch.fetch('http://ae-book.appspot.com/blog/atom.xml/',
                            allow_truncated=False,
                            follow_redirects=False,
                            deadline=10)
        newsfeed_xml = newsfeed.content
    except urlfetch.Error, e:
        # Handle urlfetch error...
```

The `fetch()` function in the `google.appengine.api.urlfetch` module calls the service to fetch a URL, waits for the response, then returns an object that represents the result. The first and only required argument to this function is the full URL, including the `http://` or `https://` and the full host name. (You cannot use a "relative" URL path to request a URL of the application doing the requesting. You can derive an appropriate hostname from the handler's own request data, if you need to.)

The remaining arguments to the function are all optional. They specify the payload (the request body, empty by default), the method (default is GET), and any additional headers to include (as a dict-like value).

The allow_truncated argument specifies what to do if the response from the remote host is larger than the maximum supported size of one megabyte. If set to True, the service truncates the response to one megabyte before returning it to the application. If False, the service raises a urlfetch.ResponseTooLargeError when this happens. The default when calling fetch() is False. Using the standard libraries (urllib2 et al.) sets this to True, so there is one fewer custom exception you need to catch.

The follow_redirects argument tells the service how to handle HTTP redirect codes (HTTP response codes 301 and 302, accompanied by a Location header specifying a new URL). If True, the service will follow HTTP redirects and return the final page to the application. If the service encounters more than five consecutive redirects, it stops at the fifth and returns the last redirect response to the app. If this argument is False, the service returns whatever the remote host returned for the requested URL, which may be an HTTP redirect. The argument's default value is True.

Lastly, the deadline argument tells the service how long to wait for the remote host to respond. The default is 5 seconds, and you can set this to anywhere from 1 to 10 seconds. If the fetch exceeds the deadline, the service raises a urlfetch.Error. (As of this writing, there is no exception class for this specific condition.)

The Python development server simulates the URL Fetch service by making HTTP connections directly from your computer. If the remote host might behave differently when your app connects from your computer rather than from Google's proxy servers, be sure to test your URL Fetch calls on App Engine.

Fetching URLs in Java

The Java runtime includes a custom implementation of the URLConnection class in the JRE-standard java.net package that calls the URL Fetch service instead of making a direct socket connection. As with the other standard interfaces, you can use this interface and rest assured that you can port your app to another platform easily.

Example 10-3 shows a simple example of using a convenience method in the URL class, which in turn uses the URLConnection class, to fetch the contents of a web page. The openStream() method of the URL object returns an input stream of bytes. As shown, you can use an InputStreamReader (from java.io) to process the byte stream as a character stream. The BufferedReader class makes it easy to read lines of text from the InputStreamReader.

Example 10-3. Using java.net.URL to call the URL Fetch service

```java
import java.net.URL;
import java.net.MalformedURLException;
import java.io.IOException;
import java.io.InputStream;
import java.io.InputStreamReader;
import java.io.BufferedReader;

// ...
        try {
            URL url = new URL("http://ae-book.appspot.com/blog/atom.xml/");
            InputStream inStream = url.openStream();

            InputStreamReader inStreamReader = new InputStreamReader(inStream);
            BufferedReader reader = new BufferedReader(inStreamReader);
            // ... read characters or lines with reader ...
            reader.close();

        } catch (MalformedURLException e) {
            // ...
        } catch (IOException e) {
            // ...
        }
```

Note that the URL Fetch service has already buffered the entire response into the application's memory by the time the app begins to read. The app reads the response data from memory, not from a network stream from the socket or the service.

You can use other features of the URLConnection interface, as long as they operate within the functionality of the service API. Notably, the URL Fetch service does not maintain a persistent connection with the remote host, so features that require such a connection will not work.

By default, the URL Fetch service waits up to five seconds for a response from the remote server. If the server does not respond by the deadline, the service throws an IOException. You can adjust the amount of time to wait using the setConnectTimeout() method of the URLConnection. (The setReadTimeout() method has the same effect; the service uses the greater of the two values.) The deadline can be between 1 and 10 seconds.

When using the URLConnection interface, the URL Fetch service follows HTTP redirects automatically, up to five consecutive redirects.

The low-level API for the URL Fetch service lets you customize several behaviors of the service. Example 10-4 demonstrates how to fetch a URL with this API with options specified. As shown, the FetchOptions object tells the service not to follow any redirects, and to throw a ResponseTooLargeException if the response exceeds the maximum size of one megabyte instead of truncating the data.

Example 10-4. Using the low-level API to call the URL Fetch service, with options

```java
import java.net.URL;
import java.net.MalformedURLException;
import com.google.appengine.api.urlfetch.FetchOptions;
import com.google.appengine.api.urlfetch.HTTPResponse;
import com.google.appengine.api.urlfetch.ResponseTooLargeException;
import com.google.appengine.api.urlfetch.URLFetchService;
import com.google.appengine.api.urlfetch.URLFetchServiceFactory;

// ...
        try {
            URL url = new URL("http://ae-book.appspot.com/blog/atom.xml/");

            FetchOptions options = FetchOptions.Builder
                .doNotFollowRedirects()
                .disallowTruncate();
            HTTPRequest request = new HTTPRequest(url, HTTPMethod.GET, options);

            URLFetchService service = URLFetchServiceFactory.getURLFetchService();
            HTTPResponse response = service.fetch(request);
            // ... process response.content ...

        } catch (ResponseTooLargeException e) {
            // ...
        } catch (MalformedURLException e) {
            // ...
        } catch (IOException e) {
            // ...
        }
```

The Java development server simulates the URL Fetch service by making HTTP connections directly from your computer. Be sure to test that your app can access the URLs it needs when running on App Engine.

Asynchronous Requests in Python

All of the calls to the URL Fetch service we've seen so far in this chapter have been *synchronous* calls: the app asks the service to fetch a URL, then waits for the service to return the result. But time is precious within a web request, and waiting for a remote host to return data is likely to be the most time-consuming part of a request handler. If the handler must fetch more than one URL, these wait times add up as the app must wait for the first host to respond before starting the next fetch. But while the service is busy fetching URLs, the app server is doing nothing. The app could be using this valuable clock time to perform other tasks.

To support this, the URL Fetch service supports *asynchronous* calls. With an asynchronous call, the app starts a URL fetch by calling the service with the request data as usual. But unlike a synchronous call, this call returns immediately, and the app can continue doing other things. When the app needs the results, it makes another call to the service, and the service returns the results. The app can fetch multiple URLs simultaneously, and the URL Fetch service performs the fetches in parallel.

Figure 10-1 shows the sequence of events for a synchronous call and an asynchronous call. As shown, if the fetch is not complete when the app asks for results, the app waits for the remainder of the duration. If the fetch is complete by the time the app asks for results, the service returns the results (or an error message) immediately.

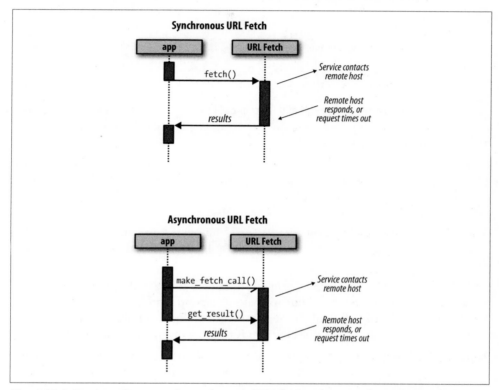

Figure 10-1. Sequence diagrams of a synchronous URL fetch and an asynchronous URL fetch

Example 10-5 demonstrates a simple asynchronous call to the URL Fetch service. The `create_rpc()` function returns an object that represents the asynchronous call ("remote procedure call," or RPC). The `make_fetch_call()` function initiates the fetch for the given URL and associates it with the given RPC object, then returns immediately. Finally, calling the `get_result()` method of the RPC object waits for the fetch to finish, and returns the result.

Example 10-5. Fetching URLs in the background using the asynchronous URL Fetch API

```
from google.appengine.api import urlfetch

# ...
    try:
        rpc = urlfetch.create_rpc()
        urlfetch.make_fetch_call(rpc, 'http://ae-book.appspot.com/blog/atom.xml/')

        # Do other things.

        newsfeed = rpc.get_result()
        newsfeed_xml = newsfeed.content

    except urlfetch.Error, e:
        # Handle urlfetch error...
```

If the app does nothing between make_fetch_call() and rpc.get_result(), it behaves as if it made a synchronous call. In fact, this is precisely how the synchronous fetch() function is implemented.

You can specify a fetch deadline of up to 10 seconds by passing a deadline argument to create_rpc(). The default deadline is five seconds. If the remote host does not respond before the deadline elapses, the fetch is canceled, and the API raises a DownloadError when you attempt to access the results.

The make_fetch_call() function accepts the same request parameters as the fetch() function, including the url, payload, method, headers, allow_truncated, and follow_redirects.

The development server simulates asynchronous calls to the URL Fetch service by performing them synchronously. If your app would respond significantly faster when using asynchronous fetches, especially if the app makes multiple simultaneous fetches, you won't notice the time savings until the app is running on App Engine.

Note that the Python standard libraries (urllib2 et al.) only support synchronous calls. To take advantage of asynchronous calls, you must use the urlfetch interface.

RPC Objects

The RPC object represents the call throughout the process. An RPC object can only represent one call. If you are fetching multiple URLs, you must create an RPC object for each fetch by calling the create_rpc() function.

The RPC object advances through four states during its lifetime:

1. Created. The object has been created, but has not been associated with a fetch call.

2. In progress. A fetch has been initiated and associated with the object.

3. Ready. The fetch has completed, either with results or with an error.

4. Checked. The status of the fetch has been reported to the application, such as by having raised an exception to represent an error.

In the simple example just given, `create_rpc()` created the object in its initial "created" state, and `make_fetch_call()` advanced it to its "in progress" state. Calling the object's `get_result()` method advanced it to the "ready" state by waiting for the fetch to finish, then advanced it to the "checked" state by verifying the results and raising an exception if necessary.

You can advance the object through the last two states manually using methods. The `wait()` method waits for the fetch to finish ("in progress" to "ready"). The `check_result()` method verifies and reports the final status ("ready" to "checked"). Calling any of these methods advances the object to the appropriate state, performing the tasks along the way. If the starting state for the method has already passed, such as calling `wait()` when in the "ready" state, the method does nothing.

Figure 10-2 illustrates the RPC object states and transitions.

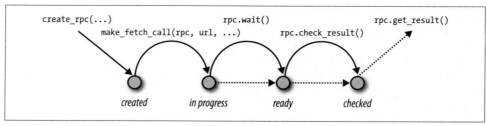

Figure 10-2. The URL Fetch RPC object states and transitions

Processing Results with Callbacks

To make the most of the parallel execution of asynchronous URL fetching, the request handler should initiate the fetch as soon as possible in the handler's lifetime. This can be as straightforward as creating the RPC objects and calling `make_fetch_call()` at the top of a routine, and calling the `get_results()` method at the point in the routine where the results are needed. If your handler uses multiple diverse components to perform tasks, and each component may require that URLs be fetched, you could have the main routine ask each component to initiate its fetches, then allow the components to get their own results as control reaches the appropriate points in the code.

The URL Fetch RPC object offers another way to organize the code that handles the results of fetches: callbacks. A callback is a function associated with the RPC object that is called when the RPC's fetch has completed, during the transition from the "in progress" state to the "ready" state. In other words, an RPC's callback function is called if the RPC is in the "in progress" state and the app calls the `wait()`, `check_results()`, or `get_results()` method.

The callback function is called without arguments. But a common use for a callback function is to process the results of the fetch, so the function needs access to the RPC object. There are several ways to give the callback function access to the object.

One way is to use a *bound method*, a feature of Python that lets you refer to a method of an instance of a class as a callable object. Define a class with a method that processes the results of the fetch, using an RPC object stored as a member of the class. Create an instance of the class, then create the RPC object, assigning the bound method as the callback by passing it as the `callback` argument to the `create_rpc()` function. Example 10-6 demonstrates this technique.

Example 10-6. Using an object method as a callback to access the RPC object

```
from google.appengine.api import urlfetch

# ...
class CatalogUpdater(object):
    def prepare_urlfetch_rpc(self):
        self.rpc = urlfetch.create_rpc(callback=self.process_results)
        urlfetch.make_fetch_call(self.rpc, 'http://api.example.com/catalog_feed')
        return self.rpc

    def process_results(self):
        try:
            results = self.rpc.get_result()
            # Process results.content...

        except urlfetch.Error, e:
            # Handle urlfetch errors...

class MainHandler(webapp.RequestHandler):
    def get(self):
        rpcs = []

        catalog_updater = CatalogUpdater(self.response)
        rpcs.append(catalog_updater.prepare_urlfetch_rpc())

        # ...

        for rpc in rpcs:
            rpc.wait()
```

Another way to give the callback access to the RPC object is to use a *nested function* (sometimes called a *closure*). If the callback function is defined in the same scope as a variable whose value is the RPC object, the function can access the variable when it is called. To allow for this style of calling, the URL Fetch API lets you assign the callback function to the RPC object's `callback` property after the object has been created.

Example 10-7 demonstrates the use of a nested function as a callback. The `create_callback()` function creates a function object, a `lambda` expression, that calls another function with the RPC object as an argument. This function object is assigned to the `callback` property of the RPC object.

Example 10-7. Using a nested function as a callback to access the RPC object

```python
from google.appengine.api import urlfetch

def process_results(rpc):
    try:
        results = self.rpc.get_result()
        # Process results.content...

    except urlfetch.Error, e:
        # Handle urlfetch errors...

def create_callback(rpc):
    # Use a function to define the scope for the lambda.
    return lambda: process_results(rpc)

# ...

        rpc = urlfetch.create_rpc()
        rpc.callback = create_callback(rpc)
        urlfetch.make_fetch_call(self.rpc, 'http://api.example.com/catalog_feed')

        # ...

        rpc.wait()
```

If you've used other programming languages that support function objects, the `create_callback()` function may seem unnecessary. Why not create the function object directly where it is used? In Python, the scope of an inner function is the outer function, including its variables. If the outer function redefines the variable containing the RPC object (`rpc`), when the inner function is called it will use that value. By wrapping the creation of the inner function in a dedicated outer function, the value of `rpc` in the scope of the callback is always set to the intended object.

Someone still needs to call the `wait()` method on the RPC object so the callback can be called. But herein lies the value of callbacks: the component that calls `wait()` does not have to know anything about what needs to be done with the results. The main routine can query its subcomponents to prepare and return RPC objects, then later it can call `wait()` on each of the objects. The callbacks assigned by the subcomponents are called to process each result.

If you have multiple asynchronous fetches in progress simultaneously, the callback for a fetch is called if the fetch finishes during any call to `wait()`–even if the `wait()` is for another fetch's RPC object. Of course, the `wait()` doesn't return until the fetch for its own RPC object finishes and its callbacks are called. A callback is only called once: if you call `wait()` for a fetch whose callback has already been called, it does nothing and returns immediately.

If your code makes multiple simultaneous fetches, be sure not to rely on a fetch's callback being called only during its RPC object's `wait()`.

## CHAPTER 11

Sending and Receiving Mail and Instant Messages

App Engine apps can communicate with the outside world in three ways. The first method we covered in Chapter 10: an app can receive and respond to HTTP requests, and an app can initiate HTTP requests and get responses with the URL Fetch service.

The second method of networked communication available to apps is email. An app can send email messages by calling the Mail service with message data and a list of recipients. An app can also receive email messages at any of several addresses monitored by App Engine.

The third method is instant messages, specifically the XMPP protocol. An app can participate in a chat dialog with a user of any XMPP-compatible chat service, including Google Talk and any Jabber server. An app can also use XMPP to communicate with custom clients via such services. App Engine does not act as an XMPP service itself; instead, it connects to Google Talk's infrastructure to participate as a chat user.

An app might send email to notify users of system events or the actions of other users (such as to send social networking invitations), confirm user actions (such as to confirm an order), follow up on long-term user actions (such as to send a shipping notice for an order), or send system notifications to administrators. The app can send email on behalf of itself, the app's administrators, or the currently signed-in user (during the request handler that's sending the email).

An app can receive email sent to specific addresses, such as to provide an email interface to the application, or to moderate or monitor email discussions. An app can reply to the email immediately, or set up work that causes a reply to be sent later.

The XMPP service is useful for chat interfaces, such as a chat-based query engine. With a custom client (like a mobile phone client, or Flash in a browser) and an XMPP server or chat service (like Google Talk), the app can use XMPP to push real-time updates to clients. App Engine doesn't run its own XMPP server, so clients would connect to the chat service (using an account on that service) to communicate with the app.

Sending email and chat messages is similar to initiating HTTP requests: the app calls a service using an API, and the service takes care of making remote connections and managing the appropriate protocols. Unlike the URL Fetch service, the Mail and XMPP services do not return a response immediately.

Receiving email and chat messages is also similar to receiving HTTP requests. In fact, they use the same mechanism: request handlers. When a service receives an email or XMPP message intended for your app, the service sends an HTTP request to the app using a specified URL with the message in the HTTP payload. The app processes incoming messages using request handlers mapped to the specified URLs. The service ignores the response for the request; if the app needs to reply to the user, it can send a message using the API.

Figure 11-1 illustrates the flow of incoming email and XMPP messages.

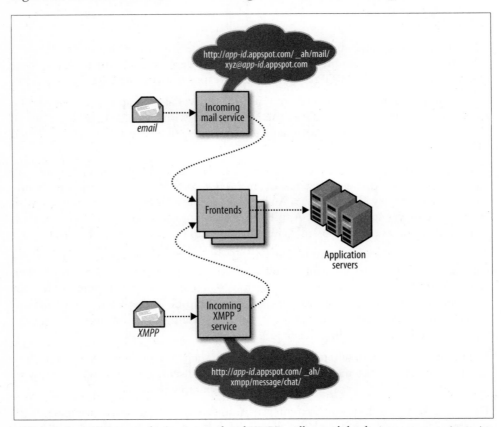

Figure 11-1. Architecture of incoming mail and XMPP, calling web hooks in response to incoming message events

Every app has its own set of email and XMPP addresses, based on its application ID. App Engine does not currently support email and XMPP addresses with custom domains.

An app can also receive messages at arbitrary addresses with an app-specific domain name. For email, the app can receive messages at addresses of these forms:

app-id@appspotmail.com

anything@*app-id*.appspotmail.com

For XMPP chat, the app can receive messages at addresses of these forms (note the differences in the domain names):

app-id@appspot.com

anything@*app-id*.appspotchat.com

In this chapter, we'll discuss the APIs for sending and receiving email and XMPP messages, and language-specific tools for creating and processing those messages.

Enabling Inbound Services

Incoming email and XMPP messages are disabled by default. If an app has an inbound service disabled, then messages sent to an app's address are ignored, and the service will never attempt to access the app at a web hook URL.

To enable inbound services, you add a section to the app's configuration file. In Python, you add a section similar to the following in the *app.yaml* file:

```
inbound_services:
- mail
- xmpp_message
```

In Java, you add a similar section to the *appengine-web.xml* file, anywhere inside the root element:

```
<inbound-services>
  <service>mail</service>
  <service>xmpp_message</service>
</inbound-services>
```

These examples enable both services. You can omit one service to keep it disabled while enabling the other.

Once your app is deployed, you can confirm that these services are enabled from the Administration Console, under Application Settings. If your app does not appear to be receiving HTTP requests for incoming messages, check the Console and update the configuration if necessary.

Sending Email Messages

To send an email message, you call the API of the Mail service. The outgoing message has a sender address ("From"), one or more recipients ("To", "Cc", or "Bcc"), a subject, a message body, and optional file attachments.

A outgoing message can have only these fields, and cannot use other email message headers. The Mail service attaches additional headers to the message for tracking purposes, such as the date and time the message is sent.

You can specify a multipart message body, such as to include both plain text and HTML versions of the message, and to include attachments. The total size of the message, including all headers, cannot exceed one megabyte.

The call to the Mail service is asynchronous. When your application calls the Mail service to send a message, the message is enqueued for delivery, and the service call returns. If there is a problem delivering the message, such as if the remote mail server cannot be contacted or the remote server says the address is invalid, an error message is sent via email to the sender address. The app is not notified of the failure by the service directly. (You can use an incoming email address for the app as the sender address. The app will have to parse the message sent by the remote server for an error.)

When your app runs in the development server, sending a message causes the server to print information about the message to the logs, and no message is sent. In the Python development server only, you can configure the server to actually send email messages using either Sendmail (if it's set up on your machine) or an SMTP server.

To configure the Python development server to use Sendmail to send email, give the server the `--enable_sendmail` flag:

```
dev_appserver.py --enable_sendmail appdir
```

To configure the Python development server to use an SMTP server to send email, use the `--smtp_host=...` (with optional `--smtp_port=...`), `--smtp_user=...`, and `--smtp_password=...` arguments:

```
dev_appserver.py \
    --smtp_host=smtp.example.com \
    --smtp_user=exmail \
    --smtp_password="t3!!t43wOr!d" \
    appdir
```

The Java development server does not support sending email; it just logs the message at the "info" log level. You can adjust the level at which outgoing mail messages are logged by running the development server with the `mail.log_mail_level` property set to a value such as `WARNING`. You can also tell the development server to log the body of the message by setting the `mail.log_mail_body` system property to `true`. From the command line:

```
dev_appserver.sh \
    --jvm_flag=-Dmail.log_mail_level=WARNING \
```

```
  --jvm_flag=-Dmail.log_message_body=true \
  appdir
```

From Eclipse, select the Run menu, Debug Configurations..., and then select your app's configuration. Select the Arguments tab, then in the "VM arguments" section, set VM properties like this:

```
-Dmail.log_mail_level=WARNING -Dmail.log_mail_body=true
```

Sender Addresses

The sender ("From") address on an outgoing email message must be one of the allowed addresses:

- The Google Account address of one of the application administrators
- The address of the user currently signed in to the app with Google Accounts (during the request handler that is sending the message)
- A valid incoming email address for the application

Replies to messages sent by the app go to the sender address, as do error messages sent by the outgoing mail server (such as "Could not connect to remote host") or the remote mail server (such as "User not found").

You can use an application developer's Google Account address as the sender address. To add accounts as application administrators, go to the Developers section of the Administration Console. If you do not want to use the account of a specific developer as the sender address, you can create a new Google Account for a general purpose address, then add it as a developer for the app. Make sure you protect the password of the address's Google account, since anyone who can sign in to that account can modify your application. You can use Gmail to monitor the account for replies, and you can set up automatic email forwarding in Gmail to relay replies to specific administrators or a mailing list (or Google Group) automatically.

 You can create a Gmail account using the application ID, and add *app-id*@gmail.com as a developer. Note that if you create the Gmail account before you register the application ID, you must be signed in using the Gmail account when you register the application ID. App Engine won't let you register an app ID that matches a Gmail account name unless you are signed in with that account.

Technically it's possible for someone else to register a Gmail account with your app ID after you have registered the app ID, though it's unlikely. If you'd like to claim your ID as a Gmail address, do it soon. Of course, the owner of the Gmail account can't administer your app unless you add the account as a developer.

You can use the email address of a user as the sender address if and only if the address is of a registered Google Account, and the user is signed in and initiated the request whose handler is sending the email. That is, you can send email on behalf of the "current" user. This is useful if the email is triggered by the user's action and if replies to the message ought to go to the user's email address. The Google Accounts API does not expose the user's human-readable name, so you won't be able to provide that unless you get it from the user yourself.

As we mentioned earlier, an application can receive email messages at addresses of the form `app-id@appspotmail.com` or `anything@app-id.appspotmail.com`, where `app-id` is your application ID and `anything` can be any string that's valid on the left side of the email address (it can't contain an @ symbol). You can use an incoming email address as the sender of an email message to have replies routed to a request handler.

The "anything" lets you create custom sender addresses on the fly. For example, a customer support app could start an email conversation with a unique ID and include the ID in the email address (`support+ID@app-id.appspotmail.com`), and save replies for that conversation in the datastore so the entire thread can be viewed by customer service personnel.

Note that the sender address will also receive error ("bounce") messages. If you use an incoming mail address as the sender, you could have the app process error messages to remove invalid email addresses automatically. Note that different remote email servers may use different formatting for error messages.

Any email address can also have a human-friendly name, such as `"The Example Team <admin@example.com>"`. How you do this is specific to the interface; we'll look at the interfaces in a moment.

You can include a separate "Reply-to" address in addition to the sender ("From") address. Most mail readers and servers will use this address instead of the sender address for replies and error messages. The "Reply-to" address must meet the same requirements as the sender address.

The development server does not check that the sender address meets these conditions because it doesn't know who the app's developers are. Be sure to test features that send email while running on App Engine.

Recipients

An outgoing email message can use any address for a recipient, and can have multiple recipients.

A recipient can be a primary recipient (the "To" field), a secondary or "carbon-copied" recipient (the "Cc" field), or a "blind carbon-copied" recipient ("Bcc"). The "To" and "Cc" recipients are included in the content of the message, so a reply intended for all recipients can be sent to the visible addresses. The "Bcc" recipients receive the message, but their addresses are not included in the content of the message, and so are not included in replies.

The "Bcc" recipient type is especially useful if you want a single message to go to multiple recipients, but you do not want any recipient to know who received the message. You can use this technique to send an email newsletter to users without exposing the users' email addresses. A common technique for newsletters is to use the sender address as the sole "To" recipient, and make everyone else a "Bcc" recipient.

The number of recipients for an email message counts toward an email recipient quota. This quota is initially small to prevent unsolicited email advertisers from abusing the system. You can raise this quota by allocating part of your budget toward email recipients.

Attachments

An app can attach files to an email message. For security reasons (mostly having to do with insecure email clients), only certain types of files are allowed as attachments. Filenames must end in an extension that reflects the file's type. Table 11-1 lists the allowed types and the corresponding allowed filename extensions.

Table 11-1. The file types allowed for email attachments, and their required filename extensions

MIME content type	Filename extension	Description
application/pdf	.pdf	Portable Document Format (PDF)
application/rss+xml	.rss	RSS feed
image/gif	.gif	GIF image
image/jpeg	.jpeg, .jpg, .jpe	JPEG image
image/png	.png	PNG image
image/tiff	.tiff, .tif	TIFF image
image/vnd.wap.wbmp	.wbmp	WAP bitmap image
image/x-ms-bmp	.bmp	Microsoft Windows bitmap image
text/calendar	.ics	iCalendar event invitation
text/comma-separated-values	.csv	Comma-separated values spreadsheet
text/css	.css	Cascading stylesheet for HTML
text/html	.html, .htm	HTML document
text/plain	.text, .txt, .asc, .diff, .pot	Plain text
text/x-vcard	.vcf	vCard electronic business card

These types are usually enough for rich email content, but not necessarily for business documents or desktop applications. If you want to deliver other kinds of files to users, one option is to send a link to a request handler that delivers the file through the browser. The link can be personalized with a temporary unique ID, or restricted using Google Accounts authentication.

Sending Email in Python

The Python API includes two ways of preparing and sending messages. One way is to call a function with the fields of the message as keyword arguments. Another is to prepare the message in an object, then call a method on the object to send the message. The Mail service API is provided by the `google.appengine.api.mail` package.

The `send_mail()` method takes the fields of the message as parameters:

```
from google.appengine.api import mail
from google.appengine.api import users

message_body = '''
Welcome to Example!  Your account has been created.
You can edit your user profile by clicking the
following link:

http://www.example.com/profile/

Let us know if you have any questions.

The Example Team
'''

# (admin@example.com is a Google Account that has
# been added as a developer for the app.)
mail.send_mail(
    sender='The Example Team <admin@example.com>',
    to=users.get_current_user().email(),
    subject='Welcome to Example.com!',
    body=message_body)
```

Alternatively, you can prepare the message using an `EmailMessage` object, then call its `send()` method. The `EmailMessage` constructor accepts the same arguments as the `send_mail()` function:

```
message = mail.EmailMessage(
    sender='The Example Team <admin@example.com>',
    to=users.get_current_user().email(),
    subject='Welcome to Example.com!',
    body=message_body)

message.send()
```

You can also set the fields of an `EmailMessage` using attributes of the object. This allows you to reuse the same object to send multiple messages with modified values.

The possible fields of a message are listed in Table 11-2.

Table 11-2. Fields of an email message in the Python interface

Field	Value	Required?
sender	The sender's email address. A string.	*Required*
to	A "To" recipient address as a string, or multiple "To" recipient addresses as a list of strings.	*Required*
cc	A "Cc" recipient address as a string, or multiple "Cc" recipient addresses as a list of strings.	*Optional*
bcc	A "Bcc" recipient address as a string, or multiple "Bcc" recipient addresses as a list of strings. "Bcc" recipients receive the message, but are not included in the content of the message.	*Optional*
reply_to	An alternate address to which clients should send replies instead of the sender address. A string.	*Optional*
subject	The subject of the message. A string.	*Required*
body	The plain-text body of the message. A string.	*Required*
html	An alternate HTML representation of the body of the message, displayed instead of body by HTML-capable email readers. A string.	*Optional*
attachments	File attachments for the message. A list of tuples, one per attachment, each containing the filename and the file data.	*Optional*

The value of an email address field (sender, to, cc, bcc, reply_to) can be a plain email address:

```
'juliet@example.com'
```

It can also be an address with a human-readable name, in the standard format (RFC 822):

```
'Juliet <juliet@example.com>'
```

When you call the send() method or the send_mail() function, the API checks the message to make sure it is valid. This includes testing the email addresses for validity, and making sure the message has all of the required fields. You can call functions to perform these checks separately. The is_email_valid(address) function returns True if it considers an email address valid. The is_initialized() method of an EmailAddress object returns True if the object has all of the fields necessary for sending.

The API includes a shortcut method that sends an email message to all administrators (developers) for the application. The send_mail_to_admins() function accepts the same arguments as send_mail(), but without the recipient fields. There is also an AdminEmailMessage class that is similar to the EmailMessage class, but with recipients set to be the app administrators automatically. When calling this function, the message size is limited to 16 kilobytes. (This is a safety limit that ensures delivery of important administrative messages.)

Example 11-1 shows a larger example using EmailMessage, with both plain-text and HTML parts, and an attachment.

Example 11-1. An example of sending an email message in Python, using several features

```python
from google.appengine.api import mail

def send_registration_key(user_addr, software_key_data):
    message_body = '''
Thank you for purchasing The Example App, the best
example on the market!  Your registration key is attached
to this email.

To install your key, download the attachment, then select
"Register..." from the Help menu.  Select the key file, then
click "Register".

You can download the app at any time from:
  http://www.example.com/downloads/

Thanks again!

The Example Team
'''

    html_message_body = '''
<p>Thank you for purchasing The Example App, the best
example on the market!  Your registration key is attached
to this email.</p>

<p>To install your key, download the attachment, then select
<b>Register...</b> from the <b>Help</b> menu.  Select the key file, then
click <b>Register</b>.</p>

<p>You can download the app at any time from:</p>

<p>
  <a href="http://www.example.com/downloads/">
    http://www.example.com/downloads/
  </a>
</p>

<p>Thanks again!</p>

<p>The Example Team<br />
<img src="http://www.example.com/images/logo_email.gif" /></p>
'''

    message = mail.EmailMessage(
        sender='The Example Team &lt;admin@example.com&gt;',
        to=user_addr,
        subject='Your Example Registration Key',
        body=message_body,
        html=html_message_body,
        attachments=[('example_key.txt', software_key_data)])

    message.send()
```

Sending Email in Java

The Java interface to the Mail service is the JavaMail standard interface (`javax.mail.*`). There is also a low-level interface, though you can access every feature of the service through the JavaMail implementation. (As such, we'll only discuss the JavaMail interface here.)

To use JavaMail, you first create a JavaMail "session." The `Session` object usually contains information needed to connect to a mail server, but with App Engine, no configuration is needed. You prepare the message as a `MimeMessage` object, then send it using the `send()` static method of the `Transport` class. The `Transport` class uses the most recently created session to send the message.

```java
import java.util.Properties;
import javax.mail.Message;
import javax.mail.MessagingException;
import javax.mail.Session;
import javax.mail.Transport;
import javax.mail.internet.AddressException;
import javax.mail.internet.InternetAddress;
import javax.mail.internet.MimeMessage;

import com.google.appengine.api.users.User;
import com.google.appengine.api.users.UserServiceFactory;

// ...
        User user = UserServiceFactory.getUserService().getCurrentUser();
        String recipientAddress = user.getEmail();

        Properties props = new Properties();
        Session session = Session.getDefaultInstance(props, null);

        String messageBody =
            "Welcome to Example!  Your account has been created." +
            "You can edit your user profile by clicking the" +
            "following link:\n\n" +
            "http://www.example.com/profile/\n\n" +
            "Let us know if you have any questions.\n\n" +
            "The Example Team\n";

        try {
            Message message = new MimeMessage(session);
            message.setFrom(new InternetAddress("admin@example.com",
                                                "The Example Team"));
            message.addRecipient(Message.RecipientType.TO,
                        new InternetAddress(recipientAddress));
            message.setSubject("Welcome to Example.com!");
            message.setText(messageBody);
            Transport.send(message);

        } catch (AddressException e) {
            // An email address was invalid.
            // ...
        } catch (MessagingException e) {
```

```
            // There was an error contacting the Mail service.
            // ...
    }
```

As shown here, you call methods on the `MimeMessage` to set fields and to add recipients and content. The simplest message has a sender (`setFrom()`), one "To" recipient (`addRecipient()`), a subject (`setSubject()`), and a plain-text message body (`setText()`).

The `setFrom()` method takes an `InternetAddress`. You can create an `InternetAddress` with just the email address (a `String`) or the address and a human-readable name as arguments to the constructor. The email address of the sender must meet the requirements described earlier. You can use any string for the human-readable name.

The `addRecipient()` method takes a recipient type and an `InternetAddress`. The allowed recipient types are `Message.RecipientType.TO` ("To," a primary recipient), `Message.RecipientType.CC` ("Cc" or "carbon-copy," a secondary recipient), and `Message.RecipientType.BCC` ("Bcc" or "blind carbon-copy," where the recipient is sent the message but the address does not appear in the message content). You can call `addRecipient()` multiple times to add multiple recipients of any type.

The `setText()` method sets the plain-text body for the message. To include an HTML version of the message body for mail readers that support HTML, you create a `MimeMultipart` object, then create a `MimeBodyPart` for the plain-text body and another for the HTML body and add them to the `MimeMultipart`. You then make the `MimeMultipart` the content of the `MimeMessage`:

```java
import javax.mail.Multipart;
import javax.mail.internet.MimeBodyPart;
import javax.mail.internet.MimeMultipart;

// ...
        String textBody = "...text...";
        String htmlBody = "...HTML...";

        Multipart multipart = new MimeMultipart();

        MimeBodyPart textPart = new MimeBodyPart();
        textPart.setContent(textBody, "text/plain");
        multipart.addBodyPart(htmlPart);

        MimeBodyPart htmlPart = new MimeBodyPart();
        htmlPart.setContent(htmlBody, "text/html");
        multipart.addBodyPart(htmlPart);

        message.setContent(multipart);
```

You attach files to the email message in a similar way:

```java
        Multipart multipart = new MimeMultipart();
        // ...

        byte[] fileData = getBrochureData();
        String fileName = "brochure.pdf";
```

```
String fileType = "application/pdf";

MimeBodyPart attachmentPart = new MimeBodyPart();
attachmentPart.setContent(fileData, fileType);
attachmentPart.setFileName(fileName);
multipart.addBodyPart(attachmentPart);

// ...
message.setContent(multipart);
```

Remember that an attachment must be of one of the approved types, and must have a filename that ends with a corresponding filename extension, as listed in Table 11-1.

You can add multiple `MimeBodyPart` objects to a single `MimeMultipart`. The plain-text body, the HTML body, and the file attachments are each part of a MIME multipart message.

When using a `MimeMultipart`, you must include a `text/plain` part to be the plain-text body of the message. The multipart object overrides any plain-text content set on the `MimeMessage` with `setText()`.

App Engine's implementation of the JavaMail interface includes a shortcut for sending an email message to all of the app's administrators. To send a message to all administrators, use a recipient address of `"admins"`, with no @ symbol or domain name.

Receiving Email Messages

With the `mail` inbound service enabled in configuration, an application can receive email messages at any of several addresses. An incoming mail message is routed to the app in the form of an HTTP request.

Email sent to addresses of the following forms are routed to the default version of the app:

app-id@appspotmail.com

anything@*app-id*.appspotmail.com

The HTTP request uses the POST action, and is sent to the following URL path:

/_ah/mail/*to-address*

The recipient email address of the message is included at the end of the URL path, so the app can distinguish between different values of "anything."

The body content of the HTTP POST request is the complete MIME email message, including the mail headers and body. It can be parsed by any library capable of parsing MIME email messages. We'll look at examples in Python and Java in the next two sections.

The development server console (`http://localhost:8080/_ah/admin/`) includes a feature for simulating incoming email by submitting a web form. The development server cannot receive actual email messages.

 If the app has the incoming mail service enabled but does not have a request handler for the appropriate URL, or if the request handler returns an HTTP response code other than 200 for the request, the message gets "bounced" and the sender receives an error email message.

Receiving Email in Python

To receive email in Python, you map the incoming email URL path to a script handler in *app.yaml* file:

```
handlers:
- url: /_ah/mail/.+
    script: handle_email.py
```

The app address used for the message is included in the URL path, so you can set up separate handlers for different addresses directly in the configuration:

```
handlers:
- url: /_ah/mail/support%40.*app-id\.appspotmail\.com
    script: support_contact.py
- url: /_ah/mail/.+
    script: handle_email.py
```

Email addresses are URL-encoded in the final URL, so this pattern uses %40 to represent an @ symbol. Also notice you must include a .* before the application ID when using this technique, so the pattern works for messages sent to version-specific addresses (such as support@dev.latest.*app-id*.appspotmail.com).

The Python SDK includes a class for parsing the POST content into a convenient object, called `InboundEmailMessage` (in the `google.appengine.api.mail` package). It takes the multipart MIME data (the POST body) as an argument to its constructor. Here's an example using the webapp framework:

```python
from google.appengine.api import mail
from google.appengine.ext import webapp
from google.appengine.ext.webapp.util import run_wsgi_app

class IncomingMailHandler(webapp.RequestHandler):
    def post(self):
        message = mail.InboundEmailMessage(self.request.body)
        # sender = message.sender
        # recipients = message.to
        # body = list(message.bodies(content_type='text/plain'))[0]
        # ...

application = webapp.WSGIApplication([('/_ah/mail/.+', IncomingMailHandler)],
                                     debug=True)
```

```
def main():
    run_wsgi_app(application)

if __name__ == '__main__':
    main()
```

The `InboundEmailMessage` object includes attributes for the fields of the message, similar to `EmailMessage`. `sender` is the sender's email address, possibly with a displayable name in the standard format (`Mr. Sender <sender@example.com>`). `to` is a list of primary recipient addresses, and `cc` is a list of secondary recipients. (There is no `bcc` on an incoming message, because blind-carbon-copied recipients are not included in the message content.) `subject` is the message's subject.

The `InboundEmailMessage` object may have more than one message body: an HTML body and a plain-text body. You can iterate over the MIME multipart parts of the types `text/html` and `text/plain` using the `bodies()` method. Without arguments, this method returns an iterator that returns the HTML parts first, then the plain-text parts. You can limit the parts returned to just the HTML or plain-text parts by setting the `content_type` parameter. For example, to get just the plain-text bodies:

```
for text_body in message.bodies(content_type='text/plain'):
    # ...
```

In the example earlier, we extracted the first plain-text body by passing the iterator to the `list()` type, then indexing its first argument (which assumes one exists):

```
text = list(message.bodies(content_type='text/plain'))[0]
```

If the incoming message has file attachments, then these are accessible on the `attachments` attribute. As with using `EmailMessage` for sending, this attribute is a list of tuples whose first element is the filename and whose second element is the data byte string. `InboundEmailMessage` allows all file types for incoming attachments, and does not require that the filename accurately represent the file type. *Be careful* when using files sent to the app by users, since they may not be what they say they are, and have not been scanned for viruses.

The Python SDK includes a convenient webapp handler base class for processing incoming email, called `InboundMailHandler` in the `google.appengine.ext.webapp.mail_handlers` package. You use the handler by creating a subclass that overrides the `receive()` method, then installing it like any other handler. When the handler receives an email message, the `receive()` method is called with an `InboundEmailMessage` object as its argument.

```
from google.appengine.ext.webapp import mail_handlers

class MyMailHandler(mail_handlers.InboundMailHandler):
    def receive(self, message):
        # ...

application = webapp.WSGIApplication([('/_ah/mail/.+', MyMailHandler)],
```

```
                              debug=True)

    def main():
        run_wsgi_app(application)

    if __name__ == '__main__':
        main()
```

Receiving Email in Java

In Java, you map the incoming email URL path to a servlet with an entry in the deployment descriptor (*web.xml*):

```
<servlet>
  <servlet-name>mailreceiver</servlet-name>
  <servlet-class>myapp.MailReceiverServlet</servlet-class>
</servlet>
<servlet-mapping>
  <servlet-name>mailreceiver</servlet-name>
  <url-pattern>/_ah/mail/*</url-pattern>
</servlet-mapping>
```

The JavaMail and servlet APIs provide everything we need to parse the MIME multipart message in the HTTP POST request. The `MimeMessage` class (in the `javax.mail.internet` package) has a constructor that accepts a `java.io.InputStream`, which we can get from the `HttpServletRequest` using its `getInputStream()` method. The `MimeMessage` constructor also needs a JavaMail `Session`, which, as with sending email, can use the default empty configuration.

```java
import java.io.IOException;
import java.util.Properties;
import javax.mail.Session;
import javax.mail.MessagingException;
import javax.mail.Multipart;
import javax.mail.Part;
import javax.mail.internet.MimeMessage;
import javax.servlet.http.*;

public class MailReceiverServlet extends HttpServlet {
    public void doPost(HttpServletRequest req,
                       HttpServletResponse resp)
            throws IOException {
        Properties props = new Properties();
        Session session = Session.getDefaultInstance(props, null);

        try {
            MimeMessage message = new MimeMessage(session, req.getInputStream());
            String contentType = message.getContentType();
            Object content = message.getContent();
            if (content instanceof String) {
                // A plain text body.
                // ...

            } else if (content instanceof Multipart) {
```

```
                // A multipart body.
                for (int i = 0; i < ((Multipart) content).getCount(); i++) {
                    Part part = ((Multipart) content).getBodyPart(i);
                    // ...

                }
            }

        } catch (MessagingException e) {
            // Problem parsing the message data.
            // ...

        }
    }
}
```

If the incoming message is a MIME multipart message (such as a message with an HTML body, or attachments), the getContent() method of the MimeMessage returns an object that implements the Multipart interface. You can use this interface to get a count of the parts (getCount()) and select parts by index (getBodyPart(int index), which returns a BodyPart).

Sending XMPP Messages

An App Engine application can send instant messages to users of XMPP-compliant chat services, including Google Talk and Jabber servers, using the XMPP service.

Each participant in an XMPP communication has an address similar to an email address, known as a *JID*. (JID is short for "Jabber ID," named after the Jabber project, where XMPP originated.) A JID consists of a username, an "at" symbol (@), and the domain name of the XMPP server. A JID can also have an optional "resource" string, which is sometimes used to identify specific clients connected to the service with the username; a message sent to the ID without the resource goes to all connected clients.

> *username* @ *domain* / *resource*

To send a message, a chat participant sends an XMPP message to its own XMPP server. The participant's chat service contacts the recipient service's host using the domain name of the JID and a standard port, then delivers the message. If the remote service accepts messages for the JID and someone is connected to the service with a chat client for that JID, the service delivers the message to the client.

Most services, including Google Talk, require that the user has established a previous relationship with a sender before it will route chat messages to the user. The user can establish this relationship with an App Engine app either by sending a chat invitation to the app, or by accepting a chat invitation sent by the app. App Engine applications can send chat invitations as well as messages.

In most cases, App Engine applications should only send a chat invitation to a user at the request of the user. Sending unsolicited chat invitations could be considered abuse and a violation of the terms of service.

App Engine's XMPP service uses the same infrastructure as Google Talk, Google's Jabber-compatible instant messaging service. You can use Google Talk directly via the Google Talk client for Windows, from Gmail's web interface, from a Google Talk web gadget, or any Jabber-compatible chat client.

You can also develop a custom client that connects to Google Talk via XMPP with a Google Account. This could be an application that runs on a desktop computer or an Internet-capable mobile phone, or it could be a Flash applet that runs in a browser window. (Web browsers do not support making an XMPP connection directly. Gmail's interface to Google Talk uses an HTTP relay hosted by Google, which does not have a public protocol.) A custom client connected in this way can have messages pushed to it from your App Engine app. For more information on developing custom Google Talk clients, see the Google Talk developer documentation:

   http://code.google.com/apis/talk/

 Any user with a Google Account can access the Google Talk service for free with any XMPP-compatible chat client. This includes users with Google Accounts on Google Apps domains.

An XMPP message includes a sender address, one or more recipient addresses, a message type, and a message body.

The sender address must be one of the app's incoming XMPP addresses. These are of the form *app-id*@appspot.com or *anything*@*app-id*.appspotchat.com, where *app-id* is your application ID and *anything* can be any string that's valid on the left side of a JID (it can't contain an @ symbol). Unlike incoming email addresses, it's not as convenient to use the "anything" form for creating IDs on the fly, since the recipient needs to accept an invitation from that ID before receiving messages, but it can still be useful for sessions that begin with an invitation, or addresses that represent specific purposes or users of the app (support@*app-id*.appspotchat.com).

If the version of the app that is sending an XMPP message is not the default version, App Engine modifies the sender address to a version-specific address, so replies go directly to the correct version: *anything*@*version*.latest.*app-id*.appspotchat.com (*app-id*@appspot.com becomes *app-id*@*version*.latest.*app-id*.appspotchat.com.)

App Engine adds a "resource" to the end of the sender JID (after the domain name) that looks like this: /bot. This is mostly just to comply with the best practice of sending messages using JIDs with resources. It isn't noticed by chat users, and is not needed when a user wishes to send a message to the app. You'll see it in log messages.

The message type can be any of the types in the XMPP standard, including "chat," "error," "groupchat," "headline," and "normal." An app can only receive messages of the types "chat" and "normal," and so cannot participate in group chats. For straightforward communication between an app and a chat user, you usually want to send "chat" messages. For an app and a custom client, you can do what you like.

When an app is running in the development server, sending an XMPP chat message or invitation causes the server to print the message to the console. The development server does not contact the XMPP service or send messages.

The APIs for calling the XMPP service are straightforward. In Python, each major action is a function in the `google.appengine.api.xmpp` module. In Java, each action is a method of an `XMPPService` object, which you get from `XMPPServiceFactory.getXMPPService()`. (There is no Java standard API for this one.)

Sending a Chat Invitation

To invite a user to chat in Python, you call the `send_invite()` method. It takes the recipient JID as its first argument, and an optional sender JID (`from_jid`) as its second argument. By default, it uses *app-id*`@appspot.com` as the sender JID.

```
from google.appengine.api import xmpp

jid = 'juliet@example.com'

xmpp.send_invite(jid)  # from app-id@appspot.com

xmpp.send_invite(jid, from_jid='support@app-id.appspotchat.com')  # from a custom JID
```

In Java, each JID is represented by a `JID` object, which you create by passing the address as a string to the `JID` constructor. To send an invitation, you call the `sendInvitation()` method with either one or two arguments:

```
import com.google.appengine.api.xmpp.JID;
import com.google.appengine.api.xmpp.XMPPService;
import com.google.appengine.api.xmpp.XMPPServiceFactory;

// ...
        XMPPService xmpp = XMPPServiceFactory.getXMPPService();

        // From app-id@appspot.com:
        xmpp.sendInvitation(JID("juliet@example.com"));

        // From a custom JID:
        xmpp.sendInvitation(JID("juliet@example.com"),
                            JID("support@app-id.appspotchat.com"));
```

Sending a Chat Message

To send a chat message in Python, you call the **send_message()** function. The function takes a JID or list of JIDs, the body of the message, and an optional sender JID (**from_jid**). It returns a success code, or a list of success codes, one for each recipient JID.

```
result = xmpp.send_message(
    'juliet@example.com',
    'Your dog has reached level 12!')

if result != xmpp.NO_ERROR:
    # ...
```

By default, this sends a message of the "chat" type. You can send a message of a different type by setting the **message_type** parameter. Acceptable values include **xmpp.MESSAGE_TYPE_CHAT** (the default), **xmpp.MESSAGE_TYPE_ERROR**, **xmpp.MESSAGE_TYPE_GROUPCHAT**, **xmpp.MESSAGE_TYPE_HEADLINE**, and **xmpp.MESSAGE_TYPE_NORMAL**.

Complete XMPP messages are sent over the network as XML data. By default, **send_message()** treats the text of the message as plain text, and knows to escape XML characters. Instead of a text message, you can send an XML stanza. This is included verbatim (assuming the stanza is well formed) in the XMPP message, so you can send structured data to XMPP clients. To tell **send_message()** that the content is an XML stanza so it doesn't escape XML characters, provide the **raw_xml=True** parameter.

The **send_message()** function returns a status code for each recipient JID, as a single value if called with a single JID, or as a list of codes if called with a list of JIDs. The possible status values are **xmpp.NO_ERROR**, **xmpp.INVALID_JID**, and **xmpp.OTHER_ERROR**.

In Java, you send a message by calling the **sendMessage()** method of the **XMPPService**. The method takes a **Message** object, which you build with a **MessageBuilder** object. **sendMessage()** returns a **SendResponse** object, which contains status codes for each intended recipient of the message.

```
import com.google.appengine.api.xmpp.JID;
import com.google.appengine.api.xmpp.Message;
import com.google.appengine.api.xmpp.MessageBuilder;
import com.google.appengine.api.xmpp.SendResponse;
import com.google.appengine.api.xmpp.XMPPService;
import com.google.appengine.api.xmpp.XMPPServiceFactory;

// ...
        XMPPService xmpp = XMPPServiceFactory.getXMPPService();

        JID recipient = new JID("juliet@example.com");
        Message message = new MessageBuilder()
            .withRecipientJids(recipient)
            .withBody("Your dog has reached level 12!")
            .build();

        SendResponse success = xmpp.sendMessage(message);
```

```
if (success.getStatusMap().get(recipient) != SendResponse.Status.SUCCESS) {
    // ...
}
```

You use the `MessageBuilder` class to assemble the (immutable) `Message` object. You can chain its methods to construct a complete message in a single statement. Relevant methods include:

`withBody(String body)`
Sets the message body.

`asXml(boolean asXml)`
Declares that the body contains a well-formed XML stanza (and not plain text).

`withFromJid(JID jid)`
Sets the sender JID.

`withRecipientJids(JID jid1, ...)`
Adds one or more recipient JIDs.

`withMessageType(MessageType type)`
Sets the message type.

`build()`
Returns the finished `Message`.

Message types are represented by the `MessageType` enum: `MessageType.CHAT`, `MessageType.ERROR`, `MessageType.GROUPCHAT`, `MessageType.HEADLINE`, and `MessageType.NORMAL`.

The `sendMessage()` method returns a `SendResponse` object. Calling this object's `getStatusMap()` method returns a `Map<JID, SendResponseStatus>`, a map of recipient JIDs to status codes. The possible status codes are `SendResponse.Status.SUCCESS`, `SendResponse.Status.INVALID_ID`, and `SendResponse.Status.OTHER_ERROR`.

Checking a Google Talk User's Status

App Engine's XMPP service supports inquiring about the availability (or presence) of a Google Talk user, whether the user is online and accepting chat messages. Querying for presence is specific to the Google Talk service and not XMPP, so this feature only works with Talk users. (XMPP chat clients use presence notification messages, which are not yet supported by App Engine.)

A Google Talk user will only appear as available to an App Engine app if the user has a prior chat relationship with the app (the user accepted an invitation from the app, or has sent the app an invitation). All other users appear as "not present."

A user's presence value has no relationship with the user's "available" status. A connected user appears as present even if her status is set to "away." Also, there is no way to read the user's status message.

To get the status of a Google Talk user in Python, you call the `get_presence()` function with the user's JID and an optional custom sender JID (`from_jid`). The function returns `True` if the user is connected and can receive chat messages from the app.

```
if xmpp.get_presence('juliet@example.com'):
    # User can receive chat messages from the app.
    # ...
```

In Java, you call the `getPresence()` method of the `XMPPService` instance with the user's JID and an optional sender JID. The method returns a `Presence` object, whose `isAvailable()` method returns `true` if the user is connected.

```
import com.google.appengine.api.xmpp.Presence;

// ...
        JID jid = new JID("juliet@example.com");
        Presence presence = xmpp.getPresence(jid);
        if (presence.isAvailable()) {
            // ...
        }
```

When running in the development server, all user addresses are present.

Receiving XMPP Messages

With the `xmpp_message` inbound service enabled, an app can receive XMPP messages sent by users and clients of XMPP chat services, such as Google Talk. Incoming messages are routed to the application in the form of HTTP requests to a specified URL. This is similar to how an app can receive email.

An app can receive two kinds of XMPP messages: "chat" and "normal." Chat messages are sent by user-operated instant messaging clients, and usually represent a conversation. Normal messages are general purpose messages, which you might use for custom clients. Notice that this means an app cannot be a participant in a group chat.

An app receives XMPP messages at several addresses. Messages sent to addresses of these forms are routed to the default version of the app:

> *app-id*@appspot.com

> *anything*@*app-id*.appspotchat.com

Messages sent to addresses of this form are routed to the specified version of the app, useful for testing:

> *anything*@*version*.latest.*app-id*.appspotmail.com

Each message is delivered to the app as an HTTP POST request to the following URL path:

> /_ah/xmpp/message/chat/

(Unlike incoming email, the sender JID is not included in the URL path.)

The body content of the HTTP POST request is a MIME multipart message, with a part for each field of the message:

from
> The sender's JID.

to
> The app JID to which this message was sent.

body
> The message body content (with characters as they were originally typed).

stanza
> The full XML stanza of the message, including the previous fields (with XML special characters escaped); useful for communicating with a custom client using XML.

The Python and Java SDKs include classes for parsing the request data into objects.

When the service is enabled, all incoming messages are accepted and routed to the app. All incoming chat invitations are accepted automatically. The app always appears as connected and available when someone inquires for the app's presence.

The development server console (`http://localhost:8080/_ah/admin/`) includes a feature for simulating incoming XMPP messages by submitting a web form. The development server cannot receive actual XMPP messages.

Receiving XMPP Messages in Python

In Python, you map the URL path to a script handler in *app.yaml* file, as usual:

```
handlers:
- url: /_ah/xmpp/message/chat/
  script: handle_xmpp.py
```

You can parse the incoming message into a **Message** object by passing a mapping of the POST parameters to its constructor. With the webapp framework, this is a simple matter of passing the parsed POST data (a mapping of the POST parameter names to values) in directly:

```
from google.appengine.api import xmpp
from google.appengine.ext import webapp
from google.appengine.ext.webapp.util import run_wsgi_app

class IncomingXMPPHandler(webapp.RequestHandler):
    def post(self):
        message = xmpp.Message(self.request.POST)

        message.reply('I got your message!')

application = webapp.WSGIApplication([('/_ah/xmpp/message/chat/',
                                       IncomingXMPPHandler)],
                                      debug=True)
```

```
def main():
    run_wsgi_app(application)

if __name__ == '__main__':
    main()
```

The `Message` object has attributes for each message field: `from`, `to`, and `body`. It also includes a convenience method for replying to the message: `reply()`, which takes the body of the reply as its first argument.

The Python SDK includes an extension for webapp that makes it easy to implement chat interfaces that perform user-issued commands. Here's an example that responds to the commands /stats and /score username, and ignores all other messages:

```
from google.appengine.api import xmpp
from google.appengine.ext import webapp
from google.appengine.ext.webapp import xmpp_handlers
from google.appengine.ext.webapp.util import run_wsgi_app

def get_stats():
    # ...

def get_score_for_user(username):
    # ...

class UnknownUserError(Exception):
    pass

class ScoreBotHandler(xmpp_handlers.CommandHandler):
    def stats_command(self, message):
        stats = get_stats()
        if stats:
            message.reply('The latest stats: %s' % stats)
        else:
            message.reply('Stats are not available right now.')

    def score_command(self, message):
        try:
            score = get_score_for_user(message.arg)
            message.reply('Score for user %s: %d' % (message.arg, score))
        except UnknownUserError, e:
            message.reply('Unknown user %s' % message.arg)

application = webapp.WSGIApplication([('/_ah/xmpp/message/chat/', ScoreBotHandler)],
                                     debug=True)

def main():
    run_wsgi_app(application)

if __name__ == '__main__':
    main()
```

The `CommandHandler` base class, provided by the `google.appengine.ext.webapp.xmpp_handlers` package, parses the incoming message for a command of the following syntax:

```
/commandname argument
```

If the message contains such a command, the handler attempts to call a method named after the command, such as `commandname_command()`. If no such method exists, it calls the `unhandled_command()` method, whose default implementation replies to the message with "Unknown command." You can override this method to customize its behavior.

The base handler calls the command method with the `Message` object as an argument. The handler annotates the object with two additional attributes: `command`, the name of the command, and `arg`, the text following the command, if any.

If the incoming message does not start with a `/commandname`-style command, the base handler calls the `text_message()` method with the `Message` as its argument. The default implementation does nothing, and you can override it to specify behavior in this case.

This package also contains a simpler handler class named `BaseHandler`, with several useful features. It parses incoming messages, and logs and ignores malformed messages. If a message is valid, it calls its `message_received()` method, which you override with the intended behavior. The class also overrides `webapp.RequestHandler`'s `handle_exception()` method to send an XMPP reply with a generic error message when an uncaught exception occurs, so the user isn't left to wonder whether the message was received. (`CommandHandler` extends `BaseHandler`, and so also has these features.)

Receiving XMPP Messages in Java

In Java, you process incoming XMPP messages by mapping a servlet to the URL path called by the XMPP service, in the deployment descriptor:

```
<servlet>
  <servlet-name>xmppreceiver</servlet-name>
  <servlet-class>myapp.XMPPReceiverServlet</servlet-class>
</servlet>
<servlet-mapping>
  <servlet-name>xmppreceiver</servlet-name>
  <url-pattern>/_ah/xmpp/message/chat/</url-pattern>
</servlet-mapping>
```

The `XMPPService` object includes a `parseMessage()` method that knows how to parse the incoming request data into a `Message` object. You access the data using the `Message`'s methods.

```
import java.io.IOException;
import javax.servlet.http.*;

import com.google.appengine.api.xmpp.Message;
import com.google.appengine.api.xmpp.XMPPService;
import com.google.appengine.api.xmpp.XMPPServiceFactory;
```

```
public class XMPPReceiverServlet extends HttpServlet {
    public void doPost(HttpServletRequest req,
                       HttpServletResponse resp)
          throws IOException {
        XMPPService xmpp = XMPPServiceFactory.getXMPPService();
        Message message = xmpp.parseMessage(req);
        // ...
    }
}
```

You access the fields of a `Message` using methods:

getFromJid()
: The sender `JID`.

getMessageType()
: The `MessageType` of the message (`MessageType.CHAT` or `MessageType.NORMAL`).

getRecipientJids()
: The app JID used, as a single-element `JID[]`.

getBody()
: The `String` content of the message.

getStanza()
: The `String` raw XML of the message.

## CHAPTER 12

Bulk Data Operations and Remote Access

The datastore is designed for retrieving and processing data at a rate suitable for interactive web applications. A single request may need to update a few entities, or query for and retrieve several dozen. Larger amounts of work triggered by interactive actions are not typically expected to be performed within a single web request. (App Engine's facility for such work, task queues, is discussed in Chapter 13.) User-initiated actions tend to fit into this model of short requests.

Administrative actions, such as one-off chores performed by the application's maintainers and staff, sometimes follow a different model. You may need to create or update thousands of entities from a datafile, or download the complete contents of the datastore for archival or offline testing. A change to a data model in a new version of the software may require modifying millions of entities to match before the software can be deployed.

You could build features into the application to do these things, and that may be appropriate for routine maintenance tasks. But App Engine has a feature that makes it easy to do ad hoc work with a live application, driven from your own computer: a remote access API.

With the remote access API, utilities running on your computer can call the live application's services, such as the datastore, using the same APIs and libraries that the application uses. Each service call becomes a web request that is processed by a request handler. Each interaction uses a secure connection and is restricted to developer accounts. Figure 12-1 shows how the remote API request handler gives transparent access to the live application's services.

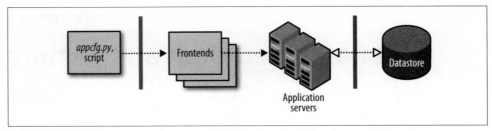

Figure 12-1. Architecture of remote API, with remote calls performed by a web hook

App Engine includes a tool for uploading and downloading data via the remote API. The tool can create new datastore entities using data from a comma-separated values (CSV) datafile (which can be exported and imported from most spreadsheet applications), and can create CSV files with data from the app's datastore. It can use the app's data models to validate data before storing it, and can be extended to perform custom transformations on the data. The tool also makes it easy to do a straight download of the entire datastore, and can upload that data back to the app, or to another app.

App Engine also has a tool for running a Python command-line session with the remote API. With this remote shell tool, you can execute arbitrary Python statements using the Python API, and service calls will operate on the live application.

These remote access features come in two parts: the remote API request handler, and the tools and libraries that call the handler. The remote API handler is available for both Python and Java applications, and is included with each runtime environment. Both versions of the remote API use the same network protocol, so any tool that works with the Python version also works with the Java version.

Currently, the remote access tools and libraries are only available for Python. You can use these tools and libraries with a Java application via the Java remote API request handler. You will need to download and install the Python SDK to get the tools and libraries. For some features, you may also need to reimplement your data models using the Python data modeling library (described in Chapter 7). See the section "Installing the Python SDK" on page 16.

In this chapter, we'll describe how to set up the remote API request handler for Python and Java apps, and how to use the bulk upload and download tools from the Python SDK. We'll also look at the Python remote shell utility. Finally, we'll look at how to use the remote API directly in your own Python scripts.

Setting Up the Remote API for Python

The Python remote API request handler is included in the runtime environment. You can set it up at a URL path of your choosing in your *app.yaml* file. Be sure to restrict this URL path to administrators using `login: admin`.

Here's an excerpt that sets up the remote API URL using the path `/remote_api`:

```
handlers:
- url: /remote_api
  script: $PYTHON_LIB/google/appengine/ext/remote_api/handler.py
  login: admin
```

The `$PYTHON_LIB` portion of the script path gets replaced by the system with the actual path to the App Engine libraries.

You can test this URL in a browser using the development server. Visit the URL (such as `http://localhost:8080/remote_api`), and make sure it redirects to a fake authentication form. Check the box to sign in as an administrator, and click Submit. You should see this message:

```
This request did not contain a necessary header.
```

The remote API expects an HTTP header identifying the remote API protocol version to use, which the browser does not provide. But this is sufficient to test that the handler is configured correctly.

Setting Up the Remote API for Java

To use the remote API tools with a Java application, you set up a URL path with a servlet provided by the SDK, namely `com.google.apphosting.utils.remoteapi.RemoteApiServlet`. You can choose any URL path; you will give this path to the remote API tools in a command-line argument. Be sure to restrict access to the URL path to administrators.

The following excerpt for your deployment descriptor (*web.xml*) associates the remote API servlet with the URL path `/remote_api`, and restricts it to administrator accounts:

```
<servlet>
  <servlet-name>remoteapi</servlet-name>
  <servlet-class>
    com.google.apphosting.utils.remoteapi.RemoteApiServlet
  </servlet-class>
</servlet>
<servlet-mapping>
  <servlet-name>remoteapi</servlet-name>
  <url-pattern>/remote_api</url-pattern>
</servlet-mapping>

<security-constraint>
  <web-resource-collection>
    <web-resource-name>remoteapi</web-resource-name>
    <url-pattern>/remote_api</url-pattern>
  </web-resource-collection>
  <auth-constraint>
    <role-name>admin</role-name>
  </auth-constraint>
</security-constraint>
```

Using the Bulk Loader Tool

The bulk loader tool is part of the Python SDK, and requires that Python be installed on your computer. The main tool is called bulkloader.py. On Windows, the Python SDK installer puts this command in the command path. On Mac OS X, the Launcher creates a symbolic link to the tool at /usr/local/bin/bulkloader.py when you first run it, which may or may not be in your command path. If you installed the SDK using the ZIP archive, the command is in the SDK's root directory.

You can verify you can run the bulkloader.py command by running it without arguments:

```
bulkloader.py
```

If you have a Python application, you can use the appcfg.py upload_data and appcfg.py download_data commands to do data uploads and downloads. These are equivalent to bulkloader.py, but can also derive the application ID and the remote API URL from your *app.yaml* file. (Future releases may make more bulk loader features available via appcfg.py; check the App Engine website for the latest.)

If you have a Java application, you just run the bulkloader.py tool, specifying the application ID and remote API URL as command-line arguments:

```
bulkloader.py --app-id=appid --url=http://appid.appspot.com/remote_api ...
```

 You can use the bulk loader tool with the development server by specifying the equivalent remote API URL for it using the --url=... argument. This is useful for testing the remote API URL configuration, for verifying data uploads before doing them with the live application, and for managing test data during development.

You must still specify an accurate --app_id=... argument when using the development server.

```
bulkloader.py --app_id=app-id \
    --url=http://localhost:8080/remote_api ...
```

The tool will prompt for an email address and password. You can enter any values for these when using the development server.

If you get an "Authentication Failed" error when using the loader with the development server, then your remote API URL is not working. Check your configuration and the development server output.

Installing SQLite

The loader tool keeps track of its progress during an upload or download in a datafile, so you can interrupt it and start it again from where it left off instead of starting the job from the beginning. To do this, the tool requires a Python module called sqlite3. You may already have this module installed in your version of Python. Verify that you have the `sqlite3` module installed by starting a Python shell and importing it. If nothing happens, the module is installed:

```
% python
Python 2.6.1 (r261:67515, Jul  7 2009, 23:51:51)
[GCC 4.2.1 (Apple Inc. build 5646)] on darwin
Type "help", "copyright", "credits" or "license" for more information.
>>> import sqlite3
>>>
```

If you do not have the module, you can get it from the SQLite website. Note that if you compiled your Python installation from source, you will need to recompile it with SQLite support.

http://www.sqlite.org/download.html

If you'd prefer not to install SQLite, you can disable the use of the progress datafile in the bulk loader tool by providing this command-line argument when running the tool: `--db_filename=skip`.

Backup and Restore

One of the easiest features of the bulk loader to use is the backup and restore feature. The bulk loader can download every entity of a given kind to a datafile, and can upload that datafile back to the app to restore those entities. It can also upload the datafile to another app, effectively moving all of the entities of a kind from one app to another. You can also use these features to download data from the live app, and "upload" it to the development server for testing (using the `--url=...` argument mentioned earlier). These features require no additional configuration or code beyond the installation of the remote API handler.

To download every entity of a given kind, run the `bulkloader.py` tool with the `--dump`, `--kind=...`, and `--filename=...` arguments:

```
bulkloader.py --dump \
    --app_id=app-id \
    --url=http://app-id.appspot.com/remote_api \
    --kind=kind \
    --filename=backup.dat
```

(This is a single command line. The \ characters are line continuation markers, supported by some command shells. You can remove these characters and type all of the arguments on one line.)

To upload a datafile created by `--dump`, thereby re-creating every entity in the file, use the `--restore` argument instead of `--dump`:

```
bulkloader.py --restore \
    --app_id=app-id \
    --url=http://app-id.appspot.com/remote_api \
    --kind=kind \
    --filename=backup.dat
```

When using `--dump` and `--restore`, entities are *not* validated using the app's model classes. They are dumped and restored directly as they appear in the datastore.

Entity keys are preserved, including system-assigned numeric IDs. Properties with key values will remain valid as long as the entities they are referring to are in the app or are part of the dump being restored. Restoring an entity with the same key as an existing entity will replace the existing entity.

Keys are preserved even if you upload to an app other than the one that originally contained the dumped entities. If you restore an entity with a system-assigned numeric ID, the ID counter for the given key path and kind is advanced past the restored ID, so future new entities will not overwrite the restored entity.

Uploading Data

The bulk loader uploads data from your computer to your application. Out of the box, the loader supports reading data from a datafile, and the loader can be customized extensively. This makes it easy to produce a set of fixed information, such as information about products in an online store, and upload it to the app as entities in the datastore. The translation is obvious: each row represents one entity, and each column represents a property of the entity. The tool reads datafiles in the CSV file format, which can be exported by most spreadsheet applications, including Microsoft Excel and Google Spreadsheets.

To perform the translation, the bulk loader needs to know the intended data types and property names for each column. You describe this in a file of Python code that defines a "loader" class for each kind to be imported. The class can define additional code to use to translate each string value from the datafile to an appropriate datastore value, and can postprocess entities before they are saved to add or delete properties and create additional entities. The loader class can even replace the CSV file reading routine to read data in other formats.

Here is a simple loader definition file. Let's call it *loaders.py*:

```python
from google.appengine.tools import bulkloader
import datetime

# Import the app's data models directly into
# this namespace.  We must add the app
# directory to the path explicitly.
import sys
import os.path
sys.path.append(
  os.path.abspath(
    os.path.dirname(
      os.path.realpath(__file__))))
from models import *

def get_date_from_str(s):
    if s:
```

```
            return datetime.datetime.strptime(s, '%m/%d/%Y').date()
        else:
            return None

class BookLoader(bulkloader.Loader):
    def __init__(self):
        bulkloader.Loader.__init__(self, 'Book',
            [('title', str),
             ('author', str),
             ('copyright_year', int),
             ('author_birthdate', get_date_from_str),
             ])

loaders = [BookLoader]
```

The loader definition file must do several things:

1. It must import or define a data model class for each kind to import, using the Python data modeling API. The loader file does not have the app directory in the module load path, so the loader file must add it. The modules should be imported directly into the local namespace.

2. It must define (or import) a loader class for each kind to import, a subclass of the Loader class in the package google.appengine.tools.bulkloader. This class must have a constructor (an __init__() method) that calls the parent class's constructor with arguments that describe the CSV file's columns.

3. It must define a module-global variable named loaders, whose value is a list of loader classes.

The loader class's __init__() method calls its parent class's __init__() method with three arguments: self (the object being initialized), the kind of the entity to create as a string, and a list of tuples. Each tuple represents a column from the CSV file, in order from left to right. The first element of each tuple is the property name to use. The second element is a Python function that takes the CSV file value as a string and returns the desired datastore value in the appropriate Python value type. (Refer to Table 4-1 for a list of the Python value types for the datastore.)

For simple data types, you can use the constructor for the type as the type conversion function. In the example above, we use str to leave the value from the CSV file as a string, and int to parse the CSV string value as an integer. Depending on the output of your spreadsheet program, you can use this technique for long, float, db.Text, and other types whose constructors accept strings as initial arguments. For instance, users.User takes an email address as a string argument.

The bool type constructor returns False for the empty string, and True in all other cases. If your CSV file contains Boolean values in other forms, you'll need to write a converter function, like this:

```
def bool_from_string(s):
    return s == 'TRUE'
```

Dates, times, and date-times usually require a custom converter function to make an appropriate `datetime.datetime` value from the string. As shown previously, you can use the `datetime.datetime.strptime()` function to parse the string in a particular format. Tailor this to the output of your spreadsheet program.

To create a multivalued property, you can use a type conversion function that returns a list value. However, the function must get all of its data from a single cell (though you can work around this by tweaking the file reader routine, described below). It cannot reference other cells in the row, or other rows in the table.

Storing a key value (a reference to another entity) is usually a straightforward matter of defining a type conversion function that uses `db.Key.from_path()` with the desired kind and a key name derived from a CSV file value.

By default, the bulk loader creates each entity using a key with no ancestors, the given kind, and a system-assigned numeric ID. You can tell the bulk loader to use a custom key name instead of a numeric ID by defining a method of your loader class named `generate_key()`. This method takes as arguments a loop counter (`i`) and the row's column values as a list of strings (`values`), and returns either a string key name or a `db.Key` object. The `db.Key` object can include an entity group parent key. If the function returns `None`, a system-assigned numeric ID will be used.

```
class BookLoader(bulkloader.Loader):
    # ...

    def generate_key(self, i, values):
        # Use the first column as the key name.
        return values[0]
```

 If an entity is uploaded with the same key as an entity that already exists in the datastore, the new entity will replace the existing entity. You can use this effect to download, modify, then reupload data to update existing entities instead of creating new ones.

You can "skip" an unused column in the CSV file by giving it a property name that begins with an underscore. The Python data modeling API does not save attributes beginning with an underscore as properties, so the final entity will not have a property with this name. You can reuse the same dummy property name for all columns you wish to skip:

```
class BookLoader(bulkloader.Loader):
    def __init__(self):
        bulkloader.Loader.__init__(self, 'Book',
            [('_UNUSED', lambda x: None),
             ('title', str),
             ('author', str),
             ('_UNUSED', lambda x: None),
             ('_UNUSED', lambda x: None),
             ('copyright_year', int),
```

```
    # ...
    ])
```

If you have a column that is to be the entity key name (via `generate_key()`) and you do not want this value to also become a property, you must "skip" the column in the column list using this technique. The bulk loader will complain if it finds more columns than are declared in the list.

The bulk loader uses the Python data modeling API to construct, validate, and save entities. If your app is written in Python, you just use the model classes of your app for this purpose, and get the validation for free.

If your app is written in Java, you have a choice to make. You can either implement Python data model classes that resemble your application's data model, or you can define Python data models that allow arbitrary properties to be set by the loader without validation. For information on defining data models in Python, see Chapter 7. To define a model class that allows all properties and does no validation, simply define a class like the following for each kind in the loader file, above the definition of the loader classes:

```
from google.appengine.ext import db

class Book(db.Expando):
    pass
```

The loader class can do postprocessing on an entity after it is created but before it is saved to the datastore. This gives you the opportunity to inspect the entity, add or remove properties, and even create additional entities based on each row of the datafile. To perform postprocessing, implement a method named `handle_entity()` on the loader class. This takes an instance of the model class as its only argument (`entity`). It should return the instance to create, a list of model instances if more than one entity should be created, or `None` if no entity should be created.

You can extend the loader class to read file formats other than CSV files. To do this, you override the `generate_records()` method. This method takes a filename (`filename`), and returns a Python generator. Each iteration of the generator should yield a list of strings for each entity to create, where each string corresponds to a property defined in the loader's constructor. You can use a `generate_records()` routine to massage the columns processed by the loader so that all the information needed for a single property appears in the column's value, such as to assemble what will eventually become a multivalued property from multiple columns in the datafile.

You can override the `initialize()` method of the loader to perform actions at the beginning of an upload. This method takes the input file's name (`filename`) and a string given on the command line as the `--loader_opts=...` argument (`loader_opts`), which you can use to pass options to this method. Similarly, you can override the `finalize()` method to do something after the upload is complete.

To start the upload for a Java app or a Python app, run the `bulkloader.py` command as follows:

```
bulkloader.py
    --app_id=app-id \
    --url=http://app-id.appspot.com/remote_api \
    --config_file=loaders.py \
    --kind=Book \
    --filename=bookdata.csv
```

If you have a Python app, you can use `appcfg.py upload_data` to do the same thing, with fewer arguments to type. (The app ID and remote API URL are derived from the app's configuration file.)

```
appcfg.py upload_data \
    --config_file=loaders.py \
    --kind=Book \
    --filename=bookdata.csv \
    app-dir
```

The `--config_file=...` argument specifies the file of Python code that defines the loader classes. The `--kind=...` argument states the kind of the entities to import from the datafile; the loader figures out which `Loader` class and model class to use using the kind. `--filename=...` is the name of the CSV file.

If your CSV file's first row is a header row and not actual data, add the `--has_header` argument to skip the first row.

If any row of the CSV file fails to translate to an entity, either because a type conversion function raised an exception or because the corresponding model class does not consider a converted value valid, the bulk loader stops the upload and reports the error. If you have `sqlite3` installed, you can start the upload from where it left off (after fixing the offending value in the CSV file) by running the command again with the same arguments.

You can do a test run of an upload without actually uploading any data by adding the `--dry_run` argument. This causes the loader to process the CSV file and construct and validate each entity object, and report any errors it finds. It doesn't upload any data or otherwise access the app.

Downloading Data

You can use the bulk loader to download data from the app's datastore as well as upload it. The download feature is symmetrical with the upload feature: it supports downloading an app's entities and adding them as rows to a CSV datafile. You provide Python code that describes how entities should be saved, and you can customize the download process to perform data transformations or output other file formats.

Similar to the loader class for uploads, the download feature uses a file of Python code that defines an exporter class for each kind of entity to download. The exporter class specifies which property goes in which column of the resulting CSV file, and can include value transformation functions to get the entity data into a format accepted by your spreadsheet program.

Here is a simple exporter definition file that is symmetric with the loader definition example in the previous section. Data downloaded with this exporter can be loaded back in with the loader. Let's call this file *exporters.py*:

```python
from google.appengine.tools import bulkloader
import datetime

# Import the app's data models directly into
# this namespace.  We must add the app
# directory to the path explicitly.
import sys
import os.path
sys.path.append(
  os.path.abspath(
    os.path.dirname(
      os.path.realpath(__file__))))
from models import *

def make_str_for_date(d):
    if d:
        return d.strftime('%m/%d/%Y')
    else:
        return ''

class BookExporter(bulkloader.Exporter):
    def __init__(self):
        bulkloader.Exporter.__init__(self, 'Book',
            [('title', str, None),
             ('author', str, ''),
             ('copyright_year', int, ''),
             ('author_birthdate', make_str_for_date, ''),
            ])

exporters = [BookExporter]
```

The exporter definition file must do several things:

1. It must import or define a data model class for each kind to export, using the Python data modeling API. The exporter file does not have the app directory in the module load path, so the exporter file must add it. The modules should be imported directly into the local namespace.

2. It must define (or import) an exporter class for each kind to export, a subclass of the `Exporter` class in the package `google.appengine.tools.bulkloader`. This class must have a constructor (an `__init__()` method) that calls the parent class's constructor with arguments that describe the CSV file's columns.

3. It must define a module-global variable named `exporters`, whose value is a list of exporter classes.

You can safely put your exporter classes in the same file as the loader classes, if you like. You can even put them in the same file as your models if that makes sense for your application. You provide the name of the file that defines the exporters using the `--filename=...` command-line argument.

The loader class's `__init__()` method calls its parent class's `__init__()` method with three arguments: `self` (the object being initialized), the kind of the entity to create as a string, and a list of tuples. Each tuple represents a column from the CSV file, in order from left to right. The first element of each tuple is the name of a property on each entity. The second element is a Python function that takes the datastore value (as a Python representation of a datastore value type) and returns the string value to add to the CSV file. For the exporter, each tuple also requires a third element that specifies the default value to use if a given entity does not have this property (a string). If the default value is `None`, then the bulk loader will consider it an error if it finds an entity without this property, and it will abort.

The desired behavior of the type conversion function depends on your spreadsheet application. In most cases, the result of passing the datastore value to the `str` constructor is sufficient. For Boolean values, you may want a converter function that emits `'TRUE'` instead of `'True'`:

```python
def make_str_for_bool(b):
    return 'TRUE' if b else 'FALSE'
```

For `datetime` value types (such as `datetime.date`), you can call the `strftime()` method of the value in a converter function to produce a string form of the date in the desired format, as in the previous example.

If you pass a `Key` value (such as a reference property) to `str`, you get an encoded key string. This value contains all of the information about the key, and you can reconstruct the `Key` object by passing this string to the `Key` constructor.

The default exporter behavior does not save the key of each entity to the CSV file. You can change the behavior of the exporter by overriding the `output_entities()` method. This method takes a generator that yields model instances in key order (`entity_generator`), and does all the work to produce a file. The output filename is accessible using the `output_filename` member of the exporter (`self.output_filename`).

You can also override the `initialize()` method to do work before the download begins. This method takes the name given by `--filename=...` and the string given by `--exporter_opts=...`, as the `filename` and `exporter_opts` arguments, respectively. There's also a `finalize()` method you can override, which is called after the download is complete (with no arguments).

To download data with the bulk loader and exporter classes, run the `bulkloader.py` command as follows (notice the `--download` option that wasn't there in the upload command):

```
bulkloader.py
    --download \
    --app_id=app-id \
    --url=http://app-id.appspot.com/remote_api \
    --config_file=exporters.py \
    --kind=Book \
    --filename=bookdata.csv
```

For a Python application, you can also start a download using `appcfg.py download_data`, like so:

```
appcfg.py download_data \
    --config_file=exporters.py \
    --kind=Book \
    --filename=bookdata.csv \
    app-dir
```

Controlling the Bulk Loader

You can control the rate that the bulk loader transfers data using command-line arguments:

`--num_threads=...`
> The maximum number of loader threads to spawn. The default is 10.

`--batch_size=...`
> The maximum number of entities to create or download with each remote API call. The loader combines puts and gets into batches to reduce the number of remote API calls needed. If you have large entities, set this number low so that the total size of a batch call does not exceed one megabyte. The default is 10.

`--bandwidth_limit=...`
> The maximum number of bytes per second to send or receive on average. The default is 250 kilobytes per second.

`--rps_limit=...`
> The maximum number of records per second to send or receive on average. The default is 20 records per second.

`--http_limit=...`
> The maximum number of HTTP requests to make per second. The default is 15 requests per 2 seconds (7.5 per second).

If you restrict your app's Google Accounts authentication to a Google Apps domain, the bulk loader needs to know the domain for authentication purposes. You provide this with the `--auth_domain=...` argument.

The bulk loader uses a temporary database file to keep track of where in a loading job it is in case it is interrupted. Rerunning the interrupted tool with the same arguments restarts the job from where it left off. By default, the name of this file is `bulkloader-progress-...`, where `...` is the timestamp of the current run. You can specify a custom name and location for this file with the `--db_filename=...` argument. If you specify a value of `skip` for this argument, the bulk loader will not use a file to record progress. (If you do not have `sqlite3` installed, you must specify `--db_filename=skip`.)

The loader also writes a log of its actions to a file named `bulkloader-log-...` (also with a timestamp in the name). You can change this name with `--log_filename=...`.

For downloads, the loader stashes downloaded entities in a temporary datafile named `bulkloader-results-...`. You can change the name of this file with `--result_db_filename=...`.

Using the Remote Shell Tool

With the remote API handler installed, you can use a tool included with the Python SDK to manipulate a live application's services from an interactive Python shell. You interact with the shell using Python statements and the Python service APIs. This tool works with both Java and Python applications using the remote API handler.

To start a shell session, run the `remote_api_shell.py` command. As with the other Python SDK commands, this command may already be in your command path.

```
remote_api_shell.py app-id
```

The tool prompts for your developer account email address and password. (Only registered developers for the app can run this tool, or any of the remote API tools.)

By default, the tool connects to the application using the domain name `app-id`.`appspot.com`, and assumes the remote API handler is installed with the URL path `/remote_api`. To use a different URL path, provide the path as an argument after the application ID:

```
remote_api_shell.py app-id /admin/util/remote_api
```

To use a different domain name, such as to use a specific application version, or to test the tool with the development server, give the domain name with the `-s ...` argument:

```
remote_api_shell.py -s dev.latest.app-id.appspot.com app-id
```

The shell can use any service API that is supported by the remote API handler. This includes URL Fetch, memcache, Images, Mail, Google Accounts, and of course the datastore. (As of this writing, XMPP is not supported by the remote API handler.) Several of the API modules are imported by default for easy access.

The tool does not add the current working directory to the module load path by default, nor does it know about your application directory. You may need to adjust the load path (`sys.path`) to import your app's classes, such as your data models.

Here is an example of a short shell session:

```
% remote_api_shell.py clock
Email: juliet@example.com
Password:
App Engine remote_api shell
```

```
Python 2.5.1 (r251:54863, Feb  6 2009, 19:02:12)
[GCC 4.0.1 (Apple Inc. build 5465)]
The db, users, urlfetch, and memcache modules are imported.
clock> import os.path
clock> import sys
clock> sys.path.append(os.path.realpath('.'))
clock> import models
clock> books = models.Book.all().fetch(6)
clock> books
[<models.Book object at 0x7a2c30>, <models.Book object at 0x7a2bf0>,
<models.Book object at 0x7a2cd0>, <models.Book object at 0x7a2cb0>,
<models.Book object at 0x7a2d30>, <models.Book object at 0x7a2c90>]
clock> books[0].title
u'The Grapes of Wrath'
clock> from google.appengine.api import mail
clock> mail.send_mail('juliet@example.com', 'test@example.com',
'Test email', 'This is a test message.')
clock>
```

To exit the shell, press Ctrl-D.

Using the Remote API from a Script

You can call the remote API directly from your own Python scripts using a library from the Python SDK. This configures the Python API to use the remote API handler for your application for all service calls, so you can use the service APIs as you would from a request handler directly in your scripts.

Here's a simple example script that prompts for a developer account email address and password, then accesses the datastore of a live application:

```
#!/usr/bin/python

import getpass
import sys

# Add the Python SDK to the package path.
# Adjust these paths accordingly.
sys.path.append('~/google_appengine')
sys.path.append('~/google_appengine/lib/yaml/lib')

from google.appengine.ext.remote_api import remote_api_stub

from google.appengine.ext import db
import models

# Your app ID and remote API URL path go here.
APP-ID = 'app-id'
REMOTE_API_PATH = '/remote_api'

def auth_func():
    email_address = raw_input('Email address: ')
    password = getpass.getpass('Password: ')
```

```
        return email_address, password

    def initialize_remote_api(app-id=APP-ID,
                              path=REMOTE_API_PATH):
        remote_api_stub.ConfigureRemoteApi(
            app-id,
            path,
            auth_func)
        remote_api_stub.MaybeInvokeAuthentication()

    def main(args):
        initialize_remote_api()

        books = models.Book.all().fetch(10)
        for book in books:
            print book.title

        return 0

    if __name__ == '__main__':
        sys.exit(main(sys.argv[1:]))
```

The ConfigureRemoteApi() function (yes, it has a TitleCase name) sets up the remote API access. It takes as arguments the application ID, the remote API handler URL path, and a callable that returns a tuple containing the email address and password to use when connecting. In this example, we define a function that prompts for the email address and password, and pass the function to ConfigureRemoteApi().

The function also accepts an optional fourth argument specifying an alternate domain name for the connection. By default, it uses *app-id*.appspot.com, where *app-id* is the application ID in the first argument.

The MaybeInvokeAuthentication() function sends an empty request to verify that the email address and password are correct, and raises an exception if they are not. (Without this, the script would wait until the first remote call to verify the authentication.)

Remember that every call to an App Engine library that performs a service call does so over the network via an HTTP request to the application. This is inevitably slower than running within the live application. It also consumes application resources like web requests do, including bandwidth and request counts, which are not normally consumed by service calls in the live app.

On the plus side, since your code runs on your local computer, it is not constrained by the App Engine runtime sandbox or the 30-second request deadline. You can run long jobs and interactive applications on your computer without restriction, using any Python modules you like—at the expense of consuming app resources to marshal service calls over HTTP.

## CHAPTER 13

Task Queues and Scheduled Tasks

The App Engine architecture is optimized for handling web requests, small amounts of work that run in a stateless environment with the intent of returning a response to the user as fast as possible. But many web applications have other kinds of work that need to get done, work that doesn't fit in the fast response model. Instead of doing the work while the user waits, it's often acceptable to record what work needs to get done, respond to the user right away, then do the work later, within seconds or minutes. The ability to make this trade-off is especially useful with scalable web applications that use a read-optimized datastore, since updating an element of data may require several related but time-consuming updates, and it may not be essential for those updates to happen right away.

Then there's the work that needs to get done independently of user actions: fetching and caching fresh data from remote sources, sending daily status email messages, respawning health packs and enemies throughout the island. For this, it would be useful to configure a schedule of work that needs to be done on a regular basis, and that gets performed regardless of web traffic from users.

App Engine provides facilities for these categories of work: *task queues* and *scheduled tasks*. With task queues, a request handler invoked by a user request can enqueue a unit of work—a *task*—and return a response to the user and exit. App Engine executes enqueued tasks at a configurable rate. If a task fails, App Engine retries the task, ensuring that tasks that fail due to transient conditions (such as datastore contention) eventually succeed.

An app can also provide a schedule of tasks to be performed on a regular basis at particular times of an hour, day, or week, and App Engine executes the tasks according to the schedule. Scheduled tasks are not retried, but a scheduled task can use a task queue to take advantage of the retry behavior.

So, what is a task? A task is a request to a request handler. The task specifies a URL path of the application to be called, and can also include data that App Engine passes to the request handler as HTTP parameters. A URL of a networked application called by a system to perform a task is known as a *web hook*.

App Engine invokes a request handler for a task in the same environment as it does a handler for a user request. This means the task handler runs with the same sandbox and resource restrictions, including the 30-second deadline. A task can enqueue another task, allowing a large unit of work to be initiated by a single task and performed in batches. By treating task handlers as request handlers, App Engine can parallelize and scale tasks using the same infrastructure it uses to scale user requests. Figure 13-1 illustrates how task queues and scheduled tasks take advantage of the request handler infrastructure.

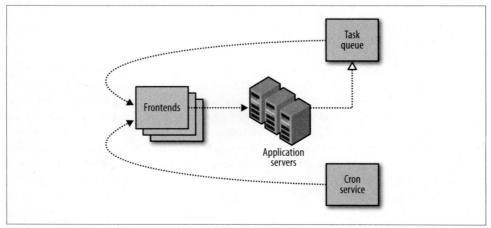

Figure 13-1. Architecture of task queues and scheduled tasks ("cron"), calling web hooks

In this chapter, we'll describe the concepts of task queues and scheduled tasks, and how to use them in Python and Java applications.

 Google initially released the task queue feature as an "experimental" feature, reserving the right to change the design, API, and resource limits before declaring the feature stable. As of this writing, the feature is still under this "experimental" status. Please refer to the official App Engine documentation for the latest information on the task queue API.

Task Queues

An app tells App Engine to perform a task by adding the task to a task queue; it *enqueues* the task. The task queue keeps track of the tasks to perform, and processes them (by issuing HTTP requests) at a particular rate. You can configure the rate for a queue to control how quickly tasks can consume resources. An app can have up to 10 different queues configured at different rates. Once a task has been enqueued successfully, the task queue ensures that the task will be performed at least once, and at least until the task reports success. Queues ensure the eventual success of tasks by retrying them until they succeed.

Enqueueing a task is fast, about three times faster than writing to the datastore. This makes tasks useful for pretty much anything whose success or failure doesn't need to be reported to the user in the response to the HTTP request that initiates the work. For example, an app can write a value to the memcache, then enqueue a task to persist that value to the datastore. This saves time during the user request, and allows the task to do bookkeeping or make other time-consuming updates based on the change (assuming it meets the application's needs that the bookkeeping happens later than the initial update).

Because tasks are just calls to application URLs, tasks are executed in parallel, just like user requests. This makes tasks useful for performing lots of work quickly. Consider a user request that needs to send 100 email messages. Without tasks, the only option would be to make 100 calls to the Mail service, one at a time, while the user waits for a response. With tasks, the user request can enqueue tasks and respond to the user right away. And if each email message is sent in a separate task, App Engine can fire up multiple application instances to send multiple messages simultaneously. With a bit of effort in the browser to check on task progress, task queues can provide a seamless and fast real-time user experience for performing large amounts of work.

Task queues are also useful for batch processing, such as converting datastore entities from one data schema to another without the use of an offline driving mechanism. A task can process a chunk of the batch (such as a range of entity IDs), then enqueue another task to process the next chunk. If processing a chunk fails, the queue can retry the chunk without restarting the entire batch job. You can combine task chaining with parallelization for fine-grained control over how quickly batch jobs execute, and how quickly they consume resources.

Processing Rates and Token Buckets

The processing rate for a queue is controlled using a "token bucket" algorithm. In this algorithm, a queue has a number of "tokens," and it spends a token for each task it executes. Tokens are replenished at a steady rate up to a maximum number of tokens (the "bucket size"). Both the replenishment rate and the bucket size are configurable for a queue.

If a queue contains a task and has a token, it usually executes the task immediately. If a queue has many tasks and many available tokens, it executes as many tasks as it can afford, immediately and in parallel. If there are tasks remaining, the queue must wait until a token is replenished before executing the next task. The token bucket algorithm gives a queue the flexibility to handle bursts of new tasks, while still remaining within acceptable limits. The larger the bucket, the more tasks an idle queue will execute immediately when the tasks are enqueued all at once.

I say it *usually* executes the tasks immediately because App Engine may adjust the method and rate of how it executes tasks based on the performance of the system. In general, task queue schedules are approximate, and may vary as App Engine balances resources.

A queue does not wait for one task to finish before executing the next task. Instead, it initiates the next task as soon as a token is available, in parallel with any currently running tasks. Tasks are not strictly ordered, but App Engine makes an effort to perform tasks in the order they are enqueued. Tasks must not rely on being executed serially or in a specific order.

Each task queue has a name and processing rate (token replenishment rate and bucket size). Every app has a queue named "default" that processes 5 tasks per second, with a bucket size of 5. If you don't specify a queue name when enqueueing a task, the task is added to the default queue. You can adjust the rate and bucket size of the default queue, and can set the rate to 0 to turn it off. Tasks enqueued to a paused queue remain on the queue until you upload the new configuration with a positive rate.

Task queues and token buckets help you control how tasks are executed so you can plan for maximizing throughput, making the most efficient use of system resources to execute tasks in parallel. Tasks inevitably share resources, even if the resource is just the pool of warmed-up application servers. Executing a bunch of tasks simultaneously may not be the fastest way to complete all of the tasks, since App Engine may need to start up new instances of the application to handle the sudden load. If multiple tasks operate on the same entity groups in the datastore, it may be faster to perform only a few tasks at a time and let datastore retries sort out contention, instead of relying on task retries to drive in all of the changes. Limiting the execution rate with token buckets can actually result in faster completion of multiple tasks.

Queue processing rates are configured using a configuration file. This file can be uploaded separately from the rest of the application. If a given queue is processing tasks too quickly, you can upload a new temporary configuration for the queue that tells it to run at a slower rate, and the change will take effect immediately. You can experiment with different rates and token bucket sizes to improve task throughput.

The maximum rate of queue processing for an application is 10 tasks per second. That's the total rate across all queues. If your queue configuration adds up to a collective rate of more than 10 tasks per second, you will get an error when you try to upload the app or the configuration file.

Elements of a Task

You define a task by specifying the aspects of the HTTP request to be made when the task is executed. This can include a URL path, a method (such as POST), and a message body or form parameters.

If the task does not specify a URL path, it assumes a URL path of the following form, based on the queue name:

/_ah/queue/*queue-name*

This is convenient for using the same handler for every task in a queue, or otherwise selecting the handler based on the queue name. The default URL for tasks on the default queue is /_ah/queue/default.

A task can include a delay, either a number of seconds from when the task is enqueued or a specific date and time in the future. The queue will not execute the task until after the delay has elapsed. The queue may not execute the task right away after the delay depending on token availability, but the queue will execute the task at the next opportunity after its delay has elapsed.

Every task has a name that identifies it uniquely. You can supply the name, or you can let the system assign a name. Task names allow you to ensure that a given unit of work is only enqueued once in situations where the app may call the task queue API more than once for the same work. If a task with a given name is already in a queue, or has been enqueued in the past seven days, an attempt to enqueue another task with the same name will fail. If you do not specify a name for a task, the system assigns a name guaranteed to be unique across all pending and completed tasks currently in the system. Completed tasks that remain in the system to prevent duplicates are called *tombstones*, or *tombstoned tasks*.

A common case where custom names and tombstones are useful is when handling a web form. Suppose clicking a button or submitting a form causes the application to perform some expensive work that ought to only be performed once. If the user accidentally clicks the button twice, the browser may send two web requests for the same action. You can prevent the work from being performed twice by rendering the form with a unique ID (such as the button's "value") and performing the work in a task with that name. Two requests to perform the work with the same name will result in only one task being created and performed.

Currently, tombstones remain in the system for about seven days. This may be configurable in a future release.

Task Handlers and Retries

When a queue executes a task, it issues an HTTP request to the app via the frontend, which routes it to a request handler according to the app's URL configuration. The frontend recognizes a request coming from a queue as if it were coming from a developer account, so you can restrict access to task URLs in the handler configuration.

The request handler for the task URL should perform the work, then return an HTTP response code of 200, indicating the work was completed successfully. If the handler returns a different response code, App Engine assumes the task failed completely, and puts it back on the queue to retry it again later. A failed task is reenqueued with a delay that gets exponentially longer the more times it has been retried so that problems caused by resource consumption or contention can be relieved automatically, up to a maximum delay of one hour.

Retries guarantee the eventual success of the task, assuming it is possible for the task to succeed. If a task enqueues successfully, it stays on the queue until it is successful. Tasks are retried indefinitely, and never expire. (Currently, there is no way to flush queues, or identify tasks that fail repeatedly, but these are being considered as future features.)

Under very rare circumstances, such as after a system failure, a task may be retried even if it completed successfully. This is a design trade-off that favors fast task creation over built-in once-only fault tolerance. A task that can be executed multiple times without changing the end result is called *idempotent*. Whether a task's code must be strictly idempotent depends on what the task is doing and how important it is that the calculation it is performing be accurate. For instance, a task that deletes a datastore entity can be retried because the second delete fails harmlessly.

Since a task is always run with its task name (assigned when the task is created, either by the application or by the system), a task can guard against reruns by storing and recognizing its task name. App Engine provides the name of the task in an HTTP header with the request, along with three other useful headers:

X-AppEngine-TaskName
: The name of the task, or the system-generated unique ID.

X-AppEngine-QueueName
: The name of the queue executing the task.

X-AppEngine-TaskRetryCount
: The number of times the task has been retried (0 for the first attempt).

The body of a response from a task's request handler is ignored. If the task needs to store or communicate information, it must do so by using the appropriate services or by logging messages.

Task queues have special behavior with regard to app versions. If the version of the app that enqueued a task was the default version, then the task uses the default version of the app when it executes—even if the default version has changed since the task was enqueued. If the version of the app that enqueued the task was not the default version at the time, then the task uses that version specifically when it executes. This allows you to test nondefault versions that use tasks before making them the default.

A call to a task handler appears in the request log, just like a user-initiated web request. You can monitor and analyze the performance of tasks just as you would user requests.

Testing and Managing Tasks

The development web server does not process task queues. Instead, it remembers tasks that are added to queues, and lets you execute them manually from the developer console. Recall that the development server console URL looks like this:

```
http://localhost:8080/_ah/admin/
```

Select Task Queues from the sidebar. Each named queue is listed with its rate and bucket size, the age of its oldest task, and the number of tasks in the queue. You can delete all tasks from the queue by clicking the Flush Queue button.

To execute tasks on a queue, click the queue's name. The Console displays a list of the tasks on the queue. For any task, click the Run button to run the task, or the Delete button to delete it without running it. If the task runs successfully, it disappears from the list.

> Be sure to have a window open showing the development server's log output when testing tasks. When you run a task, it appears as a logged request, along with its response code. If the response code is not 200, the task is considered to have failed, and it remains in the list of tasks in the Console. You can tell that something actually happened by watching the log messages.

You can inspect task queues for an app running on App Engine from the Administration Console. As of this writing, the App Engine team is still building features for managing tasks, such as the ability to flush task queues manually from the Administration Console, or the ability to delete tasks using the API. Currently, once a task is enqueued, it cannot be removed from the queue for the app or from the Administration Console. You can add logic to your task to watch the retry count (the X-AppEngine-TaskRetryCount header) and return success without performing work to bail if it is retried too many times. If your current code doesn't do this bail out trick and you have tasks enqueued and failing, just upload new code using the same app version number, and the tasks will use it when they are retried.

Using Task Queues in Python

A Python application enqueues tasks using the API provided by the google.appengine.api.labs.taskqueue module. The simplest way to enqueue a task is to call the add() function. Without arguments, the add() function enqueues a task to the default queue using the default URL for that queue:

```
from google.appengine.api.labs import taskqueue

taskqueue.add()
```

When the task queue feature is no longer considered "experimental," Google will change the package name of the Python API to `google.appengine.api.taskqueue` (moving it out of the `labs` package).

Recall that the default queue's name is `default`, and if a task does not specify its own handler URL path, it uses a URL path derived from the queue name, such as:

```
/_ah/queue/default
```

You map the URL to a request handler that performs the task in the *app.yaml* file. You can restrict the URL so that it can only be called by task queues and by the app's developers (for testing) using `login: admin`, like so:

```
handlers:
- url: /_ah/queue/default
  script: default_task.py
  login: admin
```

With this configuration, the no-argument call to the `add()` function enqueues the task on the default queue with the default URL and no arguments, and returns immediately. When the task queue processes this task, it issues an HTTP POST request with default arguments to the URL path `/_ah/queue/default`, which invokes the *default_task.py* request handler.

You can pass parameters to the task, as a set of named parameters (like a web form) or an HTTP POST message body. The `add()` function accepts either a Python `dict` of named parameters as the `params` argument, or a bytestring (`str`) message body as the `payload` argument.

```
taskqueue.add(params={'address': 'juliet@example.com'})

# ...

class DefaultQueueHandler(webapp.RequestHandler):
    def post(self):
        address = self.request.get('address')
        # ...
```

You can specify a custom URL for a task to use instead of the default URL for the queue using the `url` parameter. In fact, you can choose to ignore the default URLs entirely and just use per-task URLs.

```
taskqueue.add(
    url='/send_invitation_task',
    params={'address': 'juliet@example.com'}
)
```

You can control other aspects of the HTTP request as well. You can change the HTTP method used with the `method` parameter; the default is `POST`. (You can only use a `payload` or `params` for HTTP methods that support them.) You can also add arbitrary HTTP headers with the `headers` argument, which takes a Python `dict`.

You can set a delay for a task, such that the task does not become eligible for execution until the delay has elapsed. You can specify the delay as a number of seconds from the time the task is enqueued using the `countdown` argument, or as a `datetime.datetime` in the future using the `eta` (as in "estimated time of arrival") argument.

To set the name for a task, you specify the `name` argument. As described earlier, the name ensures that only one task with that name can be enqueued for a period of time, at least seven days with the current implementation. If you do not specify a name, the system assigns a unique name that has not been used in the past seven days.

The Python API also includes an object interface for enqueueing tasks. The `add()` function is equivalent to creating a `Queue` object that represents the default queue, creating a `Task` object with the given parameters, and adding it to the queue with the `add()` method of the `Queue`.

```
q = taskqueue.Queue()

t = taskqueue.Task(
    url='/send_invitation_task',
    params={'address': 'juliet@example.com'}
)

q.add(t)
```

An app can have up to 10 named queues, each with its own task execution rate (token replenishment rate and bucket size). In a Python app, you configure queues using a configuration file named *queue.yaml*, which looks like this:

```
queue:
- name: fastest
  rate: 10/s
  bucket_size: 10
- name: limitedemail
  rate: 1000/d
```

The file is in the YAML format, just like other Python configuration files. It contains one element named `queue` whose value is a list of mappings, one mapping for each queue. Each queue has a `name`, a token replenishment `rate`, and a `bucket_size`. The `name` and `rate` elements are required. If you omit `bucket_size`, it defaults to 5.

The `rate` is specified as a number, a slash, and a unit of time: `s` for second, `m` for minute, `h` for hour, and `d` for day. Tokens are replenished continuously over the interval, so `1/s` and `60/m` are equivalent.

The default queue uses a rate of `5/s` and a bucket size of 5. You can configure the default queue using *queue.yaml* by defining a queue named `default`.

```
queue:
- name: default
  rate: 1/s
```

To enqueue tasks to named queues, you use the object interface, passing the name of the queue to the `Queue` constructor:

```
q = taskqueue.Queue('limitedemail')

t = taskqueue.Task(
    url='/send_invitation_task',
    params={'address': 'juliet@example.com'}
)

q.add(t)
```

Remember that each named queue has a default task URL, which you can use by omitting the `url` parameter for the task. In this example, the default URL for the `limitedemail` queue is:

```
/_ah/queue/limitedemail
```

Similar to *index.yaml*, the *queue.yaml* file applies to all versions of the app. It is uploaded when the app is uploaded with `appcfg.py update`. You can update just the queue configuration for the app using `appcfg.py update_queues`:

```
appcfg.py update_queues app-dir
```

Deferring work with tasks

The Python SDK includes a handy utility that makes it easy to throw work into a task without writing a custom task handler. The utility uses a prepackaged general purpose task handler to process deferred work.

To use this utility, you create a Python function or other callable object that performs the work to be executed outside of the current request handler, then pass that callable object to the `defer()` function from the `google.appengine.ext.deferred` package. The `defer()` function takes the object to call within the task and arguments to pass to the callable object.

Here's a simple example that spans two Python modules, one containing the deferred function, and one containing the request handler that defers it. First, here's the function, to appear in a module named *invitation.py*:

```
from google.appengine.api import mail
import logging

_INVITATION_MESSAGE_BODY = '''
You have been invited to join our community...
'''

def send_invitation(recipient):
    mail.send_mail('support@example.com',
                   recipient,
                   'You\'re invited!',
                   _INVITATION_MESSAGE_BODY)
    logging.info('Sent invitation to %s' % recipient)
```

And here's the request handler script:

```python
from google.appengine.ext import webapp
from google.appengine.ext.webapp.util import run_wsgi_app
from google.appengine.ext import deferred
import invitation

class SendInvitationHandler(webapp.RequestHandler):
    def get(self):
        # recipient = ...
        deferred.defer(invitation.send_invitation, recipient)

        # ...

application = webapp.WSGIApplication([
    ('/sendinvite', SendInvitationHandler),
    ], debug=True)

def main():
    run_wsgi_app(application)

if __name__ == '__main__':
    main()
```

You set up the request handler for deferred work using the following configuration in your *app.yaml* file:

```yaml
handlers:
- url: /_ah/queue/deferred
  script: $PYTHON_LIB/google/appengine/ext/deferred/
  login: admin
```

This maps the URL path /_ah/queue/deferred to the deferred module in the API. ($PYTHON_LIB is replaced with the path to the Python directory containing the SDK on App Engine.) Tasks created with defer() use this URL path by default. login: admin restricts this handler to task queues and application developers.

The defer() function enqueues a task on the default queue that calls the given callable object with the given arguments. (Despite its use of the URL /_ah/queue/deferred for deferred tasks, this utility uses the default queue, not a queue named deferred.) The arguments are serialized and deserialized using Python's pickle module; all argument values must be pickle-able.

Most Python callable objects can be used with defer(), including functions and classes defined at the top level of a module, methods of objects, class methods, instances of classes that implement __call__(), and built-in functions and methods. defer() does not work with lambda functions, nested functions, nested classes, or instances of nested classes. The task handler must be able to access the callable object by name, possibly via a serializable object, since it does not preserve the scope of the call to defer().

You also can't use a function or class in the same module as the request handler class from which you call defer(). This is because pickle believes the module of the request handler class to be __main__ while it is running, and so it doesn't save the correct package name. This is why the previous example keeps the deferred function in a separate module.

You can control the parameters of the task, such as the delay, by passing additional arguments to `defer()`. These are the same arguments you would pass to `Task()`, but with the argument names prepended with an underscore so they are not confused with arguments for the callable.

```
deferred.defer(invitation.send_invitation,
               'juliet@example.com',
               _countdown=86400)
```

To call the callable, the task handler determines the module location of the callable from the description saved by the `defer()` function, imports the required module, recreates any required objects from their serialized forms, then calls the callable. If the module containing the callable imports other modules, those imports will occur during the task. If the deferred callable requires any additional setup, such as changes to the module import path, make sure this happens in the callable's module, or within the callable itself.

The task handler determines the success or failure of the task based on exceptions raised by the callable. If the callable raises a special exception called `deferred.PermanentTaskFailure`, the task handler logs the error, but returns a success code to the task queue so the task is not retried. If the callable raises any other exception, the exception is propagated to the Python runtime and the handler returns an error code, which causes the task queue to retry the task. If the callable does not raise an exception, the task is considered successful.

The `deferred` library is careful to raise `deferred.PermanentTaskFailure` for errors it knows will prevent the task from ever succeeding. Such errors log messages, then return success to flush the task from the queue.

Using Task Queues in Java

The Java task queue API consists of classes in the `com.google.appengine.api.labs.taskqueue` package. To enqueue a task, you use static methods of the `QueueFactory` class to get a `Queue` object that represents the queue, then you call the `add()` method on the `Queue`. This example enqueues a task on the default queue, using the default URL (`/_ah/queue`) and no data payload:

```
import com.google.appengine.api.labs.taskqueue.Queue;
import com.google.appengine.api.labs.taskqueue.QueueFactory;

// ...
        Queue queue = QueueFactory.getDefaultQueue();
        queue.add();
```

When the task queue feature is no longer considered "experimental," Google will change the package name of the Java API to `com.google.appengine.api.taskqueue` (moving it out of the `labs` package).

As usual, you map the URL to a request handler that performs the task in the deployment descriptor (*web.xml*). You can restrict the URL so that it can only be called by task queues and by the app's developers (for testing), like so:

```
<servlet>
  <servlet-name>defaulttaskurl</servlet-name>
  <servlet-class>myapp.DefaultQueueServlet</servlet-class>
</servlet>
<servlet-mapping>
  <servlet-name>defaulttaskurl</servlet-name>
  <url-pattern>/_ah/queue</url-pattern>
</servlet-mapping>

<security-constraint>
  <web-resource-collection>
    <web-resource-name>defaulttaskurl</web-resource-name>
    <url-pattern>/_ah/queue</url-pattern>
  </web-resource-collection>
  <auth-constraint>
    <role-name>admin</role-name>
  </auth-constraint>
</security-constraint>
```

This example restricts the default task URL (`/_ah/queue`) to be accessible only by administrators and task queues.

With this configuration, the no-argument call to the `add()` method enqueues the task on the default queue with the default URL and no arguments, and returns immediately. When the task queue processes this task, it issues an HTTP POST request with default arguments to the URL path `/_ah/queue`, which invokes `DefaultQueueServlet`.

You can pass parameters to the task as a set of named parameters (like a web form) or an HTTP POST message body. The `add()` method accepts a `TaskOptions` object that describes data and options for the task. You create a `TaskOptions` object using the `TaskOptions.Builder` static methods. Each builder method returns a `TaskOptions` object, and the object itself has similar methods for chaining purposes.

```
import com.google.appengine.api.labs.taskqueue.TaskOptions;

// ...
        TaskOptions taskOptions =
            TaskOptions.Builder.url("/send_invitation_task")
            .param("address", "juliet@example.com")
            .param("firstname", "Juliet");
        Queue queue = QueueFactory.getDefaultQueue();
        queue.add(taskOptions);
```

The url() method sets a custom URL for the task. If no custom URL is set, the task calls the default URL for the queue.

The param() method adds a request parameter to be included with the task's HTTP request. The method takes the name of the parameter, and either a String or a byte[] as the value of the parameter. Parameters are added to the HTTP request body URL-encoded, similar to a web form. The removeParam() method removes a parameter from the TaskOptions object; it takes the parameter name as its argument.

You can also set the HTTP request body with the payload() method. This method takes the request body as a String. You can also include a character set specification (such as "utf-8") as the second argument. You can't set both a payload and parameters for the same task.

You can control other aspects of the HTTP request as well. The method() method sets the HTTP method; the default is "POST". You can also add arbitrary HTTP headers by calling the header() method (which takes a String key and String value as arguments) for each header, or by calling the headers() method with a Map<String, String>.

You can set a delay for the task. The countdownMillis() method sets the delay as a number of milliseconds (a long) from the time the task is enqueued. The etaMillis() method sets the delay to be an absolute date and time, as a number of milliseconds from midnight, January 1, 1970, UTC.

To set the name for a task, you call the name() method. As described earlier, the name ensures that only one task with that name can be enqueued for a period of time, at least seven days with the current implementation. If you do not specify a name, the system assigns a unique name that has not been used in the past seven days.

An app can have up to 10 named queues, each with its own task execution rate (token replenishment rate and bucket size). In a Java app, you configure queues using a configuration file named *queue.xml*, in the *WEB-INF/* directory, which looks like this:

```
<queue-entries>
  <queue>
    <name>fastest</name>
    <rate>10/s</rate>
    <bucket-size>10</bucket-size>
  </queue>
  <queue>
    <name>limitedemail</name>
    <rate>1000/d</rate>
    <bucket-size>5</bucket-size>
  </queue>
</queue-entries>
```

The file includes one <queue> element per queue to be configured. Each queue has a <name>, a token replenishment <rate>, and a <bucket-size>.

The `<rate>` is specified as a number, a slash, and a unit of time: `s` for second, `m` for minute, `h` for hour, and `d` for day. Tokens are replenished continuously over the interval, so `1/s` and `60/m` are equivalent.

The default queue uses a rate of `5/s` and a bucket size of `5`. You can configure the default queue using *queue.xml* by defining a queue named `default`.

```
<queue-entries>
  <queue>
    <name>default</name>
    <rate>1/s</rate>
    <bucket-size>1</bucket-size>
  </queue>
</queue-entries>
```

To enqueue tasks to named queues, you pass the queue name to the `QueueFactory` method `getQueue()`. Tasks enqueued with the `Queue` object it returns will use the named queue.

```
Queue queue = QueueFactory.getQueue("limitedemail");
queue.add(taskOptions);
```

Remember that each named queue has a default task URL, which you can use by not setting a URL for the task. In this example, the default URL for the `limitedemail` queue is:

```
/_ah/queue/limitedemail
```

Similar to *datastore-indexes.xml*, the *queue.xml* file applies to all versions of the app. It is uploaded when the app is uploaded with `appcfg update` (`appcfg.sh update` on Mac OS X or Linux). You can update just the queue configuration for the app using `appcfg update_queues`:

```
appcfg update_queues war
```

Transactional Task Enqueueing

There's an exciting feature of tasks that had not yet been released by the time this book went to press, but is likely to be available by the time you read this: the ability to enqueue a task as part of a datastore transaction. A task enqueued within a transaction is only enqueued if the transaction succeeds. If the transaction fails, the task is not enqueued.

This opens up a world of possibilities for the datastore. Specifically, it enables easy transactions that operate across multiple entity groups.

Consider the message board example from Chapter 6. To maintain an accurate count of every message in each conversation, we have to update the count each time a message is posted. To do this with strong consistency, the count and the message have to be updated in the same transaction, which means they have to be in the same entity group—and therefore every message in the thread has to be in the same entity group. This might be acceptable for a count of messages per conversation, since it's unlikely that many users will be posting to the same conversation simultaneously, and even so, the delay for resolving concurrency failures might not be noticed.

But what if we want a count of every message on the website? Putting every message in a single entity group would be impractical, as it would effectively serialize all updates to the entire site. We need a way to update the count reliably without keeping everything in one entity group.

Transactional task enqueueing lets us update the count reliably without concern for entity groups. To post a message, we use a transaction to create the message entity and enqueue a task that will update the count. If the transaction fails, the task is not enqueued, so the count remains accurate. The task is performed outside of the transaction, so the count does not need to be in the same entity group as the message, but transactional enqueueing and task retries ensure that the count is updated, but only under the proper circumstances.

Of course, this comes with a trade-off: it must be acceptable for the count to be inaccurate between the time the message entity is created and the time the count is updated. In other words, we must trade strong consistency for *eventual consistency*. Transactional task enqueueing gives us a simple way to implement eventually consistent global transactions.

You might think that eventual consistency is suitable for the global message count, because who cares if the message count is accurate? But eventual consistency is useful for important data as well. Say Alicandria wants to give TheBarbarousBobmcgrath 1,000 gold pieces. Since any player can trade gold with any other player, it is impractical to put all players in the same entity group. So we use transactional task enqueueing: the app deducts 1,000 gold pieces from Alicandria's inventory, then enqueues a task to give 1,000 gold pieces to TheBarbarousBobmcgrath, all in a transaction. We use task names and memcache locks to ensure the system doesn't accidentally create new gold pieces if it retries the task. Also, since Bob might get angry if he doesn't get his money quickly, we configure the gold transfer queue to execute at a fast rate and with a large token bucket.

We're not able to include a tested code sample here because this feature wasn't available when this book was written. Check the App Engine website for information on the release of this feature and how to use it.

Scheduled Tasks

Applications do work in response to external stimuli: user requests, incoming email and XMPP messages, HTTP requests sent by a script on your computer. And while task queues can be used to trigger events across a period of time, a task must be enqueued by application code before anything happens.

Sometimes you want an application to do something "on its own." For instance, an app may need to send nightly email reports of the day's activity, or fetch new headlines from a news service. For this purpose, App Engine lets you specify a schedule of tasks to perform on a regular basis. In the App Engine API, scheduled tasks are also known as "cron jobs," named after a similar feature in the Unix operating system.

A scheduled task consists of a URL path to call and a description of the recurring times of the day, week, or month at which to call it. It can also include a description, which is displayed in the Administration Console and other reports of the schedule.

To execute a scheduled task, App Engine calls the URL path using an empty GET request. A scheduled task cannot be configured with parameters, headers, or a different HTTP method. If you need something more complicated, you can do it in the code for the request handler mapped to the scheduled task's URL path.

As with task queue handlers, you can secure the URL path by restricting it to application developers in the frontend configuration. The system can call such URL paths to execute scheduled tasks.

The HTTP request includes the header `X-AppEngine-Cron: true` to differentiate it from other App Engine–initiated requests. Of course, this isn't enough to ensure that the request isn't from a malicious user. To block external users, you must secure the URL in the frontend configuration.

In Python, the schedule is a configuration file named *cron.yaml*. It contains a value named `cron`, which is a list of task schedules. Each task schedule has a `description`, a `url`, and a `schedule`. You can also specify a `timezone` for the schedule.

```
cron:
- description: Send nightly reports.
  url: /cron/reports
  schedule: every day 23:59
  timezone: America/Los_Angeles
- description: Refresh news.
  url: /cron/getnews
  schedule: every 1 hours
```

In Java, the corresponding file in the *WEB-INF/* directoryis named *cron.xml*. A `<cronentries>` element contains zero or more `<cron>` elements, one for each schedule. The `<url>`, `<description>`, `<schedule>`, and `<timezone>` elements define the scheduled task.

```
<cronentries>
  <cron>
    <url>/cron/reports</url>
    <description>Send nightly reports.</description>
    <schedule>every day 23:59</schedule>
    <timezone>America/Los_Angeles</timezone>
  </cron>
  <cron>
    <url>/cron/getnews</url>
    <description>Refresh news.</description>
```

```
        <schedule>every 1 hours</schedule>
    </cron>
</cronentries>
```

The value for the schedule element (in either Python or Java) uses a simplified English-like format for describing the recurrence of the task. It accepts simple recurrences, such as every 30 minutes or every 3 hours, with a minimum interval of every 1 minutes. The parser's English isn't that good: it doesn't understand every 1 minute or every minute. It does understand every day, as an exception.

The interval every day also accepts an optional time of day, as a 24-hour hh:mm time; every day 23:59 runs every day at 11:59 p.m. You can have a task recur weekly using the name of a weekday, as in every tuesday, and can also include a time: every tuesday 23:59. In another English parsing foible, day names must use all lowercase letters. You can abbreviate day names using just the first three letters, such as every tue 23:59.

You can have a task recur monthly or on several days of a given month by specifying a comma-delimited list of ordinals (such as 2nd, or first,third) and a comma-delimited list of weekday names (monday,wednesday,friday or sat,sun). For instance, 2nd,4th sunday occurs on the second and fourth Sunday of each month. You can also include a time of day, as earlier.

Finally, you can have a task recur yearly by including the word "of" and a comma-delimited list of lowercase month names (january,july, or oct,nov,dec). Here's a schedule that uses every feature to execute at 6 p.m. on six specific days of the year:

```
3rd,4th tue,wed,thu of march 18:00
```

You can specify a timezone element to set the time zone for the time of day in a task schedule. This element is optional: if omitted, it defaults to Coordinated Universal Time (UTC). The value of timezone is a string from the "zoneinfo" standard list of time zone identifiers, such as America/Los_Angeles (also known as Pacific Time in the United States). See the App Engine documentation for a link to a list of time zone identifiers.

If you choose a time zone identifier where Daylight Saving Time (DST) is used and have a task scheduled during the DST hour, your task will be skipped when DST advances forward an hour, and run twice when DST retreats back an hour. Unless this is desired, pick a time zone that does not use DST, or do not schedule tasks during the DST hour.

Scheduled tasks are always invoked using the default version of the app. There is no way to schedule a task to execute using a specific nondefault version of the app.

The development console does not execute scheduled tasks automatically. If you need to test a scheduled task, you can visit the task URL path while signed in as an administrator. The Python version of the development console includes a Cron Jobs section that lists the URL paths in the configuration file for easy access.

As with other service configuration files, the scheduled task configuration file applies to the entire app, and is uploaded along with the application. You can also upload it separately. With the Python SDK:

```
appcfg.py update_cron app-dir
```

With the Java SDK (`appcfg.sh update_cron` on Mac OS X or Linux):

```
appcfg update_cron war
```

You can validate your task schedule and get a human-readable description of it using `appcfg.py cron_info app-dir` (Python) or `appcfg cron_info war` (Java). The report includes the exact days and times of the next few runs, so you can make sure that the schedule is what you want.

## CHAPTER 14

The Django Web Application Framework

This chapter discusses how to use a major web application framework with the Python runtime environment. Java developers may be interested in the general discussion of frameworks that follows, but the rest of this chapter is specific to Python. Several frameworks for Java are known to work well with App Engine, and you can find information on these by searching the Web and asking the App Engine Java forum.

As with all major categories of software, web applications have a common set of problems that need to be solved in code. Most web apps need software to interface with the server's networking layer, communicate using the HTTP protocol, define the resources and actions of the application, describe and implement the persistent data objects, enforce site-wide policies such as access control, and describe the browser interface in a way that makes it easily built and modified by designers. Many of these components involve complex and detailed best practices for interoperating with remote clients and protecting against a variety of security vulnerabilities.

A *web application framework* is a collection of solutions and best practices that you assemble and extend to make an app. A framework provides the structure for an app, and most frameworks can be run without changes to demonstrate that the initial skeleton is functional. You use the toolkit provided by the framework to build the data model, business logic, and user interface for your app, and the framework takes care of the details. Frameworks are so useful that selecting one is often the first step when starting a new web app project.

Notice that App Engine isn't a web application framework, exactly. App Engine provides scaling infrastructure, services, and interfaces that solve many common problems, but these operate at a level of abstraction just below most web app frameworks. A better example of a framework is webapp, a framework for Python included with the App Engine Python SDK. webapp lets you implement request handlers as Python classes, and takes care of the details of interfacing with the Python runtime environment and routing requests to handler classes.

Several major frameworks for Python work well with App Engine. Django, Pylons, web2py, and CherryPy work as is or with the help of an adapter component, and some frameworks (such as web2py) have added explicit support for App Engine. These frameworks are mature, robust, and widely used, and have large thriving support communities and substantial online documentation. You can buy books about these frameworks.

Not every feature of every framework works with App Engine. Notably, many frameworks include a mechanism for defining data models, but these are usually implemented for relational databases, and don't work with the App Engine datastore. In some cases, you can just replace the framework's data modeling library with App Engine's. Some features of frameworks also have issues running within App Engine's sandbox restrictions, such as by depending upon unsupported libraries. Developers have written adapter components that work around many of these issues.

In general, to use a framework, you add the framework's libraries to your application directory, then map all dynamic URLs (all URLs except those for static files) to a script that invokes the framework. Because the interface between the runtime environment and the app is CGI, you can use a WSGI adapter in the script to call a WSGI framework, just as we did with webapp. Most frameworks have their own mechanism for associating URL paths with request handlers, and it's often easiest to send all dynamic requests to the framework and let it route them. You may still want to use *app.yaml* to institute Google Accounts–based access control for some URLs.

Since many web developers will want to use a framework more substantial than webapp, App Engine's Python runtime environment includes the Django web application framework. You don't need to add Django's libraries to your application directory, though you may still want to use a "helper" component that simplifies setting it up.

In this chapter, we'll look at how to create an App Engine app using the Django web application framework and the Python runtime environment. We'll discuss how to set up Django for development, how to select the Django version, and how to install and use the Django App Engine Helper, an open source tool, to create an app.

For more information about Django, see the Django project website:

> *http://www.djangoproject.com/*

Installing Django

When App Engine first debuted in early 2008, the latest version of Django was 0.96. The Django project has since released version 1.0 and a significantly updated version 1.1. The 1.1 release includes many new features and changes to the API that are not backward compatible with 0.96, but the new features are substantial enough that most new apps should prefer the latest version.

Because App Engine promises not to make backward-incompatible changes to the runtime environment, the default version of Django on App Engine (in version 1 of the Python runtime) is still 0.96. However, App Engine includes a mechanism for explicitly selecting a newer version, such that all subsequent attempts to import Django modules will use the new version. You can use this mechanism in your main request handler script to use Django 1.1 for your app.

Before you do that, you must download and install Django 1.1 on your local computer. You won't need to add it to your application directory (it's available when running on App Engine), but you will need it locally while building and testing your application. Go to the Django project website and download Django 1.1:

http://www.djangoproject.com/download/1.1/tarball/

Follow the instructions to install the Python modules in your local Python environment by running the following commands. (The **sudo** command will require your computer's administrator password.)

```
tar xzvf Django-1.1.tar.gz
cd Django-1.1
sudo python setup.py install
```

Django 1.1 was the latest release when this book was published. If you see a newer version available on the Django website, be sure to check the App Engine documentation to confirm that the new version has been added to the Python runtime environment before using it locally.

If you'd prefer to use your own copy of Django instead of the one provided by the Python runtime environment (such as a newer version not yet in the environment), you can add it directly to your application directory. Doing so requires an additional step to remove the version of Django that's part of the runtime environment from the Python module search path. To do this, put this in your main request handler script prior to importing **django** modules:

```
for k in [k for k in sys.modules if k.startswith('django')]:
    del sys.modules[k]
```

Creating a Django Project

In Django, the complete set of code, configuration, and static files for a website is called a *project*. You create a new project by running a command that was installed with Django, called **django-admin.py**, like so:

```
django-admin.py startproject myproject
```

This command creates in your current working directory a new directory named after the project, in this case *myproject/*, with several starter files:

__init__.py
> A file that tells Python that code files in this directory can be imported as modules (this directory is a Python package).

manage.py
> A command-line utility you will use to build and manage this project, with many features.

settings.py
> Configuration for this project, in the form of a Python source file.

urls.py
> Mappings of URL paths to Python code, as a Python source file.

If you're following along with a Django tutorial or book, the next step is usually to start the Django development server using the `manage.py` command. If you did so now, you would be running the Django server, but it would know nothing of App Engine. To run the project in the App Engine development server, we must connect the Django project to the App Engine runtime environment using a request handler script and configuration in the *app.yaml* file.

The Request Handler Script

All that's left to do is to invoke the Django project from a handler script. Example 14-1 is a minimal script that hands the request off to Django 1.1 using the WSGI runner function from the webapp library. Create a file named *main.py* in the Django project directory you created in the previous step (e.g., *myproject/*).

Example 14-1. A simple request handler for invoking the Django framework

```
from google.appengine.dist import use_library
use_library('django', '1.1')

import os
os.environ['DJANGO_SETTINGS_MODULE'] = 'settings'

import django.core.handlers.wsgi
from google.appengine.ext.webapp import util

def main():
    # Run Django via WSGI.
    application = django.core.handlers.wsgi.WSGIHandler()
    util.run_wsgi_app(application)

if __name__ == '__main__':
    main()
```

The `use_library()` function is an App Engine utility that tells the runtime environment that version 1.1 of Django should be used when importing libraries from the `django` package. Without this call, importing from `django` would use Django 0.96.

`use_library()` does not have any effect when run in the development server, so make sure your Python installation has the correct version of Django in its module load path.

The script sets the `DJANGO_SETTINGS_MODULE` environment variable before importing anything from Django so imported modules know where to find your application's Django configuration. The value `'settings'` says this is in a file named *settings.py* in the application root directory. (This file was created by Django when you started the project.)

The rest of the handler script uses a `main()` routine (which is cached with app caching) to create the Django WSGI handler, then run it with webapp's WSGI runner utility. You could also use a generic WSGI-to-CGI adapter, but this one includes features such as smart handling of uncaught exceptions.

A typical setup routes all dynamic URLs for the site to Django via the handler script. To do this, create an *app.yaml* file in the project directory such as the following:

```
application: myproject
version: 1
runtime: python
api_version: 1

handlers:
- url: /static
  static_dir: static
- url: /.*
  script: main.py
```

Though you will use Django's own URL routing feature for most of the application, you must still use *app.yaml* to configure the App Engine frontend, and tell the App Master to serve static files using the static file servers.

There's one small tweak we must make before we can try this out. Edit *settings.py*, and look for the line that defines `ROOT_URLCONF`. By default, this is set to a module path that includes the project directory as a package name, such as `myproject.urls`. Since the project directory is our app's root directory, this path needs to be adjusted. Change this to read just `urls`:

```
ROOT_URLCONF = 'urls'
```

Run the App Engine development server (using the Launcher or the `dev_appserver.py` command), then visit the server URL in your browser. If Django says "It worked!" you're ready to develop your Django app on App Engine.

The Django App Engine Helper

Django has many useful features that work well with App Engine, but some features need a little help to work as described in the Django documentation. A few features are not supported, especially those that depend on Django's database interface, which expects to be backed by a relational database. If you develop with Django using just the minimal request handler, you'll need to be careful not to use an unsupported feature, or a feature that depends on something that is unsupported. Notably, Django's `admin` application relies heavily on the database interface, and does not work with App Engine.

Thankfully, there are several open source projects that restore and extend support for features of Django for App Engine. One such project is the Django App Engine Helper. The Helper makes it easy to use Django's maintenance tools with App Engine, such as using *manage.py* to start the App Engine development server. It provides an adapter layer so you can use App Engine data models with some Django components expecting Django's own data classes. The Helper also makes it easy to use Django's unit testing framework, including fixtures that install test data in the development server's datastore. Other features of Django are adapted to use App Engine services and infrastructure, and otherwise behave as they do in other Django apps.

To install the Helper, download it from the project website:

http://code.google.com/p/google-app-engine-django/

Click the Downloads tab, then select the revision with the highest release number. The download is a ZIP archive.

Unpack the archive, then copy all of its files to the application root directory. The Helper includes custom versions of *settings.py* and *manage.py*, its own *main.py* request handler and *app.yaml* configuration, and everything else you need to start a new project. (You can omit the documentation and auxiliary files, such as *README* and *Makefile*.) Be sure to edit *app.yaml* to use your application ID.

 The Django App Engine Helper distribution is itself a complete skeleton project. To start a new project, simply copy the Helper files to a new application directory and edit *app.yaml* to add your application ID. You don't need a separate handler script; the Helper provides one for you.

The Helper looks in several places for Django. First, it checks the application directory for a version of Django in either a *django* package directory or a *django.zip* archive containing the contents of the package. This lets you override the version of Django included with the App Engine runtime environment using a custom version.

If it doesn't find either of those, it calls `use_library()` to select an appropriate version. When run in the development server, the Helper uses whatever version is installed with Python on your computer. On App Engine, it uses the most recent version of Django supported by that specific version of the Helper. As of the "r94" release, that's Django 1.1.

You can request a specific version of Django that's supported by App Engine by editing *main.py* and *manage.py* in your project, finding the line that calls

`InstallAppengineHelperForDjango()`, and adding the version identifier as an argument to that function call. For instance, to select Django 1.0:

```
InstallAppengineHelperForDjango('1.0')
```

Now that the Helper is installed, you can start the App Engine development server using `manage.py` as you would with any other Django project:

```
python manage.py runserver
```

Thanks to the Helper, this is no different than running the `dev_appserver.py` command or using the Launcher to start the server. If you'd prefer to use those methods, you may, without losing any functionality of the Helper.

Test that the default project is working locally by visiting the server's URL in a web browser. By default, Django uses port 8000, not 8080, so this URL is:

http://localhost:8000/

The Helper adds several features to *manage.py* that work with the App Engine development server. One especially useful feature is the `shell` command, which starts a Python shell in the context of the Django project—and the development server. You can use this shell to import App Engine modules and interact with the development server, the simulated sandbox, and the simulated services.

```
python manage.py shell
```

Here is a simple shell session that demonstrates calling the development server's simulated Mail service (several harmless warning messages have been elided):

```
% python manage.py shell
Python 2.6.1 (r261:67515, Jul  7 2009, 23:51:51)
[GCC 4.2.1 (Apple Inc. build 5646)] on darwin
Type "help", "copyright", "credits" or "license" for more information.
(InteractiveConsole)
>>> from google.appengine.api import mail
>>> mail.send_mail('sender@example.com', 'to@example.com', 'my subject',
'message body')
INFO:root:MailService.Send
INFO:root:  From: sender@example.com
INFO:root:  To: to@example.com
INFO:root:  Subject: my subject
INFO:root:  Body:
INFO:root:    Content-type: text/plain
INFO:root:    Data length: 12
INFO:root:You are not currently sending out real email.  If you have sendmail
installed you can use it by using the server with --enable_sendmail
>>>
```

You can open a Python shell that connects to the live application via `remote_api` using the `console` command. This requires that you set up `remote_api` as described in Chapter 12 using a URL path of `/remote_api`.

```
python manage.py console
```

With `console`, the previous command session would actually attempt to send an email message using the Mail service. (It would fail, unless `sender@example.com` happens to be a developer of your application.)

You can deploy and manage your App Engine application using *manage.py*. The `update`, `rollback`, and `vacuum_indexes` commands all work as *manage.py* targets, and they assume that the Django project in the current directory is the intended application.

```
python manage.py update
```

You can erase the development server datastore using the `flush` (or `reset`) command. Unlike *dev_appserver.py*, the Helper is careful to maintain a separate development datastore for each Django project.

```
python manage.py flush
```

For more information on features of the Helper, see the Helper's project website and the Articles section of the App Engine documentation.

Creating a Django Application

In Django terms, a Django project consists of one or more "applications." Each application has a self-contained purpose, such as a user management application or a shopping cart application. A complete website may use multiple applications together, each of which can be reusable for other sites.

You create a Django application by running the project's `manage.py` command with the `startapp` action:

```
python manage.py startapp bookstore
```

This creates a subdirectory in the project's root directory named after the new application, in this case `bookstore`. The directory contains three files: an empty *__init__.py*, *models.py*, and *views.py*.

 Running `manage.py` uses code paths that run through the development server and that may emit warning messages about the datastore and images API, even for actions that don't start a development server. You can safely ignore these warnings.

The new app must be added to the project's configuration. Edit *settings.py* in the project root directory, and find the `INSTALLED_APPS` variable (a Python tuple). Add the module path of the app as an element of the tuple, retaining `'appengine_django'`.

```
INSTALLED_APPS = (
    'appengine_django',
    'bookstore',
)
```

A simple Django application defines request handlers ("views") and data models for performing the app's functions. The handlers are (typically) functions in the *views.py* file, and data models are classes in *models.py*. The Django project hooks up the app's handlers to the site's URLs in its *urls.py* file, and describes the appearance of the site and its applications using templates.

To see how views and URLs work, let's define a simple view that returns an HTTP response. Edit *views.py* in the *bookstore/* directory so it looks like this:

```
from django.http import HttpResponse

def home(request):
    return HttpResponse('The Book Store home page.')
```

Now edit the *urls.py* file for the project (in the project root directory) so that it looks like this:

```
from django.conf.urls.defaults import *

urlpatterns = patterns('',
    (r'^books/', 'bookstore.views.home'),
)
```

Start the server (`python manage.py runserver`) then visit the view's URL in a browser: `http://localhost:8000/books/`. The message from the view is displayed.

In this simple example, URLs that match the pattern `'^books/'` are routed to the `home()` function defined in the `bookstore.views` module. Django's URL routing facility includes many features for defining URL patterns in a modular way, including the ability to define a set of partial URL paths within each application. URL patterns can also match parts of URL paths and pass them to view functions as arguments.

A view is a function that takes a `django.http.HttpRequest` object as an argument (along with any other arguments passed in by the URL pattern) and returns a `django.http.HttpResponse`. Django has many handy ways for creating and returning response objects, including convenient ways to use its templating system.

Let's update this simple example to use a template, which we'll expand upon later. Edit *views.py* to look like this:

```
from django.shortcuts import render_to_response
import datetime

def home(request):
    return render_to_response(
        'bookstore/index.html',
        { 'clock': datetime.datetime.now() },
    )
```

Next, create a directory named *templates/* in the project root directory. Note that this is the project directory, not the *bookstore/* application directory. The project (the website) owns the appearance of the site. The project can declare multiple template directories in *settings.py*; the *templates/* directory is declared in the default settings.

Create a subdirectory in *templates/* named *bookstore/*, so the full path from the project root is *templates/bookstore/*. Inside, create the file *index.html* with the page contents to display:

```html
<html>
  <body>
    <p>Welcome to The Book Store! {{ clock }}</p>
  </body>
</html>
```

Reload the page to see the template displayed by the new view.

The `render_to_response()` shortcut function takes as its first argument the path to the template file, relative to one of the template directories specified in the `TEMPLATE_DIRS` variable of the *settings.py* file for the project. The second argument is a Python mapping that defines variables to be used within the template. In this example, we set a template variable named `clock` to be the current `datetime.datetime`. Within the template, `{{ code }}` interpolates this value as a string.

There are too many cool features of Django URLs, views, and templates to cover here. For more information, see the Django website.

Using App Engine Models With Django

Django includes a data modeling library that provides an object interface to relational databases. Since App Engine's datastore is not a relational database, there is no obvious way to translate between Django's modeling interface and the datastore. The Django data interface cannot be used with App Engine, nor can any component that relies on it, including the Django data administration application.

Instead, you can use App Engine's data modeling library, which we discussed in Chapter 7. While it's not a drop-in replacement for Django data modeling, it uses a similar API design. For instance, you can pass entities and query objects to Django templates for displaying data on web pages.

Unlike with Django data models, you do not need to run `python manage.py syncdb` or related commands when changing App Engine models. The datastore is schemaless, so there are no table definitions to update.

You can use the App Engine modeling interface directly, or you can use a feature provided by the Django App Engine Helper to define your models. The Helper includes a `BaseModel` class, a subclass of App Engine's `db.Model` that adds the ability to use an App Engine model class in a Django unit test fixture. (More on testing in a moment.)

Let's use `BaseModel` to implement some data classes for the message board. Edit *models.py* in the *bookstore/* directory to look like the following. (The Helper's version of `python manage.py startapp` has already added the import statements for the `BaseModel` class and `db` package.)

```
from appengine_django.models import BaseModel
from google.appengine.ext import db

class Book(BaseModel):
    title = db.StringProperty()
    author = db.StringProperty()
    copyright_year = db.IntegerProperty()
    author_birthdate = db.DateProperty()

class BookReview(BaseModel):
    book = db.ReferenceProperty(Book, collection_name='reviews')
    review_author = db.UserProperty()
    review_text = db.TextProperty()
    rating = db.StringProperty(choices=['Poor', 'OK', 'Good', 'Very Good', 'Great'],
                               default='Great')
    create_date = db.DateTimeProperty(auto_now_add=True)
```

Edit *views.py* to query the database for books and pass the query object to the template, like this:

```
from django.shortcuts import render_to_response
from google.appengine.ext import db
from bookstore import models

def home(request):
    q = models.Book.all().order('title')
    return render_to_response('bookstore/index.html',
                              { 'books': q })
```

Finally, edit *templates/bookstore/index.html* to display the list of books:

```
<html>
  <body>
    <p>Welcome to The Book Store!</p>
    <p>Books in our catalog:</p>
    <ul>
    {% for book in books %}
      <li>{{ book.title }}, by {{ book.author }} ({{ book.copyright_year }})</li>
    {% endfor %}
    </ul>
  </body>
</html>
```

Notice that we're passing the db.Query object directly to the template. The template uses the query object's iterator interface to fetch the Book entities from the datastore.

If you load the page right now (and feel free to do so to test the code), you'll see an empty list of books. Let's create some books from the Python shell. Stop the server (hit Ctrl-C), then start the shell:

```
python manage.py shell
```

You can create objects in the development server's datastore by typing Python code directly into the shell. Here is a complete shell session, including output, that creates several Book entities:

```
% python manage.py shell
Python 2.6.1 (r261:67515, Jul  7 2009, 23:51:51)
[GCC 4.2.1 (Apple Inc. build 5646)] on darwin
Type "help", "copyright", "credits" or "license" for more information.
(InteractiveConsole)
>>> from bookstore import models
>>> import datetime
>>> b = models.Book(title='Grapes of Wrath, The', author='Steinbeck, John',
copyright_year=1939, author_birthdate=datetime.date(1902, 2, 27))
>>> b.put()
datastore_types.Key.from_path(u'Book', 1,
_app_id_namespace=u'google-app-engine-django')
>>> b = models.Book(title='Cat in the Hat, The', author='Dr. Seuss',
copyright_year=1957, author_birthdate=datetime.date(1904, 3, 2))
>>> b.put()
datastore_types.Key.from_path(u'Book', 2,
_app_id_namespace=u'google-app-engine-django')
>>>
```

Exit the shell (press Ctrl-D), then restart the server and load the page.

Using Django Unit Tests and Fixtures

The Django App Engine Helper includes support for unit tests using Django's unit test runner and the App Engine development server. The unit test runner runs tests inside the development server's environment, so tests can access the simulated services, including the simulated datastore. The test runner supports tests defined with the standard Python libraries unittest or doctest, or other test frameworks with test runner customizations. Django provides its own class for defining unittest test cases, called django.test.TestCase, which adds several Django-specific features.

For unittest tests, the runner looks in files in the Django application directory (e.g., *bookstore/*) named *models.py* and *tests.py* for classes that inherit from unittest.TestCase or django.test.TestCase. Each method of a test case class whose name begins with test is a separate test. For each test, the runner initializes the test environment, instantiates the TestCase class, and calls the method for the test. If the class defines a setUp() method, it calls it before each test. If the class defines a tear Down() method, it calls it after each test. You can use setUp() and tearDown() to create and clean up test data and preparation for every test in a test case.

The TestCase class provides methods that cause the test to report failure if the conditions tested are not met. self.assertEqual() takes two arguments, and causes the test to fail if the arguments are not equal. self.assert_() takes one argument, and fails the test if the argument is a false value (False, None, 0, the empty string, and so forth). self.assertRaises() takes an exception class, a callable object, and arguments for the callable object, calls the callable, then fails the test if the callable does *not* raise the given exception. There are several other test methods, as well. Each of these methods takes an optional message argument that is printed in the test report if the test fails.

Here are a few trivial tests that illustrate the mechanism. Add this to *models.py*:

```
from django import test
import datetime
# ...

class TestBook(test.TestCase):
    def setUp(self):
        self.book = Book(title='test title',
                         author='test author',
                         copyright_year=1922,
                         author_birthdate=datetime.date(1900, 1, 1))

    def testCreateDate(self):
        self.assert_(self.book.author_birthdate
                     and isinstance(self.book.author_birthdate, datetime.date))

    def testAuthorMustBeAString(self):
        def badAssignment():
            self.book.author = 999
        self.assertRaises(db.BadValueError,
                          badAssignment)

    def testAuthorIsAString(self):
        self.book.author = 'Steinbeck, John'
```

The last test, `testAuthorIsAString()`, tests that assigning a `str` to the `author` property of a `Book` does not raise an exception. If it did, the test would fail.

To run all of the tests for the `bookstore` app, run the following command (from the project root directory, as usual):

```
python manage.py test bookstore
```

The tests run, and the runner prints a summary of successful and failed tests.

Real tests can get somewhat complicated, and may require that test data be present in the datastore. Django and the Helper ensure that the datastore starts out empty for each test. You can load data into the datastore in the `setUp()` routine, or in the test method itself. But for large amounts of test data, there is a better way: fixtures.

A fixture is a set of test data that is imported into the datastore at the beginning of a test. The easiest way to create test data is with the Django command `python manage.py dumpdata`. With the help of the Helper and the `BaseModel` base class, the `dumpdata` command knows how to dump the contents of the development server's simulated datastore in a format that can be used as a Django test fixture.

First, clear the datastore with the `reset` command:

```
python manage.py reset
```

Next, start up a shell:

```
python manage.py shell
```

Enter Python statements to create test data in the datastore. Here is a shell session that creates a few Book and BookReview entities:

```
% python manage.py shell
Python 2.6.1 (r261:67515, Jul  7 2009, 23:51:51)
[GCC 4.2.1 (Apple Inc. build 5646)] on darwin
Type "help", "copyright", "credits" or "license" for more information.
(InteractiveConsole)
>>> from google.appengine.ext import db
>>> from bookstore import models
>>> b1 = models.Book(title="one", author="")
>>> b1.put()
datastore_types.Key.from_path(u'Book', 1,
_app_id_namespace=u'google-app-engine-django')
>>> br1 = models.BookReview(book=b1, review_text="review1")
>>> br2 = models.BookReview(book=b1, review_text="review2")
>>> br3 = models.BookReview(book=b1, review_text="review3")
>>> db.put(br1)
datastore_types.Key.from_path(u'BookReview', 2,
_app_id_namespace=u'google-app-engine-django')
>>> db.put(br2)
datastore_types.Key.from_path(u'BookReview', 3,
_app_id_namespace=u'google-app-engine-django')
>>> db.put(br3)
datastore_types.Key.from_path(u'BookReview', 4,
_app_id_namespace=u'google-app-engine-django')
>>> b2 = models.Book(title="two", author="")
>>> b2.put()
datastore_types.Key.from_path(u'Book', 5,
_app_id_namespace=u'google-app-engine-django')
>>> b2br1 = models.BookReview(book=b2, review_text="review1")
>>> b2br2 = models.BookReview(book=b2, review_text="review2")
>>> db.put(b2br1)
datastore_types.Key.from_path(u'BookReview', 6,
_app_id_namespace=u'google-app-engine-django')
>>> db.put(b2br2)
datastore_types.Key.from_path(u'BookReview', 7,
_app_id_namespace=u'google-app-engine-django')
>>>
```

Exit the shell (Ctrl-D).

Create a directory named *fixtures/* in the *bookstore/* app directory. Now run the dumpdata command, and redirect its output to a file in this new directory:

```
python manage.py dumpdata bookstore >bookstore/fixtures/bookstore.json
```

The resulting file contains representations of all of the datastore entities for the kinds whose models are defined in the bookstore app, in the JSON format.

To load this fixture for every test in a test case, you create a class attribute for the django.test.TestCase named fixtures, whose value is a list of the names of the fixture files to load from the *fixtures/* directory. Here's another (trivial) test case that uses fixtures, which you can put in *models.py*:

```
# ...

class TestBooksAndReviews(test.TestCase):
    fixtures = ['bookstore.json']

    def testBookReviewOrder(self):
        d = Book.all().filter('title =', 'one').get()
        self.assert_(d, 'Book "one" must be in test fixture')

        q = BookReview.all().filter('book =', d)
        q.order('-create_date')
        reviews = q.fetch(3)
        self.assertEqual('review3', reviews[0].review_text)
        self.assertEqual('review2', reviews[1].review_text)
        self.assertEqual('review1', reviews[2].review_text)
```

Run the new test using the **test** command, as before:

```
python manage.py test bookstore
```

For each test in the **TestBooksAndReviews** test case, Django flushes the simulated data-store, loads the fixtures, calls the test case's **setUp()** method (if any), then calls the test method, and finally calls the **tearDown()** method (if any).

You can also load fixtures into the project's development datastore manually using the **python manage.py loaddata** command:

```
python manage.py loaddata bookstore/fixtures/bookstore.json
```

See the Django documentation for more information about unit testing and fixtures.

Using Django Forms

Django includes a powerful feature for building web forms based on data model definitions. The Django forms library can generate HTML for forms, validate that submitted data meets the requirements of the model, and redisplay the form to the user with error messages. The default appearance is useful, and you can customize the appearance extensively.

Django's version of the form library only works with the Django data modeling API, and does not work directly with App Engine models. Thankfully, the App Engine Python runtime environment includes an App Engine–compatible implementation of Django forms, in the package **google.appengine.ext.db.djangoforms**.

We won't go into the details of how Django forms work—see the Django documentation for a complete explanation—but let's walk through a quick example to see how the pieces fit together. Our example will use the following behavior for creating and editing **Book** entities:

- An HTTP GET request to **/books/book/** displays an empty form for creating a new **Book**.

- An HTTP POST request to **/books/book/** processes the book creation form, and either creates the book and redirects to **/books** (the book listing page) or redisplays the form with errors, if any.
- An HTTP GET request to **/books/book/1234** displays the form to edit the **Book** entity, with the fields filled out with the current values.
- An HTTP POST request to **/books/book/1234** updates the book with that ID, with the same error-handling behavior as the book creation form.

Edit *urls.py* to use a new view function named **book_form()** to handle these URLs:

```
from django.conf.urls.defaults import *

urlpatterns = patterns('',
    (r'^books/book/(\d*)', 'bookstore.views.book_form'),
    (r'^books/', 'bookstore.views.home'),
)
```

The regular expression '**^books/book/(\d*)**' captures the book ID in the URL, if any, and passes it to the view function as an argument.

Edit *views.py* to create the **BookForm** class and the **book_form()** view function:

```
# ...
from google.appengine.ext.db import djangoforms
from django.http import HttpResponseRedirect

# ...
class BookForm(djangoforms.ModelForm):
    class Meta:
        model = models.Book

def book_form(request, book_id=None):
    if request.method == 'POST':
        # The form was submitted.
        if book_id:
            # Fetch the existing Book and update it from the form.
            book = models.Book.get_by_id(int(book_id))
            form = BookForm(request.POST, instance=book)
        else:
            # Create a new Book based on the form.
            form = BookForm(request.POST)

        if form.is_valid():
            book = form.save(commit=False)
            book.put()
            return HttpResponseRedirect('/books/')
        # else fall through to redisplay the form with error messages

    else:
        # The user wants to see the form.
        if book_id:
            # Show the form to edit an existing Book.
            book = models.Book.get_by_id(int(book_id))
            form = BookForm(instance=book)
```

```
        else:
            # Show the form to create a new Book.
            form = BookForm()

    return render_to_response('bookstore/bookform.html', {
        'book_id': book_id,
        'form': form,
    })

# ...
```

The BookForm class is a subclass of google.appengine.ext.db.djangoforms.ModelForm. It can examine an App Engine model class (a subclass of db.Model) and can render and process forms with fields based on the model's property declarations. It knows which model class to use from the Meta inner class, whose model class attribute is set to our Book class. The ModelForm has useful default rendering and processing behavior for each of the default property declaration types, and you can customize this extensively. For now, we'll use the defaults.

The book_form() view function takes the HTTP request object and the book_id captured by the regular expression in *urls.py* as arguments. If the request method is 'POST', then it processes the submitted form; otherwise it assumes the method is 'GET' and just displays the form. In either case, the form is represented by an instance of the BookForm class.

If constructed without arguments, the BookForm represents an empty form for creating a new Book entity. If constructed with the instance argument set to a Book object, the form's fields are prepopulated with the object's property values.

To process a submitted form, you pass the dictionary of POST parameters (request.POST) to the BookForm constructor as its first positional argument. If you also provide the instance argument, the instance sets the initial values—including the entity key—and the form data overwrites everything else, as provided.

The BookForm object knows how to render the form based on the model class and the provided model instance (if any). It also knows how to validate data submitted by the user, and render the form with the user's input and any appropriate error messages included. The is_valid() method tells you if the submitted data is acceptable for saving to the datastore. If it isn't, you send the BookForm to the template just as you would when displaying the form for the first time.

If the data submitted by the user is valid, the BookForm knows how to produce the final entity object. The save() method saves the entity and returns it; if you set the commit=False argument, it just returns the entity and does not save it, so you can make further changes and save it yourself. In this example, a successful create or update redirects the user to /books/ (which we've hardcoded in the view for simplicity) instead of rendering a template.

To display the form, we simply pass the `BookForm` object to a template. There are several methods on the object for rendering it in different ways; we'll use the `as_p()` method to display the form fields in `<p>` elements.

Create that template now, named *templates/bookstore/bookform.html*:

```
<html>
  <body>

    {% if book_id %}
      <p>Edit book {{ book_id }}:</p>
      <form action="/books/book/{{ book_id }}" method="POST">
    {% else %}
      <p>Create book:</p>
      <form action="/books/book/" method="POST">
    {% endif %}
        {{ form.as_p }}
        <input type="submit" />
      </form>

  </body>
</html>
```

The template is responsible for outputting the `<form>` tag and the Submit button. The `BookForm` does the rest.

Before we test this, let's make one more change to the book-listing template to add some "create" and "edit" links. Edit *templates/bookstore/index.html*:

```
<html>
  <body>
    <p>Welcome to The Book Store!</p>
    <p>Books in our catalog:</p>
    <ul>
    {% for book in books %}
      <li>{{ book.title }}, by {{ book.author }} ({{ book.copyright_year }})
      [<a href="/books/book/{{ book.key.id }}">edit</a>]</li>
    {% endfor %}
    </ul>
    <p>[<a href="/books/book/">add a book</a>]</p>
  </body>
</html>
```

Restart the development server, then load the book list URL (`/books/`) in the browser. Click "add a book" to show the book creation form. Enter some data for the book, then submit it to create it.

 The default form widget for a date field is just a text field, and it's finicky about the format. In this case, the "author birthdate" field expects input in the form `YYYY-MM-DD`, such as `1902-02-27`.

Continue the test by clicking the "edit" link next to one of the books listed. The form displays with that book's data. Edit some of the data, then submit the form to update the entity.

Also try entering invalid data for a field, such as nonnumeric data for the "copyright year" field, or a date that doesn't use the expected format. Notice that the form redisplays with your original input, and with error messages.

The main thing to notice about this example is that the data model class itself (in this case Book) completely describes the default form, including the display of its form fields and the validation logic. The default field names are based on the names of the properties. You can change a field's name by specifying a **verbose_name** argument to the property declaration on the model class:

```
class Book(BaseModel):
    title = db.StringProperty(verbose_name="Book title")
    # ...
```

See the Django documentation for more information about customizing the display and handling of forms, and other best practices regarding form handling.

## CHAPTER 15

Deploying and Managing Applications

Uploading your application to App Engine is easy: just click a button or run a command, then enter your developer account email address and password. All of your application's code, configuration, and static files are sent to App Engine, and seconds later your new app is running.

Easy deployment is one of App Engine's most useful features. You don't have to worry about which servers have which software, how servers connect to services, or whether machines need to be rebooted or processes restarted. Other than your developer account, there are no database passwords to remember, no secret keys to generate, and no need to administer and troubleshoot individual machines. Your application exists as a single logical entity, and running it on large-scale infrastructure is as easy as running it on your local computer.

App Engine includes features for testing a new version of an app before making it public, reverting to a previous version quickly in case of a problem, and migrating the datastore and service configuration for the app from one version to another. These features let you control how quickly changes are applied to your application: you can make a new version public immediately to fix small bugs, or you can test a new version for a while before making it the version everyone sees.

Service configuration is shared across all versions of an app, including datastore indexes, task queues, and scheduled tasks. When you upload the app, the service configuration files on your computer are uploaded as well, and take effect immediately for all app versions. You can also upload each configuration file separately. This is especially useful for datastore indexes, since new indexes based on existing entities take time to build before they are ready to serve datastore queries.

Notice that service configuration is separate from the application configuration, which includes URL mappings, runtime environment selection, and inbound service activation. Application configuration is bound to a specific app version.

App Engine provides rich facilities for inspecting the performance of an app while it is serving live traffic. Most of these features are available in the Administration Console, including analytic graphs of traffic and resource usage, and browsable request and message logs. You can also use the Console to inspect and make one-off changes to datastore entities.

You also use the Administration Console to perform maintenance tasks, such as giving other developers access to the Console, changing settings, and setting up a billing account.

In this chapter, we'll discuss how to upload a new app, how to update an existing app, and how to use App Engine's versioning feature to test a new version of an app on App Engine while your users continue to use the previous version. We'll look at how to migrate the datastore and service configuration from one version to another. We'll also look at features of the SDK and the Administration Console for inspecting, trouble-shooting, and analyzing how your live application is running. And finally, we'll discuss other application maintenance tasks, billing, and where to get more information.

Uploading an Application

We introduced uploading an application way back in Chapter 2, but let's begin with a brief review.

If you're developing a Python app using the Launcher for Windows or Mac OS X, you can deploy your app by selecting it in the app list then clicking the Deploy button. The Launcher prompts for your developer account email address and password. The Mac version can remember your account credentials on your Keychain, but it always prompts in case you want to specify a different account. The upload begins, and the Launcher opens a window to display status messages emitted by the uploader tool.

If you're developing a Java app using Eclipse and the Google Plugin, you can deploy your app by clicking on the Deploy App Engine Project button in the Eclipse toolbar (the one that looks like the App Engine logo, a gray airplane engine with blue wings). It prompts for your developer account email address and password. The upload begins, and an Eclipse progress window reports on the status.

You can also upload a Python or Java app using the AppCfg command-line tool from the SDK. For Python, the tool takes the **update** action and a path to your application root directory (the directory containing the *app.yaml* file):

```
appcfg.py update clock
```

For Java, the tool takes the **update** action and a path to the WAR directory:

```
appcfg update clock/war
```

(For Mac OS X or Linux and a Java app, use **appcfg.sh**.)

We said this earlier, but it's worth repeating: there is no way to download the app's files once they have been uploaded. We strongly advise that you keep backups and use a revision control system.

Using Versions

The upload tool determines the application ID from the appropriate configuration file. For Python, this is the `application` element in the *app.yaml* file. For Java, this is the `<application>` element in the *appengine-web.xml* file.

The tool also uses this file to determine the version ID to use for this upload, from the `version` element. If App Engine does not yet have a version of this app with this ID, then it creates a new version with the uploaded files. If App Engine does have such a version, then it replaces the existing version. The replacement is total: no remnants of the previous version's code or static files remain. The new app has only the files present in the project directory on your computer at the time of the upload. Of course, data stored by the services for the app remain, including the datastore, memcache, log data, and enqueued tasks.

The version of the app that is visible on your app's primary domain name—either *app-id*.appspot.com or your Google Apps domain—is known as the *default version*. When you upload your app for the first time, the initial version becomes the default version automatically. If you subsequently upload a version with a different version ID, the original version remains the default until you change the default using the Administration Console.

Recall from Chapter 3 that each version has its own `appspot.com` URL that includes the version ID as well as the application ID:

    version-id.latest.app-id.appspot.com

 Remember that there are no special protections on the version URLs. If the app does not restrict access using code or configuration, then anyone who knows an unrestricted URL can access it. If you don't want a user to be able to access a version other than the default, you can check the `Host` header in the app and respond accordingly. You can also upload the nondefault version with configuration that restricts all URLs to administrators. Be sure to upload it again with the real configuration before making it the default version.

When you replace an existing version by uploading the app with that version ID, App Engine starts using the uploaded app for requests for that version within seconds of the upload. It is not guaranteed that every request after a particular time will use the new code and static files, but it usually doesn't take more than a few seconds for the App

Master to update all of the frontend servers. The App Master ensures that all of the files are in place on a frontend server before using the new files to handle requests.

Internally, App Engine maintains a "minor" version number for each version ID. When you upload the app, App Engine creates a new minor version for the app ID and version ID mentioned in the app's configuration file, and associates all code, static files, and frontend configuration with that minor version. When it is done creating the new minor version, it declares the new minor version the latest for the version ID, and the frontend starts to use it. Minor version numbers are an internal implementation detail, and are not exposed to the app or the Administration Console. You cannot access previous minor versions or the latest minor version number, and you cannot revert to previous minor versions. (This explains the word `latest` in the version URL, but you can't actually replace the word with a minor version number to access other minor versions.)

If you upload the app with the same version ID as that of the version that's currently the default, your users will start seeing the updated app within a few seconds of uploading. This is fine for small, low-risk changes that don't depend on changes to your data schemas or datastore indexes.

For larger changes, it's better to upload the app with a new version ID (in the application configuration file), test the app using the version URL, then switch the default version to direct traffic to the new version. To switch the default version, sign in to the Administration Console, then select Versions from the sidebar. Select the radio button next to the desired version, then click the Make Default button. This is shown in Figure 15-1.

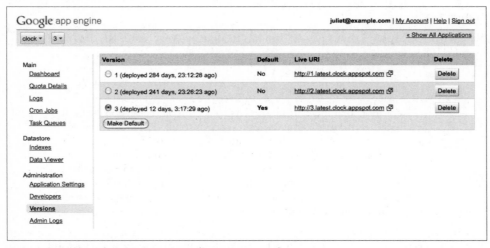

Figure 15-1. The Administration Console Versions panel

App Engine can host up to 10 different version IDs per app at one time. You can delete unused versions from the Administration Console by clicking the Delete button on the appropriate row.

Many actions in the Administration Console refer to a specific version of the app, including usage statistics and the log viewer. You can control which version you're looking at by selecting it from the drop-down menu in the top-left corner of the screen, next to the application ID. The version ID only appears as a drop-down menu if you have more than one version of the app. Similarly, the application ID appears as a drop-down menu if you have more than one app associated with your developer account.

Managing Service Configuration

All versions of an application use the same services. Service configuration and application data are shared across all versions of the app.

An app can have several service-related configuration files:

index.yaml or *datastore-indexes.xml*
> A description of all of the required datastore indexes.

queue.yaml or *queue.xml*
> Configuration for task queues.

cron.yaml or *cron.xml*
> The schedule for scheduled tasks (cron jobs).

Whenever you upload the app, these configuration files are uploaded from your computer to the services and take effect for the entire app, replacing any configuration that was once there. This is true regardless of whether the app version ID is new or already exists, or whether the version ID is the default.

You can update the configuration for each service without uploading the entire app using the AppCfg tool. To update just the index configuration, use the `update_indexes` action, with the project directory (e.g., `app-dir`):

```
appcfg.py update_indexes app-dir
```

To update just the task queue configuration, use `update_queues`:

```
appcfg.py update_queues app-dir
```

And to update just the scheduled task schedule, use `update_cron`:

```
appcfg.py update_cron app-dir
```

Managing Indexes

When you upload the datastore index configuration for an app, the datastore begins building indexes that appear in the configuration but do not yet exist. This process is *not* instantaneous, and may take many minutes for new indexes that contain many rows. The datastore needs time to crawl all of the entities to build the new indexes.

You can check on the build status of new indexes using the Administration Console, in the Indexes section. An index being built appears with a status of "Building." When it is ready, the status changes to "Serving." Figure 15-2 shows a simple example of the "Indexes" section.

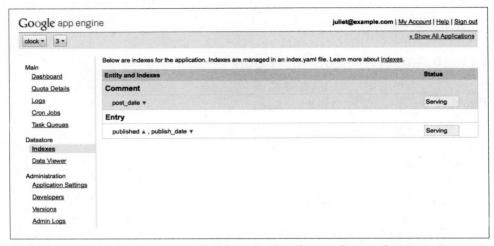

Figure 15-2. The Administration Console Indexes panel, with two indexes in the "Serving" status

If an index's build status is "Error," the index has exploded (as described earlier in "Exploding Indexes" on page 159). To clear this condition, you must first remove the index from your configuration, then upload the new configuration. You can change the definition of the index so that it is no longer an exploding index, or you can delete the entities that are causing the problem. Once that is done, you can add the index configuration back and upload it again.

If your application performs a query while the index for the query is building, the query will fail. You can avoid this by uploading the index configuration, waiting until the index is built, then making the app that uses that query available. The most convenient way to do this depends on whether you upload the new application in a new version:

- If you are uploading the new application using the version identifier that is currently the "default" version, upload the index configuration alone using the `appcfg.py update_indexes` command. When the indexes are built, upload the app.

- If you are uploading the application as a new version, or as a version that isn't the default and that nobody is actively using, you can safely upload the application and index configuration together (`appcfg.py update`). Wait until the indexes are built before making the new version the default.

If you upload index configuration that does not mention an index that has already been built, the datastore does not delete the unused index, since it might still be in use by an older version of the app. You must tell App Engine to purge unused indexes. To do this, run the AppCfg command with the `vacuum_indexes` option. For instance, in Python:

```
appcfg.py vacuum_indexes app-dir
```

App Engine will purge all custom indexes not mentioned in the index configuration uploaded most recently. This reclaims the storage space used by those indexes.

Browsing and Downloading Logs

Once your app is up and running on App Engine, you'll want to monitor, analyze, and manage its behavior. The Administration Console and the AppCfg tool include several important features for doing this. One of the most important is the application's request and message log.

App Engine maintains a log of every request for the app, including the date and time of the request; the IP address of the client; the URL requested; the HTTP status the server returned; and information provided by the client, such as the user agent (the browser identification string) and the referrer (if the user followed a link, which page contained the link). App Engine also records resource usage for each request.

An application can also write its own messages to the log, to associate diagnostic information with the request. We looked at the interfaces for doing this back in Chapter 3.

You can browse your application's logs using the Administration Console. To do so, visit the Console, select your app, then choose Logs from the sidebar menu. Separate logs are maintained for each version of the app, so make sure the version whose logs you want to browse is selected.

The log browser can show all recent requests for the app, or just recent log messages emitted by the app at a given log level. Each entry can be expanded to view the request details. Figure 15-3 shows an example of the "Info"-level messages for an app, with one request expanded.

You can perform advanced filtering in the log viewer by clicking the Options widget. Here you can limit the view to messages before a specific date and time, and can filter for textual patterns in the app's log messages or in specific fields in the request logs.

You can download your application's log data for offline analysis using the AppCfg tool from the SDK. This command works similarly with both the Python SDK (*appcfg.py*) and the Java SDK (*appcfg* or *appcfg.sh*).

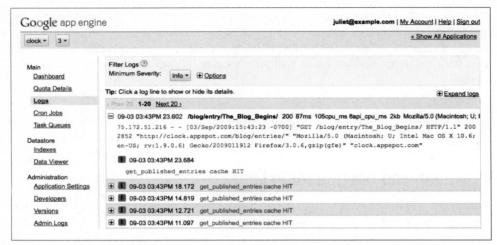

Figure 15-3. The Administration Console log browser

The following command downloads request logs for the app in the development directory *clock*, and saves them to a file named *logs.txt*:

```
appcfg.py request_logs clock logs.txt
```

Request data appears in the file in a common format known as the Apache Combined (or "NCSA Combined") logfile format, one request per line (shown here as two lines to fit on the page):

```
127.0.0.1 - - [05/Jul/2009:06:46:30 -0700] "GET /blog/ HTTP/1.1" 200 14598 -
"Mozilla/5.0 (Macintosh; U; Intel Mac OS X 10_5_8; en-us)...,gzip(gfe)"
```

From left to right, the fields are:

- The IP address of the client
- A - (an unused field retained for backward compatibility)
- The email address of the user who made the request, if the user is signed in using Google Accounts; - otherwise
- The date and time of the request
- The HTTP command string in double quotes, including the method and URL path
- The HTTP response code returned by the server
- The size of the response, as a number of bytes
- The "Referrer" header provided by the client, usually the URL of the page that linked to this URL
- The "User-Agent" header provided by the client, usually identifying the browser and its capabilities

By default, this data does not include the domain name (the "host") of the request. You can add it by giving the `appcfg.py request_logs` command the `--include_vhost` option. The host field is added at the end of the line:

```
appcfg.py request_logs clock logs.txt --include_vhost
```

You can download just the requests for a given host using the `--vhost` option. This is useful if you are using multiple `appspot.com` domain names for different purposes, or if you want to see log data for requests directed at specific versions of the app.

```
appcfg.py request_logs clock logs.txt --vhost msgs.example.appspot.com
```

The command above downloads request data only. To download log messages emitted by the application, include a minimum severity level specified as a number, where 0 is all log messages ("debug" level and up) and 5 is only "critical" messages, using the `--severity` argument:

```
appcfg.py request_logs clock logs.txt --severity=1
```

Application messages appear in the file on separate lines immediately following the corresponding request. The format for this line is a tab, the severity of the message as a number, a colon, a numeric timestamp for the message, then the message:

```
1:1246801590.938119 get_published_entries cache HIT
```

Log data is ordered chronologically by request, from earliest to latest. Application messages are ordered within each request by their timestamps.

The downloaded log data is the combined log data for all versions of the app. For requests to specific versions using the versioned `appspot.com` URL, you can use the `--include_vhost` or `--vhost` options to differentiate between requests for different versions. There is no built-in way to tell the difference between a request for a previous default version and a newer default version, though the app could add such an indication to its log messages if desired.

By default, `appcfg request_logs` downloads log data for the current calendar day, back to midnight, Pacific Time. You can use the `--num_days` option to request more than one day's worth of logs, or specify 0 to download all of the log data available. You can also specify an alternate end date with the `--end_date=...` option, whose value is of the form YYYY-MM-DD (such as 2009-11-04).

For the purposes of `appcfg request_logs`, App Engine retains up to 90 days of request log data, and about 1,000 application log messages for each log level. You can keep a running archive of all messages using the `--append` option. If this option is provided, `appcfg request_logs` will check your local logfile for the latest message it has, then download all available log messages since that message and append them to the file. How often you need to do this for a complete data set depends on how fast the log data grows, based on how often the application writes messages to the log.

Log data does not count toward your storage limits, and there is (currently) no way to increase the amount of log data retained by App Engine.

Inspecting the Datastore

You can use the Administration Console to inspect and modify entities in the datastore of your live application. You can view all entities of a kind, perform queries using GQL, edit the properties of existing entities, and create new entities based on existing ones. These features are in the Data Viewer section of the Console.

The editing facilities of this interface are somewhat limited. You can't create new properties, delete properties, or change value types. New entities created through the Console have properties and value types derived from other examples of the given kind. You cannot create new kinds. You also can't view or edit binary ("blob") data. In most cases, these abilities go beyond the needs of inspecting a live app's data—most apps can't use kinds they don't already know about—but you might notice if the app relies on the existence or nonexistence of properties.

You can perform real-time queries on entities from the Console using GQL, even for Java applications. However, you can only perform queries for which the app already has indexes (built-in or custom). If you try to perform a query that needs an index that the app doesn't have, the Console displays a helpful error message.

Refer to the section "GQL" on page 123 for more information about the Administration Console's data viewer.

Application Settings

The Application Settings panel of the Administration Console lets you change or view several miscellaneous aspects of your application.

This panel lets you view the application ID and the authentication method (Google accounts or Google Apps) that you set when you registered the application ID. These cannot be changed. If you need different values, you must register a new application ID.

The application title is the user-visible name of your application. It appears on the Google Accounts sign-in screen. You set this when you created the application, and you can change it at any time from this panel.

The "cookie expiration" time is the amount of time a user signed in with a Google account will remain signed in. If the user signs in to your app, he will not have to sign in again from the computer he is using until the expiration time elapses.

Also on this screen, you can view which optional services are enabled for this application. Optional services are those that have passive behavior that affect the app, specifically the inbound services of incoming email and incoming XMPP. You can enable these for an app in the app's configuration file, as discussed in previous chapters.

This screen offers an alternate path for setting up a domain name for an app using Google Apps. Instead of adding the app as a service within Google Apps, you can use this setup procedure to associate the app with an Apps domain with default settings.

Either setup procedure has the same effect, and you must still register the domain and create the Google Apps account separately. (There is a link to set up Google Apps on this screen.)

Managing Developers

When you register an application ID, you become a developer for the application automatically. You can invite other people to be developers for the application from the Developers section of the Administration Console.

To invite a developer, you enter the person's email address in the appropriate field and click Invite. App Engine sends an email to the developer inviting her to set up an account. If the email address you invited is for a Google account, the developer can use the existing account to access App Engine, though she must still accept the invitation by clicking on a link in the invitation email message. If the email address does not have a corresponding Google account, the developer can create a Google account for that address by following the instructions in the message. The developer cannot accept the invitation from a Google account with a different address; you must invite the alternate address explicitly.

An invited developer who has not yet accepted the invitation appears in the list with a status of "Pending." After the developer accepts the invitation, she appears with a status of "Active."

You can remove any developer from the list by clicking the Remove button for the developer. The developer loses all access immediately.

All developers of an application have the same rights and access. They can access the Administration Console, upload new application files, create and delete versions, change the default version, access logs, and inspect and tweak the datastore. They can even remove your administrator access, take over billing, and disable or delete the app. When a developer signs in to the application itself via Google Accounts, the app recognizes her as an administrator, allowing her to access URLs configured as administrator-only and telling the app about the administrator status when the app inquires via the API.

While you can only register up to 10 application IDs yourself, you can be a developer on as many applications as you like, assuming you can get invited. Of course, it's against the Terms of Service to create fake accounts just to be able to create more apps and invite your main account to them, so don't do that.

Every administrative action performed by a developer adds a corresponding entry in a special log. Any developer can view this log in the Admin Logs section of the Console. This log cannot be edited or erased. Activities that get logged include app updates, version changes, developer invites and removals, index changes, settings changes, and changes to datastore entities made from the Console.

Quotas and Billing

The first thing you see when you visit the Administration Console and select an app is the "dashboard." This handy screen provides a visual overview of your app's traffic, resource usage, and errors. For an example of the dashboard for a new app, refer back to Figure 2-11 in Chapter 2.

The topmost chart displays time-based data over the past 24 hours. You can select from several data sets to view via the drop-down menu, including requests per second, clock time or CPU time per request, bandwidth, errors, and quota denials. You can adjust the period for this chart by clicking on the buttons (such as "6 hr").

Below the chart is a graph showing how much of the billable quotas have been consumed for the calendar day, and how much of your daily budget has been spent for each quota. A message at the upper-right of the chart indicates how much of the calendar day is remaining. If any of the bars look like they might fill up before the next reset, you may need to increase your budget for that quota to avoid quota denials.

Near the bottom of the dashboard are lists of popular URL paths and URLs that are returning errors. You can click on a URL to view the detailed request logs for that URL path.

The dashboard's time-based chart and URL traffic lists show data for the version of the app selected by the drop-down menu in the upper-left corner of the screen. When you first sign in to the Console, the default version is selected. To view data for a different version of the app, select it from the drop-down menu.

You can view a more comprehensive chart of how the app is consuming resources with quotas from the Quota Details section of the Administration Console. This chart shows billable quotas as well as several fixed quotas, such as API calls and service bandwidth. If your app is having quota-denial errors, check this screen for information on how the app is consuming resources.

The resource usage chart on the dashboard and the quota details screen show the total of all resource usage for all versions of the app. All versions of an app share the same budget and quotas.

When your app is ready to outgrow the free quotas, you can set up billing and set a budget for additional resources. App Engine allocates more resources as needed according to the budget you establish, and you are only billed for the resources actually consumed. To set up billing for an application, you select the Billing Settings panel in the Administration Console and click the Enable Billing button. The developer account used to enable billing becomes the "billing account," and the owner of that account is solely responsible for setting the budget and paying for resources consumed.

When you enable billing, the Console prompts you for billing information and authorization to charge via Google Checkout, Google's payment service. The process looks as though you're making a purchase via Google Checkout, but no money is charged right away. You set the budget for the app, a maximum amount of money that can be charged to your account, then authorize Google Checkout to charge up to that amount. If you increase the budget at a later date, you must reauthorize the amount with Google Checkout.

Once you have set the budget amount, you can allocate that budget across the billable quotas. You can select from several presets, or select Custom to set the values directly. Figure 15-4 is an example of the budget settings screen.

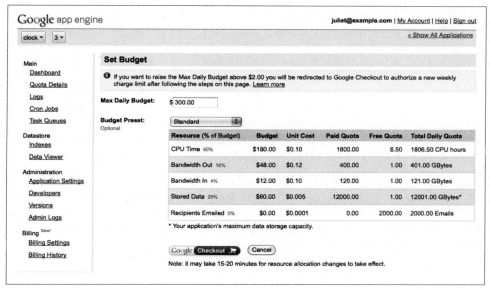

Figure 15-4. Setting the budget in the Administration Console (rates shown may not be current)

You can view a history of charges made to the billing account, including a breakdown of the billed resource usage for each calendar day, in the Billing History panel.

Getting Help

If you have questions not answered by this book, you may find your answers in the official documentation on Google's website:

http://code.google.com/appengine/

The documentation includes complete references for the APIs and tools for both the Python and Java runtime environments; a list of frequently asked questions and answers (the FAQ); and a large collection of articles describing best practices, interesting features, and complete working examples.

You may also want to browse the contents of the SDK, as installed by either the Eclipse plug-in or the Python Launcher, and also available as a ZIP archive from the website.

The source code for the Python SDK serves as supplementary documentation, and includes several undocumented (and unsupported) features and extensions. Both SDKs also include a set of functional example applications.

All App Engine developers should subscribe to Google's App Engine downtime mailing list. This low-traffic, announcement-only list is used by the App Engine team to announce scheduled times when services are taken down for maintenance, and also to report the status of unexpected problems:

http://groups.google.com/group/google-appengine-downtime-notify

You can check the current and past health of App Engine and its services by consulting the system status site:

http://code.google.com/status/appengine

If you believe you have found a bug in App Engine, the SDK, or the Administration Console, or if you have a feature you'd like to request, you can post to the App Engine issue tracker. You can also see features others have requested, and vote for your favorites. (The App Engine team does indeed consider the highly requested features in this list when determining the product road map.)

http://code.google.com/p/googleappengine/issues/list

Google hosts several mailing lists where the large and vibrant App Engine community gathers to post questions and discuss techniques. The App Engine team is also subscribed to these lists, and they often answer questions directly. This page has more information on the mailing lists and other community resources:

http://code.google.com/appengine/community.html

Index

We'd like to hear your suggestions for improving our indexes. Send email to *index@oreilly.com*.

django.core.handlers.wsgi module, 316
django.http module, 321
django.http.HttpRequest object, 321
django.shortcuts module, 321
domain names, 69
domains
    App Engine applications, 2
    setting up app domain name using Google
        Apps, 343
    setting up custom domain name for
        application, 58
    site identification by, secure connections
        and, 81
    using custom domain names, 12
    using custom domain other than
        appspot.com when registering
        application, 56
dot notation for embedded fields in property,
    214
DownloadError class (Python), 246
DuplicatePropertyError class (Python), 198
dynamic properties, 185

E

Eclipse IDE, 10
    installing Java SDK with Google Plugin, 21
    Packagae Explorer, 39
    uploading Java app, 61
    versions for Mac, 32-bit and 64-bit, 21
editors, 16
email and instant messages, 251–276
    checking email addresses for validity, 259
    email and XMPP addresses for applications,
        253
    enabling inbound services, 253
    flow of incoming mail and XMPP messages,
        252
    receiving email messages, 263–267
      in Java, 266–267
      in Python, 264–266
    receiving XMPP messages, 272–276
    sending email messages, 254–263
      attachments, 257
      in Java, 261–263
      in Python, 258–261
      recipients, 256
      sender addresses, 255
    sending email using remote shell tool, 290
    sending XMPP messages, 267–272

EmailAddress class (Python), 259
EmailMessage class (Python), 258
    example of sending email in Python, 259
Embeddable class (javax.persistence), 214
embedded objects, JPA, 214
enhancement process (JPA), 48, 209
entities, 5, 6, 104
    (see also datastore entities)
Entity class (Java), 113
    getKey( ) method, 114, 172
    methods to inspect the entity, 117
    results from keys-only queries, 134
    setUnindexedProperty( ) method, 151
entity groups, 7, 164
    batch updates and, 179
    keys, paths, and ancestors, 166
    kinds of entities and, 167
    managing in JPA, 216
    related objects in, 224
    transactions with, 169
entity ID, 104
entity properties (see properties)
EntityManager class (javax.persistence), 45,
    208, 214
    find( ) method, 215
    persist( ) method, 214
    remove( ) method, 215
EntityManagerFactory class
    (javax.persistence), 45, 208
    createEntityManager( ) method, 214
EntityTransaction class (javax.persistence),
    216
environment variables, 85
    set by App Engine at beginning of requests,
        87
equality filters
    combining with inequality filters, 145
    multivalued properties and, 155
    query using multiple equality filters, 147
Error class (Python), 242
error handler for memcache, 238
ErrorHandler class (Java), 238
exceptions, property validation errors, 188
Expando class (Python), 106, 183
    classes based on, inheritance from, 198
    difference from Model class, 185
Expiration class (Java), 235
exploding indexes, 159
Exporter class (Python), 287

exporter class for downloads, 287–289

downloading and installing Python SDK,
17
installing Java SDK with Google Plugin for
Eclipse, 21
testing App Engine Java SDK installation,
23

X

Y

Z

About the Author

Dan Sanderson is a technical writer and software engineer at Google Inc. He has worked in the web industry for more than 10 years as a software engineer and technical writer for Google, Amazon.com, and the Walt Disney Internet Group. He lives in Seattle, Washington. For more information about Dan, visit his website at *http://www .dansanderson.com*.

Colophon

The animal on the cover of *Programming Google App Engine* is a waterbuck (*Kobus ellipsiprymnus*), a type of antelope found in western, eastern, and southern Africa. Waterbucks stand at about five feet at the shoulder and have reddish-brown coats that become darker in color as the animals age. Long, sinuous horns distinguish male waterbucks, while a ring of white hair around the tail distinguishes both genders from other antelopes.

Waterbucks live in savannas and other vegetative areas, where they graze on rough grass and leaves from trees and bushes. Contrary to its name, the waterbuck spends most of its time on land, but it will often take refuge in a body of water to avoid predators.

African myth claims that the meat of the waterbuck is inedible, but this isn't so. Although the waterbuck's sweat glands produce a strong odor reminiscent of turpentine in order to better protect itself from predators, the animal's meat—while not especially flavorful—is safe to consume.

Male waterbucks frequently use their horns as a means of defense against their enemies. As the males are polygamous and highly possessive of their mates, they are especially prone to fatally goring other male waterbucks who enter their territories and try to steal members of their harems.

The cover image is from Wood's *Animate Creations*. The cover font is Adobe ITC Garamond. The text font is Linotype Birka; the heading font is Adobe Myriad Condensed; and the code font is LucasFont's TheSansMonoCondensed.